HOW TO DO THINGS WITH FORMS

How to Do Things with Forms

with Forms

The Oulipo and Its Inventions

CHRIS ANDREWS

McGill-Queen's University Press
Montreal & Kingston • London • Chicago

© McGill-Queen's University Press 2022

ISBN 978-0-2280-1141-5 (cloth)
ISBN 978-0-2280-1163-7 (paper)
ISBN 978-0-2280-1242-9 (ePDF)
ISBN 978-0-2280-1243-6 (ePUB)

Legal deposit third quarter 2022
Bibliothèque nationale du Québec

Printed in Canada on acid-free paper that is 100% ancient forest free
(100% post-consumer recycled), processed chlorine free

Library and Archives Canada Cataloguing in Publication

Title: How to do things with forms: the Oulipo and its inventions /
Chris Andrews.

Names: Andrews, Chris, 1962– author.

Description: Includes bibliographical references and index.

Identifiers: Canadiana (print) 20220216770 | Canadiana (ebook) 20220216819
| ISBN 9780228011637 (paper) | ISBN 9780228011415 (cloth) |
ISBN 9780228012429 (ePDF) | ISBN 9780228012436 (ePUB)

Subjects: LCSH: Oulipo (Association) | LCSH: Mathematics and literature. |
LCSH: Literature, Experimental—France—History and criticism. |
LCSH: French literature—20th century—History and criticism.

Classification: LCC PQ22.O8 A53 2022 | DDC 841/.9140936—dc23

This book was typeset by Marquis Interscript in 10.5/13 Sabon.

In memory of Barbara Wright

Contents

Tables and Figures ix

Acknowledgments xi

Abbreviations xiii

Note on Translations xvii

Members of the Oulipo xix

Introduction 3

1 What the Oulipo Was Not 14

2 Kinds of Rules 39

3 Automation, Craft, and Imitation 73

4 Manipulation, Translation, and Composition 97

5 Meaningful Forms and Clinamen 127

6 Revelation and Dissimulation 163

7 Games Gone Wrong 192

8 Potentiality, Uptake, and Spread 221

9 What Has Become of the Oulipo? 245

Notes 279

Bibliography 311

Index 347

Tables and Figures

TABLES

2.1 Kinds of constraints 51
2.2 Lengths of paragraphs in Jouet's *Fins* 69
4.1 Queneau's normalization of Tutuola's English in *The Palm-Wine Drinkard* 102
4.2 Perec's translation of characters' names in Mathews's *Tlooth* 107
6.1 Anne Breidel's calorie notebook 186
7.1 Garréta's "decomposition" of Proust 216
7.2 Garréta's "corrective citation" 217
7.3 Ducasse inverting Pascal 218
9.1 Phonemes in Bénabou's classification of constraints 259

FIGURES

2.1 The spiral permutation 68
4.1 Coded messages in *Tlooth* 109
4.2 Transposition of phonemes in *Tlooth* 110
4.3 Transposition of phonemes in *Les verts champs de moutarde de l'Afghanistan* 111
4.4 Métail's reconstruction of Su Hui's "The Map of the Armillary Sphere," courtesy of the Chinese University of Hong Kong Press 115
4.5 Métail's reading of the central square in "The Map of the Armillary Sphere" 122
5.1 From Forte's *Dire ouf* (Paris: POL, 2016) 129

5.2	Lécroart, "Portrait en creux (Jacques Jouet)," courtesy of Étienne Lécroart 133
5.3	The Desargues configuration 144
5.4	The eodermdrome 157
5.5	"étoile, ortie" 160
5.6	"ai radio, dora" 160

Acknowledgments

First of all, I would like to thank Michelle de Kretser for all her encouragement and her keen-eyed editorial suggestions.

I am very grateful to Richard Ratzlaff for the care and generosity with which he welcomed *How to Do Things with Forms* at McGill-Queen's University Press, to the two anonymous readers for their acute and helpful suggestions, to Paula Sarson for her meticulous and resourceful copyediting, and to Stephen Ullstrom for writing the index with understanding and expertise.

The writing of this book was supported by a Discovery Project grant from the Australian Research Council. My "partner investigators" in that project – Christelle Reggiani, Christophe Reig, and Hermes Salceda – have been a fund of critical insights and good humour. Caroline Boulom provided precious research assistance and administrative support.

My thanks to David Bellos and Mridula Chakraborty for their invitations to speak and for their hospitality. Over many years, friends and colleagues have helped me write this book with their comments, questions, and support. In particular, I would like to thank Esther Allen, Hani Ashtari, Peter Asveld, Jan Baetens, Mary-Lise Billot, Marc Bruimaud, Christopher Clarke, Peter Consenstein, Claude Debon, Dave Drayton, Véronique Duché, Farz Edraki, Natalie Edwards, Ben Etherington, Suzanne Gapps, Valentina Gosetti, Zahia Hafs, Christopher Hogarth, Vandad Jalili, Julie Koh, Marc Lapprand, Suzanne Meyer-Bagoly, Ryan O'Neill, Sophie Patrick, Jean-Jacques Poucel, Carol Sanders, Michael Sheringham, Anthony Uhlmann, Sonia Wilson, and Barbara Wright.

Material from a number of articles has been reworked for inclusion here, and I am grateful to the following editors and presses for permitting separate publication: "Constraint and Convention: The Formalism of the Oulipo," *Neophilologus* 87 (2003): 223–32; "Inspiration and the Oulipo," *Studies in Twentieth and Twenty-First Century Literature* 29, no. 1 (2005): 9–28; "Paranoid Interpretation and Formal Encoding," *Poetics Today* 30, no. 4 (2009): 669–92; "Poetry, Play and Constraint in Jacques Roubaud's *Parc sauvage*," *Australian Journal of French Studies* 41, no. 1 (2012): 142–52; "Intertextuality and Murder: Anne F. Garréta's *La décomposition* and *À la recherche du temps perdu*," *Australian Journal of French Studies* 54, no. 1 (2017): 71–83; and "Craft and Automation," *Contemporary French and Francophone Studies: Sites* 5, no. 5 (2021): 530–8.

Permission to quote poems has been granted as follows:

For Auden's poem "Rimbaud" in North America and the Philippines: copyright 1940 and © renewed 1968 by W.H. Auden; from *Collected Poems* by W.H. Auden, edited by Edward Mendelson. Used by permission of Random House, an imprint and division of Penguin Random House LLC. All rights reserved. And in the rest of the world: copyright © 1939 by W.H Auden, renewed Reprinted by permission of Curtis Brown, Ltd. All rights reserved.

For Harryette Mullen's "Variations on a Theme Park," from *Sleeping with the Dictionary*: copyright © 2002 by Harryette Mullen. Used by permission of University of California Press. All rights reserved.

Abbreviations

COLLECTIVE WORKS

NA   *The noulipian Analects*
PBO   *The Penguin Book of Oulipo*

WORKS BY MICHÈLE AUDIN

FS   *La formule de Stokes*

WORKS BY MARCEL BÉNABOU AND GEORGES PEREC

PP   *Presbytère et prolétaires: Le dossier* PALF

WORKS BY MARCEL BÉNABOU, JACQUES JOUET, HARRY MATHEWS, AND JACQUES ROUBAUD

AS   *Un art simple et tout d'exécution*

WORKS BY ANNE F. GARRÉTA

D   *La décomposition*
NOD   *Not One Day*

WORKS BY MICHELLE GRANGAUD

G   *Geste*
TT   *Les temps traversés*

xiv   Abbreviations

WORKS BY JACQUES JOUET

RP   *Ruminations du potentiel*

WORKS BY DANIEL LEVIN BECKER

MSC   *Many Subtle Channels*

WORKS BY HARRY MATHEWS

CPM   *The Case of the Persevering Maltese*
T   *Tlooth*
VCM   *Les verts champs de moutarde de l'Afghanistan*

WORKS BY MICHÈLE MÉTAIL

VOS   *Le vol des oies sauvages*
WGR *Wild Geese Returning*

WORKS BY THE OULIPO

AES   *All that is Evident is Suspect*
ALP   *Atlas de littérature potentielle*
AO   *Anthologie de l'Oulipo*
BO 1 *La bibliothèque oulipienne*, volume 1
BO 2 *La bibliothèque oulipienne*, volume 2
BO 4 *La bibliothèque oulipienne*, volume 4
BO 5 *La bibliothèque oulipienne*, volume 5
BO 6 *La bibliothèque oulipienne*, volume 6
BO 7 *La bibliothèque oulipienne*, volume 7
GO   *Genèse de l'Oulipo 1960–1963*
LP   *La littérature potentielle: Créations, re-créations, récréations*
MO   *Moments oulipiens*
OC   *Oulipo Compendium*
OL   *Oulipo Laboratory*
OPPL *Oulipo: A Primer of Potential Literature*
PM   *Paris-Math*

WORKS BY GEORGES PEREC

53D   *53 Days*
BO   *La boutique obscure*

EC I	*Entretiens et conférences I*
EC II	*Entretiens et conférences II*
IR	*I Remember*
JSN	*Je suis né*
LUM	*Life: A User's Manual*
O I	*Œuvres I*
O II	*Œuvres II*
SS	*Species of Spaces*
TH	*Three*
WMC	*W or the Memory of Childhood*

WORKS BY RAYMOND QUENEAU

B	*Bords*
EGC	*Entretiens avec Georges Charbonnier*
ES	*Exercises in Style*
LNF	*Letters, Numbers, Forms: Essays 1928–1970*
O	*Odile*
OC I	*Œuvres complètes I*
OC II	*Œuvres complètes II*
OC III	*Œuvres complètes III*
VG	*Le voyage en Grèce*
WG	*Witch Grass*
ZM	*Zazie in the Metro*

WORKS BY JACQUES ROUBAUD

BW	*La Bibliothèque de Warburg*
DBP	*La dernière balle perdue*
GFL	*The Great Fire of London*
IC	*Impératif catégorique*
L	*The Loop*
P	*Poésie:*
PE	*Peut-être ou la nuit de dimanche*
PECH	*Poetry, etcetera: Cleaning House*
PEM	*Poésie, etcetera: Ménage*
PS	*Parc sauvage*

Note on Translations

When an English translation of a text has been published, the translated title is given first, followed by the original title in brackets: *The Loop* (*La boucle*). In subsequent references only the English title is used, except where an original date of publication is indicated. When a translation has not been published, the original title is given first, followed by a translation of the title in brackets: *Parc sauvage* (Wild grounds). In subsequent references only the original title is used. Where I have cited a work for which there is no published English translation, the translation is my own. Where I have modified a published English translation, I have added the mention "(translation modified)." Such modifications have been made in a small number of cases to preserve a feature of the original that is important for the critical argument.

Members of the Oulipo
(by Year of Co-optation)

François Le Lionnais (1901–1984): founder
Raymond Queneau (1903–1976): co-founder
1960 Noël Arnaud (1919–2003)
Jacques Bens (1931–2001)
Claude Berge (1926–2002)
Jacques Duchateau (1929–2017)
Latis (1913–1973)
Jean Lescure (1912–2005)
Jean Queval (1913–1990)
Albert-Marie Schmidt (1901–1966)
1961 André Blavier (1922–2001)
Paul Braffort (1923–2018)
Ross Chambers (1932–2017)
Stanley Chapman (1925–2009)
1962 Marcel Duchamp (1887–1968)
1966 Jacques Roubaud (1932–)
1967 Georges Perec (1936–1982)
1970 Marcel Bénabou (1939–)
Luc Étienne (1908–1984)
1972 Paul Fournel (1947–)
1973 Harry Mathews (1930–2017)
1974 Italo Calvino (1923–1985)
1975 Michèle Métail (1950–)
1983 François Caradec (1924–2008)
Jacques Jouet (1947–)

1992	Hervé Le Tellier (1957–)
	Oskar Pastior (1927–2006)
	Pierre Rosenstiehl (1933–2020)
1995	Bernard Cerquiglini (1947–)
	Michelle Grangaud (1941–2022)
1998	Ian Monk (1960–)
2000	Anne F. Garréta (1962–)
	Olivier Salon (1955–)
2003	Valérie Beaudouin (1968–)
2005	Frédéric Forte (1973–)
2009	Michèle Audin (1954–)
	Daniel Levin Becker (1984–)
2012	Étienne Lécroart (1960–)
2014	Eduardo Berti (1964–)
	Pablo Martín Sánchez (1977–)
2017	Clémentine Mélois (1980–)

HOW TO DO THINGS WITH FORMS

Introduction

In his interviews with Georges Charbonnier, Raymond Queneau briefly recounts the foundation of the Oulipo (Ouvroir de littérature potentielle, or Workshop for Potential Literature): "I had written five or six of the sonnets in *Cent mille milliards de poèmes* (A hundred thousand billion poems, 1961), and I wasn't too sure whether or not I should persist; I was feeling a little discouraged, because of course it was increasingly difficult, and then I ran into Le Lionnais, who's a friend, and he suggested setting up a sort of research group to work on experimental literature. This encouraged me to go on with my sonnets; in a way, that collection of poems is the first concrete manifestation of the group's activities" (EGC 116). The book consists of ten sonnets printed on ten successive pages, which are slitted between the lines of verse. The sonnets all have the same rhyme scheme and basic syntactic structure, so the first line of any of the ten initial or "parent" sonnets can be combined with any of the second lines, which can, in turn, be combined with any of the third lines, and so on. There are $10 \times 10 = 10^2 = 100$ combinations of the first two lines, $10^3 = 1000$ combinations of the first three lines, and 10^{14} combinations of all the lines, which makes, in total, a hundred thousand billion poems. Queneau writes in his introduction: "If it takes forty-five seconds to read a sonnet and fifteen seconds to change the strips, someone reading eight hours a day for 200 days a year would have material for more than a million centuries" (OC I 334).

Queneau's anecdote does not give a full account of the Oulipo's foundation, but it combines elements that have turned out to be characteristic of the group's enterprise: a mathematically inspired idea for a literary work, uncertainty as to the idea's feasibility and aesthetic validity, friendship, encouragement, and the unleashing of potential.[1] The division of labour in the story is also indicative of the roles that the co-founders of the group would play: Queneau as inventor and craftsman, François Le Lionnais as organizer and galvanizer.

Since 1960, the writers, mathematicians, and scholars of the Oulipo have been conducting a uniquely systematic series of experiments with literature. Those experiments, by virtue of their radicality (one might even say in some cases their extremism), raise fundamental questions for the theory and practice of literary writing. Among other things, the Oulipo is a deep resource for thinking about what literature is, how it works, and what it can do. The principal aim of this book is to draw on it as such.

Generalizing about a literary group is hazardous, especially when that group is still active and does not have a unified doctrine to which its members must subscribe. But the Oulipo is a "community of practice," to cite Camille Bloomfield, despite the differences that have traversed it.[2] The practice of the Oulipo is unified by a constructive experimentalism, which rejects the alternative between neoclassical attachment to established forms and the avant-garde ideal of sweeping those forms aside and starting over. For the Oulipo, the real renewal of literature requires the invention of new forms that will build on but also rearrange those of the past. The group aims to stimulate such invention by establishing contacts with a complementary discipline that has often been seen as opposed to literature: mathematics.

This project sets the Oulipo apart from other experimental writing groups in the late twentieth- and early twenty-first centuries (with the exception of satellite groups like the Italian Oplepo). All the Oulipians have been and are committed to the project as characterized in the very broad strokes of the previous paragraph. But they have differed as to how it is to be executed. Two key questions on which the Oulipians do not agree are whether or not constraints or precisely pre-formulated writing rules should be revealed to the reader, and whether or not they should be applied to the semantic domain. These questions are discussed in chapters 7 and 10 respectively. There have also been interesting differences of emphasis within the group. For example, some Oulipians have regarded projects and processes as instrumental, while others have granted them intrinsic value, as I show in chapter 2. Oulipians differ, too, in their approach to the clinamen or deviation from a constraint, and in their attachment to constraints

Introduction

in the strict sense as opposed to a more intuitive shaping of forms (see chapters 2 and 5). While remaining firm friends, the co-founders of the Oulipo, Queneau and Le Lionnais, had quite different approaches to literary experimentation, and in chapter 8 I underline the skepticism regarding constraints that Queneau expressed in various subtle ways toward the end of his life. The Oulipo has never been a monolith, and it has evolved continuously since its foundation in 1960. This book explores its internal variety and acknowledges the open-endedness of its venture.

In the English-speaking world, the work of divulging the Oulipo's project has been done by Warren Motte's *Oulipo: A Primer of Potential Literature*, Harry Mathews's and Alastair Brotchie's *Oulipo Compendium*, Daniel Levin Becker's *Many Subtle Channels*, and two recent anthologies: *All that is Evident is Suspect* and *The Penguin Book of Oulipo*. I refer frequently to these indispensable books, which gather many exercises illustrating the Oulipo's inventions. But the members of the Oulipo have also produced an important body of fully developed works. The distinction between exercises and works remains pertinent for the group, as I argue in chapter 1, and the idea that readers have of the Oulipo will depend to a large extent on which kind of Oulipian text they are most familiar with. The Oulipo's exercises are often witty and technically nimble; they tend to privilege a single constraint. Oulipian works can be deeply serious and affect-laden; they generally combine constraints or construct forms that are not strictly constraint-based. In the first four chapters, the discussion often bears on exercises and constraints. In chapter 5, the emphasis shifts to works and forms. Criticisms of the Oulipo as excessively cerebral and flippant lose much of their force when works are given due consideration.[3]

For the purposes of this study, Oulipian works are conceived broadly as works published by members of the Oulipo, regardless of their date of publication. So I discuss works published before the author was recruited (like Anne Garréta's *Sphinx*) or even before the group existed (like Queneau's *Witch Grass*). It is true that works may be more or less Oulipian, and that some members of the group, like Jacques Jouet, identify some of their works as non-Oulipian. But I treat the Oulipo as a genuine affinity group, whose members have been drawn to it by a commitment to the general project set out above, and in attempting to give an account of that project's powers and limits, it is helpful to consider all of their works as potentially informative.

The exercises and works examined in detail have been determined by the questions guiding my inquiry. At the highest level of generality, those questions are:

1 What kind of group is the Oulipo?
2 What kinds of writing rules have the members of the Oulipo invented?
3 How are craft, automation, and imitation related in the Oulipo's practice?
4 How are text manipulation, translation, and composition related?
5 How do forms and their irregularities signify in Oulipian works?
6 How do the Oulipians play hide-and-seek with the reader?
7 What do their works reveal about play in general and its darker side?
8 Which Oulipian inventions have been most widely taken up and why?
9 What unrealized potentials does the Oulipo have?

In chapter 1, "What the Oulipo Was Not," Queneau's negative definitions of the Oulipo, proposed in 1964, are used as pointers to the group's specificity but are also revised in the light of its evolution. A sustained comparison with the surrealist group (to which Queneau belonged in the 1920s) highlights the ways in which the Oulipo differs from the historical avant-gardes. A key difference is that the Oulipo's collective agenda has been tightly focused, excluding political discussion and action. The Oulipo's statutes, designed to pre-empt internal conflict, also set the group apart. But like the avant-gardes, the Oulipo has a strong orientation toward the future, albeit a future of inventions rather than revolutions.

The Oulipo has consistently declined to take itself too seriously, but it has done serious work at the interface of mathematics and literature, and its approach poses a serious challenge to the distinction between play and research. Unlike surrealism and some of the neo-avant-gardes of the 1960s, the Oulipo has not privileged chance operations, but it has not excluded them altogether. While disenchanting the chance encounter in *Exercises in Style* (*Exercices de style*), Queneau sees chance as both "an essential element of artistic activity" (LNF 164) and subordinate to the writer's judgment. In 1964, he was at pains to distance the Oulipo from the aleatory approach of Max

Bense, for whom unpredictability was the key to aesthetic merit. Queneau and Le Lionnais subscribe to a more traditional and pragmatic account of creativity, which requires an artwork to prove its value and its usefulness to other artists, as well as its originality. Unlike Bense's approach, the Oulipo's is based on crafting rather than broad-scope theorizing.

Chapter 2, "Kinds of Rules," begins by distinguishing between two kinds of literary experimentalism: the clastic, which breaks down conventional units or breaks rules governing their combination, and the constructive, which builds new patterns. These tendencies are not sharply separable but the constructive tendency predominates in the practice of the Oulipo. The group's principal tool for building is what its members call the constraint. The Oulipo has attempted to overcome resistance to the constraint by arguing that it is no more artificial or arbitrary than the conventions governing spelling, grammar, syntax, or genre. This has been a rhetorically useful move, but it is also potentially misleading. Careful comparison of constraints and conventions reveals a series of important differences, in the light of which it is reasonable to say that constraints are relatively artificial. But the constraint's artificiality is precisely what makes it a powerful tool for unsettling the conventional.

Constraints can be classified according to what they constrain: the process of a text's production, the text produced, its performance, or publication. Such a classification allows us to see how the Oulipo's practice has evolved since 1960. Process constraints have become more important, and certain Oulipian projects have fostered improvisation and the "artification of life," at the risk of failing to achieve a rewarding level of density in the product. Product constraints have a series of distinctive powers, which the Oulipo continues to exploit: they allow the writer to get to work straight away; they can screen potentially paralyzing worries about content; and they can divert attention productively, opening a space for "incubated cognition."

Constraints, however, are not the only means of realizing literary potential. The Oulipians also invent and employ forms, that is, arrangements or rearrangements of elements, often developed by trial and error, in a process that Jacques Jouet has nicknamed "organizational tinkering" (AS 34). Because constraints are abstract and conceived a priori, at a distance from the work of composition, they can jolt writing out of stylistic and generic ruts. Forms, by contrast, draw their power from plasticity and their capacity to adapt as composition unfolds. In explaining her departure from the Oulipo, Michèle Métail rejects constraints, defending a conception of form that resonates with the conclusion of Queneau's 1937 essay "Technique of the Novel" (LNF 29).

Chapter 3, "Automation, Craft, and Imitation," considers how constraints are used by the Oulipo. Are they a first step toward automation? Can they stand in for the work itself, as in conceptual art? The Oulipo's affinities with conceptual art are real if limited, but the group's interest in effectively automating the production of literature has waned over the years. This has disappointed some advocates of computational creativity, but it is not altogether surprising if, as Jacques Roubaud asserts, the Oulipo's activities are essentially craftlike, since craft and automation are at odds in key respects. Nevertheless, some members of the Oulipo have used their craft to simulate automation, presenting the handmade as the machine-made. Georges Perec and Marcel Bénabou's PALF (Automatic Production of French Literature) project, and Perec's radio play *Die Maschine* (*The Machine*) illustrate this strategy in different ways. The PALF project, presented by Perec and Bénabou as "entirely and really automatic," was automatic only in that it relied on relations of homonymy or synonymy codified by a dictionary. It required laborious manipulations and was abandoned once it had served to make a point about the slipperiness of lexical meaning. By contrast, *Die Maschine* presents itself as a simulation. It mimics the outputs of an autonomous machine transforming and desacralizing a canonical poem.

It turns out that the Oulipo's most fruitful engagements with automation have been imaginary, as in science fiction. The machine has appealed to the Oulipians as a metaphor for control, partly because, like other writers, they must contend with the frustrating intermittence of literary composition. Not immune to writer's block, they disparage its opposite, inspiration. Queneau is often cited as an authority in the campaign against inspiration, but he does not simply replace it with technique, and he stresses the importance of the unknown and the unpredictable in composition. As well as inventing and employing constraints to prompt creativity, the Oulipians make ample use of traditional techniques, such as memory-based imitation, which classical rhetoricians saw as a way of being inspired by a precursor.

Chapter 4, "Manipulation, Translation, and Composition," pursues the examination of the Oulipo's practice by asking what translation has meant for the group. The Oulipo works with an extended concept of translation, covering various manipulations of existing texts. Many of the Oulipo's writers have also been serious translators in the conventional sense of the word, and in some cases there have been strong connections between their translating and their original writing. I examine three such cases. Queneau's translation of Amos Tutuola's *The Palm-Wine Drinkard* chimes with his defence of an oral literature in French and with the inclination toward magical causation in his later fiction. Translating Harry Mathews's *Tlooth* gave Perec intimate familiarity with a novel based on a complex system of constraints before he undertook such construction himself in *Life: A User's Manual* (*La vie mode d'emploi*). *Tlooth* also provided textual material for implicit citation in Perec's masterwork. Métail's translation of Su Hui's "The Map of the Armillary Sphere," underpinned by philological research, is part of a long engagement with Chinese poetry, which has led away from the Oulipo and provided models for a kind of writing that is at once cosmological in scope and biographically anchored. In each of these three cases, the translations respect the limits on creativity imposed by the conventions of publishing and scholarship, but they are creative at the macro level, entering into the composition of the authors' bodies of work.

The first part of chapter 5, "Meaningful Forms and Clinamen," looks at a range of ways in which the forms of Oulipian works bear meaning. The "look and feel" of a text can quickly convey a writerly posture, helping orient readers. Forms can also signify in less immediate and more specific ways, which I classify according to Charles S. Peirce's typology of signs. When the form straightforwardly resembles what is signified by the work, it functions like a Peircian image, as in Étienne Lécroart's "Portraits en creux" (intaglio portraits). When the likeness between signifier and signified depends only on relations of parts, the form is what Peirce would call a diagram. Michelle Grangaud's anagram poems are diagrams of equality in that each line is composed of exactly the same letters as the others. When there is a "factual, existential" contiguity between signifier and signified, the sign is an index in Peirce's system. The structures based on the numbers eleven and forty-three in Perec's work are indices in this sense, as they allude to the deportation of the author's mother to Auschwitz on 11 February 1943. Finally, a form may be a symbol when the relation between signifier and signified is based on a social convention. Numerical structures are symbolic when they mobilize meanings traditionally associated with certain integers, as in Roubaud's *Some*

Thing Black (*Quelque chose noir*). It turns out that the forms employed by the Oulipo in works are almost always motivated. As Jouet puts it, with a variation on a theme by Francis Ponge: "form is the tautest string of meaning."[4] The motivation, however, need not be semantic. In the literary writing of Michèle Audin, for example, the significance of forms is primarily mathematical.

The irregularities of forms, produced by deviations from constraint, can also be meaningful. Perec introduced the term "clinamen" to name such deviations. His use of the clinamen illustrates the range of its functions: as well as encoding meanings, it can mask constraints, break symmetry, and afford greater flexibility in composition. In Perec's collection *La clôture et autres poèmes* (The enclosure and other poems, 1980), the clinamen is not only a way of loosening rigid constraints in individual poems. When the structure of the whole book and Perec's trajectory as a poet are considered, clinamen emerges as a way of regulating the approach to an unconstrained encounter with traumatic material. In Roubaud's *Parc sauvage* (Wild grounds), a very difficult constraint (the eodermdrome) yields to multiple clinamens. Formal rigour is sacrificed to narrative and poetic effect. This is justified in the story by attributing the eodermdromes to a pair of ten-year-olds, but it also points to the provisional status of constraints in fully fledged works.

Chapter 6, "Revelation and Dissimulation," examines strategies employed by the Oulipians to show and hide significant patterns in their work, rewarding but also frustrating the reader's hermeneutic efforts. Often the hidden patterns are related to the author's personal life. Writing under Oulipian constraints or in Oulipian forms does not exclude the emotive function of language or self-expression. In fact, constraints and forms can help the writer to elude self-censorship and personal taboos, and there is a significant corpus of Oulipian autobiography. The psychoanalytic relationship is an important theme in the autobiographical writing of Queneau and Perec in particular. Tracing the ramifications of that theme is facilitated by studying posthumous archives, which continue a game of hide-and-seek that the authors played throughout their writing lives, encoding meanings in the forms of their works. This formal encoding is conducive to overreading or paranoid interpretation, which may be an appropriate reaction to certain discursive situations, but is potentially harmful when generalized, as Umberto Eco has argued. The kind of paranoid reading to which expert readers of the Oulipians are prone produces three specific hazards. It can lead to a devaluation of a work's evident features; it tends to yield progressively less interesting results; and it can impoverish the context of interpretation by encouraging the reader to specialize obsessively. While the fictions of Perec and Queneau can induce interpretive paranoia, they also warn against it. Both *53 Days* and *Witch Grass* contain parables that illustrate the dangers of being hypnotized by a hypothesis that promises to crack the code of the work or deliver its unique key.

In chapter 7, "Games Gone Wrong," I turn from how the Oulipians play with the reader to how they represent play in their fictions. As a group, the Oulipo tends to celebrate play, and its exercises are generally conducted in a playful spirit. This has shaped the group's image and prompted unsympathetic critics to dismiss the Oulipo as a band of literary jokers. In their own defence, the Oulipians rarely point to the often serious themes of their works, preferring to challenge the distinction between play and seriousness in a range of ways. They appeal to the instrumental value of play as a motor of cognitive discovery and as a psychological defence mechanism. They also advocate its intrinsic value as a source of delight, perhaps even a basic human right. But this does not entail an idealization of play. In their fictions, Roubaud, Perec, and Garréta register play's deep ambiguity, showing how it can be corrupted by the aggression that it should ideally serve to sublimate.

In Roubaud's *La dernière balle perdue* (The last lost ball) and Perec's *W or the Memory of Childhood* (*W ou le souvenir d'enfance*), games are corrupted by a cheat and a class of oppressors respectively. In both cases, what Bernard Suits calls the "lusory attitude" – acceptance of the rules just because they make the game possible – is suppressed. In Garréta's *La décomposition* (Decomposition), the narrator-protagonist maintains a lusory attitude to a game that is both criminal and technically flawed. Gamifying murder in a way that prefigures recent acts of terrorism, he loses his grip on the limits of the game. The protagonist's quest to depopulate both the real world and *In Search of Lost Time* might seem to be mirrored by Garréta's irreverent treatment of Marcel Proust's novel, but *La décomposition* is also a recomposition, a homage as well as a desecration.

The last two chapters of this book examine the fortunes of the Oulipo's inventions. Chapter 8, "Potentiality, Uptake, and Spread," begins by reflecting on what the Oulipo means by potentiality. Following Roubaud, I distinguish between "predisposed potentiality" as exemplified by Queneau's *Cent mille milliards de poèmes*, and "potentiality in actuality," which is manifested in texts that transform a constraint or a structure by means of variations and mutations. Three striking examples of potentiality in actuality are considered: Queneau's *Exercices in Style*, Perec's *I Remember* (*Je me souviens*), and his story "The Winter Journey" ("Le voyage d'hiver"). All three of these works take their places in a chain of imitations and adaptations rather than being based on an imported mathematical structure. They also invite the reader to write a continuation without imposing strict or difficult constraints. At first glance, the case of the new form in the first part of Queneau's *Elementary Morality* (*Morale élémentaire*) seems quite different. On closer inspection, however, the differences recede. The "elementary morality" form has roots in the Chinese poetic tradition, and Queneau was at pains to point out that it was not a constraint-based invention. His public presentation of the form in the *Nouvelle revue française* provoked a subtly defiant response from Perec. This contributed to launching the elementary morality within the Oulipo. The form itself is supple and simple, allowing for variations and the addition of supplementary constraints.

The most productive Oulipian forms and constraints may not be the most complex or the most interesting from a mathematical point of view, and transposing mathematically interesting patterns into literature is not at all straightforward, as Queneau implied with his last published text, "The Foundations of Literature (after David Hilbert)." This text can be read as an ironic reduction to absurdity of the amalgamation of literature and mathematics.

Chapter 9, "What Has Become of the Oulipo?," takes up the historical perspective of chapter 1, arguing that while the Oulipo's influence has become more diffuse as it has spread, the group itself still has a range of unrealized potentials. Although it is widely felt that the Oulipo is past its prime, it is worth remembering that some Oulipians had the same impression before the publication of *Life: A User's Manual* in 1978. Since the composition and concerns of the group are subject to ongoing metamorphosis, any global assessment of its achievements must be provisional. The group is both widely known and underknown. Much of what it has published still awaits careful reading, appreciation, and translation. Many of the constraints and structures proposed by the Oulipo have not been carefully tested yet, and there are aspects of literature, such as sound patterning and semantics, that the group has not explored extensively.

Literary invention in the spirit of the Oulipo has spread beyond the confines of the group. Some para-Oulipian writing is highly orthodox; some plays freely with Oulipian ideas. For many contemporary writers of an experimental bent, the Oulipo is a precedent that legitimates literary play, and a source of techniques to be drawn on occasionally. The Oulipo is also a social invention, and it has the potential to influence the practice of writing and art-making in other groups. In particular, it can serve as a model of interdisciplinary collaboration. Rather than spreading, it has "sporulated," stimulating the creation of separate, more or less closely related collectives. While there is no particular political agenda inscribed in the Oulipo's inventions, the group's activities do have an important metapolitical dimension. They show that change can be effected straight away in limited domains by inventing new non-conventional rules, by shaping new literary forms and forms of life.

1

What the Oulipo Was Not

"IT IS NOT A MOVEMENT OR A LITERARY SCHOOL"

From the start, the Oulipo has defined itself negatively. In a talk given at Jean Favard's seminar in quantitative linguistics at the Institut Henri Poincaré on 29 January 1964, Raymond Queneau said of the Oulipo: "1. It is not a movement or a literary school. We situate ourselves prior to all notions of aesthetic value, which isn't to say that we care nothing for them. 2. Nor is it a scientific seminar, a 'serious' working group between quotation marks [...] Finally, 3. It has nothing to do with experimental or aleatory literature (such as is currently being practiced by the Max Bense group in Stuttgart, for example)" (LNF 181–2). This was an attempt to forestall likely confusions. The confusions were likely because in some ways the Oulipo did resemble a literary school, a scientific seminar, and an experimental literature group. How was it different from those three things? Are Queneau's demarcations still valid, more than sixty years later, given the considerable changes that the Oulipo has undergone? Not entirely. Nevertheless, they are still useful pointers to the Oulipo's specificity, and that is how I will use them in this chapter, considering each in turn.

With the first denial, Queneau was marking a boundary between the collective activities of the Oulipo and the literary writing done by its members as individual authors. In 1964, little of that individual writing was clearly based on precisely pre-formulated constraints or procedures. The elaborate numerical structuring of Queneau's early novels (as explained by the author in "Technique of the Novel" [LNF 26–9]) anticipates the Oulipo's concerns, and *Witch Grass* (*Le chiendent*, 1933) has often been seen by the group's members as a proto-Oulipian text. But as Le Lionnais wrote in the afterword to Queneau's *Cent mille milliards de poèmes* (1961), it was with that work and its predecessor, *Exercises in Style* (*Exercices de style*, 1947), that what would soon be called potential literature emerged from semi-secrecy to affirm its legitimacy, proclaim its ambitions, constitute its methods, and align itself with "our scientific civilization" (AO 882).

In 1964, no member of the Oulipo apart from Queneau had published a wittingly Oulipian book. It was therefore not disingenuous to say that the group was not a movement or a literary school. By 1981, when the *Atlas de littérature potentielle* (Atlas of potential literature) was published, things had changed. Georges Perec's *Life: A User's Manual* (*La vie mode d'emploi*, 1978) had won the Prix Médicis in France. Italo Calvino's *If on a Winter's Night a Traveller* (*Se una notte d'inverno un viaggiatore*, 1979) was well on its way to international renown. And Harry Mathews's *The Sinking of the Odradek Stadium* (1971) had been serialized in *The Paris Review* and translated into French by Perec. All three novels were categorized as "Oulipian" or "partly Oulipian" in the bibliography of the *Atlas*. The Oulipo was already beginning to look very much like a movement or a literary school, and one with wide international reach.

Nevertheless, the boundary marked by Queneau between the collective and the individual is still pertinent. The group's core collective activity – the invention of new rules and structures for literary composition – remains temporally "prior to all notions of aesthetic value": rules and structures are proposed and tried out in exercises to test their potential, in a playful way, suspending aesthetic judgment. Some are later taken up by individual writers, to be employed in literary works, usually in complex combinations. The Oulipo has not abandoned the distinction between exercise and work.[1]

For Perec, exercises had a preparatory function, as he explained to Jean-Marie Le Sidaner in 1979: "I use a certain number of these routine tasks to warm up; that's particularly true of crosswords and texts written under strict (Oulipian) constraints, which I do a bit like a pianist practicing scales" (EC II 96). Jacques Roubaud employs a similar musical metaphor in "The Oulipo and Combinatorial Art": "Where the composition of Oulipian works is concerned, it is clearly in the resort to complex systems of constraints, to strategies of progressive demonstration, and to ceremonials of revelation and dissimulation that the distinction is created between the 'five finger exercises' of elementary pieces written according to constraints and creation that is truly literary" (OC 42). Roubaud is also echoing Queneau's insistence, in his interviews with Georges Charbonnier (1962), on the difference between the Oulipo's collective activity as a think tank and literary elaboration: "The genuinely new forms and structures won't be interesting until they have been used in original texts, but we're not aiming to create literature, not at all; we're only aiming to propose forms [...] it's not about conditioning writers' inspiration; that's none of our business. But there are writers among us, and, of course, they can do that on their own behalf, as writers" (EGC 146). This working principle still holds, although, as the group's notoriety has grown, its members increasingly tend to be perceived as writing not "on their own behalf" but as members of the Oulipo. One sign of this is the way in which the Oulipo's name has been used as a brand in marketing recent translations of books by Anne Garréta, Michèle Audin, Eduardo Berti, and Pablo Martín Sánchez in the United States.[2]

In distinguishing the Oulipo from movements and literary schools, Queneau was, to recapitulate, marking conceptual boundaries between the collective and the individual, the exercise and the work, the free play of ideas and making art. But he was also indirectly signalling a historical difference between the group that he had co-founded and another to which he had belonged in his youth.

Queneau was a surrealist from 1925 to 1929. This experience is fictionalized in the novel *Odile* (1937), which by Queneau's own admission comes close to being a *roman à clef* (LNF 175). *Odile* looks back at surrealism from a point in Queneau's intellectual itinerary at which, under the influence of the esoteric metaphysician René Guénon, he had come to see the group led by André Breton as engaged in a far-from-harmless form of "pseudo-initiation."[3] Like Pierre Drieu La Rochelle's *Gilles* and Louis Aragon's *Aurélien*, Queneau's *Odile* affords fascinating insights into the daily life of the surrealist group and its internal tensions.[4] What the novel does not reveal, however, is Queneau's former zeal as an adherent. A surrealist communiqué dated 30 October 1925 reads: "the principle of *suspension* (which, contrary to expulsion, does not imply a breakdown of trust) was adopted by 15 votes for and 2 against: Breton, Queneau."[5] For Queneau, in 1925, there could be no intermediate space between inclusion and exclusion. And in 1929, he acted as secretary to Breton and Aragon, gathering the responses to a letter sent to past and present surrealists, as well as members of other groups, asking for their opinion on the possibility of joint as opposed to individual action in the political domain. This letter served to prepare a meeting held at the Bar du Château on 11 March, ostensibly to discuss the fate of Leon Trotsky, who had been exiled from the USSR by Stalin in February.

The response of Michel Leiris indicates that he thought Queneau was being manipulated: "The policy of a united front doesn't look at all promising to me, and if there is one thing I have always detested it's patching things up. Consider that, if you like, a response to your (?) questionnaire."[6] By this stage, Leiris and a number of Queneau's other friends in the group (including Pierre Naville and Robert Desnos) had tired of Breton's authoritarianism. Queneau himself, however, was still loyally abetting manoeuvres that he would come to regard, for a time at least, as sinister.[7] At the meeting on 11 March, Breton turned out to be far more interested in local literary politics than in the exile of Trotsky. He proceeded to attack Roger Gilbert-Lecomte and Roger Vailland, who belonged to a group called Le Grand Jeu, which, with its journal of the same name, was emerging as a significant force among the Parisian avant-gardes.[8] Breton had previously failed to recruit Gilbert-Lecomte and his friends René Daumal and André Rolland de Renéville to the surrealist cause.[9] Leiris, André Thirion, and Georges Ribemont-Dessaignes all later said that the meeting on 11 March was organized with the intent of discrediting Le Grand Jeu.[10]

In *Odile*, the group leader Anglarès is satisfied with the outcome of a similar meeting: "There hasn't been any real realignment [*regroupement*] but we've had excellent results [...] Salton's group has disbanded" (O 96; OC II 596). The "excellent" result of a meeting called ostensibly to federate a multiplicity has been to produce further fragmentation. When, during the formation of the Oulipo, Queneau insisted on ground rules designed to defuse conflict, in particular the permanency of membership, he may have been reacting not only to the formative trauma of his rupture with Breton, sealed by his contribution to the pamphlet *Un cadavre* (A corpse) in January 1930, but also to his earlier collaboration.

For historical reasons, surrealism has served as an anti-model for the Oulipo, but it was not, of course, an isolated phenomenon, having much in common with other roughly contemporaneous avant-gardes, such as Dada, the Russian and Italian futurisms, and Spanish ultraism, to name just a few. In "The Oulipo and Combinatorial Art," Roubaud adopts an alternative, national perspective, inscribing surrealism in a line of French literary groups since the Renaissance, which he contrasts with the Oulipo. The typical group, says Roubaud:

> (a) views the literature being produced around it as "having deteriorated to an appallingly low level" and (d) "thoroughly despises all its contemporaries";
> (b) it subscribes to the motto: "everything done prior to us is worthless; everything done after us can only exist because of us";
> (c) it is organized into ranks, with "leaders, designated successors, and 'second fiddles'";
> (e) it works through self-destructive "splits, divergences, 'deviations,' and exclusions"; and
> (f) it has developed "earmarks typical of a sect, a mafia, a gang, or, more modestly, a mutual admiration society." (OC 37)

I have slightly rearranged Roubaud's characterizations in order to show that some (those in the first set) relate to how the typical group engages with the outside world, while others (those in the second set) concern its internal organization. In its "foreign policy" the group is dismissive, arrogant, and aggressive (a, b, d); in "domestic affairs" it is hierarchical, unstable, and jealous of its members' loyalty (c, e, f).

The main lines of Roubaud's caricatural sketch coincide with the model of avant-garde group formation and dissolution proposed by Pierre Bourdieu in *The Rules of Art*. Bourdieu argues that the coherence of the avant-garde group in its early days is largely negative:

> Whereas the occupants of the dominant positions [...] are very homogenous, the avant-garde positions, which are defined mainly negatively, in opposition to the dominant positions, bring together for a while (in the phase of the initial accumulation of symbolic capital) writers and artists who are very different in their origins and their dispositions and whose interests, momentarily coming together, will later start to diverge. As small isolated sects whose negative cohesion is reinforced by an intense affective solidarity, often concentrated in the attachment to a leader, these dominated groups tend to enter into crisis, by an apparent paradox, when they achieve recognition – the symbolic profits of that recognition frequently going only to a few, or even only one of them – and when the negative forces of cohesion are weakened.[11]

This model draws on detailed studies of the symbolists, decadents, and surrealists, and it has been used persuasively in a sociological study of situationism.[12] But its applicability to the Oulipo is limited. Explaining why will help clarify the senses in which the Oulipo is not an avant-garde group.

To begin with, the recognition achieved by the group has not led to a major crisis. The minor crises recently documented by Camille Bloomfield – the "dissidence of 1974," the withdrawals of Jean Lescure, Michèle Métail, and Paul Braffort – have not seriously threatened the Oulipo's stability and continuity.[13] More recently, Roubaud has disavowed the group in *Peut-être ou la nuit de dimanche* (Perhaps or Sunday night), one of whose narrative strands (chapters 5, 10, and 15) is a settling of scores in the form of a mini *roman à clef*. The Oulipo is disguised as "L'Appentis de Science Plausible" (Lean-to of Plausible Science) or Apsipla. Marc Lapprand notes that the name carries a pejorative charge: an *appentis* or lean-to is a place for storing tools and materials, not a place where work is actually done, and plausible science may well be unsound.[14] Roubaud indirectly accuses identifiable Oulipians of having abandoned the original task of exploring potentiality and constraints while continuing to profit from the group's international renown (PE 75–81), and of having manoeuvred disloyally to commandeer the Oulipo for personal and political ends (PE 157–65). Given Roubaud's public stature and the symbolic violence of his targeted attacks, *Peut-être ou la nuit de dimanche* was bound to rock the Oulipo, but the group has not capsized.[15]

When comparing the Oulipo to the avant-gardes, it is important to bear in mind that the group was not launched by young aspirants, but by a pair of men in their late fifties – Queneau was fifty-seven, Le Lionnais fifty-nine – who were well established in their respective fields.[16] Queneau occupied a position of influence at France's leading literary publishing house, Gallimard. Le Lionnais was the presenter of the radio program "La science en marche" (Science on the move) on the public radio station France III (now France Culture). The average age of the founding members was forty-five, according to Marc Lapprand's calculations.[17] Camille Bloomfield contrasts these ages tellingly with those of avant-garde leaders: Tristan Tzara and Hugo Ball were twenty at the inception of Dada; André Breton and Philippe Soupault were twenty-three and twenty-two respectively when they wrote *The Magnetic Fields* (*Les champs magnétiques*, 1920), which would come to be regarded as the founding text of surrealism;

Guy Debord was twenty-six when he broke with Isidore Isou to launch L'internationale lettriste, which would become L'internationale situationniste.[18] In a review of Levin Becker's *Many Subtle Channels* (2012), Lauren Elkin asked, "Is the Oulipo really just a lot of old men sitting around doing word games?"[19] The author of the book under review, then the Oulipo's newest recruit, was not yet thirty. But Elkin put her finger on something: numerically, the group has been and still is dominated by older men.

A third difference with respect to Bourdieu's model is that the Oulipo was relatively homogenous in social terms at its foundation and has become somewhat less so, inverting the tendency to homogenization over time and with increasing institutionalization.[20] A simple way to grasp this gradual diversification is to consider gender and nationality. There were no women in the group until the co-optation of Michèle Métail in 1975. There are now five (although Métail and Garréta are no longer active members).[21] The founding members were all French. At the third meeting, foreign "corresponding members" were elected: Ross Chambers (Australia), André Blavier (Belgium), and Stanley Chapman (Great Britain) (GO 43). In 1976, the hierarchical distinction between active and corresponding members was dropped.[22] And since the co-optation of Pablo Martín Sánchez and Eduardo Berti in 2014, there are now ten members out of forty-two whose nationality is not French. (Following Oulipian practice, this last tally includes members excused from meetings on account of death).

Finally, there is a fourth difference underlying the three indicated above: the Oulipo has a strong positive principle of cohesion. Its members have been drawn to it not so much by common antipathies (which may temporarily mask destabilizing social differences) as by a common attachment to the technical aspects of literary composition. Asked to define the Oulipo, Levin Becker once responded: "I usually go with some variation of 'a research group of writers and scientists whose collective subject of inquiry is the literary potential of mathematical structures.' Sometimes – okay, often – I replace 'research group of writers and scientists' with 'bunch of nerds.'"[23] Levin Becker, too, has his finger on something here, and at the risk of spoiling a joke, it is worth trying to say precisely what. Benjamin Nugent identifies five characteristics of the stereotypical nerd. Only the first fits the Oulipo well: "Being passionate about some technically sophisticated activity that doesn't revolve around emotional confrontation, physical confrontation, sex, food or beauty." The activity in this case is writing in accordance with precisely pre-formulated rules. Interestingly, the fifth characteristic – "working with, playing with, and enjoying machines more than most people do" – does not apply.[24] The Oulipo's early enthusiasm for computing has waned, as I explain in chapter 3.

The Oulipo, then, is composed of a particular kind of nerd: linguistically focused, mathematically curious, not necessarily technophile, stimulated by the challenges of restrictive form. A self-definition recorded in the minutes of the meeting held on 17 April 1961 captured the mindset memorably: "Oulipians: Rats who construct the labyrinth from which they propose to escape" (OC 201; GO 49). This is certainly not everyone's idea of fun. Some find the mere idea of constraints repellent. Asked about Perec's novel *A Void* (*La disparition*), written without using the letter *e*, the Argentine writer César Aira replied: "Just thinking about it makes me feel anxious [...] I write in order to have more freedom, not less."[25] Mathews's initial reaction to the idea of the book was more extreme: "I sat down in a corner by myself and put my hands over my eyes, tormented by the question, Why would any writer wish to inflict upon himself the linguistic equivalent of Oedipal blindness and castration?"[26] But Mathews was soon converted. And if building a labyrinth to escape from *does* happen to be your idea of fun, there is comfort in discovering like minds. Levin Becker recounts how the Oulipo allowed him to emerge from a word-nerd closet: "The involuntary workings of my mind suddenly made a little more sense, thanks to a certain safety in numbers. This was not, I later learned, a unique experience. Harry Mathews, for many years the only American-born member of the group, recalls that 'being welcomed into the Oulipo made me feel like someone who has been denying a shameful habit only to discover that it is perfectly honourable'" (MSC 12).

The Oulipo's community of practice is based on deep and durable pattern-making, puzzle-solving dispositions. Certainly, the exercise of those dispositions is favoured or hindered by social factors, and whether they are shamefully hidden or proudly flaunted may depend on a writer's connection to a socially recognized group, as the examples of Levin Becker and Mathews show. But the dispositions themselves are not purely social effects, and they furnish a positive principle of cohesion that is unlikely to lose its force as the group's position shifts within the literary field.

I have distinguished the Oulipo from the avant-garde group as modelled by Bourdieu, claiming that its cohesion is not primarily negative. It might be objected that Bourdieu overlooked the cohesive force of the desire for revolution shared by many of the historical avant-gardes. That desire, however, did not always give rise to a durable community of practice. The surrealists are a case in point. Far from consolidating the group, debate about how to engage in the revolutionary struggle, and what the precise objects of that struggle were, led to a series of exclusions and departures, including those of Antonin Artaud and Pierre Naville in 1926, and Aragon in 1930.[27] Roubaud has said that in the early days of the Oulipo, Queneau and Le Lionnais were careful to keep discussions away from politics: "As it happened, there were quite different tendencies within the Oulipo. Hervé Le Tellier [...] was a member of the Ligue Communiste. I was fairly close to the Communist Party when I was little, Arnaud was a Trotskyist, and Claude Berge was to the right of the UMP. Lescure was a left-wing Gaullist, but a Gaullist. If we had gotten into that sort of discussion, it would obviously have led to a break-up."[28] In a letter to Jean Verdure in 1992, Noël Arnaud explained that all discussions of a political nature are statutorily forbidden within "the institution," each member being free to take up the position that he or she believes to be just, but outside the Oulipo and without, in any way, committing the group.[29]

This quarantining of the explicitly political distinguishes the Oulipo markedly from the historical avant-gardes as influentially theorized by Peter Bürger, who formulated their program as "the destruction of art as an institution set off from the praxis of life."[30] This destruction was imagined as prefiguring and sometimes even precipitating a sweeping revolution in pursuit of which many avant-gardes lent their collective support to political parties and organizations, not always on the left.[31]

The Oulipo has never had a political program. To borrow terms from the work of Christian List and Philip Pettit, it is a group agent with a restricted agenda, like many clubs and societies.[32] This is not to say that the Oulipo's members are apolitical as citizens or writers, or that they do not *also* belong to political communities. Roubaud, for instance, was a founding member of the collective Change, formed in 1968 at the initiative of Jean-Pierre Faye, who had been a member of the editorial board of *Tel Quel* and fallen out with Philippe Sollers. The very name of the collective declares an ambitious political program, which links the changing of representations to a changing of social reality, as explained in the liminary statement in the first number of the group's journal.[33] Roubaud, however, was happy to leave that program aside when collaborating with his fellow Oulipians. In the interview with Camille Bloomfield cited above, speaking as a member of the Oulipo, he said: "I don't think it's our job to have political positions."[34]

The father of the Oulipian Michèle Audin died under torture at the hands of the French army during the Battle of Algiers.[35] The struggle for justice in this case (which began in 1957), and led to President Emmanuel Macron's official recognition in 2018 that the murder of Maurice Audin was a state crime, benefited from the support of numerous public figures, including the historians Pierre Vidal-Naquet and Michelle Perrot, and the mathematicians Laurent Schwartz and Cédric Villani. The Oulipo was not involved, as a group, in this campaign, although there can be little doubt that all its current members believe in the justice of the cause.

This restriction of the agenda has perplexed and disappointed some admirers of the Oulipo's inventions. Jean-Jacques Poucel has remarked that "the one recursive criticism" of the Oulipo "that never seems to tire" in North America is that the group refuses to align its research with an explicit ideological or political program." The criticism, Poucel observes, rests on the presumption that "the Oulipo should behave militantly, like one of the historical avant-gardes."[36] Christian Bök, for example, is surprised that the Oulipo does not operate in this way, given the political backgrounds of many of its prominent members.

> Oulipo in fact never deigns to make explicit its political attitudes, even though the conceptual foundation of *contrainte* (with all its liberatory intentions) might lend itself easily to political agitation – and this lacuna in the artistic practice of the group seems even more odd, when we consider that many of the earliest members of the group have participated in left-wing, militant activism, fighting for Resistance during WWII, and some of these poets have even survived internment as political prisoners. Oulipo at its inception almost resembles a cell of decommissioned revolutionists, yet the group has never published a political manifesto about literature (in the way that a writer like Breton – a wartime veteran – has done, for example, on behalf of surrealism). (NA 157)

Bök is right to point to the Resistance activities of the first generation of Oulipians. In 1944 and 1945, Calvino fought with the Communist partisans of the Garibaldi Brigades in the Maritime Alps, an experience reflected in his first novel, *The Path to the Nest of Spiders* (*Il sentiero dei nidi di ragno*, 1947).[37] Le Lionnais was arrested by the Gestapo in April 1944 for his activities in the Marco Polo Resistance network. He was interrogated, tortured, and deported first to Buchenwald, then to the Mittelbau-Dora concentration camp. A brief memoir, *La peinture à Dora* (Painting at Dora), recounts how, for the benefit of a young fellow prisoner, he created an imaginary museum by describing favourite paintings and extracting from each a luminous detail, then recombining these elements in an evanescent "mental painting." Like the "Canto of Ulysses" chapter in Primo Levi's *If This is a Man* (*Se questo è un uomo*, 1947), *La peinture à Dora* testifies to the defensive power of artworks remembered and shared in conditions designed to dehumanize.[38]

Le Lionnais and Calvino were truly at the front line. Other members of the Oulipo put themselves at risk in organizational roles. As one of the editors of the clandestine surrealist journal *La main à plume*, Arnaud was the first publisher of Paul Éluard's famous poem "Liberté" ("Freedom"), and Lescure was the editor of the Resistance journal *Messages*.

Unlike his friend Le Lionnais, Queneau did not engage in high-risk clandestine activities, such as blowing up transformers or forging identity papers, but he chose his side at the beginning of the Occupation.[39] His journals record how, after his demobilization in 1940, he was repeatedly encouraged to contribute to the *Nouvelle revue française* under the new editorship of the pro-German Pierre Drieu La Rochelle. Jacques Audiberti, Drieu La Rochelle himself, Jean Paulhan, Gaston Gallimard, and finally Queneau's psychoanalyst, Adrien Borel, all tried to persuade him to adapt to the new normal. "He thinks I'm 'resisting,'" Queneau noted after a session with Borel, "a 'polite and smiling resistance' but stubborn all the same."[40] During the Occupation, Queneau published only in journals closely allied with the Resistance: *La main à plume*, *Messages*, and *Fontaine*. After the liberation of Paris, he wrote a literary column for *Front national* (the journal of the Resistance organization of the same name, not to be confused with the political party founded by Jean-Marie Le Pen). He was also a member of the National Writers' Committee, which blacklisted writers who had collaborated with the occupying forces.[41]

These are some of the backgrounds against which the Oulipo's political reticence surprises Bök, who also notes that Oskar Pastior survived internment in a Soviet labour camp (NA 77). In 2005, Bök could not have been aware of the full complexity of Pastior's case. In 2010, after Pastior's death, it was revealed that from 1961 to 1968, he had served as an informer for the Rumanian state security service (Securitate). This news dismayed his friends, in particular the Nobel laureate Herta Müller, whose novel *The Hunger Angel* (*Atemschaukel*) is largely based on Pastior's memories of deportation and imprisonment. Müller herself had resisted the Securitate's attempts to recruit her in the late 1970s.[42] In an earlier and harsher phase of the repression, Pastior, author of poems judged to be hostile to the regime and vulnerable to prosecution for homosexuality, seems to have faced a choice between returning to prison and signing a confession and an agreement to inform.[43] For those of us who have been spared such choices, reading *The Hunger Angel* and particularly the pages about the prospect of "redeportation," should at least slow the impulse to sit in judgment.[44]

There are two things to say in response to Bök's disappointed surprise at the Oulipo's political disengagement. The first has been said by Jean-Jacques Poucel: it is not quite true that the Oulipo never deigns to make explicit its political attitudes. In 1997, Roubaud, along with Jouet, Grangaud, and Le Tellier, signed a declaration condemning the Front National.[45] And Roubaud's most widely diffused and translated text is the eminently political "Le Pen est-il français?" ("Is Le Pen French?"), which demonstrates with implacable rigour that Le Pen is not French according to his own definition of Frenchness (PECH 13–14).

The second thing to say is that it may have been precisely their experience of political conflict that inclined Le Lionnais and Queneau to design the Oulipo as a special kind of group, with a focus on "research and friendship" as Poucel puts it.[46] In the 1920s and '30s, Queneau had been revolted by the use of serious political questions as pretexts for intrigue and domination in the small world of the Parisian avant-gardes. Le Lionnais returned from the Dora concentration camp to find that he was indeed a "decommissioned revolutionist": he had been expelled from the French Communist Party for reasons that remain unclear.[47] The original disengagement of the Oulipo, which set a lasting tone, was motivated if not by an Orwellian "horror of politics," then by a wariness more common in societies that have been torn apart by political violence than in durably stable democracies.[48]

The separation between art and politics in the social life of the Oulipo indicates something more general about the group: it does not have a totalizing project; it does not propose what Alain Viala, discussing the literature of French gallantry, has called a "global model" for behaviour.[49] Here again the contrast with surrealism is sharp. On the death of Breton, Queneau wrote in a brief but serene homage: "For many ill-informed people, the name of André Breton is synonymous with surrealism. They are right. Without Breton, surrealism, if it had even existed, would only have been a literary school. With him, it was a way of life."[50] The Oulipians, as remarked above, share dispositions to the playful patterning of words, but the group does not prescribe a way of life or a single existential style. Indeed, more than one new recruit has wondered how the Oulipo coheres, given the widely varying manners and styles of its members. Remembering a conversation with Roubaud, Paul Fournel has written: "It became clear to us that the Workshop was a novel by Queneau *in vivo*. An improbable assembly of heterogeneous characters, brought together by their differences much more than their resemblances, drawn from different and supposedly impermeable worlds, all rather surprised to be there, organized according to an unspoken rule, which was respected all the more strictly because it didn't officially exist."[51]

If the Oulipo is an unwritten novel by Queneau, it does not imprison its characters. They can live outside it, like the title character in Queneau's last novel, *The Flight of Icarus*, who escapes from the pages of a work in progress by the *belle époque* novelist Hubert Lubert. The Oulipo does not require exclusive adherence. The "crisis of 1974," as Camille Bloomfield has called it, was precipitated by a fraction of the old guard (Jacques Bens, Claude Berge, Jacques Duchateau, Jean Lescure) humorously proposing disciplinary measures against any Oulipian found to be associating with a number of "supposedly 'literary' journals" (the list includes *Change* and *La Quinzaine littéraire*, to which Roubaud and Perec respectively were frequent contributors).[52] The "dissidents" were not supported in this censure by the founders: concerned by the tension, Queneau asked Braffort to act as a pacifying intermediary, which, with the help of Lescure, he successfully did.[53] Neither Queneau nor Le Lionnais, it seems, had any wish to make monopolizing claims on the allegiance of the Oulipo's members. Both belonged to several intellectual communities themselves, Le Lionnais in particular, who collected the most diverse memberships, and lived under the sign of "the disparate."[54]

If staying off political terrain is an unwritten rule in the Oulipo, there are also rules that have been formulated, if not gravely. Roubaud summarized them as follows in a talk given at Western Sydney University in April 2014:

RULE ONE: No one can be expelled from the Oulipo. [...]

RULE TWO: Conversely, no one can resign from the Oulipo or stop belonging to it. Rule two is based on the principle: you can't have something for nothing. Rules one and two have an important consequence: once a member of the Oulipo, always a member. This, in turn, implies that the dead members continue to belong to the Oulipo. Marcel Duchamp, for example.

RULE THREE: Lest Rule two seem unduly coercive, an exception to it is provided. One may relinquish membership of the Oulipo under the following circumstances: suicide may be committed in the presence of an officer of the court, who then ascertains that, according to the Oulipian's explicit last wishes, his suicide was intended to release him from the Oulipo and restore his freedom of manoeuvre for the rest of eternity.

RULE FOUR: The Oulipo is not a closed group; it must be constantly enlarged through co-optation of new members.[55]

Rule two cannot of course prevent a member from withdrawing from the group's activities, whether by simply ceasing to attend meetings, or by explicitly signalling a break, as Métail, Braffort, and most recently Roubaud himself have done.[56] The "enlargement" prescribed by rule four has been slow: the Oulipo now has eighteen living members, not all of whom are active, as opposed to fifteen in 1962 (including the "corresponding members"). This cautious growth has been conditioned by the group's mechanisms of inclusion.

New members must be introduced by a member and co-opted unanimously. Fournel has also said that charm is a requisite.[57] This may sound like a pretext for arbitrariness, but it points to an important characteristic of the Oulipo: it is a group of friends. As Alexander Nehamas has argued, it is not possible to give an exhaustive account of what draws us to a friend, and Montaigne's famous answer to the question of why he was friends with La Boétie – "Because it was he, because it was I" – is not lazy or evasive but marks a genuine limit to what can be articulated. According to Nehamas, this is because friendship is based on a commitment to the future, "the hope for a better life that remains unknown for now," a hope that may be disappointed.[58] The commitment to an open future is evident in the Oulipo's co-optation of young members (like Fournel, Métail, or Levin Becker, all in their mid-twenties at the time of their entry into the group) more on the basis of promise than of achievements.

Friendships, of course, can fail and go sour. No group of friends is immune to irritation, rivalry, and resentment. But as opposed to the surrealists, who were happy to broadcast their fallings-out and made an art of the public insult, the Oulipo has remained discreet about its moments of internal turbulence. That is, until the publication of Roubaud's *Peut-être ou la nuit de dimanche*. It is a measure of the Oulipo's difference from the historical avant-gardes that it has not responded publicly to Roubaud's attack.

The "exclusion of exclusion" (rule one) and the barriers to inclusion (particularly unanimous co-optation) have slowed movement in and out of the Oulipo. Here again, the contrast with surrealism is illuminating. Breton's group was something of a revolving door: many writers and artists passed through it, and not all the brief participations ended acrimoniously. Francis Ponge, for example, appears as a signatory on only one surrealist document (the second manifesto), but as he explained in his interviews with Philippe Sollers, he stopped participating in the group's activities for practical reasons: in order to marry, he took a job with very long working hours.[59] Whatever one thinks of Breton's fondness for intrigue and his domineering tendencies, it is a testament to his charisma and assiduity as an organizer that he was able, over the decades, to keep attracting new recruits to replace the renegades.

In spite of the contrasts that I have been stressing so far in this chapter, there is an important respect in which the Oulipo resembles the historical avant-gardes, including surrealism: its activities are strongly oriented toward the future. This is especially clear in Le Lionnais's manifestos (curiously, like Breton, he published two manifestos and failed to finish a third). At the end of the "Second Manifesto" he writes: "One may ask what would happen if the Oulipo suddenly ceased to exist. In the short run, people might regret it. In the long run, everything would return to normal, humanity eventually discovering, after much groping and fumbling about, that which the Oulipo has endeavoured to promote consciously. There would result however in the fate of civilization a certain delay which we feel it our duty to attenuate" (OPPL xxvii). The Oulipo is seen here, in 1973, as an avant-garde formation, ahead of the advancing army. The goal, however, is not revolution but an augmentation of creative power through the synthesis of viable artificial structures, that is, newly invented literary forms which might live and multiply outside the laboratory environment of the Oulipo. Le Lionnais compares the invention of such forms to the synthesis of living matter, and remarks that it would seem to be "infinitely less complicated and less difficult" (OPPL xxv).

"NOR IS IT A SCIENTIFIC SEMINAR, A 'SERIOUS' WORKING GROUP BETWEEN QUOTATION MARKS"

Le Lionnais's manifestos are animated by the innovative spirit that drives scientific research. The progressive empirical successes of science encourage scientists in the belief that their theories are advancing toward truth, and Le Lionnais saw no reason why the arts should not be drawn into this great enterprise. His "messianic" vision seems to belie the modest negations with which Queneau introduced the Oulipo in 1964, particularly the second: "Nor is it a scientific seminar, a 'serious' working group between quotation marks."[60] This is a counterpart to the first negation: the Oulipo is neither a literary movement nor a scientific seminar. Just as it is not part of the Oulipo's collective brief to compose literary works, the group has not set out to make mathematical or scientific discoveries. Rather than intervening in a field of knowledge production, it works at an interface, specifically the interface between mathematics and literature.[61]

No one would dispute this second negation, which is just as valid now as ever. The number of the Oulipo's members who have or have had professions in scientific disciplines is not as high as one might suppose from some brief presentations of the group. Four of the group's eighteen living members have professional backgrounds in mathematics: Roubaud, Le Tellier, Audin, and Olivier Salon. The last two have disconcerted some of their fellow Oulipians by "converting" from mathematics to literature, becoming active writers since retiring from teaching mathematics in tertiary institutions. Of the fifteen members in 1962, three (Berge, Braffort, and Le Lionnais) were similarly qualified. Explaining the Oulipo to a correspondent in 1990, Arnaud wrote that it "gathers [...] an equal number of scientific and literary people," but the literary people have always been in the majority.[62]

Although Queneau stressed that the Oulipo was not a "serious" working group from a scientific point of view, he put "serious" in inverted commas to qualify his negation. One way not to be "serious" is not to take oneself too seriously. This is not a risk-free strategy. It may result in not being taken seriously at all by critics and the public. That risk is augmented, in the Oulipo's case, by success in domains beyond the strictly literary: education and radio. The Oulipo is a source of effective and enjoyable writing exercises, widely used in classrooms both within and beyond the French-speaking world. A number of the group's members – Bens, François Caradec, Fournel, Jouet, Le Tellier, Clémentine Mélois, and Ian Monk – have also participated in the popular and consistently light-hearted radio program "Des Papous dans la tête" on France Culture. These public faces of the Oulipo have shaped and perpetuated an image of the group as a band of literary jokers. One of the refrains of this book will be that beneath and alongside all the joking, many of the Oulipians, and not the least of them in literary terms, are also haunted and driven by serious concerns.

Queneau's fame, in particular, rests on a persistent misunderstanding or misrepresentation: for many he remains essentially a comic writer, the author of *Zazie in the Metro* and *Exercices in Style.* The vast intellectual hinterland of his fiction and poetry, never advertised in the work itself, but uncovered by critics such as Alexandre Kojève and Alain Calame, remains the preserve of specialists.[63] For Queneau as for other writers of the Oulipo, humour, like the foregrounding of form, is often a kind of tact, and sometimes, in Chris Marker's words, "the politeness of despair."[64]

At the meeting of the Oulipo on 28 April 1961, Queneau said: "We are not jokers. We set about our work *very seriously*" (GO 57). Almost every month since November 1960, the group has met and proposed at least one new structure or constraint under the "Creation" rubric. The bibliothèque oulipienne comprises 239 fascicles as of April 2022. The list of constraints proposed by the Oulipo on its official website runs to 138. Literary works written on Oulipian principles have won major prizes, most recently Le Tellier's *L'anomalie* (The anomaly, Prix Goncourt 2020).

It has become difficult to deny the significance of the Oulipo's contribution to contemporary writing, although the group still declines to take itself too seriously and generally sets a light or comic tone when presenting itself to the public. Another way not to be "serious" is to devote time to games. Queneau was well aware that in mathematics problems arising from games have often fed into fundamental research. In his 1964 talk, he proposed an analogy: "We should recall that topology and number theory grew, in part, from what were once called 'mathematical diversions,' 'recreational mathematics.' [...] We should also remember that probability began as a simple 'diversion,' [...] Like game theory, until von Neumann came along" (LNF 182). The suggestion here is that the exercises of the Oulipo could similarly raise fruitful questions for literary theory and practice. Such effects may require long gestation, as Queneau pointed out at the meeting of the Oulipo on 27 August 1971: "The Oulipo is like topology. [...] For two hundred years, it was just mental exercises. And then, all of a sudden, it revolutionized mathematics. So we shouldn't lose heart."[65]

It appears that in spite of his precautionary negations, Queneau, like Le Lionnais, had long-term hopes for the Oulipo. It may not have been a literary school or a scientific seminar, but its "recreational" work at the interface of literature and mathematics had the potential, he felt, to stimulate both, and perhaps even to revolutionize the former. That potential, however, would not be realized by a surrender to chance.

"IT HAS NOTHING TO DO WITH EXPERIMENTAL OR ALEATORY LITERATURE"

Queneau's third negation is surprising at first. More specific than the first two, it aims to distinguish the Oulipo from a particular tendency in the literature of the time and from a specific school. The tendency associated experimentation with the use of aleatory or chance-governed methods. Alison James has pointed out that such methods were used intensively during two periods in the twentieth century: the 1910s and '20s, and the 1950s and '60s.[66] In the first period, they were championed in literature by Dada and surrealism; in the second, music came to the fore, largely through the influence of John Cage. The renewed appeal of the aleatory paradigm across artistic media is apparent in an anthology edited by La Monte Young, whose publication in 1963 was an important step toward the formation of the Fluxus group. The book's full title was *An Anthology of chance operations concept art anti-art indeterminacy improvisation meaningless work natural disasters plans of action stories diagrams music poetry essays dance constructions mathematics compositions.*

In 1964, Queneau was at pains to distinguish the Oulipo from this trend. The group's general hostility to aleatory methods springs partly from its reactive stance in relation to the surrealists, who flung the gates open to chance, embracing automatic writing techniques and games involving blind collaboration, such as the "exquisite corpse" and "the one in the other."[67] Breton also exalted the coincidence as a manifestation of "objective chance," a notion that emerges progressively in three texts: *Nadja* (1928), *The Communicating Vessels* (*Les vases communicants*, 1932), and *Mad Love* (*L'amour fou*, 1937). Reflecting in *Mad Love* on the answers to a surrealist questionnaire ("What do you consider the essential encounter of your life? To what extent did this encounter seem to you, and does it seem to you now, to be fortuitous or foreordained?"), Breton proposes a definition of chance according to "the modern materialists": "*chance is the form making manifest the exterior necessity which traces its path in the human unconscious* (boldly trying to interpret and reconcile Engels and Freud on this point)."[68]

The founding members of the Oulipo did not share the surrealists' openness to chance, whether in literary composition or in the conduct of everyday life. In 1962, Berge said that in his opinion the Oulipo was "essentially *anti-chance*" (GO 146). This remark has often been repeated by other members of the group.[69] But as Alison James points out in *Constraining Chance*, on hearing Berge's formula Queneau proposed a loyal amendment: "We are perhaps not so very *anti*. I would prefer to say that we display a certain suspicion with regard to chance."[70] This is consistent with Queneau's disenchantment of the chance encounter in *Exercises in Style*, which Le Lionnais considered to be one of the founding texts of potential literature.

The *Oulipo Compendium* describes *Exercises in Style* as "a series of texts by Raymond Queneau in which the same inconsequential story is told in ninety-nine different ways" (OC 144). The description is more subtly appropriate than it might seem at first. Here is the first text, in Barbara Wright's translation:

Notation

In the *S* bus, in the rush hour. A chap of about twenty-six,
felt hat with a cord instead of a ribbon, neck too long, as if
someone's been having a tug-of-war with it. People getting off.
The chap in question gets annoyed with one of the men standing

next to him. He accuses him of jostling him every time anyone goes past. A snivelling tone which is meant to be aggressive. When he sees a vacant seat he throws himself on to it.

Two hours later, I meet him in the Cour de Rome, in front of the Gare Saint-Lazare. He's with a friend who's saying: "You ought to get an extra button put on your overcoat." He shows him where (at the lapels) and why. (ES 3–4)

The story is made up of two parts separated by a temporal gap, and the relation between them is not consequential: there is no evident causal chain leading from the first encounter to the second. In a city the size of Paris, a coincidence such as this double sighting is remarkable in the non-evaluative sense of the word: unlikely enough to be worth remarking.

A similar coincidence is the subject of Breton's short text "The New Spirit." Breton recounts how both Aragon and he were struck by the sight of a young woman whose path they crossed in the rue Bonaparte one afternoon. Meeting André Derain later at Les Deux Magots, they communicated their impressions only to learn that Derain had just seen the same woman by the railing beside the church of Saint-Germain-des-Prés. The coincidence in this case is not so remarkable from a spatio-temporal point of view: the locations of the sightings are close to one another, and they occurred over a relatively short period. The young woman is described as beautiful and behaving oddly, so it is not surprising that the three friends should have noticed her. It is perhaps curious that Breton saw her board a Clichy-Odéon bus shortly before she was seen not far away by Derain, but she had already given the impression of being "extraordinarily lost": under the influence of a drug, or reeling from a catastrophic event. What fascinated Aragon, Breton, and Derain most of all may have been that she interacted with three other men – "an unbelievable, utterly vile passer-by," "a mediocre-looking character," and "a black man" – but paid the poets and the painter no attention at all.[71]

For Breton, this triple sighting constitutes a "riddle," never to be solved. In *Exercises in Style*, Queneau dissociates his double sighting from the surrealist mystique of the encounter: the person sighted is portrayed in most of the texts as annoying. The second sighting is remarkable but not especially welcome. It is as if Queneau were saying: a coincidence can also be banal. The chance encounter is not necessarily a vessel of the marvellous. At the same time, by recasting the banal material with comic and rhetorical ingenuity, he exalts the transformative power of stylistic variation.

The "certain suspicion" or distrust with which the Oulipo regarded chance did not imply a total hostility but a vigilant filtering of what chance might throw up. In a radio talk broadcast in 1953, Queneau affirmed that "the unknown and the unpredictable" must intervene to confirm the efforts and intentions of the poet.[72] The complement to this remark is to be found in Le Lionnais's and Queneau's responses to the question of whether the Oulipo was for or against mentally ill writers ("fous littéraires"): "Le Lionnais: 'We're not against them, but the literary vocation is what interests us above all.' Queneau: 'The only literature is intentional literature" (GO 42). In other words, literary effects produced accidentally in the discourse of the mentally ill are not a part of literature. The writer must, at the very least, pick and choose. Or to put it in the terms of Queneau's radio talk, the intentions of the poet must confirm particular products of chance.

In a 1947 essay on the painting of Joan Miró, the role that Queneau assigns to chance is essential and perhaps even primordial: "But the use of chance is an essential element of artistic activity; it might even be the point on which is balanced – in an admirably unstable and marvellously paradoxical equilibrium – the swaying pyramid of the arts conceived as techniques, procedures, and recipes" (LNF 164). The Oulipo has focused its efforts on elaborating techniques, procedures, and recipes but all things considered, it cannot be said to have banished chance or even attempted to do so. As Alison James has written: "some Oulipian methods may be deemed aleatory (in accordance with the musical application of the term) in the place that they assign to the reader. [...] Furthermore, even a rule-based method such as S + 7 [...] involves a certain suspension or at least displacement of authorial intention."[73]

The S + 7 or N + 7 method replaces each noun in a text with the noun that comes seven places further on in a given dictionary. In using this method, the Oulipians defer their authorial intentions to a later moment of evaluation. Introducing the method in his interviews with Georges Charbonnier, Queneau said: "The results are of varying quality. A certain amount of chance is involved ... Well, it depends on the texts. It seems there are – and this, precisely, is one of the first results of this work – some texts that are very good, that is, very manipulatable, which produce very good results when treated in this way, and others that produce nothing at all" (EGC 125). The "certain amount of chance" is neither ruled out nor trusted to produce a marvellous result. Recently, as if to test the limits of the Oulipian mistrust of chance, Eduardo Berti proposed a chance-based variant on the N + 7 method: S + dé, or N + die, which replaces each noun in a text with another noun x places further on in a given dictionary, where x is determined by the roll of a die. It is hard to imagine this aleatory method being endorsed by the Oulipo in the 1960s, but in 2016 it was added to the official list of constraints on the Oulipo's website. This goes to show that the very notion of constraint is evolving, as I argue in chapter 2.

For Queneau in 1964, Max Bense's group in Stuttgart exemplified the aleatory tendency from which he emphatically distinguished the Oulipo. The philosopher Max Bense was a polymath, like Queneau. He too was particularly interested in the relations between mathematics and literature. A friend of Le Lionnais (GO 309), he was a mentor to two of Queneau's German translators, Ludwig Harig and Elisabeth Walther. And in 1958, he invited Queneau to give a lecture in Stuttgart. (The invitation was not taken up.)[74] The two men would seem to have had much in common, yet Queneau insisted on the difference between the Oulipo and the Stuttgart School. Why? Was this a missed opportunity, as Hans Hartje has suggested?[75] Or was there a substantive divergence of views?

In Bense's theoretical writings, influenced by Claude Shannon's mathematical theory of communication, planning and chance are at the service of what he sees as the key requirement for aesthetic merit: unpredictability.[76] Although the Oulipo does not have a systematically worked-out aesthetics, it clearly does not value unpredictability as highly as Bense did. Both Queneau in his interviews with Charbonnier and Le Lionnais in his manifestos subscribe to a more traditional account of creativity, requiring the artwork to be valuable to a community as well as original. Unpredictability and novelty are not enough. This dual account of creativity goes back at least as far as Kant's *Critique of Judgment*, where it is argued that the products of genius must be exemplary, "since nonsense too can be original."[77] And although Queneau said that the Oulipo situated itself "prior to all notions of aesthetic value," he was careful to point out that "prior to" does not imply "indifferent to." In fact, it is the aim of the Oulipo's collective work to be *preparatory* to the production of aesthetic value.

For Queneau and Le Lionnais, the value of an invented form is related to its use and adoption by writers. Queneau said: "We think that it would be useful and pleasant for present-day writers to be provided with new forms, new structures, which, with use, will turn out to be more or less interesting" (EGC 140). And Le Lionnais wrote, in the "Second Manifesto": "The efficacy of a structure – that is, the extent to which it helps a writer – depends primarily on the degree of difficulty imposed by rules that are more or less constraining" (OL xxiii). The emphasis on utility, efficacy, and help shows how pragmatic the founders of the Oulipo were. As good dance music must make people dance whatever else it does, a good invented form, for Queneau and Le Lionnais, is one that is useful and efficacious for other writers, a form that they will reuse because it has helped them.

The usefulness of a literary invention can only be assessed in retrospect, since it depends on the varying purposes that subsequent writers bring to it. And if the value of an invention depends on its usefulness, it cannot be an intrinsic quality; it must be relational and historically variable. Queneau was keenly aware of this, and must have been reminded of it frequently by his work as a member of the editorial committee at Gallimard and as director of the Encyclopédie de la Pléaide. In an interview about the Encyclopédie, he reacted strongly to Christian Mégret's supposition that the literary canon was stable up to 1900: "Not at all, there are lots of authors from the sixteenth and seventeenth centuries who don't even figure in Lanson but are now considered to be major poets. And for the contemporary period, the problem of which writers really count is even thornier" (B 115).

It is not surprising, then, that Queneau maintained a skeptical distance from Bense's "information aesthetics," which drew on the speculations of the mathematician George D. Birkhoff.[78] Birkhoff proposed what he took to be an ahistorical, objective, mathematical formula for the beautiful: $M = O/C$ (where M is "aesthetic measure," O is order, and C complexity).[79] Bense integrated this formula into an aesthetics that aspired to complete objectivity, drawing also on Noam Chomsky's generative grammar, and, as mentioned, on Shannon's communications theory. He envisaged art as a process reversing the physical world's tendency toward entropy.[80]

Even admirers like Frieder Nake admit that Bense's "heroic experiment" "turned out to be reductive and schematic."[81] In retrospect, it seems that his thinking rested on what Christopher Watkin would call a "pantasm," that is, an attempt to route our understanding of being, or humanity, or, in this case, art, through one particular element or discourse.[82] The discourse in Bense's case is that of information theory:

everything is information. Queneau was wary of such maximal-scope theorizing, which often relies either on the kind of overextended analogies analyzed and criticized by Jacques Bouveresse in *Prodiges et vertiges de l'analogie* (Marvels and fevers of analogy) or on faith that the explanation of all phenomena will be reducible to a certain base at some time in the future. Queneau, by contrast, placed his hope in precisely located points and zones of contact between disciplines and fields: edges or *Bords*, as his book of essays on "mathematicians, precursors, and encyclopedists" is significantly entitled. If the Oulipo is not a "serious" working group, Queneau seems to have been implying with his third negation that it was more serious in its respect for specialist knowledge than the Stuttgart School.

It might be objected here that the Oulipo thinks pantasmatically too, although it has never been particularly attached to information theory. Doesn't a mathematical pantasm underlie the group's practice? Don't the Oulipians act on the belief that, as Michel Serres writes in *Hominescence*, "everything is number"?[83] Watkin points out that there are two ways of understanding the claim that "everything is number," only one of which is pantasmatic.

> The non-pantasmatic way to read "tout est nombre" is as a claim that there is no object, experience or event that cannot be understood digitally, but that this digital understanding does not monopolise anything it touches and should not a priori be considered the privileged discourse for accessing any object, experience or event simpliciter. The "everything," in this case, is an "everything without distinction." There is nothing that mathematics cannot touch, but it does not exhaust anything it touches.
> The second, pantasmatic understanding also includes this "everything without distinction," but it goes further, to say that the digital is the only (strong pantasm) or privileged (weak pantasm) discourse to give direct access to what it discusses. This is not only "everything without distinction" but, in addition, "everything without remainder."[84]

While Queneau said that all Oulipian constraints were mathematizable, he was not in the grip of a mathematical pantasm.[85] His circular classification of the sciences undoes the hierarchy that would regard the less mathematized sciences as backwards, follows Piaget in regarding mathematical logic as "the axiomatics of thought itself," and proposes a continuity between logic and psychology, which has often been seen as the most backward science of all (B 126–8). Moreover, Queneau does not see mathematization as a one-way process, applying acquired mathematical knowledge to less enlightened fields. The problems that arise in any field can stimulate the production of new mathematical knowledge, and this need not be accomplished by reducing the social to the biological or the biological to the chemical (B 127).

The practice of the Oulipo is not founded on the presumption that all is number, without remainder. It does not attempt to absorb literature into the master discourse of mathematics, but searches rather for edges along which literary but also mathematical invention may be stimulated by interdisciplinary contact. The group's approach is piecemeal and artisanal. As Queneau said in his 1964 talk, the Oulipo's research is naïve in the "peri-mathematical sense, as in naïve set theory. We go forward without dwelling too much on the details [*sans trop raffiner*]. We're trying to prove movement by walking" (BCL 322; LNF 182). This privileging of practice distinguishes the group very clearly from the Stuttgart School, inspired by the charismatic Bense with his sweeping theoretical ambitions.[86]

In outliving its founders, the Oulipo has changed and will continue to change in ways that are hard to foresee. Nevertheless, certain features have endured. While the group has become much more like a literary school, at least in the perception of the reading public, it still approaches the collective invention of forms as a pre-aesthetic activity. It is not a scientific seminar, but it has worked seriously at the interface between mathematics and literature, steadily producing a large corpus of constraints and forms, implemented in exercises and works. The Oulipo is clearly experimental in its commitment to systematic invention. When Queneau said that the group had nothing to do with experimental literature, he was marking its distance from the experiments with chance operations that the neo-avant-gardes of the early 1960s were bringing once again to the fore.

The Oulipo's main way of establishing contact between mathematics and literature has been to propose new writing rules, which have sometimes been derived from mathematical structures and can always be formulated in mathematico-logical terms, although this is not always necessary or useful.[87] Before examining how Oulipian rules operate in works, it is important to clarify their relations with other kinds of rules that govern and shape literary writing. That is the task of the following chapter.

2

Kinds of Rules

CLASTIC AND CONSTRUCTIVE

The literary inventions of the early twentieth century were often deliberately disruptive. Ezra Pound felt that to "make it new" (as he translated a neo-Confucian injunction that he found in a commentary on the *Da xue* or *Great Learning*), certain things would have to be broken.[1] "To break the pentameter, that was the first heave," he wrote in Canto 81, enacting the break with a line that bunches two of its five stresses in the last two positions.[2] And Pound was by no means alone in the conviction that artistic freedom required destruction. The historical avant-gardes often advocated a clastic experimentalism: one that breaks down certain elements of the literary work, or breaks with the conventions governing their use. Clastic experimentalism has a long and prestigious history in French literature, which can be sketched by mentioning and dating a series of disruptive gestures.

In a letter to Eugène Lefébure (1867), Stéphane Mallarmé declared: "I have created my Work solely by elimination [...] Destruction was my Béatrice."[3] Pascal Durand has pointed out that the objects of the destruction and elimination mentioned here were, in part, the anecdotal elements that Mallarmé purged from "Hérodiade" ("Herodiad") and "L'Après-midi d'un faune" ("The Afternoon of a Faun") in pursuit of purity.[4] But in the same letter Mallarmé claims that he has destroyed his own self as well.[5] And the culmination of his project in *Un coup de dés* (*One Toss of the Dice*, 1897) has a destructive force underlined by Roland Barthes in *Writing Degree Zero*: "The whole effort of Mallarmé was exerted toward the destruction of language, with Literature reduced, so to speak, to being its carcass."[6] Barthes seems to have been thinking primarily of the way in which *Un coup de dés* distends conventional syntactic relations by scattering sentence fragments across the double page. It is often very hard to tell precisely how to relate one fragment to another, although they display a strong thematic coherence.

Mallarmé's experiment followed the challenge to metrical convention issued by the poets whom he identified in "Crisis of Verse" as having loosened the hold of the alexandrine and begun the move toward free verse in the 1880s: Henri de Régnier, Jules Laforgue, Gustave Kahn, Jean Moréas, and Francis Viélé-Griffin.[7] One of the most prominent inheritors of these *vers-libristes* in the following generation was Guillaume Apollinaire. Just before his book *Alcools* (*Alcools*) went to press in 1913, Apollinaire decided to strip out all the punctuation marks, perhaps under the influence of Blaise Cendrars's very lightly punctuated "Prose du transsibérien et de la petite Jehanne de France" ("The Prose of the TransSiberian and of Little Jeanne of France") published in the same year.[8] In 1919, Breton and Soupault undertook the sustained exercise in automatic writing that produced *The Magnetic Fields*, the inaugural text of surrealism, ignoring as best they could the co-occurrence restrictions that conventionally limit the words or expressions that we expect to find after a particular lexical unit.[9]

Each of the gestures that I have mentioned breaks rules relating to a particular aspect of literary composition: meter, syntax, punctuation, semantics. Although the gestures have a history, they are not strictly cumulative. Mallarmé integrates the liberties taken by the *vers-libristes* and goes a step further, but the poems in Apollinaire's *Alcools* (1913) rarely present the degree of syntactic indeterminacy to be found throughout *Un coup de dés* (1897). As opposed to the poems in *Alcools*, the sentences in *The Magnetic Fields* (1920) are punctuated normally. They are also syntactically well formed, but they are not coherent with respect to the situation referred to or each other. They constitute what certain discourse linguists, following Michael Halliday and Ruqaiya Hasan, would call non-text: "The nearest we get to non-text in actual life, leaving aside the works of those poets and prose writers who deliberately set out to create non-text, is probably in the speech of young children and in bad translations."[10]

Clastic experimentalism can go further still. Isidore Isou, the founder of Lettrisme, took a hammer to the word, outdoing James Joyce's *Finnegans Wake* by breaking words down not just into more or less recognizable morphemes but into letters. For Isou, the word was an oppressive stereotype and had to be smashed to set letters free.[11] Why letters are not also stereotypes he does not explain. In its most radical variants, clastic experimentalism aspired to a clean sweep, as in Filippo Tommaso Marinetti's literally incendiary "The Foundation and Manifesto of Futurism": "We want to free our country from the endless number of museums that everywhere cover her like countless graveyards [...] Set fire to the library shelves! ... Divert the canals so they can flood the museums! ... Oh what a pleasure it is to see those revered old canvases, washed out and tattered, drifting away in the water! ... Grab your picks and your axes and your hammers and then demolish, pitilessly demolish, all venerated cities."[12]

Futurism and Dada were far fiercer and more sweeping in their rejection of the artistic and literary pasts than surrealism. Indeed one of surrealism's important legacies was the recovery of neglected work, as Queneau stressed in his response to the death of Breton, where he pointed out that in 1923 the leader of the surrealists had lauded a series of writers, including the Marquis de Sade, G.W.F. Hegel, and Lautréamont, who were little known or held in contempt at the time, but would join the canon by the mid-1960s. "Breton changed the scale of values, not according to a system or a doctrine, but as he pleased, by Olympian decision, by an intuition that rarely erred."[13]

It is instructive to compare the scores (in a range from -25 to 25) given by Breton and the Dadaist Tristan Tzara to a series of writers, artists, musicians, and public figures in a survey entitled "Liquidation" and published in the eighteenth number of *Littérature* (1921). While not using the very top of the range, Breton gives many scores over 10, including 20 for Ducasse (Lautréamont), 19 for Sade and Jacques Vaché, and 18 for Charles Baudelaire, André Derain, Arthur Rimbaud, Soupault, and Tzara. Tzara's favourite score, by far, is -25, and he attributes scores of over 10 only to a handful of contemporaries (including Breton).[14] Marinetti was equally determined to declare his independence from the past, violently rejecting the neo-Nietzschean label often applied to him and his friends. In "Against Academic Teachers," he writes, targeting Nietzsche: "Shame on those who allow themselves to be seduced by the demon of admiration. Shame on anyone who admires and imitates the past! Shame on those who prostitute their own genius."[15]

Nevertheless, as Camille Bloomfield has pointed out, the tabula rasa is more often a feature of the avant-garde's provocative rhetoric than of its actual practice.[16] The sweep is never truly clean. It is hard to see how it could be: the past has made us the way we are and forgetting cannot alter that. As Roubaud writes in *Poetry, etcetera: Cleaning House*: "The Tabula Rasa is not an effective arm against the weight of the past" (PECH 177). This does not invalidate clastic experimentalism, whose destructions are usually selective and temporary. Placing strategic bans on overused resources can effect real and salutary change in literary practice. But the bans themselves can become thoughtless reflexes, and accumulate to impoverishing effect, as Jacques Jouet notes with a certain exasperation in his *Ruminations du potentiel* (Ruminations on potential), where he associates literary modernity with an "aesthetic miserliness": "no attributive adjectives, no past historic tense, no subjunctive imperfect, none of this, none of that ... war on syntax, all hail parataxis! Shortness of breath, ellipses everywhere ..." (RP 71).

Proscriptions of this sort, of course, are not the only way to change how writing is done. Positive rules can also be laid down, and the repertoire of resources extended. The historical avant-gardes prescribed as well as proscribed, often simultaneously, or almost. For example, in the first surrealist manifesto, Breton proposes a formal rule as a way of correcting a possible dysfunction of his method for automatic writing: "If silence threatens to settle in if you should ever happen to make a mistake – a mistake, perhaps due to carelessness – break off without hesitation with an overly clear line. Following a word the origin of which seems suspicious to you, place any letter whatsoever, the letter 'l' for example, always the letter 'l,' and bring the arbitrary back by making this letter the first of the following word."[17] Here the rule is a corrective to spontaneity, employed when the automatic text begins, suspiciously, to make too much sense. The Oulipo inverts this arrangement, putting the rule first and resorting to spontaneity, in the form of the clinamen or deviation from the constraint, to correct an overly rigid regulation of the text, as I explain in chapter 5. Insofar as the group multiplies positive rules, privileging prescription over proscription, it engages in a constructive rather than a clastic experimentalism.

This is not to say that the practice of the Oulipo is not sometimes clastic in its effects. Certain constraints, especially those that bear on letters, can disrupt linguistic norms to such a degree that the resulting texts are opaque in the extreme. Perec's *ulcérations* constraint, a kind of isogram, is a case in point: "(1) only the eleven most frequent letters of the language are used (in French those included in *ulcérations*, in English those in *threnodials*); (2) no letter is repeated until the set of eleven letters is complete; (3) the completed poem comprises a sequence of eleven such sets. This grid is then rearranged in lines conforming to poetic intent and ordinary syntax" (OC 60). This constraint is constructive in that it builds patterns of letters, and clastic in that it leads to the violation of co-occurrence restrictions and syntactic norms. Here is the illustrative example given by Mathews:

> This lean rod
> Threads lion roads the linnet hails
> (Ordinal hod-rest, hard line to set),
> Oils hard nails. Hot nerd,
> I, Stendhal or not,
> Heard slither a solid *n*. (OC 60)

It is almost always hard, though never impossible, to make head or tail of poems written under this constraint. But their opacity is a side effect, not an objective, and Perec's choice of relatively clear examples for the *Atlas de littérature potentielle* suggests that he would have been happy with a result that combined formal rigour and perfect clarity, like his monovocalic motto, "*Je cherche en même temps l'éternel et l'éphémère*" ("I seek at once the eternal and the ephemeral," or, in Ian Monk's monovocalic translation, "We seek the essence where the end meets the endless").[18]

It would be simplistic to label literary groups as either clastic or constructive, for there is a tension between these tendencies wherever there is striving to make it new. But if the destructive urge is strongest in Italian futurism and Dada, the Oulipo and the short-lived Literary Center of the Constructivists in the Soviet Union exemplify the predominance of the drive to build.[19] In order to understand how the Oulipo builds, it is important to look carefully at its central tool, the constraint, and ask what kind of rule it is.

CONSTRAINT AND CONVENTION

The members of the Oulipo have often used the term "constraint" in a broad way, to cover any kind of rule involved in writing. In the first Oulipian manifesto, Le Lionnais mentions "constraints of vocabulary and grammar, constraints of the novel (division into chapters, etc.) or of classical tragedy (rule of the three unities), constraints of general versification, constraints of fixed forms (as in the case of the rondeau and the sonnet), etc." (OPPL 26–7). For Le Lionnais, Oulipian constraints are the logical extension of the rules already governing vocabulary, grammar, fixed forms, and genres; they are the next stage in the evolution of human expression.

This broad use of the term, which has been maintained by the younger generations of Oulipians, has two notable effects. First, it obscures the specificity of the Oulipian constraint, even if one distinguishes between Oulipian constraints and other kinds, as Roubaud does in "Notes sur l'Oulipo et les formes poétiques" (Notes on the Oulipo and poetic forms) (AS 22–7). Second, it naturalizes the constraint, even if one maintains that all constraints are arbitrary in relation to the language of composition, as Roubaud also does in the article just cited (AS 22). For if the alexandrine, which Roubaud calls a "traditional constraint," is arbitrary and only seems necessary and natural because it has been massively used as a result of a series of historical contingencies, it follows that Oulipian constraints are not fundamentally any more arbitrary than the alexandrine. If Queneau was right to say "nothing more artificial than the sonnet" (EGC 140), the Oulipian constraint cannot logically be accused of abnormal or excessive artificiality. This is the conclusion reached by Bénabou in "Rule and Constraint": "Now it is actually in the passage from the rule to the constraint that the stumbling block appears: people accept the rule, they tolerate technique, but they refuse constraint [...] It is precisely this boundary, wholly arbitrary, that must be challenged in the name of a better knowledge of the functional modes of language and writing" (OPPL 41).

When the Oulipians put generic conventions and their own constraints into the same category they are making a move that is at once modest and bold. It is modest because it implies that the Oulipo is simply systematizing and formalizing what literature has always done intuitively. But this is not such a simple step to have taken. As Roubaud has remarked, the Oulipo thinks about forms and constraints in a new way (BW 244). Its members often begin to invent by reflecting on abstract structures rather than employing the messier and more common method of trial, error, and refinement, which Jouet has labelled "organisational tinkering" ("le bidouillage organisationnel" [AS 34]).[20]

Putting conventions and constraints into the same category is a bold move too because it implies the following syllogism: All literature is governed by constraints. We are the specialists in constraints. Therefore, our specific knowledge applies potentially to all literature, and beyond literature to a great variety of creative activities, if one takes into account the various Ou-x-Po groups formed in the image of the Oulipo to invent analogous constraints for cartoons, cooking, cinema, detective fiction, history, mathematics, music, painting, photography, politics, radio, tragicomedy, and translation (OC 319–36).[21]

In a literary field that continues to privilege the "natural," and in which style is often regarded as the expression of an innate nature, the paradoxical naturalization of the constraint, which begins by affirming the arbitrariness of all compositional rules, has been strategically useful to the Oulipo. As Christelle Reggiani has argued, the "cultural insertion" of writing under constraints has had to resort to strategies that accommodate the dominant textual ideology.[22] But naturalizing the Oulipian constraint has obscured certain aspects of its functioning and blocked the way to a deeper understanding of its productivity and its limits.

At least one Oulipian has acknowledged this. In "L'auteur oulipien" (The Oulipian author), Roubaud, contrasting what he calls Oulipian and traditional constraints, writes: "The constraint here differs doubly from the traditional constraint (in spite of the obvious resemblances, *which were perhaps overly stressed by the founders, in a polemical spirit*)" (my emphasis).[23] The two differences according to Roubaud are, first, that traditional constraints can rarely be defined in a way that satisfies the strict criteria of formalization (especially the criteria of stability and non-ambiguity), and, second, that Oulipian constraints have not yet given rise to what he calls "transmissible forms of life," such as the sonnet.[24] There are, however, other differences, which collectively tell against the broad use of the term "constraint."

In order to grasp these differences, it is important to recognize that a regularity in behaviour need not be the effect of an explicitly promulgated rule. According to Paul Ziff, linguistic behaviour is not rule-bound in the legalistic sense: "the regularities found in or in connection with a language are not sources of constraint."[25] Of course, linguistic rules can be codified and interpreted prescriptively, but a language can function perfectly well without such codification. Linguistic and literary purisms are late formations. In this connection, W.V.O. Quine distinguishes between "the rule that fits," that is, accounts for an observed regularity in behaviour, and "the rule that guides."[26]

The Oulipian constraint is always a rule that guides. The generic or linguistic convention is usually a rule that fits. Oulipian rules are explicitly formulated by an individual writer before the composition of exemplifying texts, whereas conventions are inferred by critics or linguists after the fact, when they have noticed recurring features in a corpus of works or utterances.[27] In the foundational text of Western genre criticism, the *Poetics*, Aristotle observes the regularities that characterize tragedy, much like a naturalist studying the features of an animal species.[28] His rules are a posteriori and principally descriptive.[29]

Roubaud has written that most traditional constraints are anonymous, while Oulipian constraints have a unique creator: the Oulipo (AS 25, 31). He implies that Oulipian constraints are collective inventions, but they are almost always clearly attributed to an individual in the group's publications, and some bear the name of their inventor ("The Quenine," "Mathews's Algorithm," "Delmas's constraint").[30] Alastair Fowler calls this kind of invention "monogenesis" and points out that it is the exception rather than the rule for genres.[31]

Since the constraint precedes the exemplifying text, it cannot exist unless it has been formulated in abstract terms. Conventions, on the other hand, normally exist before they are described by a critic or linguist and often operate unconsciously.[32] The initially implicit nature of conventions is no obstacle to their transmission, for they are normally assimilated by direct imitation, without need of explicit description, whereas a constraint must be apprehended consciously and rationally before it can be used in writing. Conventions as described by critics and linguists are attempts to account for imperfect regularities, and they never exactly match the complex reality of the corpus. They admit exceptions, and do not cover every case. Constraints, by contrast, are formulated precisely, and according to Roubaud and Jouet, good Oulipian constraints are simple (ALP 54).[33]

Because conventions are described approximately there may be rival descriptions, each claiming to be the most accurate. For example, there are various ways of describing the conventions that govern the iambic pentameter in English. In a vigorous exchange in the journal *Language and Literature*, Derek Attridge and Nigel Fabb defend the merits of beat prosody and generative metrics respectively. For Fabb, Keats's line "How many bards gild the lapses of time" is unmetrical because it contravenes the stress maximum condition, according to which a stress maximum, that is, "a syllable bearing primary stress in a polysyllabic word provided that it is preceded and followed in the same line by a syllable without primary lexical stress," may not occupy a weak (odd-numbered) position in the line.[34] The offending syllable in this case is the first of "lapses," in the seventh position. For Attridge, this line exemplifies a rare but attested metrical variation, which he describes in terms of promotion and demotion of unstressed and stressed syllables.[35] More broadly, he argues against metrical theories that assume a clear division between metrical and unmetrical lines. Disagreements such as this do not arise when the rule in question is an Oulipian constraint, for it always already has an authoritative and clear formulation. Departures from the constraint can therefore be identified without controversy. It is only when those departures become very numerous that the text's overall conformity to the constraint may be called into question.

Over time, the ways in which a convention is described may be revised and refined. The convention itself may be modified too, as writers deviate from it in practice. Browning's free use of the double offbeat in iambic pentameter, for example, would have been unacceptable to Pope and his contemporaries.[36] Statistical trends appear among the deviations, leading to drift or evolution in certain directions. Generic conventions are, as Rosalie Colie has put it, metastable.[37] A convention can drift, but a constraint cannot, because it is anchored by a highly precise formulation. Conventions evolve whereas constraints fall from and return to favour.

Constraints may be, and often are, employed singly in a text, like the lipogrammatic constraint that forbids the use of the letter *e* in Perec's *A Void*. Conventions, by contrast, operate in bundles. A convention is always associated with several others, which bear on different aspects of the text. These aspects may be grouped into the broad categories of form and content (Alastair Fowler), or mode and theme (Gérard Genette), or formal organization, rhetorical structure, and thematic content (John Frow).[38]

Following Graham Hough, Alastair Fowler argues that the search for an invariant set of conventions, common to all examples of a genre and not to be found elsewhere, is fruitless.[39] Roubaud reaches a similar conclusion regarding the sonnet, pointing out that there are so many exceptions to the defining "rules" that, "by Oulipian standards no precise definition of the form can be said to exist" (oc 229). To describe the association of conventions in a genre, Hough, Fowler, and Roubaud adopt the notion of "family resemblance," developed by

Ludwig Wittgenstein in his *Philosophical Investigations* to explain what we mean when we use the concepts "language" and "number": "We extend our concept of number as in spinning a thread we twist fiber on fiber. And the strength of the thread does not reside in the fact that some one fiber runs through its whole length, but in the overlapping of many fibers."[40]

The following list sums up the differences between Oulipian constraints and generic or linguistic conventions:

the constraint is formulated before a text is written in accordance with it, whereas a convention is described retrospectively by a scholar who has noticed a regularity in a corpus of texts or utterances;

the constraint does not need to be exemplified by a text in order to exist, while a convention cannot exist independently of the corpus in which it is observed;

a constraint is apprehended rationally and consciously by the writer and cannot be grasped and reproduced intuitively, through imitation, as a convention can;

the formulation of a constraint is necessarily precise, unique and definitive, while the description of a convention may be approximate, can be challenged by rival descriptions, and is often revised as literary or linguistic practices evolve;

a constraint is generally an individual invention, while conventions are almost always produced collectively and anonymously.

An analogy may help clarify further the distinction between conventions and constraints. Constraints may be compared to axioms in mathematics; exemplifying texts are "deduced" from them like theorems, whereas conventions are "induced" from a corpus of examples.[41]

In spite of the Oulipo's attempts to naturalize the constraint, the differences set out above indicate its relative artificiality compared to linguistic and generic conventions. The constraint's abstraction and simplicity, its indifference to the patterns that have sedimented in a language or a literary tradition, make it a powerful tool for jolting composition out of stylistic and generic ruts. A non-naturalizing defence of the constraint could emphasize this productive artificiality.

In contrasting the convention with the constraint, I may seem to have characterized conventions in a way that implies an unrealistic

Kinds of Rules

unselfconsciousness on the part of most writers. Taking the iambic pentameter as an example, it could be objected that the poet who writes according to this metrical scheme is aware that each line should contain five iambs or at least five beats. The iambic pentameter, however, in all of its historical incarnations, has been more than a sequence of five iambs or beats, insofar as it has allowed for certain variations on the metrical base. Using the *wswswswsws* pattern (where *w* is a weak syllable and *s* a strong syllable) as an Oulipian constraint would produce very monotonous verse. And although poets who write in iambic pentameter may think of their lines as sequences of five feet or beats, not all of them, by any means, would be able to describe the subsidiary rules governing the variations that they find acceptable. Some poets, like Thomas Campion, Robert Bridges, and Roubaud, have been metrical theorists, but most are not. And the majority do not seem to be at a practical disadvantage.

Like linguistic conventions, the conventions of versification are generally propagated by imitation, or reproduction, as the philosopher Ruth Garrett Millikan would say: a new iambic pentameter, for example, reproduces certain aspects of its models, and certain aspects only (such as the distribution of stressed syllables).[42] Versification also satisfies the second condition for conventionality according to Millikan: the regularities that dominate at a given moment in literary history are not the only ones compatible with the characteristics of the language; they have come to dominate for contingent and historical reasons; they proliferate partly due to weight of precedent.[43] Although conventions often operate without being explicitly described, or formulated as rules, such formulation may of course occur, as in pedagogical grammars and manuals of etiquette. But, according to Millikan, "this evaluative kind of normativity is something added to mere conventionality."[44]

The fact that generic conventions may harden into prescriptive rules and end up functioning like constraints does not mean that conventions necessarily precede constraints, or that constraints are exclusively modern and conventions always traditional. Ancient formal rules such as those governing lipograms, anagrams, palindromes, acronyms, and chronograms should be classed as constraints in my view, while new genres and generic conventions continue to emerge. The members of the Oulipo are justified in claiming certain poems by the Grands Rhétoriqueurs and the Troubadours, or by Fulgentius, Ausonius, and Optatianus Porfirius as "anticipatory plagiarisms."[45] There are numerous precedents for the Oulipo's setting up of formal challenges, and for the resistance to such an approach, from Martial's mockery of laboured trifles in the first century CE to Calvin Bedient's critique of the "cerebral avant-gardes" in 2013.[46]

The constraint is not a superior level of regulation, on top of genre, as it were, but a way of formalizing one aspect of a text's construction, at a range of possible levels, from the letter to the chapter, from sememe to global theme. Constraints do not replace or transcend generic conventions; they operate along with them in all but the briefest texts. The modes of this co-operation are various. Where constraints and conventions work on the same level, there may be interference or reorganization of conventional patterns. In his exploration of "the relation x mistakes y for z," for example, Queneau uses matrices to formalize the conventional misidentifications of vaudeville and classical tragedy, then proposes a methodical survey of the narrative possibilities suggested by other (mathematically interesting) matrices (OC 247–8).

Where the constraint operates on a level not directly affected by generic conventions, as in Perec's *A Void*, the relation between constraint and conventions is more complex. The lipogram comes in "under" novelistic conventions, applying to letters, but the banning of a letter limits vocabulary and the use of the present and compound past tenses in French, and these effects, in turn, severely restrict access to the registers of plain speaking. In *Clés pour* La disparition (Keys to *A Void*), Hermes Salceda has shown how the lipogrammatic constraint contributes to what he calls the novel's "narrative atomisation": the multiplication of minor characters and subsidiary plot strands, but also moments of implausibility, imprecision, and incoherence.[47] Patient analysis of this kind still has much to teach us about how constraints and conventions interact.

PROCESS, PRODUCT, PERFORMANCE

It is time now to ask what constraints constrain. Citing the lipogram as a paradigmatic constraint, as I have done, may be misleading, for it can imply that constraints always constrain a feature of the finished literary work. Their domain of application is, in fact, considerably broader. Constraints may bear on the process of writing, its product, and the performance or publication of the text. Three broad types of constraint can thus be distinguished, as shown in table 2.1.

Table 2.1
Kinds of constraints

			Types and examples
What the constraint bears on	Process	of transforming an existing text	1a N + 7 procedure
		of composing a new text	1b Jacques Jouet's "subway poems"
	Product		2 lipogram
	Performance/publication		3 Jacques Jouet's "chronopoems"

A constraint may determine a process for transforming an existing text (type 1a). The N + 7 procedure, for example: take a text, take a dictionary, replace each noun in the text by the seventh subsequent noun in the dictionary (OC 198–9). Another early procedure of this kind, invented by Queneau, consisted of lopping the beginnings and middles off all the lines of a poem, and keeping only the ends, to make a more or less coherent "haikuized" version. Queneau's experiments on sonnets by Mallarmé led him to conclude that there was "almost as much in the restriction as in the entire poem," which is why he titled his results "Redundancy in Phane Armé" ("La redondance chez Phane Armé") (OPPL 58–61; PBO 141–5). As an illustration, here is Mathews's haikuized version of W.H. Auden's sonnet about Rimbaud:

[The nights, the railway arches,] The bad sky
[His horrible companions] did not know it:
[But in that child,] the rhetorician's lie
[Burst like a pipe: the cold] had made a poet.

[Drinks bought him by his weak and] Lyric friend,
[His five wits systematically] deranged,
[To all accustomed nonsense] put an end,
[Till he from lyre and weakness was] estranged

[Verse was a special illness] of the ear.
[Integrity was not enough; that] Seemed
[The hell of childhood:] he must try again.

[Now, galloping through Africa,] He dreamed
[Of a new self, a son, an] the engineer
[His truth acceptable] to lying men. (OC 216)[48]

The punctuation of the original text has been modified, and a definite substituted for an indefinite article in the second-last line. Grangaud's "Poèmes fondus" (Melted poems) haikuize sonnets more literally, trimming them down to the space of the Japanese form: three lines of five, seven, and five syllables respectively.[49]

A constraint may also determine a process for composing a new text (type 1b). The first poem in Jouet's *Poèmes de métro* (Subway poems) explains the process constraint according to which all the poems in the book were written:

> What is a subway poem?
>
> From time to time, I write subway poems. This poem being
>   an example.
> Do you want to know what a subway poem consists of?
>   Let's suppose you do. Here, then, is what a subway poem
>   consists of.
> A subway poem is a poem composed during a journey
>   in the subway.
> There are as many lines in a subway poem as there are stations
>   in your journey, minus one.
> The first line is composed mentally between the first two stations
>   of your journey (counting the station you got on at).
> It is then written down when the train stops at the
>   second station.
> The second line is composed mentally between the second and
>   the third stations of your journey.
> It is then written down when the train stops at the third station.
>   And so on.
> You must not write anything down when the train is moving.
> You must not compose when the train has stopped.
> The poem's last line is written down on the platform
>   of the last station.
> If your journey necessitates one or more changes of line,
>   the poem will then have two or more stanzas.
> An unscheduled stop between two stations is always an awkward
>   moment in the writing of a subway poem.[50]

In this case the constraint regulates the place and time of composition.

Kinds of Rules

The constraints that guided Perec's unfinished *Lieux* (Places) project also determined when and where the writing was to be done, over a much longer period, as the author explained in a letter to Maurice Nadeau in 1969:

> I have selected twelve places in Paris – streets, squares and cross-roads connected to important events or moments in my existence. Each month, I describe two of these places: one *in situ* (in a café or in the street itself), relating "what I can see" in the most neutral manner possible, listing the shops, architectural details, micro-events (a fire engine going by, a lady tying up her dog before going into the charcuterie, a removal in progress, posters, people, etc.); the second I write anywhere (at home, in a café, in the office), describing the place from memory, evoking the memories that are connected to it, the people I knew there, and so on. Each text (which may come down to just a few lines or extend over five or six pages or more), once completed, is put away in an envelope that I seal with a wax seal. After one year, I will have described twelve places twice over, once in memory mode, once *in situ* in real descriptive mode. I shall begin over again in the same manner each year for twelve years, permuting my pairs of places according to a table (12 x 12 mutually orthogonal Latin squares) provided for me by an Indian mathematician working in the United States.[51]

Perec hoped that the texts written according to this protocol would record a triple process of aging: the aging of the places, of his writing, and of his memories (SS 56).

Type 2 constraints in table 2.1 determine an aspect of the finished text. This is the kind of constraint most commonly associated with the Oulipo. All the constraints in Queneau's "Classification of the works of the Oulipo," familiarly known as Queneleyev's Table, by analogy with Mendeleyev's periodic table of the chemical elements, belong to this category (ALP 74; OC 217–19). The handiest example, because it is simple to explain, is the lipogram: a text that does not include a particular letter of the alphabet. But the lipogram does not begin or end with the Oulipo. As Perec himself points out in his essay "History of the Lipogram," the constraint can be traced as far back as the sixth century BCE in ancient Greece (OPPL 100). A variant of the lipogram is the monovocalic text, which eliminates all the vocalic letters except for one. Perec wrote a short novel without using *a, i, o,* or *u*: *Les revenentes* (1972), translated by the Oulipian Ian Monk as *The Exeter Text: Jewels, Secrets, Sex*. Monk has written monovocalic texts of his own, like the sassy "Iris" from his "Homage to Georges Perec: An Entertainment in Six Univocalisms":

Winking, I light his cig.
– I'm Iris, I lisp.
– Hi, I'm Mick McGinnis. Drink?
– Mmmm ... Gin sling?
– Right. Sid! sling this girl's gin!
– Chin chin!
Whilst sipping, I drink him in. I find him, sinking his brimming Irish mild, simplistic, timid, his big limbs, his smiling lips inviting. I grin:
– This gin sling's insipid piss, isn't it?
– Might I finish it?[52]

The Canadian poet Christian Bök used this constraint to dazzling effect in *Eunoia* (2001), a book that is deeply and explicitly indebted to Perec.[53]

Constraints of type 3 in table 2.1 are relatively new in the work of the Oulipo; they determine an aspect of the text's performance or publication. An example is the baobab, invented by Roubaud, which bears on the pitch of the performers' voices. The original baobab is a "soft constraint," requiring a text to multiply the occurrences of the sounds corresponding to the French words *bas* [ba] and *haut* [o], meaning "low" and "high." Three readers are required for the performance: one reads most of the text neutrally; another utters the [ba] sounds in a deep voice, while a third pronounces the [o] sounds at a high pitch.[54] Jouet's chronopoems are governed by constraints that limit the duration of their performance. They are read aloud with a timer, which goes off just after the last word. Jouet has written a nine-second poem entitled "100 meters," and a forty-six-second poem entitled "400-meter hurdles," in which the sound of the word *haie* ['ɛ], meaning "hurdle," recurs more or less regularly.

Since 1 April 1992, Jouet has been observing the type 1b constraint of writing a poem every day, but more recently he has adopted type 3 constraints determining the individuals to whom certain of his daily poems are to be addressed in the first instance. On 29 May 2013, he inaugurated his "projet poétique planétaire" (planetary poetic project), whose aim – to address a different poem to every person on the planet – could be realized only if the open invitation to collaborate were taken up epidemically. Jouet has begun working through the telephone directory of the Ain (01) department in France, sending his poems by post along with an explanation of the project. With the help of other poets, he has extended the operation to different sectors of the world's population, always maintaining the principle of singular address.[55] In this case the constraint determines how the text is transmitted in written form rather than its oral performance.

The three broad kinds of constraints that I have distinguished, which regulate the process of composition, the written product, and its publication or performance, are not mutually exclusive. They can be combined and often are. For example, Jouet defines his landscape monostichs as follows, formulating process, product, and performance constraints:

> A landscape monostich is a poem composed in situ: a landscape.
>   [type 1b: process constraint]
> It is a one-verse panoramic poem, which has between 40 and
>   50 syllables (more than 20 words). [type 2: product constraint]
> It is composed on a single line. [type 2: product constraint]
> It is read aloud as the reader's eye sweeps across the audience
>   from left to right or from right to left. [type 3:
>   performance constraint]

In the following example, the movement of the seer / performer's eyes mirrors a movement in the seen landscape:

> the tractor on the left, there, see it? when I begin the landscape
> monostich with my eyes, by the time I finish it on the right, it's
> there, the tractor[56]

If the three types of constraints are not always separate in practice, one might wonder if it is worth distinguishing them conceptually. One advantage of the classification is that it gives us a handle on how the Oulipo's practice has evolved. The group began with product constraints (type 2) and constraints for transforming existing texts (type 1a). Perec, who was co-opted in 1967, introduced process constraints for composing new texts (type 1b), for example in his unfinished *Lieux* project, which he first described publicly in *Species of Spaces* (*Espèces d'espaces*, 1974). And Jouet, who joined the group in 1982, just after Perec's death, has been, so far, the main inventor of performance and publication constraints (type 3).

PROCESS CONSTRAINTS AND PROJECTS

Process constraints organize the writer's life. When this organization covers significant periods of time, we speak of projects. The first phase of Perec's *Lieux* project would have taken twelve years to complete had he persisted. Roubaud worked on the grand "Project" whose failure is narrated in *The Great Fire of London* for more than twenty years (GFL 1). Jouet's commitment to writing a poem each day, made in 1992, is lifelong.[57]

Projects can be reassuring, both for writers and for those who support and rely on them (spouses, relatives, publishers, patrons, funding bodies). Jacques Roubaud's *Description d'un projet* (Description of a project, 1979) was written and published both for the author's friends, as "a kind of sign," and for himself, "to see, perhaps, where I have got to; and, perhaps, to help me keep going."[58] The long letter that Perec sent to Maurice Nadeau in July 1969, outlining his projects for the years to come, was an attempt to take stock and clarify his intentions, but also a bid for support: he asked if Nadeau would publish *W or the Memory of Childhood* as a serial in *La Quinzaine littéraire* (JSN 64). This appeal was successful.[59] Similarly, the "Tentative de description d'un programme de travail pour les années à venir" (Attempt at a description of a work program for the years to come) that Perec prepared in 1976 for the publisher Paul Otchakovsky-Laurens supported a request for "advances on royalties to be paid in monthly instalments, like a salary, and a commitment in principle to take on board his entire writing life, in all the nineteen parts laid out in the prospectus."[60] These terms were granted.

The project is a way of controlling the future, if only in imagination. Comparing Perec's *Lieux* project with that of his character Bartlebooth in *Life: A User's Manual*, Philippe Lejeune writes: "Long-term planning of a work (paintings and puzzles, or writing) seems to have the function of protecting oneself from the future by occupying it in advance and hypothetically postponing death to a time beyond the project's completion date."[61] The project also limits the writer's freedom in obvious ways. The constraints of *Lieux*, for example,

Kinds of Rules

obliged Perec to be present in Paris for at least one day a month for twelve years. And an organizing structure can come to feel like a futile burden, as Perec confessed in a radio interview with Gérard Macé: "I think I was circling around these texts, looking for something that wasn't in the protocol, with the result that I became lazier and lazier, got further and further behind [...] once [...] I went all the way across Paris to Avenue Junot, which was one of the places, wrote on my sheet of paper, 'Avenue Junot gives me the shits,' put the paper in an envelope and left."[62]

The *Lieux* project was abandoned. For Perec, the protocol or process constraint was a fallible instrument. *Lieux* had an undeclared objective to which the protocol turned out to be ill adjusted. It emerges from Philippe Lejeune's patient chronological analysis of the manuscripts that Perec was obliquely approaching childhood memories of his mother, who was deported to Auschwitz in 1943 and did not return. He would finally confront those memories in two very different ways in the mid-1970s: directly (or at least without a formulated constraint) in the autobiographical strand of *W or the Memory of Childhood*, and through the grille of the isogram in the poems of *La clôture* (The enclosure, 1976).[63]

> When I was writing *W*, a book in which I evoke childhood memories, I opened the envelopes containing the descriptions of the rue Vilin. I looked at the photos that a friend had taken for me when I was writing the descriptions; I used them, and since I was thinking a lot about the street, which was being destroyed, I wrote a set of poems, illustrated with photographs. I made a sort of art book, called *La clôture*, and after that I was done with the idea of coming back regularly to describe what I could see in the rue Vilin; there was no point going on.[64]

For Perec, the process constraints could not guarantee the value of the product. The proof of the pudding was in the eating, not the recipe. This is no longer the case for all writers and readers. There are two reasons why the primacy of the product may be less self-evident now than it was forty or fifty years ago. First, competitive project funding favours artists skilled at talking up as yet unrealized work. It encourages them to exaggerate their foresight, and penalizes the abandonment of funded projects. Second, conceptual art and writing have increasingly blurred the distinction between project description and artwork. As César Aira notes in *Birthday*, "The genre of 'preparatory notes' has its own aesthetic and its own kind of finish."[65] But in spite of these historical factors, the hierarchical distinction between work and project, or between product and process, still has adherents, not all of whom can be dismissed as dinosaurs. Dorothea Lasky's 2010 pamphlet *Poetry Is Not a Project* mounts a spirited defence of what a project cannot be relied upon to produce: "Just because you have constructed a project does not mean you have written a poem. You can plan a party, but you have to make the people show up for it to really be a party. Any other way, all you have created is just a decorated empty room. You can blast the music as loud as you want to, but if there is no one there to dance to it, there will be no dancing."[66]

A writer's orientation toward process or product may be influenced by historical factors, but it is also a question of temperament. The writers of the Oulipo vary considerably along this dimension. Some (Queneau, Perec, Roubaud) regard process constraints and projects instrumentally, subordinating them to the finished work. For others the distinction is not so clear. Frédéric Forte, for example, has launched the form that he describes and exemplifies in "99 Preparatory Notes to 99 Preparatory Notes" (AES 222–6). His notes are not in fact strictly preparatory; they have been prepared for publication and compose finished works. On a quick first reading they might seem to have been thrown down in a jumble, but artfully drawn-out threads soon appear:

4. Jean Queval never finished his sentences.
18. There is a Quevallian form to the 99 preparatory notes.
26. Jean Queval is the main character in "99 preparatory notes to 99 preparatory notes."

5. What would 99 preparatory boats be – sketches for an armada?
11. What would 99 preparatory coats be – homework for a theatrical costuming course?
17. What would 99 preparatory goats be – a petting zoo? (AES 222–3)

Forte's contradictions are also carefully set up:

16. There are more or less than 36 ways to write 99 preparatory notes.

Kinds of Rules

22. Contradiction is potential.
36. There are exactly 36 ways to write 99 preparatory notes.
    (AES 222–3)

Nevertheless, the very gesture of turning preparatory notes into a form indicates an openness to the aesthetic potential of the unfinished and the imperfect: "63. The '99 preparatory notes' form is imperfect, which is perfect'" (AES 224). In his "99 notes préparatoires à ma vie avec Raymond Queneau" (99 preparatory notes to my life with Raymond Queneau), Forte writes: "Would he have been interested in the 99 preparatory notes form? I'm not so sure!"[67] Forte is right to be doubtful, considering what Queneau wrote in 1938, fulminating against the "glorification of the unfinished": "Shame, three times shame on those who delight in the fact that death prevented Pascal from completing his Apology. And ninety-nine times shame on those who write their own 'Pascalian thoughts' because they're incapable of producing a finished work" (LNF 38).

The project is privileged boldly in Jouet's poetry and fiction, which often relies on process constraints. The constraint in *Poèmes de métro* is not fallible as much as exhaustible. At the end of the book, Jouet writes:

If twelve months of metro poems are coming to an end,
coming to an end without beginning again as such,
it is because I am beginning to feel I could compose fake subway
poems without leaving my room.[68]

Peter Poiana comments: "Abandonment is not failure. It is rather the acknowledgement that a particular episode in the Oulipian exploration of potential literature has reached its logical conclusion."[69] Jouet has similarly exhausted a series of other constraints and thematic specifications governing particular sequences of daily poems (some of which have been inspired by genres of painting: still life, portrait, historical) but, as noted above, his overarching commitment to writing a poem each day is ongoing.

This two-level approach is a way of sustaining productivity while allowing for adjustment to change both in the poet (learning, aging, shifting of interests) and in their environment (due to geographical displacement, political events, ecological disturbances, and other factors). A long-term writing project that is detailed and rigidly structured is almost certain to lose these two kinds of responsiveness, as Roubaud discovered in persisting with his "Project." Jouet's projects, by contrast, are modular rather than architectonically unified. They are also less instrumental and fallible (from the writer's point of view) than those of Roubaud and Perec. He has declared his admiration for artists such as Sophie Calle and Roman Opalka, whose long-term projects contribute to the construction of a life-work which undoes the distinction between living and making art.[70] Jouet's decision to publish all of his daily poems converts them into documentation: proof of his commitment to the project, which distinguishes him as an author, and draws sympathetic readers into the life-work's gradual unfolding.

But this effect depends crucially on a prior sympathy with a partly conceptual approach. A reader who has no interest in *how* Jouet writes is far less likely to be gripped by *what* he writes. Peter Poiana asks: "Why should readers be interested in a text composed on the basis of an arbitrary rule that has no relevance to them or their lives? Why should they care if a poem was written in one minute, one hour or one day?"[71] Although rhetorically put, these questions can be answered. Jouet's arbitrary rules can be relevant to the lives of readers who are particularly curious about writing processes, and who may wish to adopt or adapt his process constraints, participating in what he has called "the Republic of Forms."[72] Such readers certainly exist, although their number is modest as yet.

Jouet's productivity has been so great that it may, in one sense, have been counterproductive. Camille Bloomfield has suggested that some readers are put off by the sheer abundance of his work, which is hard to keep up with or choose a way into.[73] As well as overwhelming certain readers, writers who publish much more frequently than their peers put themselves at a certain disadvantage with regard to literary institutions: when not all the published titles can be chosen for reviewing or prize submission, gatekeepers may simplify their lives by choosing not to make the extra choice and simply leaving the hyper-productive writer aside.

As well as publishing very frequently, Jouet has exhibited the process of his writing. He has performed live in Paris, Beirut, Medellín, and Metz, obliging himself to complete one narrative episode per hour, and projecting the work in progress on a screen.[74] These performances, which fold a process constraint into a performance constraint, have been limited in time, but they issue a provocative challenge to the habitual separations between private and public, preparation and finished work, life and art. Indeed they could be seen as steps toward a totalizing artification of life, to use a neologism proposed by Ossi Naukkarinen and Yuriko Saito.[75] They abolish, or at least suspend, the private life of writing.

In discussing process, as they are often encouraged to do, contemporary artists and writers are usually drawing attention to themselves and away from the work. And by making ongoing projects public, they are bidding for future attention and support as well. If art requires an audience, to artify one's whole life is to ask for attention all the time. And unless one believes that such attention is granted perpetually to everyone by a divine being, this is a lot to ask, even of a large set of followers.

Human attention is scarce, as teachers and internet companies know, and it wanders in search of rewards. There is enormous variety, of course, in what readers find rewarding, but, in general, writing projects that privilege concept and process run an increased risk of failing to reward attention to their products. As the champion of conceptual writing Kenneth Goldsmith is quick to admit, those products can be boring to sit down and actually read. "The idea of making a text intentionally flat and boring," he writes, "flies in the face of everything we've come to expect of 'good' literature." He goes on to cite as examples of this strategy: Tan Lin's *Ambient Fiction Reading System 01: A List of Things I Read and Didn't Read for Exactly One Year*, Thomas Claburn's *i feel better after i type to you*, and Perec's "Attempt at an Inventory of the Liquid and Solid Foodstuffs Ingurgitated by Me in the Course of the Year Nineteen Hundred and Seventy-Four."[76]

There is a significant difference between Perec's "Attempt at an Inventory" and Goldsmith's first two examples. Lin's and Claburn's pieces are chronologically organized, while Perec's inventory groups foods and drinks consumed into categories – soups, charcuterie, seafood, and so on – presented in an order corresponding to a typical menu. The last and sparsely populated category is non-alcoholic drinks:

N coffees
one tisane
three Vichy waters (ss 245)

The final word in the original is "Vichy," which also names the government that collaborated with the German occupying forces in the arrest and deportation of Perec's mother.[77] The "Attempt at an Inventory" belongs to the sociological strain that Perec identified in his own work (ss 141), but it is further from being a mass of raw data than his attempts at exhausting places in Paris, which obliged him to write or record without revision, adhering to the order of things perceived.[78] He hoped that the deliberately flat stenographic notation of his various "attempts" ("tentatives") would capture what he dubbed the infraordinary: that which we fail to perceive even as ordinary because we are so accustomed to it (ss 209–11).

Bernard Magné has pointed out the similarity between Perec's descriptions of places and Jouet's subway poems, grouping them in the category of "real-time description."[79] Such writing, like Goldsmith's *Soliloquy* (an unedited record of every word spoken by the author in the course of a week), renounces one of literature's distinctive powers: to condense and reorganize experience.[80] "Real-time description" is comparable to data gathering as opposed to analysis in the social sciences, or to musical improvisation as distinct from composition. Like the conceptual writing advocated by Goldsmith, it courts the risk of boring the reader by abandoning the criteria of the product's density and internal organization.

The experience that literary composition has traditionally condensed is experience of writing as well as of life: the final version of a text brings together ideas that occurred to the writer in successive drafts. This means that the subject of literary composition is temporally extended, or if, like Galen Strawson, one sees selves as short-lived entities, it is a self collaborating with earlier selves.[81] Sometimes the extension or collaboration facilitated by writing covers a long period. When tidying up papers in 1974, Queneau discovered the notes that he had taken when reading Philastre's translation of the *I Ching* fifty years earlier. Those notes suggested a structure for the as yet unwritten third part of his last book, *Elementary Morality*, whose sixty-four prose poems allude systematically to the sixty-four hexagrams of the ancient Chinese classic (oc 1 1455–58).

There are traditions of improvised poetry in many languages, but in text-based cultures, composition prepares most writers to say something richer, denser, more strongly patterned, and more memorable than anything they could say from scratch in real time. Often it also prepares them to say something wilder and more surprising. Creative writers need to surprise both themselves and their readers to some degree, but the surprises of composition and of reading need not mirror one another, and the latter may be carefully engineered.

One advantage of real-time description or recording is that it disposes of the thorny practical question of how long to go on revising. Most writers, however, must find a way between the sworn enemies of revision and the victims of acute perfectionism. A process constraint could settle the question: the work is finished when it has been through so many drafts, or when so many hours have been spent on its drafting. But few writers would be prepared to let process alone determine the moment of completion. Most rely on an intuitive judgment of the work's rightness, or their own incapacity to improve it significantly. Their decision is based on a state of the product, or a state of the relation between the text and its writer. A poet, for example, might choose to regard a poem as provisionally finished when the whole text hangs together stably in their mind and can be confidently recited from memory without the appearance of "soft spots," that is, places where hesitation among variants persists.[82]

When a text is written under product constraints, one criterion of completion will be its conformity to the "design specifications" (Perec spoke in these terms of his system of constraints for *Life: A User's Manual,* referring to his *cahier des charges*). The conformity need not be absolute for the constraints to give the writer a handle on how the work is proceeding. This is just one of the advantages of the constraint as it is most frequently understood: a precisely pre-formulated rule that bears on the product of writing (type 2).

PRODUCT CONSTRAINTS AND ATTENTION

A product constraint does not specify a procedure for its own satisfaction. There are various ways to write a lipogram, for example. One may draft a text using the full alphabet and then "translate" it by searching for synonyms and periphrases that do not contain the proscribed letter. Or one may collect words and phrases that already satisfy the constraint and use them as building blocks. If product constraints do not specify a procedure, why have they proven to be useful both to creative writers and teachers of writing?

Constraints focus the writer's attention on a particular aspect of the text's construction, transforming it into a problem or a game, while their practical know-how – acquired gradually by reading and imitation – takes care of the rest. The concreteness of the problem or the game makes it easy to get to work straight away. It may be difficult to write a lipogram of any length, but it is easy to grasp what a lipogram is. Simple constraints are highly effective in the classroom because they presuppose very little prior literary knowledge or experience. To start writing a lipogram, a student needs to know only what letters and the alphabet are. By contrast, a working knowledge of the iambic pentameter requires a student either to have read a good many examples or to have securely grasped the notions of syllable and stress, and then understood a theoretical account of the line. To exaggerate slightly, the constraint works in the classroom because it enables the student to write without having read. In many classrooms, this advantage is not to be sniffed at.

Writing under constraints reorders the parts of traditional rhetoric, in which *inventio* (invention, discovery) is followed by *dispositio* (organization, arrangement) and *elocutio* (style). Constraints usually oblige the writer to begin with problems of style or organization, the solutions to which determine – in a certain measure – the invention or discovery of the content. This can be a relief. We live in what Vincent Descombes has called "the age of expressivist individualism," which requires artists to aim for originality.[83] And since originality in this age is defined primarily in terms of content, the pressure to have something new to say is constant and pervasive. It can be paralyzing. Constraints defer this ill-defined, high-stakes problem by finding problems of lesser moment with smaller sets of possible solutions. They redirect attention and redistribute work among the writer's faculties. While, for example, the writer is busy searching for an adjective that might plausibly qualify a gin sling and containing no vocalic letter other than *i*, the problem of "what to say" recedes into the background. Which is not to say that it is abandoned. On the contrary, as psychological studies have shown, distracting attention from an unsolved problem often initiates a phase of "incubation" during which implicit cognition proceeds decisively.[84]

By opening and protecting a space in which incubated cognition can work, the constraint can sometimes help a writer overcome a blockage or repression. Bénabou has given an explanation of this phenomenon:

> This paradoxical effect of constraint, which, rather than stifling the imagination, serves to awaken it, can actually be explained very readily. The choice of a linguistic constraint allows one to

Kinds of Rules

skirt, or to ignore, all these other constraints which do not belong to language and which escape from our control. Leiris seized this point perfectly, regarding the method used by Raymond Roussel, of whom he said: "His voluntary subjugation to a complicated and difficult rule was accompanied, as a corollary, by a distraction regarding all the rest, leading to a lifting of censorship [*levée de la censure*], the latter being far better skirted by this means than by a process such as automatic writing" (*Brisées*, 59–60). (OPPL 42–3, translation modified)[85]

Perec and Mathews also subscribe to this account of the constraint as a means of eluding self-censorship. Describing the process of writing *A Void*, Perec said: "it was so hard to find a way forward at the sentence level that all the other systems of censorship or inhibition were removed."[86] The constraints that Mathews set up for *Cigarettes* had a similar effect: "I had concocted an elaborate formal scheme in which abstract situations were permuted according to a set pattern. This outline suggested nothing in particular, and for a time it remained utterly empty and bewildering. It then began filling up with situations and characters that seemed to come from nowhere; most of them belonged to the world I had grown up in. I had never been able to face writing about it before, even though I'd wanted to make it my subject from the moment I turned to fiction" (CPM 81). In the process of composition, then, constraints may screen negative feelings that can have a paralyzing effect: anxiety about having nothing new or significant to say, embarrassment or shame regarding the subjects "given" by the writer's circumstances, fear of engaging with traumatic material.

In this section and the previous one, I have been discussing the practical benefits of process and product constraints (types 1 and 2) for the writer. Performance constraints (type 3) are obviously oriented toward the audience. They enrich the experience of hearing and seeing the texts performed. But product and process constraints have a similar effect on reading insofar as the reader is aware of them: they prompt us to notice patterns in the work or to imagine scenes of writing. They can convey more or less deeply encrypted meanings, as I show in chapter 6. And they put a stamp of rationality on the texts written under them, however weird or oracular their content. In the terms with which I began this chapter, they manifest a constructive design however clastic their semantic effects.

CONSTRAINTS AND FORM

In chapter 8, I tackle the question of what potentiality means for the Oulipo. The group has not theorized the concept. There is no entry for potentiality in the *Oulipo compendium* or *L'abécédaire provisoirement définitif* (Provisionally definitive alphabet primer). Roubaud admits in *La dissolution* (The dissolution) that the principles of a general conception of potentiality have yet to be clearly identified.[87] But in *La Bibliothèque de Warburg* he writes: "Potentiality, for me, is associated with a formal project that can be made explicit and generalized; one particular case of this is form, another is the text under constraints [...] I think it would be good to go easy on the connection between the constraint and the Oulipo" (BW 242). Frédéric Forte also relativizes the importance of the constraint in his "99 Preparatory Notes to 99 Preparatory Notes": "Constraint is a means, but there are other means" (AES 222).

I have been using "constraint" in this book as a technical term to mean a precisely pre-formulated writing rule. The term "form" has a messier cluster of meanings, whose complex and contradictory evolution has been traced by Angela Leighton in the first chapter of *On Form*.[88] One way to wrangle the cluster is to open the concept of form to admit "all shapes and configurations, all ordering principles, all patterns of repetition and difference," as Caroline Levine has done in *Forms: Whole, Rhythm, Hierarchy, Network*.[89] Wittgenstein's "forms of life" (*Lebensformen*) come under this broad definition, along with all other social arrangements. This has the advantage of neutralizing the pejorative connotations of formalism: "The traditionally troubling gap between the form of the literary text and its content and context dissolves. Formalist analysis turns out to be as valuable to understanding sociopolitical institutions as it is to reading literature. Forms are at work everywhere."[90] The evident risk of broadening the definition in this way is that it may encourage us to overestimate our analytic capacities. Skills in the formal analysis of literature are not straightforwardly transposable to sociology or political science.

For the purposes of my argument here, I propose a restriction of Levine's definition: a literary form is a pattern or arrangement of linguistic elements, at a range of scales down to the single sentence or verse line (taking in the aphorism and the monostich as minimal forms). This, of course, is still very broad, but form thus defined does not englobe the constraint. A constraint is a rule; a form is a pattern.

Kinds of Rules

A form may result from the application of a constraint. Jacques Jouet's novel *Fins* (Endings), for example, uses the spiral permutation that governs the movement of end-words in a sestina to determine paragraph lengths. In a sestina the end-words are repeated in the following order (the numbers correspond to end-words and the rows to stanzas):

1	2	3	4	5	6
6	1	5	2	4	3
3	6	4	1	2	5
5	3	2	6	1	4
4	5	1	3	6	2
2	4	6	5	3	1

The new order produced by the permutation can be read off figure 2.1 by following the spiral rather than the straight line.[91]

Jouet's novel consists of 216 paragraphs. The first 6 paragraphs contain one, two, three, four, five, and six sentences respectively. In the next set of 6 paragraphs there are six, one, five, two, four, and three sentences. The numbers of sentences have been subjected to the spiral permutation. This is repeated to produce a prose "sestina" of 34 paragraphs, as shown in the first part of table 2.2. The permutation is then applied to sequences of 6 paragraphs (labelled with letters), as in the second part of the table. And so on, up to the 216th paragraph, which completes a "sestina of sestinas." Thus a rule applied recursively produces a pattern of paragraph lengths.[92] A constraint determines a form.

But this does not always happen, as Reggiani has recently pointed out.[93] Texts written under the constraint of the lipogram, for example, may take many different forms. Perec demonstrates this in *A Void* by including a little anthology of formally diverse poems translated to eliminate the letter *e*.[94] The lipogram sets a stamp on the texture of the work, but not its structure, to use an opposition theorized by Monroe Beardsley.[95] Conversely, forms may be constrained, like the form of Jouet's *Fins*, but need not be, since an arrangement of elements in a literary work is not always produced by the application of a rule. A new form may be modelled on one that already exists, and the model for a literary form is not always literary: Queneau drew his inspiration for *Exercises in Style* from musical variations, as I explain in chapter 8. A form may also be fashioned by trial and error combinations. Jouet calls this "organizational tinkering": "The constraint is therefore something

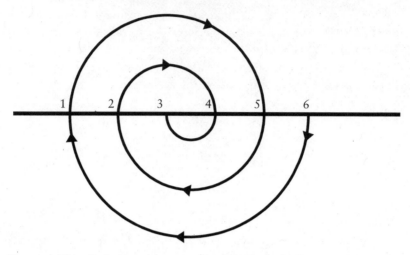

Figure 2.1 The spiral permutation

quite different from a writer's organizational tinkering [*le bidouillage organisationnel du travail littéraire*]. And there is nothing wrong with organizational tinkering!" (AS 34). The difference resides in the constraint's pre-formulation and fixity as opposed to the tinkered form's gradual emergence in the process of composition.

In practice, modelling and imitation are often hard to distinguish from tinkering. Jouet's metaphor is a salutary reminder that writers, like tinkers, are always recycling. Following Levine, I characterized a literary form as an arrangement of elements, but since writers make nothing out of nothing, it would perhaps be more accurate to say that a form is a rearrangement. The sonnet, whose first recognizable exemplars are attributed to the Sicilian court poet Giacomo da Lentini in the years 1220–1250 CE, seems to have been produced by modifying forms in circulation at the time, although precisely *which* forms is a matter of speculation and disagreement. Roubaud argues that the sonnet emerged as a variant of the *cobla* as it was developed by the Provençal troubadours.[96] Hassanaly Ladha has made a case for the influence of the Arabic *qasīdah* at the court of Frederick II, who had learned Arabic as a child in Palermo.[97] Whatever the contributions of the possible models, it is clear that the sonnet was not invented from scratch. Nor, once launched, has it conformed to a set of precise and fixed formal rules, as I pointed out earlier in this chapter. It is true that a standard sonnet comprises fourteen lines,

Table 2.2
Lengths of paragraphs in Jouet's *Fins*

¶ 1: 1 sentence	¶ 7: 6 sentences	¶ 13: 3 sentences	¶ 19: 5 sentences	¶ 25: 4 sentences	¶ 31: 2 sentences
¶ 2: 2 sentences	¶ 8: 1 sentence	¶ 14: 6 sentences	¶ 20: 3 sentences	¶ 26: 5 sentences	¶ 32: 4 sentences
¶ 3: 3 sentences	¶ 9: 5 sentences	¶ 15: 4 sentences	¶ 21: 2 sentences	¶ 27: 1 sentence	¶ 33: 6 sentences
¶ 4: 4 sentences	¶ 10: 2 sentences	¶ 16: 1 sentence	¶ 22: 6 sentences	¶ 28: 3 sentences	¶ 34: 5 sentences
¶ 5: 5 sentences	¶ 11: 4 sentences	¶ 17: 2 sentences	¶ 23: 1 sentence	¶ 29: 6 sentences	¶ 35: 3 sentences
¶ 6: 6 sentences	¶ 12: 3 sentences	¶ 18: 5 sentences	¶ 24: 4 sentences	¶ 30: 2 sentences	¶ 36: 1 sentence
a	b	c	d	e	f
¶ 37: 2 sentences	¶ 43: 1 sentence	¶ 49: 4 sentences	¶ 55: 6 sentences	¶ 61: 5 sentences	¶ 67: 3 sentences
¶ 38: 4 sentences	¶ 44: 2 sentences	¶ 50: 5 sentences	¶ 56: 1 sentence	¶ 62: 3 sentences	¶ 68: 6 sentences
¶ 39: 6 sentences	¶ 45: 3 sentences	¶ 51: 1 sentence	¶ 57: 5 sentences	¶ 63: 2 sentences	¶ 69: 4 sentences
¶ 40: 5 sentences	¶ 46: 4 sentences	¶ 52: 3 sentences	¶ 58: 2 sentences	¶ 64: 6 sentences	¶ 70: 1 sentence
¶ 41: 3 sentences	¶ 47: 5 sentences	¶ 53: 6 sentences	¶ 59: 4 sentences	¶ 65: 1 sentence	¶ 71: 2 sentences
¶ 42: 1 sentence	¶ 48: 6 sentences	¶ 54: 2 sentences	¶ 60: 3 sentences	¶ 66: 4 sentences	¶ 72: 5 sentences
f	a	e	b	d	c

but there are poems with fewer or more lines that are widely recognized as sonnets, such as Gerard Manley Hopkins's "curtal sonnets" (ten and a half lines) and the sixteen-line sonnets of George Meredith's *Modern Love*.[98]

It has been the Oulipo's ambition from the outset to invent a new form that would be widely adopted by writers outside the group, spreading as the sonnet did from the Sicilian court in the thirteenth century through the literatures of Western Europe and beyond. This is the Oulipo's Holy Grail, a language game that would also be a transmissible form of life, to use Wittgenstein's terminology. As Roubaud admits, the Grail has proved elusive.[99] Nonetheless, I show in chapter 8 that certain Oulipian inventions have demonstrated a remarkable potential for uptake and spread, and I emphasize the sonnet-like nature of their genesis, in which variation and tinkering have played primordial roles. If the power of the constraint lies in its abstraction and simplicity, which enable it to cut across conventions, forms draw their power from plasticity. More readily than constraints, they can respond and adjust to the messiness of human behaviour, and in particular to "those mathematically 'dirty' objects, natural languages," to quote Roubaud in *Impératif catégorique* (Categorical imperative) (IC 238).

Explaining her departure from the Oulipo in an interview with Camille Bloomfield, Métail opposed forms to constraints: "I started getting tired of those constraints, which allow you to produce a text, even if you've got nothing to say. I started to question the fundamental principle of inventing a constraint that can be reused by other authors, even if they make it evolve. All my later work attests to my approach: the choice of a form (I never use the word 'constraint') is intrinsically tied to the content; the form alone permits the meaning to 'crystallize.' I never reuse a form created for a text; it remains unique, like the content."[100]

Métail's trajectory lends force to her critique: she was a prolific inventor of constraints, especially in the mid-1980s, publishing three consecutive fascicles in the bibliothèque oulipienne in 1986 (OC 78–9). Her first point in the passage quoted above sounds like common sense: a writer needs to have something to say. But it would be a mistake to reduce this something to a paraphrasable message that exists prior to writing. Readers looking for such a message will be disappointed by Métail's poems. What she means is that a literary work needs to have a necessity of its own and not to be a mere exercise.

Métail's second point – that forms should be unique – also sounds like common sense, and similar positions are frequently held by advocates of open or organic forms, many of whom are indebted, directly or indirectly, to a famous passage from Samuel Taylor Coleridge's "Shakespeare's Judgment Equal to his Genius," itself based on a passage from August Wilhelm Schlegel's lectures on dramatic art: "The form is mechanic, when on any given material we impress a pre-determined form, not necessarily arising out of the properties of the material; – as when to a mass of wet clay we give whatever shape we wish it to retain when hardened. The organic form, on the other hand is innate; it shapes, as it develops, itself from within, and the fulness of its development is one and the same with the perfection of its outward form. Such as the life is, such is the form." [101]

It is tempting to say that the reused form is mechanic and the unique form organic, but that would be simplistic, for the forms that prosper and are widely taken up generally allow for a good deal of flexibility. They set a few parameters, such as the number of lines in a sonnet, but only a few: there are no conventions governing the number of words or sentences in a sonnet. And even the parameters that forms do set can often be altered, as with the sonnet's fourteen lines. In the words of Le Lionnais, the mechanics of the sonnet leave room for choice (GO 83–4). The innovative sonnet sequences of the twentieth and twenty-first centuries by Jacques Roubaud, Ted Berrigan, Bernadette Mayer, Wanda Coleman, Emmanuel Hocquard, and Terrance Hayes – to mention only poets from France and North America – demonstrate that the reuse of a form need not be mechanical. [102]

Métail's opposition to the reuse of forms puts her in substantive disagreement with the other members of the Oulipo, and particularly Jouet. [103] But her privileging of form over constraint chimes with Roubaud's call to "go easy on the connection between the constraint and the Oulipo" (BW 242). It also echoes the end of Queneau's essay "Technique of the Novel," published in 1937: "Rules disappear once they've outlived their usefulness. But forms go on eternally. There are forms that confer all the virtues of the Number onto the novel's subject, and so, born of the story's various aspects and of its very expression, connatural with its central idea, at once daughter and mother to all the elements that it polarizes, a structure takes shape, transmitting to the work the last gleams of the Universal Light and the last echoes of the Harmony of the Worlds" (LNF 29).

This often-cited passage is open to various readings. Its mystical, Pythagorean resonance, evident in the capitalized expressions, has been underlined by Claude Simonnet, Alain Calame, Claude Debon, and Alison James among others.[104] Roubaud sets the question of eternity aside, and finds a prefiguration of the Oulipo's project:

> The exhaustion of tradition, represented by rules, is the starting point in the search for a second foundation, that of mathematics. [...]
> *Proposition 18*: Mathematics repairs the ruin of rules.
> [...]
> 33. Once the "shift" has been made, from the rule to the constraint by axiom, mathematics then furnishes another substitutive concept [*concept de substitution*]: for replacing "form." After the 1937 statement that we used for proposition 17. Queneau wrote:
> "*But forms subsist eternally.*"
> The notion then substituted for this "eternity," leaving the question of "eternity" in darkness, is of course the keystone of the Bourbakian edifice, the notion of *structure*. (ALP 66; OPPL 93, translation modified)

In this reading, "rules" are traditional, outworn conventions, to be replaced by constraints, which are analogous to axioms in mathematics, and the notion of form is to be replaced by structure "in its Quenellian or Oulipian sense," which is analogous to structure as the term is used by the group of mathematicians who published under the collective pseudonym Bourbaki (OPPL 93).

If the passage from "Technique of the Novel" is read in its immediate context, however, the rules in question appear to be those that Queneau set for himself when writing his novel *The Last Days* (*Les derniers jours*): "I've said that the number of *The Last Days* is 49, although in its published form, it contains only thirty-eight chapters. This is because I've removed the scaffolding and syncopated the rhythm" (LNF 29). "Rules disappear [*Il n'y a plus de règles*] once they've outlived their usefulness" (OC II 1240) can be read not as a comment on literary history but as the statement of a practical precept: pre-formulated rules lose their binding force once they cease to serve the interests of the emerging work.

3

Automation, Craft, and Imitation

THE CONCEPTUAL AND THE AUTOMATIC

In "La nueva escritura" ("The New Writing," 1998) César Aira claims: "The great artists of the twentieth century are not those who produced a body of work, but those who invented procedures so that works could make themselves, or not."[1] Procedures, he says in effect, open up two avenues: automatically produced art and conceptual art. The procedure can be implemented automatically, or a formulation of the procedure can stand in for the artwork. How far has the Oulipo gone in these two directions? The short answer is: further in the conceptual direction. Which is hardly surprising, since the conceptual is built into the foundational notion of potential literature, enshrined in the group's name.

Marcel Duchamp, a leading figure in conceptual art broadly conceived, was an Oulipo member, although never active. It could be said that Le Lionnais was a conceptual writer, since he was happy to propose literary ideas and leave their realization to others. At the meeting of the Oulipo on 28 August 1961, the mood seems to have been merry, but Le Lionnais was not speaking ironically when he said: "The method is sufficient in itself. There are methods without examples. The example is a supplementary treat, for oneself and for the reader" (GO 88).

A number of Oulipians have produced works with an important conceptual dimension. Michelle Grangaud's *Souvenirs de ma vie collective: Sujets de tableaux sans tableaux* (Souvenirs of my collective life: subjects for pictures without pictures), for example, consists of 2,357 brief descriptions of imaginary or potential artworks.

How to Do Things with Forms

Engels raising the illegitimate son of Marx as his own.
Nuclear fission releasing an immense amount of energy.
Gypsy dancing the fandango on a packet of cigarettes.
Roughneck soldier getting drunk in the castle cellar.
Thomas Aquinas creating the exercise known in the Schools
as "the dispute."[2]

In the original, the final syllable of each sentence is repeated at the beginning of the next:

Engels élevant le fils illégitime de Marx comme si c'était son
propre **fils**.
Fission du noyau atomique dégageant une énorme quantité
d'éner**gie**.
Gitane dansant le fandango sur un paquet de ciga**rettes**.
Reître se saoulant dans la cave du châ**teau**.
Thomas d'Aquin créant l'exercice appelé "la dispute" dans
les écoles.

Each description is a single sentence, and the main verb is very often a present participle. These features make for a strong formal resemblance between *Souvenirs de ma vie collective* and the catalogue of people and stories swirling around in the mind of Georges Perec's character Valène as he imagines the painting of the apartment building that *Life: A User's Manual* purports to describe:

1 The Coronation at Covadonga of Alkhamah's victor, Don Pelage
2 The Russian singer and Schönberg living in Holland as exiles
3 The deaf cat on the top floor with one blue & one yellow eye
4 Barrels of sand being filled by order of the fumbling cretin
5 The miserly old woman marking all the expenses in a notebook
  (LUM 228)

These pictures "all around" the picture (LUM 228) are also "pictures without pictures," since Valène's execution of the projected work has barely even begun: "The canvas was practically blank: a few charcoal lines had been carefully drawn, dividing it up into regular square boxes, the sketch of a cross-section of a block of flats, which no figure, now, would ever come to inhabit" (LUM 500). So *Life: A User's Manual* itself has one of the characteristic features of conceptual art identified by Peter Goldie and Elisabeth Schellekens: "Conceptual art replaces illustrative representation by what some call 'semantic representation' – semantic not only (not necessarily) in the sense of words appearing on or in the work of art itself but in the sense of depending on meaning being conveyed through a text or supporting discourse."[3] But to categorize the novel as a conceptual artwork would be a stretch. The framing fiction of the picture is so gradually rendered explicit, and so overpowered by the detail of the descriptions and stories within the frame, that Valène comes to seem the author's negative avatar, who has failed to represent with paint what Perec has depicted so intricately with words. In this way, *Life: A User's Manual* stages the triumph of writing as the art of the not materially made.

In a "Declaration of Intent," the Fluxus artist Lawrence Weiner writes: "The work need not be built."[4] But if it is *only* conceived, it remains strictly private. To exist intersubjectively, it must at least be sketched or described. And the description of an unbuilt work need not give any impression of incompleteness if it is read as literature. César Aira develops this thought in his novel *Ghosts*: "It is possible to imagine an art in which the limitations of reality would be minimized, in which the made and the unmade would be indistinct, an art that would be instantaneously real, without ghosts. And perhaps that art exists, under the name of literature."[5]

In their privileging of the constraint and the procedure, of conception over execution (in some cases), and in their fondness for describing imaginary, unmade artworks, the writers of the Oulipo have enduring affinities with conceptual art. But they have shown only a moderate interest in what for Craig Dworkin is the central feature of contemporary conceptual writing: "the use of found language in ways that go beyond modernist quotation or postmodern citation."[6] And although the Oulipo has an indispensable website, it has not reacted to the appearance of the internet as a given that is, according to Kenneth Goldsmith's analogy, revolutionizing literary writing just as photography changed the game for painting.[7]

What of the other direction signalled by Aira's manifesto-essay, that is, automation? Some progress toward the automatic production of literary texts was made in the first two decades of the Oulipo's activity. Queneau's *Cent mille milliards de poèmes* (1961) and, on a much more modest scale, his branching story "A Tale for Your Shaping" ("Un conte à votre façon," 1973) resemble plans for combinatorial machines (OC 15–33; PBO 455–7). Although originally published on paper and requiring manual manipulation (turning pages or paper strips), they soon lent themselves to automation. An automatic system for combining the lines of the sonnets in *Cent mille milliards de poèmes* was devised in 1961 by Dimitri Starynkevitch, who went on to automate the N + 7 procedure in 1963, generalizing it to N + n (GO 79).[8] Dominique Bourguet programmed a computerized version of "A Tale for Your Shaping" for the ARTA (Atelier de Recherches et Techniques Avancées) project at the Pompidou Centre in 1975.[9]

When the Alamo (Atelier de Littérature Assistée par la Mathématique et les Ordinateurs, or Workshop for Literature Assisted by Mathematics and Computers) was founded in 1981 by Paul Braffort and Jacques Roubaud as a "computing arm" ("prolongement informatique") of the Oulipo, automation was naturally a part of its brief.[10] But the design of automatic systems that can produce innovative and valuable literary texts is, of course, a very complex task. In the database for Bot or Not, an online Turing Test for poetry set up by the Australian poets Oscar Schwartz and Benjamin Laird, there were computer-generated poems that over 50 percent of the thousands of visitors attributed to a human.[11] Many readers, however, would want to distinguish between the human-like and the valuably innovative.

In May 2019, Ross Goodwin, who is employed by Google Arts & Culture, began posting poems generated by "OpenAI's GPT-2 architecture for ML (Multitask Learner) language models." When he posted this fragment on Twitter on May 6:

> Work is not the same
> for all of us.
> People change everything
> into potatoes.
>   change
>   everything into soups.
>   change
> everyone in the room.
> First, change the person
> they are with.
> Then change the expression
> that they allow
> to rest on their bones.[12]

Oscar Schwartz responded: "I've been reading computer generated poems for 6 years now and this one … is my favourite."[13]

To reach this technologically impressive but aesthetically modest level, Ross Goodwin relied on corporate support (from Google and OpenAI) and the processing of large data sets. Research of this kind requires solid financial backing. Without sustained industrial or institutional sponsorship, neither the Oulipo nor the Alamo was ever really in this race. As Roubaud said in an interview with Camille Bloomfield: "computing is very expensive, and Oulipians are not big spenders."[14]

The Alamo developed a number of computer-assisted writing systems in the 1980s and '90s, which are freely available on the group's site, but since 1998 it has been most active in running workshops and public events.[15] The Oulipo's recent inactivity in computational creativity has disappointed some people in the field but is not entirely surprising. Apart from the external (institutional and economic) reasons mentioned above, there has also been a certain lack of engagement, notably on the part of the Alamo's co-founder, Roubaud. According to Braffort, Roubaud was never really interested in the Alamo.[16] A paragraph from "Mathematics in the Method of Raymond Queneau," first published in 1977, foreshadows that disinterest: "*Proposition 10*: Oulipian work is craftsmanlike. Queneau's commentary seems here to mask something: '*this* [the craftsmanlike nature of Oulipian work] *is not essential. We regret having no access to machines.*' I would take it [the proposition] in a slightly different manner, and machines would be irrelevant. It seems to me […] that it is a case of a trait which is, on the contrary, essential. The claim to craftsmanship reflects an affirmation of amateurism; it is a voluntary archaism (and perhaps, here again, an anticipation)" (OPPL 85; ALP 53).

This is not necessarily a disavowal of the Oulipo's original brief, which privileged mathematics over other potential complementary disciplines (such as linguistics). As the eminent computer scientist and mathematician Donald Knuth writes: "there is no such thing as 'mathematical thinking' as a single isolated concept; mathematicians use a variety of modes of thought, not just one."[17] And not all mathematicians prefer to use the modes most suited to computer science and algorithmics. Having pondered the question of why the Oulipo has not pursued computer-assisted writing, Natalie Berkman concludes that the group's mathematical inclinations (rather than technophobia) led it elsewhere, toward "abstract mathematical thought – patterns and structure – rather than the procedural tendencies of applied mathematics."[18]

Because of the graphic complexities of mathematical notation, many mathematicians, even today, spend less time at computer interfaces than their colleagues in the humanities. Andrew Wiles, who published his proof of Fermat's last theorem in 1995, was reported to have used a computer only to write up his results.[19] In 2002, the Fields medallist Timothy Gowers wrote that most of his colleagues did not use computers in their work in a fundamental way.[20] This is changing, as Gowers believed it would. Computers are frequently used to verify proofs in the field of experimental mathematics, which has had its own journal since 1992.[21] Automation is advancing in mathematics as it is in natural language processing. But individuals and groups may have reasons for not contributing to its advancement. To dismiss such reasons automatically as "innovation resistance" is to assume that automation is manifestly destined to spread without limits. As Quassim Cassam reminds us: "Many innovations have turned out to be not fit for purpose and those who resisted their adoption have been proved right in the end."[22] If tasks are neither boring nor onerous, there might be good reasons not to automate them, even if we can. Crafts, after all, have made something of a comeback, and the Slow movement is set to last for as long as the destructive logic of productivism keeps pushing us in the opposite direction.

If the Oulipo's activity is essentially craftlike, as Roubaud argued, it is unsurprising that the group has not become a leader in automation, for craft and automation are fundamentally at odds in certain key respects. A simulation of craft production can be automated, but craft itself, by definition, cannot. Inversely, automatic production must, by definition, run without human intervention, but a simulation of it can be crafted. A famous example is Wolfgang von Kempelen's chess-playing "Turk": a false automaton, operated by a hidden chess master, which defeated numerous challengers in Europe and America from 1770 to the early nineteenth century, and was the subject of a debunking essay by Edgar Allan Poe.[23] Von Kempelen and Johann Nepomuk Mälzel used the Turk as an elaborate illusionist's prop, to fascinate and amaze. In literature as in live entertainment, machines may have imaginary uses, as science fiction abundantly shows. Some members of the Oulipo have used their craft to simulate automation, building literary "mechanical Turks."

THE PALF PROJECT

Perec and Bénabou's Production automatique de littérature française (Automatic production of French literature) or PALF project – on the strength of which they were invited to join the Oulipo – is one such invention (PP 10). "Automatic production" can mean a variety of things, depending on the kind of mechanisms understood to be driving the process: physical, psychological, or linguistic. Bénabou and Perec appeal to the third kind of mechanism, emphatically rejecting psychological automatism as exemplified by surrealism: "Here the notion of automatism has no relation at all to Breton's so-called 'automatic' writing" (PP 25–6). Breton acknowledged his debt to Freud's free association techniques, and defined surrealism in the first manifesto as "psychic automatism in its pure state."[24] Bénabou and Perec, writing in the time of structuralism and generative grammar, appeal to a new paradigm. But can the two kinds of mechanisms (psychological and linguistic) be so sharply dissociated? Jacques Lacan, whose name figures in the "draft table of contents" (1967) as the author of a projected "letter / preface" (PP 98), would not have thought so.[25]

The PALF project was manual and time-consuming, as Bénabou reveals in his introduction to the published dossier. It was not manual by default; it was never designed to be mechanizable. The procedure consists essentially of replacing lexical words in a given sentence with definitions chosen from Littré's dictionary, as in the following example:

La marquise sortit à cinq heures.
[The marchioness went out at five o'clock.]

marquise: toit avancé soutenu par des piliers
[marchioness: extended roof supported by pillars]

sortir: être mis en vedette
[to go out: to be given star billing]

cinq heures: l'heure du thé
[five o'clock: tea time]

Donc, "La marquise sortit à cinq heures" = le toit avancé soutenu par des piliers fut mis en vedette à l'heure du thé

[So "the marchioness went out at five o'clock" = "the extended
roof supported by pillars was given star billing at tea time"]

toit: couche supérieure (d'un filon)
[roof: upper layer (of a mineral vein)]

avancé: qui touche à sa terme
[extended: reaching its end]

soutenu: sans familiarité
[supported: without familiarity]

pilier: fourche patibulaire
[pillar: gallows]

être mis en vedette: être en sentinelle
[to be given star billing: to be on guard duty]

à l'heure: exact
[at ... time: exact]

thé: (arbrisseau) qui croît à la Chine
[tea: (bush) which grows in China]

Donc, "La marquise sortit à cinq heures" = La couche supérieure
qui touche à son terme sans familiarité avec les fourches patibulaires est la sentinelle exacte qui croit à la Chine

[So, "The marchioness went out at five o'clock" = The upper
layer reaching its end without familiarity with the gallows is the
exact guard who believes in China] (PP 27)

Human choice intervenes at two levels: choosing among dictionary
definitions, and making various adjustments to ensure a minimum
of semantic coherence. The definitions chosen are obviously not
the most obvious. Bénabou and Perec declare that they are seeking the
greatest possible "automatism" and the greatest possible "diffraction."
In the absence of a working definition of automatism, they resort to
"synonymy, metonymy, the use of set expressions (formulae, quotes,
proverbs)" (PP 29). They maximize "diffraction" by choosing the

definition in the semantic field most remote from that of the word in its initial context. Leaving aside the question of how remoteness is to be measured, the principles of automatism and diffraction are likely to pull in different directions: a remote (and antiquated) synonym, such as "fourche patibulaire" (gallows) for *pilier* (pillar) is presumably less automatic than one that figures in a stock metaphor such as "pillar = regular customer or frequenter," which is also given by Littré ("Habitué ne bougeant pas plus d'un lieu public qu'une des colonnes de l'établissement").[26]

As Bénabou and Perec note, the procedure quickly overloads the syntax of the sentence, which is allowed to buckle: "The syntactical structure of the initial utterance does not constitute an absolute constraint; the only obligation is to follow rigorously the order of the words" (meaning the *lexical* words) (PP 28). Thus "soutenu par des piliers" (supported by pillars) becomes "sans familiarité avec les fourches patibulaires" (without familiarity with the gallows), *avec* (with) replacing *par* (by) to ensure a minimum of coherence. The simple past tense of "*fut* mis en vedette" ("*was* given star billing") is shifted to the present: "*est* la sentinelle" ("*is* the guard"). Otherwise the verb *croire* (to believe) would have had to be in the imperfect tense ("qui croyait à la Chine"), which would have eliminated the homonymy *croît* (grows) / *croit* (believes), on which the final substitution hinges. Note that the word *arbrisseau* (bush) in Littré's definition has simply been left out.

The examples of their procedure that Bénabou and Perec give have been carefully handcrafted. The basic point of the exercise is to show that any two lexical items in the French language are linked by a chain of synonymic or homonymic substitutions passing via subsidiary meanings, and that by the same procedure any two strings of comparable length can be made to converge on a third. Thus Bénabou and Perec offer a tongue-in-cheek demonstration that the punning first and last sentences of Raymond Roussel's story "Parmi les noirs" ("Among the Blacks") – "Les lettres du blanc sur le bandes du vieux billard" ("The chalked letters on the cushions of the old billiard table") and "Les lettres du blanc sur les bandes du vieux pillard" ("The white man's letters about the old plunderer's gangs") – are "rigorously equivalent" since they can both be transformed into the sentence: "Les bandes de la lettre sur les pillards du vieux blanc," which might be translated as: "The strips of the letter about the old white man's plunderers" (PP 40–1; LP 138–40).

Bénabou and Perec worked on the PALF project intermittently from 1966 to 1973. As Bénabou writes in his introduction, "finir la PALF" ("finish the PALF") became a catchphrase in their conversations and letters, but the projected content kept changing, and eventually frustration at the delays gave way, on Perec's part at least, to "skepticism and lassitude" (PP 7). Having spent many hours mining the Littré and producing a handful of witty exercises demonstrating the procedure and variants thereof, the point seems to have been made, and the friends abandoned their ambitious plans for a "semantic map" of the French language and a novel based on the transformation of "Prolétaires de tous les pays, unissez-vous" (Proletarians of all countries, unite) into "Le presbytère n'a rien perdu du son charme ni le jardin de son éclat" (The vicarage has lost none of its charm, nor the garden its splendour) (PP 98).[27] Somewhat ironically, the "Automatic Production of French Literature," presented by Perec and Bénabou as "entirely and really automatic," faltered and stalled (PP 22). But like a number of Perec's unfinished projects, it nourished others that did come to fruition. According to Bénabou, "it opened the way to what would be the long and brilliant series of Perec's Oulipian works. Moreover, insofar as a part of the exercise consisted in seeking out unexpected definitions, it also anticipated, long in advance, the later series of his crosswords" (PP 8).

The PALF system produces literature not from raw materials but from fragments of finished works: emblematic sentences from *In Search of Lost Time* by Marcel Proust, "Among the Blacks" by Raymond Roussel, *The Communist Manifesto* by Karl Marx and Friedrich Engels, *The Mystery of the Yellow Room* by Gaston Leroux, *Phaedra* by Jean Racine, and André Breton's "First Surrealist Manifesto." This was part of the point: literature is made by transforming what has already been written; like language, it "goes round in circles and functions in a closed circuit" (PP 9). In the context of the PALF, the operators of the circulation were dictionary-manipulating human beings, but while that project was still a going concern, Perec embarked on another, which simulated an autonomous machine transforming a canonical work. This was the radio play *Die Maschine*, translated by Eugen Helmlé in close and creative collaboration with the author for the German broadcaster Saarländische Rundfunk.[28]

Automation, Craft, and Imitation

DIE MASCHINE

In *Die Maschine*, Johann Wolfgang von Goethe's famous "Wanderers Nachtlied II" ("Rambler's Lullaby II") is analyzed, manipulated, and finally related to other poetic texts, supposedly by a machine consisting of three processors responding to "system control." The machine works through a series of protocols: statistical, linguistic, semantic, critical, and poetic. Although comic and desacralizing effects predominate in the sections governed by the first three protocols, there are uncanny and uncomfortable moments. These result from apparent dysfunction. "Aleatory recreation" falters and recreates *other* texts:

üb

üb immer treu und redlichkeit

stop

[...]

überalle

überalle

über alles

in der welt

TON[29]

"Üb immer Treu und Redlichkeit" (Always practice fidelity and honesty) is the first line of a song by Ludwig Christoph Heinrich Hölty, often cited as an encapsulation of the "Prussian virtues." From there, the processors drift to the second line of the "Deutschlandlied," Germany's national anthem since 1922, although only the third stanza has been sung on official occasions since the Second World War, the others, and especially the first two lines ("Deutschland, Deutschland über alles, / über alles in die Welt") bearing the taint of association with the Nazi regime. Ulrich Schönherr's translation adds the word "germany" to conserve the salience of the allusion for English-speaking readers:

overall

above all

germany above everything

in the world

SOUND.[30]

A little later, system control intervenes just in time to stop processor 2 completing a reflex action from a former time:

```
h
ha
hai
hai
heil hi
      stop[31]
```

In an early article on *Die Maschine*, J.J. White remarks: "This anthropomorphic process [...] shows what overtones certain arrangements of Goethe's phonetic material and the poem's vocabulary may have now acquired."[32] The process is anthropomorphic in that the machine betrays traces of all-too-human history, but the mistakes in *Die Maschine* function in a way that Perec intended to be specifically machine-like. He often quoted Paul Klee's dictum, "Genius is the error in the system" (EC I 240–1). Such an "error" is no mistake; it is a designed irregularity. Via Klee, Perec implies that the truly accomplished writer is the one who knows how to dispose such irregularities to the best effect.

It was in these terms that he began to think about his radio play. In a letter to Helmlé, he wrote: "To begin with I wanted to explore the relationship between system and error (since genius is the error in the system). First I thought: This is where poetry lies. Then it occurred to me that the genius of a machine is the precise opposite – to be a system based on error."[33] This is a neat conceptual chiasmus (from the error in the system to the system in the error), which reinforces the distinction between human and computer ("so there would be no intersection at all between the two kinds of genius," writes Perec). It is hard to discern, in the finished radio play, a unified "system based on error," but there are certainly significant patterns in the products of supposedly random or undirected processes.

I showed above how the "aleatory reconstruction" of an iconic German poem drifts toward expressions of German nationalism. In the fourth section of *Die Maschine*, the machine "free associates," releasing an "explosion of quotes," which are connected to Goethe's poem more or less obliquely by mentions (in most cases) of trees, silence, birds, mountaintops, or night. Even works of genius, it is implied, are not absolutely original, since they recombine thematic components circulating over long periods, to be found not only in the writing of canonical authors (Schiller, Hölderlin, Baudelaire, Verlaine, Neruda, and Borges are quoted), but also in that of minor figures such as Fernand Séverin or Stuart Merrill, and even in the work of writers nobody has heard of, perhaps for good reason. Arthur Paugris, author of the following lines, seems to have been invented specially by Perec and Helmlé for the machine's little anthology:

> kein windhauch regt sich mehr in dem geheimen grün
> der zweige. stumm hat der mond ihre stimm' gemacht
> doch durch die trauer der halboffnen blätter glühn
> die küsse kalt und blau der sterne in der nacht ...[34]

> no breath of wind stirs any longer the branches'
> clandestine green, the moon has silenced their voices,
> but through the grief of the half-open leaves cold kisses
> and blue stars are glowing in the night[35]

Paugris anticipates Hugo Vernier, the putative secret genius of nineteenth-century French poetry, whose existence cannot be proved in Perec's story "The Winter Journey," which I discuss in chapter 8.

The PALF project was presented, albeit light-heartedly, as research. Bénabou and Perec claimed that the procedure was "entirely and really" automatic. In fact, it was automatic only in that it relied on relations of homonymy or synonymy codified by a dictionary. This did, however, strictly limit the freedom of the operators. Directing the semantic drift in interesting or predetermined directions required laborious, circuitous manipulations, and the project stalled. *Die Maschine*, by contrast, presents itself from the outset as a simulation: "This radio play seeks to simulate the functioning of a computer programmed to analyse and decompose Johann Wolfgang von Goethe's 'Rambler's Lullaby II.'"[36] It is a work of science fiction.[37] This gave Perec great freedom in determining how the analysis and decomposition would unfold. The work was commissioned, promptly completed, and went on to enjoy remarkable success on the airwaves.[38]

MACHINE VERSUS INSPIRATION

The machine has appealed to the writers of the Oulipo as a metaphor for the process of literary composition because it serves as a corrective to the idea of a discontinuous inspiration beyond the writer's control. Machines are designed and built according to rational plans; they can be switched on and off at will; and, barring breakdowns, they operate in a predictable and continuous fashion. Literary machines promise to realize a "phantasm of continuity," as Le Tellier has remarked.[39] For Calvino, in his essay "Cybernetics and Ghosts," the literature machines of the future will emulate what writers already do "when things are going well."[40] And according to Bénabou this is to be achieved by refining and combining constraints: "It is thus the paradox of writing under constraint that it possesses a double virtue of liberation, which may one day permit us to supplant the very notion of inspiration" (OPPL 43).

The notion to be supplanted can be understood in a weak or a strong way. Fournel invokes a weak inspiration in the following definition of the Oulipo's aim: "to explore the means by which a writer might be inspired at all times, always in a position to produce."[41] That is, always capable of producing *something*. If this is the aim, constraints are already a very effective tool for achieving it. They can be, as Jouet has put it, a "vaccine against the blank page" (AS 35). But Jouet himself remarks that this is a rather limited conception of the constraint. The contents of a page filled with the help of a constraint are not necessarily creative according to the widely accepted definition of creativity as the capacity to produce things that are both original and valuable.[42] A strong conception of inspiration, however, implies the production of just such things.

Aiming higher than mere continuity, the writers of the Oulipo have sometimes expressed their desire to supplant this stronger inspiration. In this they are distant inheritors of Plato's wary attitude to poets and rhapsodes. In Plato's *Ion*, Socrates argues that poetry is not an art or craft (*techne*), as it does not have a unitary object of its own (unlike divination, arithmetic, medicine, painting, sculpture, or music) about which poets could speak with special authority (531a–33c). It is, he says, a divine gift (534b, 536d). But being possessed by the Muse completely deprives the poet of reason (535b–e). In the *Phaedrus*, Socrates contrasts the merely proficient with the inspired poet: "But anyone who approaches the doors of poetic composition without the Muses' madness, in the conviction that skill alone will make him a competent poet, is cheated of his goal. In his sanity both he and his poetry are eclipsed by poetry composed by men who are mad" (245a).[43] This passage was central to the Renaissance theory of *furor poeticus*, as elaborated by Marcilio Ficino and other neo-Platonists, and subsequently to certain Romantic theories of inspiration, such as that of Percy Bysshe Shelley.[44] But, as Penelope Murray has shown, the *Phaedrus* as a whole is consistent with Plato's project of subordinating poetry to philosophy, and conquering Homer's central position in the Greek education system.[45] This project is explicit in the *Republic*, where Socrates famously recommends that Homer and his fellow poets be banished from the ideal society (398b2–3, 401b1–3).

The Oulipo would like to rid us not of poets but of the idea that only the inspired and insane can reach perfection in the art of poetry. One of the staunchest opponents of inspiration in the group is Roubaud, who began to write poetry under surrealism, as it were, and soon found the powerful influence of Paul Éluard, in particular, debilitating (P 104). The romantics had already internalized inspiration; the surrealists located it in the unconscious, and they followed Plato faithfully in opposing it to technique.[46] They resemble the rhapsode Ion at the end of the dialogue that bears his name, gladly accepting the qualification "divinely inspired" even though this entails a complete lack of skill and reason (542b). For Roubaud, the surrealist attempt to liberate inspiration by abolishing the border between conscious and unconscious thought was not a viable option. The poetic project that he formulated in the early 1960s demanded sustained and intensive technical work precisely in order to patrol that border and keep certain thoughts out of consciousness: the memory of his brother's suicide and the temptation of despair (P 109–10).

Roubaud found support for his rejection of inspiration in an idea implicitly underlying Bourbaki's mathematical research: intuition is dangerous and leads mathematicians astray; David Hilbert's axiomatic method is the only guide they need (P 107). In line with this idea, Roubaud formulates the following "severe axiom" in *Poésie*: (Poetry:): "I am not inspired in mathematics; I don't need inspiration in poetry" (P 107, underlining in original). He even converts the lack of mathematical inspiration into a literary advantage:

And yet, when I see how truly creative mathematicians (much more creative than I ever was myself) often speak about the mental and material operation of mathematical creation, I am convinced that, as a poet, I would have been unable to part with the worn-out idea of inspiration [...] if I had known what it was like to come up with, say, algebraic inventions; for they

88 How to Do Things with Forms

> have the same poor, sad vision, and, brimming with enthusiasm, hand on the most banal received ideas about CREATION, ideas that circulate unimpeded by disciplinary boundaries and cheerfully fill in the gulf between the two cultures (literary and scientific). (P 109)

Here it seems more important to Roubaud not to subscribe to a cliché about inspiration than to have made a mathematical discovery that might be qualified as inspired. His position seems to be determined more by reaction to a commonly held opinion than by a conviction about the facts of the matter, the matter in this case being how creation or invention works.[47]

Roubaud's hostility to the notion of inspiration is overdetermined: due in part to a materialist outlook, it stems also from a personal argument with surrealism, specific psychological necessities, and a strong aversion to received ideas. But of course he is not alone in repudiating inspiration. As Timothy Clark writes at the beginning of *The Theory of Inspiration* (1997): "To anyone with knowledge of the current state of literary studies, nothing sounds more trite, mystifying and even embarrassing than talk of writers as 'inspired'. 'Inspiration' seems a spurious and exploded theory of the sources of literary power."[48] Reasons for the discredit into which the notion has widely fallen are not hard to find, and three at least are bound to carry weight with writers who have declared their allegiance to science and the Enlightenment: the idea of inspiration has been used irrationally to attribute agency to mythological agents; it has been used in anti-egalitarian ways to designate a privilege of the writer as member of an élite; and it has been used lazily, to justify lack of rigour and refusal to work. Such uses or abuses have made the notion suspect and embarrassing. But it is not exactly obsolete. As Clark shows, although the theory of inspiration seems "spurious and exploded," critics and philosophers keep reassembling its parts in different ways to grapple with a "crisis in subjectivity" that has been associated with literary composition from Plato to the present day.[49]

Clark's "crisis in subjectivity" is fundamentally a crisis of control: the process of writing is not entirely subject to the writer's will; it tends to proceed by fits and starts; it is often jerky, spasmodic, threatening to come to a definitive halt. The enemies of inspiration may regret this, but few would deny it. In the current state of the art, a writer who claimed to possess a fail-safe and self-sufficient method for literary composition would inspire little more confidence than one who claimed to be inspired.

The flip side of inspiration is writer's block in its various forms, to which the members of the Oulipo are by no means immune. Queneau's best-known novel, *Zazie in the Metro*, was the one that took him longest to complete, partly because he stopped "hearing" the voice of the protagonist, as he explains, addressing her in a draft: "Sometimes you took a long time to pipe up. For about six months – nothing, not a word. Gallimard wasn't happy. What's with that novel, he said: Coming along? Getting there? Nearly done? What was I supposed to say, the girl's shut up on me. [...] It was awkward. You must have been sleeping. Or something" (OC III 1697). The extremely productive Roubaud is also prone to bouts of literary debilitation, as he confesses in *La dissolution*: "I break down. I try and I try, but I get nowhere: not a line, not a sentence, not a word, not a letter, not even a punctuation mark: nothing. No alternative solution in view."[50] And for many years, Bénabou suffered from a kind of paralysis that is eloquently explored and overcome in his literary début, *Why I Have Not Written Any of My Books*.

Given the Oulipo's commitment to extending rational control over literary production, it is not surprising that inspiration and its lack have become, along with chance, conceptual foils for the group. In their attacks on inspiration, the Oulipians often refer back to two closely related passages in Queneau's work, from his 1937 novel *Odile* and his 1938 essay "Plus and Minus." Both passages contain an apparent paradox, voiced in the first instance by the character Vincent N. in *Odile*: "The really inspired person is never inspired: he's always inspired" (O 101; OC II 600); "he [the poet] is never inspired because he's always inspired" (LNF 40; VG 126). For Le Tellier, it is the constraint that supplies the continuous inspiration of the truly inspired person: "Far from interrupting, far from restricting freedom, the constraint turns out to be infinitely fertile, and confirms Queneau's affirmation that 'the really inspired person is never inspired: he's always inspired.'"[51]

Lescure quotes the "famous sentence" from *Odile* and comments: "What does this mean? What? This thing so rare, inspiration, this gift of the gods which makes the poet, and which this unhappy man never quite deserves in spite of all his heartaches, this enlightenment coming from who knows where, is it possible that it might cease to be capricious, and that any and everybody might find it faithful and compliant to his desires?" (OPPL 34). On this Oulipian reading, Queneau was foreshadowing, in the late 1930s, the supplanting of inspiration that Bénabou envisaged as the group's long-term goal in "Rule and Constraint." Constraints, Le Tellier, Lescure, and Bénabou suggest, are the key to democratizing inspiration.

But if we put the famous sentences back into their contexts, two obstacles to this reading appear. First, although Queneau sees technique as a plus and inspiration as a minus, he does not imagine the first replacing the second. Rather, the true poet effects a dialectical superseding of the opposition between them: "Quite the opposite, I don't believe that a true poet is ever 'inspired': both the lowest and the highest denominator are beneath him, he's above technique and inspiration, which come to the same thing as far as he's concerned, because he's in full possession of both of them" (O 100–1). True poets are not only superior technicians, they are also, in some sense, above technique.

The first time Vincent uses the word "inspired," Queneau puts it in scare quotes to make it clear that he is talking about the surrealist (or Platonic) version of inspiration: a supposed surrender to the unconscious (or to the possessing muse). He imagines that for the "true poet" technique is a plus and this sort of inspiration a minus. Nevertheless the true poet possesses both "supereminently" ("suréminemment" [OC II 600]). Such a poet does not reject the contributions of the unconscious but considers them from a point of view metaphorically above or beyond the Platonic opposition of inspiration to technique. When Vincent says that the truly inspired poet is never inspired, he means that such a poet has already left that opposition definitively behind. Dennis Duncan brings this out in his alternative translation: "*The truly inspired person never* becomes *inspired: he is* always *inspired.*"[52]

When Vincent says that the truly inspired poet is always inspired, he is attributing a new meaning to the word. Inspiration in this second sense refers to decisions made from the point of view above or beyond the inspiration / technique opposition: decisions about the relative values of unconscious givens, and about which techniques to use and when to depart from them. These decisions are intuitive by necessity. As Kevin Hart has remarked, if the possibilities that open up at each step of composition all had to be tested and their merits compared, no text would ever be finished.[53] For Vincent N., truly inspired writers not only have more possibilities to work with (possessing technique and irrational "inspiration" to an uncommon degree), their intuitive decisions about which possibilities to realize are also consistently felicitous.

The second obstacle to the Oulipian interpretation of the famous sentences is that, when read in context, they do not promise to give everyone access to a demystified inspiration. Vincent N.'s interlocutor in the scene from *Odile*, Roland Travy, is reminded of a man he saw sitting contemplatively by the road in Morocco, and speculates: "No doubt the Arab that I'd seen one day on the road from Bou Jeloud to Bab Fetouh was just such a poet" (O 101). In "Plus and Minus," however, the "true poet" is scarcely to be found:

> And should someone claim that such poets don't exist, I will answer: the fact that modern poets have been reduced to a discontinuous inspiration doesn't mean we must console them by calling the minus that afflicts them a plus [...] The true poet requires no consolation, then, and no form of intoxicant. He's never inspired not only because he knows the powers of language and rhythm, but also because he knows what he is and what he's capable of: he isn't a slave to free association. If this is no longer how things are, it's time we convinced ourselves that it is how they should be. (LNF 41)

Here Queneau is echoing an article by René Daumal on Indian poetics, which he goes on to quote at length and with full approval: "Do such poets exist? Certainly, they have walked the earth. And if the classic poets of post-Buddhic India are not such poets any more than our own are, it is nevertheless this idea of the poet that has guided and fertilized the efforts of the best among them" (LNF 42).

In the late 1930s, Queneau did not situate his ideal poet in a future of formalized poetics. Nor did he follow Daumal in attempting to graft his own writing onto an ancient tradition with origins beyond Europe. His models were Homer and Dante, but also his near-contemporaries Marcel Proust and James Joyce (LNF 30–2). Having set out his ideas on inspiration in "Plus and Minus," Queneau went on, in his next essay for *Volontés*, to cite Joyce's *Ulysses* and *Work in Progress* as examples of the "continuous and transcendent inspiration" that he held up as an ideal (VG 133). He presented Joyce not as a technical innovator but the legitimate heir to Homer: "I hope to explain in a further article how his direct link to Homer expresses the ultimate truth [*la vérité dernière*] of Western literature" (VG 134). The Second World War intervened, and the "further article" was never published, but it is clear that for Queneau, during this phase of his writing life, inspiration was more a matter of transmission and tradition than of rupture and innovation. And he saw "the really inspired person" as a rare specimen at best. There is no suggestion in *Odile* or in "Plus and Minus" that true inspiration will soon be freely available to all. On the contrary, it is envisaged as a grail which only a few may approach at the cost of great effort: "Yes, long and hard is the struggle to become and to be a poet. You who now claim to be poets, humble yourselves before what you should be" (LNF 42).

While attempting to approach this forbiddingly remote ideal, the aspirant presumably has to make do with a more or less intermittent flow of genuinely creative ideas. Queneau admits this implicitly when, in "Plus and Minus," he compares the poet to a hunter: "He doesn't wait for inspiration to drop from the heavens like roasted ortolans. He *knows how to hunt*, and puts into action the irrefutable proverb 'Heaven helps those who help themselves'" (LNF 40). Even the best hunter has lean days and weeks. Even those who help themselves need help from heaven or the world. Queneau made this point humorously in a poem originally entitled "L'inspiration," and later included as part V of "Pour un art poétique" (For a poetic art). The poem begins, "Good lord good lord how I'd like to write a little poem / Hold on here's one right now passing by," and ends, "damn / it got away."[54] It is implied that such an eventuality is more likely if the as yet unwritten poem is treated with a lack of respect, not as an individual but as an addition to a series – like a new pearl on the string of a necklace or a tablet in a tube – and approached as inert material to be formatted according to the poet's desires (OC I 107).

In a radio talk broadcast in 1952, Queneau returned to this theme: "You don't write poems to turn them into songs, or even to turn them into poems, you write what you can – and what you must. What you can, because in this, as in other things, the finest efforts and the best intentions are worthless unless the unknown and the unpredictable intervene to confirm, as it were, the effort – and the intention."[55] Effort and intention are necessary but insufficient, and must be confirmed by that which escapes the rational control of the individual writer: the unknown and the unpredictable. This confirmation often comes in the form of an illumination preceded by phases of preparation and incubation, to employ terms proposed by Graham Wallas in

The Art of Thought (1926) and widely taken up in psychological studies of creativity.

In literary writing, illumination need not occur in a grand flash; it can be produced by a series of adjustments and expansions prompted by encounters with relevant stimuli in the writer's environment. In the context of insight problem-solving, Colleen Seifert and her colleagues have called this mechanism "opportunistic assimilation."[56] Queneau gives a brief account of how it works for the novelist in his preface to Faulkner's *Mosquitoes*: "Once the 'work' is well underway, once the author is immersed in the writing, then everything can be thrown into it, everything fits, everything seems to fall into place and offer its own contribution, a grain of salt or calcium, a clump of seaweed or a little fish; coincidences accumulate, as do intuitions, insights, sudden revelations, endowing the conscious 'plan' of the novel with the necessary thicknesses and densities" (LNF 157). This kind of experience is by no means the preserve of genius.

IMITATION

Constraints, as I argued at the end of chapter 2, are problem-finding tools, which can distract attention productively and protect spaces for incubated cognition. They also hook in or throw up adventitious elements for the writer's consideration, sometimes serendipitously. In this double sense, they serve as "inspiration pumps," to quote Perec (EC II 288). They have amply proved their efficacy, both in the work of experienced writers and in the classroom. But there is no all-purpose tool, and no tool is best used in a continuous and exclusive way. As Paul Dourish, one of the pioneers of tangible computing, reminds us: "effective use of tools inherently involves a continual process of engagement, separation and re-engagement."[57]

The writers of the Oulipo do not always use constraints, and Jouet, reflecting on his own practice, has suggested that an alternation of constrained and unconstrained writing maintains a generative conflict: "Meaning is born from confrontation with the absence of meaning. The constraint should find its reason for being in its opposite, the absence of constraint" (AS 50). The absence of constraint does not, however, imply a lack of method, and the writers of the Oulipo make abundant use of the techniques accumulated by the traditions in which they work, some of which "pump inspiration" from human sources in the past.

Roubaud is a prolific inventor of constraints, but his writing is also deeply informed by the traditional practices of memorization, recitation, and mental composition. These are all part of imitation as it was broadly conceived by Dionysius of Halicarnassus, Quintilian, Seneca, and other scholars in ancient Greece and Rome. In *Poésie:* Roubaud explains how over many years he selected poems to form a personal canon, copied them out by hand, learned them by heart, and repeated them to himself to maintain their mnemonic traces (P 38–40). In this way he incorporated a portable library that constitutes the background against which his own poems have been written. As a rule he composes mentally and orally, while walking (P 15). For him, poetry is, or should be, a bodily activity like playing a musical instrument: "Many people have a great deal of trouble imagining the art of poetry as an art of the hand and the mouth, requiring exercises, training, and application. Learning to 'play' poetry, by which I mean lodging poems in one's head and reproducing them for oneself and for others, should be as natural as taking up the violin, the viola da gamba, the guitar, the saxophone, or the computer" (P 228).

Roubaud's "playing" of poetry is guided by a set of procedures, some of which were formalized by the arts of memory from antiquity to the Renaissance (P 37–49). But, like playing music, it is not simply procedural. Since both kinds of playing are bodily practices, they are necessarily affected by the player's physical particularities, which change as the body ages, and by emotional and metabolic states, which vary over shorter spans of time. Memorized models, for example, cannot always be retrieved intact at will, as Roubaud admits (P 47). Indeed they are inevitably subject to erosion and distortion (P 58–61). Models may also be lodged in memory unconsciously.

Roubaud has little to say about how the physical performance of existing poetry conditions the composition of new poems. But clearly it does so in ways that cannot be reduced to the rule-based transformations practised by the Oulipo, such as the N + 7 procedure and other "homomorphisms." The traditional memory-based imitation that Roubaud defends alongside the formulation and use of constraints is a quasi-dialogical activity, in which the precursor is felt to be present as a personal style that may be extrapolated to new kinds of material. As Roubaud remarks in an aside, "a style is neither a form, nor a 'something to say' or 'to mean'" (P 92).

This accompaniment by a precursor was underlined by Dionysius of Halicarnassus in a fragment from his trilogy on imitation: "by constant observation, the reader's soul attracts a likeness of the style."[58] Similarly, in *On the Sublime*, Longinus states that writers can be possessed and inspired by their precursors as well as by the Muses.[59] Inspiration of this kind is familiarly known as channelling. The metaphor is an ancient one, to be found in both of the sources just cited.[60] Channelling may not be entirely enviable, for it threatens to confine a writer to the condition of the epigone. Once this problem arises, attempting to solve it by rejecting influence altogether is likely to leave the repudiated precursor in a dominant position, negatively but powerfully determining the work of the former disciple. A more promising strategy is to multiply influences: as they conflict and compete, the influenced writer is obliged to assume a measure of independence in deciding whom to listen to and when. In *The Loop*, Roubaud writes:

It was really only after Queneau's death that I claimed the title of Oulipian without reticence. Raymond Queneau is my master, but I am the only one who knows and decides how, in what sense, and to what extent.

I will add, since this touches on an essential feature of the conception of my Project, that in this general refusal of obedience, I adopted a particular strategy, which was not to imitate a revolutionary gesture but to seek and to choose a multiplicity of master figures (the fatal illusion par excellence, in politics as in art, is the "tabula rasa"), hence Queneau, but also Raimbaut d'Orange, Cavalcanti, and Mallarmé, but also Gertrude Stein and Trollope and Kamo no Chomei [...]

In each case, the choice was as much that of a "counter-mastery" as of an example to follow without reservation. It was Queneau against surrealism, Raimbaut d'Orange and Mallarmé against the sing-song conception of poetry, Cavalcanti against Dante, Gertrude Stein against Joyce [...] I took on certain masters in order to refuse others that everyone accepted. (L 252)

In the early stages of his career, Perec was adept at channelling, which he induced by "excessive reading" ("la lecture à outrance") (EC I 83–4). He too had a library of memorized models: touchstone sentences from favourite novels, which his friend Jacques Lederer remembers him reciting as "so many spurs to emulation."[61] And, like Roubaud, Perec found freedom in a multiplicity of influences. In a text on his debt to Flaubert, he writes: "The reasons for these borrowings have never been very clear to me. In the first case (*Things*), I was probably under a dominating influence, wanting to be Flaubert [*un accaparement, un vouloir-être Flaubert*]; in the case of *Life: A User's Manual,* I think it's more like placing survey marks or tracing a network: Flaubert, like Kafka and Calvino, Sterne and Jules Verne, Roussel and Rabelais, Leiris and Queneau, etc., is now a part of the fictional space in which I try to move, just as I do in physical space" (O II 680).

Perec and Roubaud declare their independence by signalling multiple allegiances. This move is not unprecedented. Indeed it recalls the accompanying text that Queneau wrote for his book of poems *L'instant fatal* (1948): "My favourite poets are Rutebeuf, Villon, Jacques Jacques, Chénier and Péguy. I have imitated them (as well as a number of others) with all my heart, and I hope it's obvious in these poems [...]" (OC I 1169). And Queneau, in turn, was inscribing himself in a long rhetorical tradition that saw the multiplication of models, or eclectic imitation, as a means of producing novelty.[62] Seneca compared this practice to a bee's gathering of pollens to make honey: "we should so blend those several flavours into one delicious compound that, even though it betrays its origin, yet it nevertheless is clearly different from that whence it came."[63]

A number of the Oulipo's eminent writers are imitators in the Senecan sense: Queneau, Roubaud, and Perec, as I have suggested, but also Garréta, whose "imitation" of Proust (and many other authors) in *La décomposition* is simultaneously homage and profanation, as I argue in chapter 7. In the work of these Oulipians there is a strong complementarity between using constraints to find and define problems, and imitating models that set a standard for solutions.

4

Manipulation, Translation, and Composition

MANIPULATION AND TRANSLATION

In the *Oulipo Compendium*, Harry Mathews writes: "Translation. A principle central to Oulipian research, although not in its usual sense of translation between two languages: with one exception, Oulipian techniques of translation are used within a single language. Each technique manipulates an element of the text that has been artificially isolated from the whole, whether it be meaning, sound, grammar or vocabulary" (OC 234). These techniques, which Mathews goes on to list (antonymic, grammatical, homolexical, homophonic, homosemantic, and translexical translation, homosyntaxism, semo-definitional literature, and transplants), are based on what, in chapter 2, I called process constraints of type 1a, that is, rules for transforming an existing text. With the one exception mentioned by Mathews (homophonic translation), they might be viewed, at a stretch, as methods of intralingual translation, which Roman Jakobson defined as "an interpretation of verbal signs by means of other signs in the same language."[1] But this is a stretch. Consider the emblematic N + 7 procedure, which is a special case of homosyntaxism: each noun in a text is replaced by the seventh subsequent noun in a given dictionary. Meaning is altered more or less radically. Sometimes, if a large dictionary is used, nouns are replaced by cognate words. The method depends for its effect on familiarity with the source, which is parodied by the substitutions. Using C.K. Ogden's Basic English word list, a famous declaration yields, "We hold these verses to be self-evident, that all mists are created equal, that they are endowed by their curve with certain unalienable rooms, that among these are Liquid, Lip, and the rain of Head."

Can we call this a translation? An extreme translation, perhaps? It stretches even Jakobson's definition of intralingual translation, since it is hard to see how the substitutions interpret the original. It would be clearer to speak of manipulation, as Georges Perec does in his prefatory remarks on "35 variations sur un thème de Marcel Proust" (35 variations on a theme by Marcel Proust).[2] Mathews himself uses the verb "to manipulate" in his translation entry: "Each technique manipulates an element of the text that has been artificially isolated from the whole." This in fact points to a difference: whereas manipulations bear on a single element, translations "in the usual sense" attempt to match multiple elements of the source text, generally privileging denotative meaning.

In *Palimpsests*, Gérard Genette discusses the Oulipo as a workshop for manipulation, which he calls transformation. According to Genette there are two distinct ways of deriving one text from another: transformation and imitation. The first modifies one of the source's elements; the second expresses a different idea in the manner of the source.[3] The first process can be accomplished by the application of a simple rule; the second is more indirect, since it passes via an abstract notion of what the manner (or genre) is. This is a useful distinction, and it lines up with the one that I drew in chapter 2 between the Oulipian constraint and the generic convention. Nevertheless, Genette's treatment of the Oulipo is drastically reductive: "I shall therefore consider only one aspect of this Oulipic activity: namely its transformational aspect. That is, after all, its principal feature in a sense, especially if one takes into account the Oulipisms that consist first of an ad hoc textual production followed by systematic transformation. The palindrome obviously falls within this category, or the holorhyme."[4] As Arnaud remarks, Genette seems to confuse Oulipian exercises and works.[5] The only work that he mentions, briefly, is Perec's *A Void*, even though *Palimpsests* was published in 1982, four years after *Life: A User's Manual*. And Genette effectively ignores all the Oulipian exercises that are not transformational, that is, all except those based on constraints of type 1a.

This reduction is what allows him to qualify Oulipian writing as "mechanical," generalizing a formulation that Jean Lescure used to describe the writer's role in applying the N + 7 procedure: "the said operator, whose function is purely mechanical" (AES 40).[6] While Genette admires the work of Queneau and Calvino, and includes their names in a list of modern or postmodern authors who reconnect with pre-modern traditions via hypertextuality, he is clearly less enthusiastic about the rest of the Oulipo.[7] Although his opinion is not thoroughly informed, as Arnaud demonstrates, it is worth considering as a symptom, and as the index of a risk. Many readers, some very well read, have reacted similarly over the years, from Jean Paulhan, who shrank from the "sordid boredom" given off by the group's first collective publication (GO 180), to Calvin Bedient, who sees the Oulipo as fundamentally affect-shy and risk-averse.[8]

Readers tend to come to the Oulipo via its exercises. Because those exercises can be exemplified concisely they are well suited to illustrating the group's rule-based approach in collective publications. They can also be used in writing workshops without lengthy apprenticeship. Exercises are the public face of the Oulipo, the major source of its pedagogical and performative success. But they can pall, seeming parasitic in the case of manipulations, or overly effect-driven when composed for public readings. The ludic can lose its flavour when practised systematically, as Genette points out at the end of *Palimpsests*: "Texts that are 'purely playful' in their purpose are not always the most captivating or even the most amusing. Premeditated and organized games (those that are played with a deliberate 'purpose') sometimes induce a deadly boredom, and the best jokes are often unintentional."[9] If the Oulipian exercise at its most routine can resemble party entertainment, the Oulipian work at is best matches Genette's ideal for the hypertext: "an indeterminate compound, unpredictable in its specifics, of seriousness and playfulness (lucidity and ludicity), of intellectual achievement and entertainment."[10]

Contrary to the impression given by *Palimpsests*, manipulation or, as Mathews calls it, "translation," is only one of the things that the writers of the Oulipo do with texts. One of the others, and not the least significant, is translation in the conventional sense of the word. According to the calculations of Camille Bloomfield and Hermes Salceda, seventeen out of forty-one members of the Oulipo have translated or co-translated at least one book.[11] The Oulipo has often translated itself. To cite just a few examples: Calvino translated Queneau's *The Blue Flowers* (*Les fleurs bleues*) into Italian; Perec translated Mathews's *Tlooth* and *The Sinking of the Odradek Stadium* into French; Monk translated Perec's *A Gallery Portrait* (*Un cabinet d'amateur*), *The Exeter Text* (*Les revenentes*), and *Which Moped with Chrome-Plated Handlebars at the Back of the Yard?* (*Quel petit vélo au guidon chromé au fond de la cour?*) into English; and Martín

Sánchez translated Le Tellier's *L'anomalie* into Spanish. The Oulipo has been an international group if not from the start at least from the recruitment of Mathews and Calvino in 1973 and 1974 respectively, and the group's self-translation has boosted the international projection of its works.

Oulipian translators have also ranged much further afield. Queneau translated *The Palm-Wine Drinkard and his Dead Palm-Wine Tapster in the Deads' Town* by the Nigerian writer Amos Tutuola. Roubaud has translated indigenous North American and medieval Japanese poetry, and Métail has translated Chinese poems dating from the third to the nineteenth centuries CE. These were elective translations, prompted by aesthetic affinities with authors remote in space or time or both. They also fed into original projects and works. Thus translation by Oulipians has served not only to diffuse the work of the Oulipo, but also to nourish that work with the literatures of the world. In its projection and influence, but also in the breadth of its curiosity, the Oulipo is a "world group" as Camille Bloomfield has called it, although its members are still mainly French, and Paris remains the centre of its activities.[12]

Before examining some interactions between translation and original writing, I want to ask *how* Oulipians have translated in the conventional sense of the word. As already indicated, a large corpus could inform the answer to this question. I will consider three contrasting cases, which reveal both the variety of the group's translation practice and, in each case, an ongoing engagement with certain strategies exemplified by the source text.

CASE I: QUENEAU'S TRANSLATION OF TUTUOLA'S *THE PALM-WINE DRINKARD*

In his "By the same author" lists, Queneau included three translations: of *Twenty Years A-Growing* by Maurice O'Sullivan, *Peter Ibbetson* by George du Maurier, and *The Palm-Wine Drinkard* by Tutuola. Queneau heard about *The Palm-Wine Drinkard* in 1952, the year of its publication by Faber and Faber, from his friend the translator Jean Rosenthal.[13] The book made a genuine splash, thanks in part to an early and enthusiastic review by Dylan Thomas, who underlined its departures from the conventions of British English and realist narrative: "This is the brief, thronged, grisly and bewitching story, or series of stories, written in young English by a West African, about the journey of an expert and devoted palm-wine drinkard through a nightmare of indescribable adventures, all simply and carefully described, in the spirit-bristling bush [...] nothing is too prodigious or too trivial to put down in this tall, devilish story."[14]

Given Queneau's commitment to spoken language in literature, passionately defended in essays from the 1930s, '40s, and '50s, it is natural to assume that what attracted him to Tutuola's novel was its orality.[15] But what Thomas called Tutuola's "young English" is not strictly speaking oral, for Tutuola chose to write down in English stories that were familiar to him from the oral tradition of his mother tongue, Yoruba. The distinctiveness of his English at the phrase level is largely an artifact of mental translation into a language learnt during a fairly brief period of formal schooling and later used in his work as a messenger with the Labour Department in Lagos.[16] The novel's true orality resides in its style from the sentence level up and in its narrative structure.

In a review of *L'ivrogne dans la brousse* (as Queneau translated Tutuola's title), Alexandre Vialatte wrote: "Three-quarters of the charm come from the translator's talent [...] Queneau translated him like a god, with an incomparable fruity flavour. He doesn't translate, he reinvents, raves, and prophesies as if he were speaking with native ease in the tongue of a land that has never existed."[17] Queneau's translation is undeniably skilful and resourceful, but the degree of reinvention is limited. In fact, he erases many of Tutuola's originalities at the word and phrase level, as we can see by comparing the instances of non-standard usage in the original with the translations shown in table 4.1. In each of these cases, Queneau's translation accurately captures the meaning as clarified by the context. It also normalizes grammar and usage, but here it is important to remember that this is what translation normally does, if not usually to the same extent. David Bellos has written of the "general tendency of all translations to adhere more strongly than any original to a normalized idea of what the target language should be."[18] It turns out that this rule applies even to translations done by Queneau, whom no one could accuse of linguistic purism.

Why do translations adhere more strongly to the norm? "Translators," Bellos writes, "are instinctively averse to the risk of being taken for less than fully cultivated writers of their target tongue."[19] They also want their translations to be widely read, so they are averse to the risk of accumulating abnormalities to the point where

Table 4.1

Queneau's normalization of Tutuola's English in *The Palm-Wine Drinkard*

The Palm-Wine Drinkard	L'Ivrogne dans la brousse	Back translation
drinkard	ivrogne	drunk
I lied down on the middle of the roads (11)	alors je me couche au Carrefour (13)	so I lie down at the Intersection
and he could jump a mile to the second before coming down (22)	et il pouvait faire un saut tel qu'en une seconde il retombait un kilomètre plus loin (23)	and he could jump so that in one second he landed a kilometre further on
when the people in the town saw his havocs and bad character (34)	Les gens de cette ville, en voyant tous ses méfaits et son caractère méchant (34)	The people of this town, seeing all his misdeeds and his bad character
I was sweating as if I bath in water for overloading (37)	je suais comme dans un bain de vapeur à cause de cette charge (37)	I was sweating as if in a steam bath because of that load
they laughed at us as if bombs explode (45)	ils éclatent de rire comme des bombes (45)	they burst out laughing like bombs
we began to snuff the sweet smelling (51)	nous nous mettons à renifler la bonne odeur (51)	we begin to sniff the good smell

readers become alienated and give up. This is especially the case in first translations. An author's first chance in translation is often also their last. Once their reputation and readership in the target language have grown, a translator may be less nervous about adhering more closely to deviations from the norm in the original. First, however, it may be necessary for a freer translation to "domesticate" a local readership as well as the source. Friedrich Schleiermacher pointed this out in 1813: "free imitations should first awaken and whet readers' appetites for foreign works, and paraphrase prepare for a more general understanding, so as to pave the way for future translations."[20]

Tutuola himself encouraged his editor at Faber and Faber, Alan Pringle, to do some strategic domestication: "I shall be very much grateful if you will correct my 'WRONG ENGLISH' etc. and can alter the story itself if possible."[21] Pringle replied: "We agree that your English is not always conventional English as written in this country, but for that very reason we think it would be a great pity to make it conform to all the rules of grammar and spelling. [...] We propose therefore that our reader should go through the manuscript before it is set up

Manipulation, Translation, and Composition 103

in type, correcting what are evidently copying errors, accidental omissions, confusions or inconsistencies, but leaving intact all those expressions which, though strictly speaking erroneous, are more graphic than the correct expressions would be."[22] A manuscript page in facsimile is included in the published book, showing the editor's restrained "corrections," which in the following transcription are indicated using strikethrough and italics:

> I could not blame the lady for following the Skull as a complete gentleman to his house [~~atall~~] *at all.* Because if I were a lady, no doubt I would follow him to [~~where-ever~~] *wherever* he would go, and still as I was a man I would jealous him more than that, because if this gentleman [~~go~~] *went* to the battle field, surely, enemy would not kill him or capture him and if bombers [~~see~~] *saw* him in a town which was to be bombed, they would not throw bombs on his presence, and if they *did* throw it, the bomb itself would not explode until that gentleman would leave that town, because of his beauty.[23]

Here is the corresponding passage from Queneau's translation with the most significant revisions shown in the same way:

> Je ne pouvais vraiment pas blâmer la demoiselle d'avoir suivi Crâne quand c'était un gentleman complet, parce que, si j'avais été une demoiselle, [~~sans doute que~~] *pas de doute,* je l'aurais suivi n'importe où il aurait voulu aller, et même, en tant qu'homme, [~~j'étais jaloux de lui~~] *je l'enviais* encore plus que ça parce que [~~si ce gentleman allait~~] *à supposer que ce gentleman se trouve* sur un champ de bataille, sûrement l'ennemi ne le tuerait pas et ne le ferait pas prisonnier et, si les avions le voyaient dans une ville qui devait être bombardée, ils ne lâcheraient pas leurs bombes, s'il se trouvait là, et, s'ils [~~la lâchaient~~] *en lâchaient,* la bombe elle-même n'exploserait pas avant que ce gentleman n'ait quitté la ville, à cause de sa beauté.[24]

The use of "jealous" as a verb (where standard English would use "envy") was preserved by the English editor. It is as if he had tidied up details of spelling and tense in order to make such larger-scale deviations from the norm stand out all the more clearly. In the translation and its revision, "I would jealous him" becomes "j'étais jaloux de lui"

("I was jealous of him") and then "je l'enviais" ("I envied him"). As for "throw bombs on his presence," Queneau has taken the object of the possible bombing to be understood, and written simply: "ils ne lâcheraient pas leurs bombes" ("they would not drop their bombs"). This is an accurate reading, but sidesteps the unusual combination of the concrete ("bombs") and the abstract ("presence") in the original.

In the translation, then, normalization is extended from spelling and adjustments of tense to lexis and phrase construction. Anything that could be construed as erroneous in the original is smoothed away, but Tutuola's characteristic sentence-level syntax, with its insistent repetitions, is respected. Neither Pringle nor Queneau goes so far as to "alter the story itself." Queneau does, however, do *some* inventing or at least some inventive borrowing: to translate *tapster*, which figures in the full title of the novel, he chooses *malafoutier*, although, as he writes in his preface, this term is used in the Congo and not in West Africa.[25] He also engages in compensation, as in the following example:

> he commanded the drum with a kind of voice that the strings
>   of the drum should tight me there (12)

> d'une voix spéciale, il ordonne au tambour de me ligoter sur
>   place avec ses cordes (au tambour) (14)

The addition of "(au tambour)" at the end is far from arbitrary. It extends a syntactic habit that runs right through Tutuola's novel: specifying the identity of a participant between parentheses, and it allows Queneau to repeat the word, as "drum" is repeated in the original. In the following examples a jocular phonetic spelling ("fouteballe") and a familiar expression (the adverbial "toute chose") sustain the overall oral tone, although they do not correspond to specific colloquial features in the source:

> I was seriously sat down in my parlour (8)
> je reste assis toute chose dans mon salon (10)

> it was cleared as a football field (61)
> il était bien dégagé, comme un terrain de fouteballe (61)

And Tutuola's systematically inclusive language is maintained throughout:

they would catch him or her and begin to cut the flesh of his
or her body into pieces while still alive (59)

ils l'attrapent et ils le (ou la) coupent vivant (ou vivante)
en morceaux (59)

In short, Queneau's *L'ivrogne dans la brousse* is nimble and confident, but to describe it as a wholesale reinvention is to undervalue Tutuola's storytelling powers. *L'Ivrogne* is a translation, straightforwardly so, respecting the "story itself" and the tone of its telling – "candid and clever," as Queneau describes it in his preface – while dissolving much of the original's idiosyncrasy at the word and phrase level.[26]

The oralized "neo-French" for which Queneau became famous with *Zazie in the Metro* and what Dylan Thomas called Tutuola's "young English" are both non-standard language varieties, but to draw a parallel between them, as some critics have done, may obscure an important disanalogy between the two writers' projects.[27] The whole thrust of Queneau's campaign for neo-French was to encourage writers in France to write in their true mother tongue: French as it was really spoken. In the very different context of 1950s Nigeria, Tutuola, whose mother tongue was Yoruba, chose to write in the language of colonization that he had learned at school. But as he points out in the essay "My Vernacular," English for him is a thin or translucent medium: "Although I wrote in English (and still do), my writings, looking back now, are still *in* Yoruba. *In* here is deliberately put in italics. The medium in which my ideas are expressed is English, but what I write, the ideas I express, the atmosphere I create, and as reviewers of my works (perhaps rightly) maintain, the gestures readers encounter on the pages of the books I write are *Yorubaish*."[28] It was the Yorubaish ideas, atmosphere, and gestures that Queneau valued in *The Palm-Wine Drinkard* and prioritized in his translation, rather than the fine texture of the linguistic medium as transformed by Tutuola.

CASE 2: PEREC'S TRANSLATION OF MATHEWS'S *TLOOTH*

My second case differs starkly from the first, because the source and target texts are strongly oriented toward the written rather than the spoken word. Perec would not have subscribed to Queneau's assertion that "only the phoneme counts in Western languages" (LNF 84).

For him, the written sign was crucial. His preoccupation with the letter is clearest in *A Void* but evident also in his translation of Mathews's *Tlooth*.

It was friendship that led Perec to embark on his first book-length translation. He agreed to translate *Tlooth* in 1971, before he had read it, and the formal ingenuity that he discovered there prompted him to introduce Mathews to the Oulipo.[29] In the set of rules underlying *Tlooth*, as partially explained by the novel's author, Perec found a model for what David Bellos has called a formal "multiplex": a complex system of constraints operating at different levels.[30] Perec would go on to build systems of similar complexity in the radio play *Konzertstück für Sprecher und Orchester* (Concertino for speaker and orchestra) and, on a grander scale, in *Life: A User's Manual*.

Mathews spoke of his friendship with Perec and their mutual translation in an interview with Mariacarmela Mancarella: "I admired his work as a writer, but it inspired me far less than the man himself. It was to him that I was totally devoted. If we happily agreed to translate each other's work [...], it's because we had such faith in one another: questioning one another's motives or talents was inconceivable."[31] Perhaps this was the best way to approach the translation of a book as deeply strange and perplexing as *Tlooth*. Perec once described Mathews's narrative world as one "determined by rules from another planet."[32] In the absence of a posthumous explanatory text analogous to Raymond Roussel's *How I Wrote Certain of My Books* (*Comment j'ai écrit certains de mes livres*), those rules remain mysterious. Naturally Perec was curious about them, and we know from Mathews's *Le Verger* (*The Orchard*) that he entertained a mistaken hypothesis about the book's hidden structure, imagining that it was based on a palindrome of secret words.[33] This is somewhat discouraging for interpreters who do not have the benefit of Perec's privileged access to the author. But perhaps it is possible to glimpse some of the figures in *Tlooth*'s carpet by comparing the original with the translation. Where there is a departure from the original whose motivation is not apparent, it *may* have been dictated by a compositional rule. For example, almost all the characters' first names are completely different in the translation, as shown in table 4.2.

Once all these names are put together it becomes clear that most of them are epicene, that is, they may be given to boys or girls, although not always in the same language. This quasi-systematic gender ambiguity applies to the first-person protagonist as well, whose name and

Table 4.2
Perec's translation of characters' names in Mathews's *Tlooth*

Characters with first names in Tlooth	Corresponding characters in Les verts champs de moutarde de l'Afghanistan
Sydney Valsava (T 3)	Jacky Valsava (VCMA 7)
Lynn Petomi (3)	Jean Petomi (7)
Hilary Cheyne-Stokes (3)	Céleste Cheyne-Stokes (7)
Tommy Withering (3)	Jo Withering (7)
Evelyn Roak (3)	Louison Roak (7)
Cecil Méli (3)	Andrea Meli (8)
Lee Donders (4)	Lou Donders (8)
Marion Gullstrand (4)	Michou Gullstrand (8)
Leslie Auenbrugger (4)	Alix Auenbrugger (8)
Yana (12)	Oona (15)
Robin Marr (35)	Dominique Hoffnung (38)
Laurence Hapi (35)	Claude Hapi (38)
Beverley Zuckerkandl (35)	Camille Zuckerkandl (38)
Joan (107)	Gabriele (107)
Claude Morora (114)	Cecil Mora (114)
Lou, Jean, Jerry, Désiré(e), Babe (151)	Gaby, Loulou, Lulu, Jacky, Désiré(e), Bébé (158)

gender are revealed very late in the piece. *Tlooth* falls therefore into the category of "ungendered narrative," defined by Khuman Bhagirath Jetubhai and Madhumita Ghosal as "fiction where the gender of one or more characters is kept undisclosed throughout the entire work, or in a significant portion of it."[34] Levin Becker remarks that in this respect, *Tlooth* anticipates Garréta's *Sphinx*, in which the indeterminacy is maintained throughout for the protagonist and the beloved (MSC 292). It should be noted, however, that Garréta's erasure of gender marking is much more than a device for maintaining suspense or springing a surprise: it is part of a campaign against sexual difference, largely inspired by the work of Monique Wittig.[35]

Preserving certain connotations of a name may entail quite substantial alterations to the denotative meaning of the source text. In *Tlooth*, we are introduced to "a young man of extraordinary beauty" named Joan, from Vich in Catalonia (107). In *Les verts champs de moutarde de l'Afghanistan*, this character is named Gabriele, and comes from Ivrée in the Piémont. The Catalan has been transformed into an Italian because Joan does not look like a woman's name to a French reader, whereas Gabriele with a final *e* might (although it is missing a double *ll* or a grave accent on the penultimate *e*). In a later chapter entitled "Love in the Mountains" ("Amours alpines") Joan / Gabriele's past as a smuggler is transposed from the Pyrenees to the Alps.

Mathews's fondness for encoding leads him to invent various proto-Oulipian constraints in *Tlooth*. These create challenges for the translator, which Perec takes up with glee. Three coded messages sent between the narrator and her lover Yana (T 29) are shown in figure 4.1. Despite the rounded sans-serif font, the *w*'s give it away: we are looking at inverted letters. And on the following page, the narrator says: "It would have vexed the local cryptologists to learn that there was no true cipher, only simple inversion" (30). Not all letters can be read upside down, and writing in this "code" means using a restricted alphabet of fourteen letters: *b, d, h, i, m, n, o, p, q, s, u, w, x, y*. This is a hard constraint, since it eliminates the vowel letters *a* and *e*, unlike the Oulipian prisoner's constraint, which also restricts the alphabet to fourteen letters, forbidding the use of any letter extending above or below the line (OC 215). Small wonder then that the "decoded" messages remain fairly opaque.

X swoons poop puny moos you unbosom mounds

IS sop poop owns synonymous homo I show no snow

SOS powwow now 9 by moon (T 29)

Small wonder too that Perec's versions depart substantially from the originals (literal back translations are given in brackets):

nous bondissons: don quoiqu' hypo sommons un don moins
    mou du bouquin
(we jump: gift although hypo we summon a less soft gift of
    the book)

oui nous pouvons: individu d'un nom ibid in ms pq non bidon
(yes we can: individual of an ibid name in ms [manuscript] bc
    [because] not phony)

SOS symposium voyons-nous 9h in disp
(SOS symposium let's meet 9 o'clock in disp[ensary]) (VCM 32)

spunou̸ ɯosoqun noh soom hund dood suooms X

I replied,

mous ou moys I oɯoy snoɯhuouhs sumo dood dos SI

Two days later she wrote,

uooɯ hq 6 mou mommod SOS

Figure 4.1 Coded messages in *Tlooth*

Only at the end of the second message and in the final one do original and version converge semantically.

A further formal challenge for the translator arises in the description of a "blue film," for which the narrator-protagonist of *Tlooth* has been hired to write a scenario. In Mathews's novel, increasingly complicated spoonerisms throw a semi-transparent veil over the pornographic action, but even without unscrambling the phonemes, the general idea is clear enough: "I hood teasing oarward, sfeening into her, but when my kite slew to its wool hock and she gruddenly began stinking lard on it, my legs gave fey" (T 121). The overall effect of Perec's translation is very similar. In other words, it satisfies the requirement of functional equivalence: "Je flémençais à agencer fentement, me pentant en elle, mais quand ma rheuh assaignit sa maille stinale et que Fella se tit toudain l'aspiquer de touches ses lorces mes vambes cochirent" (VCM 122).

Looking more closely, however, it becomes apparent that the reorganization of phonemes works quite differently. Figure 4.2 shows how the phonemes may have been transposed from one numbered position in Mathews's sentence to another. Not all the anomalies are resolved by reversing the transpositions. My reconstruction was influenced by Perec's translation, which is considerably easier to decipher, because as Isabelle Vanderschelden has shown, it is based on a symmetrical scheme, represented in figure 4.3.[36] Thus Perec extends the procedure – exchanging phonemes over greater textual distances – and refines it, introducing symmetry, while preserving the general effect. In addition, his refinement is a personalization or appropriation in that it connects with the many instances of bilateral symmetry in his own work, which have been catalogued by Bernard Magné.[37]

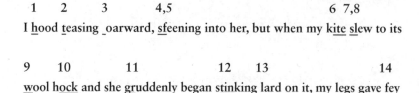

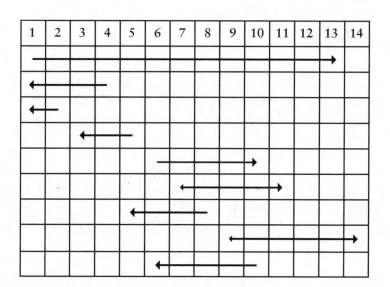

Figure 4.2 Transposition of phonemes in *Tlooth*

Even when only one translator is involved, translation is always a negotiation, as Umberto Eco has argued.[38] Sometimes negotiators need to apply a little pressure. In his essay "Fearful Symmetries," Mathews recounts how the French title of *Tlooth* came to be so different: "One day Perec suggested as a title *Les verts champs de moutarde de l'Afghanistan,* words that end a chapter more or less half way through the novel; I did not approve; so he waited until I was safely on the other side of the Atlantic before announcing, after the book had been sent to the printer that he and Geneviève Serreau had agreed that *Les verts champs de moutarde de l'Afghanistan* was indeed the best possible title for the French edition" (CPM 57). Mathews goes on, with hindsight, to admit that the French title works "every bit as well as the original *Tlooth*: its significance is no less mysterious, its

Manipulation, Translation, and Composition

```
     1           2   3            4                        6    7
Je flémençais à agencer fentement, me pentant en elle, mais quand ma rheuh assaignit

  7    8         9     10 11           12          13        14
sa maille stinale et que Fella se tit toudain l'aspiquer de touches ses lorces mes

15    16
vambes cochirent.
```

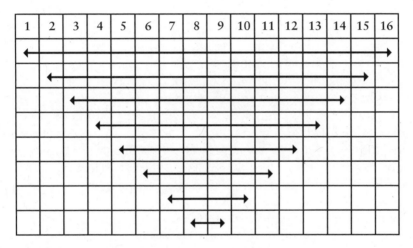

Figure 4.3 Transposition of phonemes in *Les verts champs de moutarde de l'Afghanistan*

emergence in the text no less abrupt" (CPM 57). It is also visually evocative, and it gives extra resonance to one of the most poetic and memorable moments in the narrative, when the fugitives from a prison camp in the USSR finally reach a place of greater safety, and their weeks of hiding are over:

> At three in the afternoon Robin, walking about thirty yards ahead of us, stopped at the far edge of a grove we were crossing to call back,
> "Alley-alley infree!"
> We ran through the trees. Beyond, the ground fell sheerly to an expanse that stretched away into horizon haze: the green mustard fields of Afghanistan. (T 97)

From its title on, *Les verts champs de moutarde de l'Afghanistan* shows that translation can be loyal while departing from the source's propositional meaning at many points, and that a translator can be scrupulous while setting a strong personal stamp on the work.

Mathews's collaboration on the translation indicates that he wanted to maintain the perceptibility of the traces left by his secret rules. A formally blind translation, ignoring the rules entirely, would have obscured those traces. That is what Aira recommends, with characteristic radicality, in an essay on Roussel: "The sole function of the procedure is to generate the plot. Once the story is written, the procedure disappears, is hidden, and is as relevant to the reading and interpretation of the work as the fact that the author used blue or black ink [...] Translating Roussel is not only possible but advisable, and reading him in translation [...] is the only way to appreciate him fully, insofar as removing his work from the language in which it was born consummates the occultation of its genesis."[39] Reading *Les verts champs de moutarde de l'Afghanistan* does not do this, since Perec and Mathews strove to maintain the degree of obscurity in which the work's genesis was originally shrouded, rather than increase it. And comparing translation and original does give us some tantalizing glimpses behind the scenes. Like Queneau, Perec, and Calvino, Mathews plays hide-and-seek with the reader, but he remains even harder to find than his Oulipian colleagues.

CASE 3: MÉTAIL'S TRANSLATION OF SU HUI'S "THE MAP OF THE ARMILLARY SPHERE"

In an interview with Laure Adler, Métail told the story of how she decided to learn Chinese:

> It's very strange because it's related to the Oulipo in a way, it's related to Georges Perec: he was the one who introduced me to the Oulipo because I knew him already. And when Georges Perec died and I went home after his cremation, I took a book from the shelf at random to try to distract myself from my dark thoughts, and it was a book by François Cheng about Chinese poetic writing, which I found absolutely fascinating, and on that day, that is, the day of Georges Perec's funeral, I decided to learn Chinese, but I was already thirty-three. At the beginning of the following academic year, I enrolled at INALCO, the National

Institute of Asian Languages and Cultures, and started learning Chinese, without knowing how far I would take it. In the end I went on to write a doctoral thesis and I worked on reversible Chinese poems, that is, on a kind of palindrome (Perec holds the record for palindromes in France).[40]

Métail's doctoral research, prompted by the serendipitous reading of two pages in François Cheng's *L'écriture poétique chinoise* (*Chinese Poetic Writing*), gave rise to an annotated anthology of reversible poems from the third to the nineteenth centuries with French translations: *Le vol des oies sauvages*, which has been translated into English by Jody Gladding as *Wild Geese Returning*.[41] In her introduction, Métail explains that the recurrent image of migrating geese in flight symbolizes both the content and the structure of *huiwenshi* (回文诗) or reversible poems, which "from the very beginning were associated with an actual story of separation" and "tied to Taoist cosmological speculations" (WGR xxxv, xxxvii). The earliest examples in Métail's anthology, written by the wives of government officials sent to remote territories, are both, in a sense, spells to reverse the geographical and emotional separation between spouses. The second, Su Hui's "The Map of the Armillary Sphere," dating from the fourth century CE, is a classic of dizzying complexity.

According to an account written by the Tang dynasty empress Wu Zetian, when Su Hui's husband Dou Tao took a concubine with him on a mission to Xianyang, Su Hui embroidered her square-shaped, reversible poem in five colours and sent it to him. Tao found it to be "a wonder without equal," dismissed his concubine and "with great ceremony [...] had a carriage prepared to fetch Su Hui" (WGR 11). Not surprisingly, the embroidery was lost. Copies of the text survived, but without the colour scheme.

The first step in the restoration of the poem was to map the parts of an armillary sphere onto a square. A record left by Zhu Shuzhen shows that this was accomplished in the early thirteenth century (WGR 16).[42] Putting together the accounts of the last people to see the embroidery, it was also possible to reconstruct the distribution of the colours, characters of a particular colour belonging to rhyming poems of a particular length. The reconstructed colour scheme worked neatly except for certain poems in seven-syllable lines attested in the ancient commentaries, some of whose characters feature in other poems with different metrical schemes. How could the "double allegiance" of those characters be made visible and readable in the coloured square? Métail came up with an original solution to this problem, suggested by a Han dynasty compass: encasing the characters that do double service between red lines (red being the colour that corresponds to poems in seven-syllable lines) running diagonally across the square, as can be seen in figure 4.4's black-and-white reproduction.

Having thus completed the restoration of "The Map of the Armillary Sphere" in *Wild Geese Returning*, Métail proceeds to offer a sample of the poems that can be read within it. Estimates of the total number vary widely. Métail writes:

> Was Su Hui herself able to calculate the exact number of poems engendered by her creation? That seems unlikely. The art of the combinatory developed very early in China, thanks to *The Book of Changes*, but we are confronted here with a particularly difficult case, because of the number of parameters. The important thing is not so much the exact number of poems, nor how exhaustively we read them, as it is the vertigo that grips the reader facing the open work, facing the infinity of unfurling meaning. Three thousand one hundred and twenty is the number of poems I have actually read that follow all three rules of isometry (same number of syllables per line), rhyme, and metrical / colour correspondence. (WGR 29; VOS 39, translation modified)

The Oulipo has claimed Su Hui's "Map" as an "anticipatory plagiarism," and its combinatorial structure does anticipate Queneau's *Cent mille milliards de poèmes*.[43] But there are significant differences. Even by the most generous estimate, Su Hui's "Map" generates far fewer combinations: 14,005 compared to a hundred thousand billion.[44] Yet it is more complex in that there are more "parameters," more ways of combining. And it may not have been based on precise preliminary calculations.

Métail's work on "The Map of the Armillary Sphere" has been saluted by scholars of Chinese literature. Reviewing *Wild Geese Returning* along with the book that kindled Métail's desire to learn Chinese, Nan Z. Da wrote: "François Cheng's *Chinese Poetic Writing* and Michèle Métail's *Wild Geese Returning* offer two of the most scholarly, yet lucid, introductions to Chinese poetry I have ever

Manipulation, Translation, and Composition

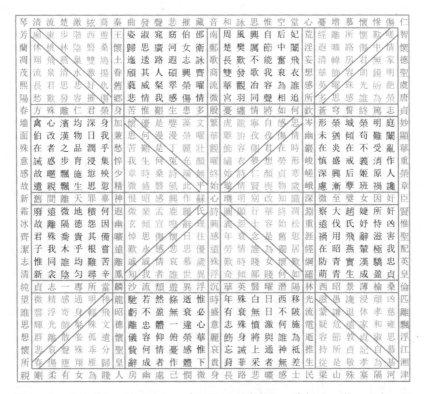

Figure 4.4 Métail's reconstruction of Su Hui's "The Map of the Armillary Sphere"

encountered, because and not in spite of the double translation (Chinese-French-English) involved in their production."[45] David Hinton used Métail's reconstruction of the map for his partial English translation, entitled "Star Gauge."[46] If we follow Sheldon Pollock in defining philology as "making sense of texts," *Wild Geese Returning* is an exemplary contribution to that discipline as well as a work of scrupulous translation.[47]

MAGICAL CAUSATION AND THE ORAL NOVEL

In each of the cases that I have presented, the translated text is linked to the original work of the translator by marked affinities if not by demonstrable influence. In 1953, the year in which *L'ivrogne dans la brousse* was published, Queneau began working seriously on his thirteenth novel, *Zazie in the Metro* (*Zazie dans le métro*, 1959). As

Dominique Jullien points out, there are structural analogies between *Zazie* and Tutuola's *The Palm-Wine Drinkard*: in both, linear episodes are suspended from a circular frame narrative (the hero or heroine's return to the starting point).[48] Both books also recount an unsuccessful underworld or otherworld journey: the narrator of *The Palm-Wine Drinkard* sets off to find his dead tapster and bring him back from the "Deads' Town," but the tapster, when eventually found, informs him that "a dead man could not live with alives" (100). As for Zazie, her ambition to see the metro is finally foiled: by the time she reaches that dreamed-of realm, she has fallen asleep. Jullien develops a convincing analogy between the ways in which the plots of the two novels function: like the originally oral tales of the *Thousand and One Nights*, both privilege metamorphoses over psychological depth, and resort unashamedly to god-from-the-machine resolutions.[49] Toward the end of his novel-writing career, in *Zazie in the Metro*, *The Blue Flowers*, and *The Flight of Icarus*, Queneau was increasingly inclined to dispense with psychological motivation. He seems to have agreed with Jorge Luis Borges that, in the novel, "the only possible integrity" lies in magical causation.[50]

The episodes that make up *The Palm-Wine Drinkard* recount escapes from the clutches of sorcerers, evil spirits, and harmful creatures – Death, Skull, the half-bodied baby, the Spirit of Prey, the Red-People, and others – with occasional assistance from helpers such as Faithful-Mother and the Invisible-Pawn. In the climactic scene of *Zazie in the Metro*, it is confirmed that a series of adversaries – Pedro-Surplus, Trouscaillon, Bertin Poirée, Haroun al Rations – who have threatened and attempted to prey upon Zazie and Marceline, are one and the same: "'Yes,' said the man with the (new) brolly, 'it is I, Haroun al Rations. I am I, he whom you cognized and, at times, hardly recognized. Prince of this world and of several related territories, I take pleasure in traversing my domain under various guises, taking on the appearances of incertitude and error which, in any case, are mine own'" (ZM 153). The machine that saves Zazie, her uncle Gabriel, and their band from this explicitly diabolical antagonist at the head of "two armoured divisions of night watchmen and a squadron of jurassic spahis" is not a crane, as in Euripedes's *Medea*, but a service elevator operated by Marceline / Marcel, which takes them down to safety in the underworld of the metro. This escape repeats the lesson of the fairy tale, as explained by Walter Benjamin in "The Storyteller": "The wisest thing – so the fairy tale taught mankind in olden times, and teaches children to this day – is to meet the forces of the mythical world with cunning and with high spirits. (This is how the fairy tale polarizes *Mut*, courage, dividing it dialectically into *Untermut*, that is, cunning, and *Übermut*, high spirits.)"[51]

The magical causation and episodic structure that *The Palm-Wine Drinkard* shares with *Zazie in the Metro* are oral features, which characterize the Yoruba tales that Tutuola drew upon. *The Palm-Wine Drinkard* is an oral novel, as the Nigerian writer Emmanuel Egudu says in J.M. Coetzee's *Elizabeth Costello*, but not only because Tutuola "wrote as he spoke."[52] It is oral also because he retold what he had heard, and artfully rearranged the materials of an oral tradition, imposing his own design on them, as Ato Quayson has shown.[53] Elizabeth Costello regards the idea of the oral novel as "muddled at its very core": "*A novel about people who live in an oral culture*, she would like to say, *is not an oral novel. Just as a novel about women isn't a women's novel.*"[54] She thinks that all Emmanuel's talk of an oral novel is "just another way of propping up the mystique of the African as the last repository of primal human energies."[55] But she is not a reliable commentator, having unfinished business with Egudu, and the idea of the oral novel need not be muddled, unless one takes an absolutist position and considers that writing itself is fatal to orality.

Queneau had a clear idea of what the oral novel could be. He believed that in literate cultures with alphabetical scripts the oral still had primacy, not as a repository of primal energies but as a motor of linguistic and literary evolution. This view is made clear in the essay "The Writer and Language," which concludes: "Literature is like the whitecaps on the undulating sea: the immortal, transfigured spume of the ocean that is the thousand words spoken by a people in the course of its history. By all people in the course of their histories" (LNF 86). In *The Palm-Wine Drinkard*, Queneau found examples of this trans-figuration of speech, which does not set the oral writer apart in an exotic or primitive reserve, since it is the universal process by which literature everywhere is or should be made. For Queneau, all good novels are oral, that is, speakable (as opposed to Mallarmé's prose [LNF 83]), and responsive to how people really speak, no matter how literate the cultures depicted. His last novel, *The Flight of Icarus*, is set among writers in late nineteenth-century Paris. It is also entirely composed of dialogue.

The Palm-Wine Drinkard was the last novel that Queneau translated, but he followed Tutuola's later work, reading My Life in the Bush of Ghosts (1954), Simbi and the Satyr of the Dark Jungle (1955), and Feather Woman of the Jungle (1962), each in the year of its publication or the following year. And in 1976, the last year of his life, he read Michèle Dussutour-Hammer's biography of the Nigerian author.[56] His affinity with Tutuola's work may not have been close, but it was real and lasting.

ALLUSION, CITATION, AND GAPS

In my second case study, collaborative translation fed directly into the translator's original work. Tlooth / Les verts champs de moutarde de l'Afghanistan is one of the texts that Perec drew on systematically in writing his longest and most ambitious novel. In Life: A User's Manual, the family name of Bartlebooth's servant Mortimer Smautf is borrowed from the doctor Vetullio Smautf in Tlooth, famous for his achievements in the treatment of the rare skin disease Mortimer's malady (105–7). There are fourteen further allusions to or citations from Tlooth in Life: A User's Manual, varying in scale from one to twenty-one words. Names, expressions, symbols, objects, minor characters, and even the description of a building and business are transferred from one book to the other.[57]

All these borrowings enrich the décor of Life: A User's Manual, adding to its splendid clutter. But there may be a larger and more diffuse debt. In both novels the central plot, to which many subplots are attached, is a story of long-delayed revenge. In Tlooth the motive is revealed off-handedly in a footnote on the first page: the surgeon Evelyn Roak removed, "together with a troublesome spur of bone, the index and ring fingers" of the narrator's left hand, ending her career as a violinist (3). In Life: A User's Manual, the motive for Gaspard Winckler's revenge on his employer Percival Bartlebooth is mysterious, although ingenious attempts have been made to fill that tantalizing gap, as I indicate in chapter 6.

Tlooth is just one of many texts solicited by Life: A User's Manual, which is an intertextual labyrinth, as scholars from Bernard Magné to Raoul Delemazure have shown. Perec laid claim to intertextuality as a motor, and conceptualized original composition as emergence from a gap in the field of the already written. In a talk given at the University of Warwick in 1967, he said: "There is [...] an image of literature [...] as a puzzle. [...] Butor explained this very well. He explained that every writer is surrounded by a mass of others [...] and [...] this puzzle that is literature, in the mind of the writer, always has a gap in it, and that gap is obviously the one that the work in progress will fill" (EC I 83). The puzzle metaphor was clearly a useful conceptual tool for Perec: it helped him claim control of the means of literary production and reject a model of the writer as host to an intermittent and mysterious inspiration. Perhaps it also helped neutralize anxiety by encouraging him to work through influences rather than attempting to avoid or repress them. Nevertheless, it is potentially misleading. The puzzle metaphor may suggest that composition comes down to solving a problem that is already constituted by a state of the field. The relations between existing works and authors are not, however, objectively given and simply waiting to be noticed. There is a degree of creative thought involved in bringing works and authors into proximity. Michel Butor acknowledges this when he projects the puzzle metaphor into an architectural space in "La critique et l'invention" (Criticism and invention): "The library becomes a dungeon. By adding new books, we attempt to redistribute the whole surface so that windows open up in it."[58] It is not simply a matter of seeing gaps but also of making them.

In his Warwick talk, Perec represented the constellation that gave rise to *Things* (*Les choses*) like this:

FLAUBERT   NIZAN
              Les Choses
ANTELME   BARTHES (EC I 82)

The connection between *Things: A Story of the Sixties* and Robert Antelme's *The Human Species* (*L'espèce humaine*), an account of the author's imprisonment in the concentration camp at Gandersheim, is particularly oblique, as Perec himself admitted: "it was really the most unconscious help there could have been because, in the end, I know there is a relation between *Things* and Antelme's *The Human Species*, but I find it very hard to specify" (EC I 82). Perhaps there is something especially productive about gaps between texts whose intuited affinities are far from obvious. The work of Métail as translator and poet might supply examples to support this hypothesis, for she has pursued her intuitions patiently, spanning gaps that few others are equipped even to perceive.

COSMOLOGY AND BIOGRAPHICAL ANCHORING

The long project of investigating Chinese reversible poems led to the first of Métail's many trips to China, which in turn provoked a conversion or turning of her gaze, not from the visible world to the Forms, as Plato recommends in the *Phaedo*, but from language to the perceptible world.[59] In her interview with Laure Adler, Métail said:

> I went there for the first time in 1985, and it was a real cultural shock. And that's when I began to move away from the formalism that I had practised with the Oulipo, because it opened my eyes to the world [...] I had this very powerful experience of a cultural shock, and I began really to look at the world [...] because with hindsight I realize that in the ten years before going to China, during which I frequented the Oulipo, I never wrote about Paris, for example. I walked around Paris a lot but I never wrote any texts about Paris. I was working exclusively on language, on language games [...] And it changed my perception, and my writing; it was a turning point, you might say, in my writing.[60]

This turning point marks the beginning of a turning away from the Oulipo, which was completed by the late 1990s. It is curious that Métail's early formalism was so pure as to exclude writerly attention to the city in which she was living, especially given the precedents of Perec's attempts to exhaust places in Paris, and Queneau's collection of peripatetic poems *Hitting the Streets* (*Courir les rues*, 1967). It may be that the grounding effect of the "detour via China," to borrow an expression from François Jullien, was related to Métail's early training in music, and her involvement with the sound poetry scene in France. Perhaps having a radically different environment and scriptworld to *look at* jolted her poetry out of its preoccupation with the sounds of signs and into a greater visual attentiveness to the world beyond.[61]

In any case, the result of the trip was that she added the atlas to the dictionary: her poetry became cartographic and topographic. And her approach to the constraint changed: she abandoned constraints in the Oulipian sense (precisely pre-formulated rules), allowing her forms to emerge instead from accumulations of material collected intuitively. Rather than constraints, she speaks now of *cadres*: frames. Frames and forms are significant for Métail; they carry meaning, as for Su Hui, whose multiply reversible poem is a spell to reverse separation.

Su Hui signed her map with the central block of nine characters:

平	始	璇
píng	shǐ	Xuán
to calm	to begin	(star)

蘇	心	璣
Sū	xīn	Jī
Su	heart	(star)

氏	詩	圖
Shì	shī	tú
Shi (Hui)	poem	map

This block poses a problem in that its nine characters and syllables cannot be broken down into isometric lines as required by the conventions of classical Chinese verse. There are also two groups of non-reversible characters "Sū Shì" (Su Hui) and "Xuán Jī" (two stars in the Northern Dipper, associated with the armillary sphere). Métail conjectures that the central place may have been left vacant in Su Hui's embroidery, although the heart character would have been clearly implied, and she proposes that the other characters should be read in the order indicated by figure 4.5.

This makes a rhyming poem in two lines of four syllables:

璇	平	蘇	氏
shǐ	píng	Sū	Shì
to begin	to calm	Su	Shi (Hui)

璇	璣	圖	詩
Xuán	Jī	tú	shī
(star)	(star)	map	poem

which Jody Gladding translates from Métail's translation as: "Begun to calm Su Shi / The poem of the Map of the Armillary Sphere" (WG 57).

If Su Hui's poem began in the torments of an individual heart, it reaches far out into the cosmos, as far as the astronomy of the time allowed. David Hinton translates the seven-syllable lines that run diagonally from the centre to the top right-hand corner as follows:

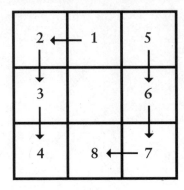

Figure 4.5 Métail's reading of the central square in "The Map of the Armillary Sphere"

   my star-gauge poem dreams of you, wounding thoughts
     with delight
        thoughts wounded, dreaming of you, my poem gauges
          the starry heart

      such countless star-glimmers: they contain all your grief
        and love
  in the midst of my grief, your face: such countless star-glimmer
     delights[62]

The resonance between the intimate and the cosmological that is so striking in Su Hui's map characterizes Métail's own work from the mid-1980s on. In no sense a confessional poet, she nevertheless anchors her writing in a particular life unfolding in particular places and times, while looking far beyond the self to processes at work in the universe as a whole. For example, the collaborative book, *L'un l'autre: L'esperluette* (The one the other: The ampersand), composed with her partner, Louis Roquin, combines Roquin's calligraphic representations of the ampersand symbol (*l'esperluette*), with minimal poems by Métail consisting of two nouns linked by an ampersand. The relation between the nouns is one of subtle complementarity rather than straightforward antonymy. The pairs include concentration & silence, flesh & emptying, weight & suspension. The ampersand, treated by Roquin like an ideogram, comes not only to operate as a conjunction but also to stand for interaction and articulation in general. In this case, the autobiographical anchoring is provided photographically. At the end of the sequence of couplings, necessarily abstract because they are limited to one-word elements, comes a sequence of three images: Roquin, arm through a gate, hands clasped and legs crossed; Roquin and Metail embracing in the same place; and finally Métail with her hands behind her back.

This combination of anchoring and sweep can also be found in Métail's immense poem *Noun Complements* (*Compléments de noms*), begun in 1972 and still under construction, whose point of departure was a notoriously long compound noun in German: Der Donaudampfschiffahrtsgesellschaftskapitän (the captain of the company for excursions by steamboat on the Danube). Having translated the compound into a series of French genitives ("le capitaine de la compagnie des voyages en bateau à vapeur du Danube"), Métail had the idea of animating the concatenation by adding a noun at the beginning and dropping one off the end, and repeating the operation indefinitely. In Tom La Farge's translation, the poem opens as follows:

> the captain of the company for excursions by steamboat
>   on the Danube
> the wife of the captain of the company for excursions
>   by steamboat
> the daughter of the wife of the captain of the company
>   for excursions by boat
> the dog of the daughter of the wife of the captain of the company
>   for excursions
> the kennel of the dog of the daughter of the wife of the captain
>   of the company
> the carpet of the kennel of the dog of the daughter of the wife
>   of the captain
> the color of the carpet of the kennel of the dog of the daughter
>   of the wife[63]

This might remind us of the house that Jack built. Métail's admittedly utopian project was initially to use all the nouns of the French language. Although she has not yet reached that goal, she has written sections in German, English, Chinese, and Esperanto. She has also written the last line, or *her* last line – for there is nothing to stop others taking the baton – ending with the word *métail*, which as well as being her family name, is a rare noun in French meaning an alloy. Again, a work of totalizing scope is anchored autobiographically.

TRANSLATION, COMPOSITION, AND ORIGINALITY

Distinguishing between adaptation and translation, Umberto Eco writes: "a translator has always to tame, in some way, his or her 'creative' impetus."[64] In the three cases that I have examined, as opposed to the manipulations mentioned in the first section of this chapter, Queneau, Perec, and Métail exercised such restraint. Working within the institutional contexts of commercial publishing and scholarly research, they observed the norms in place.

The philosopher Maria Kronfeldner has written: "Originality amounts to partial independence from the causal influence of an original."[65] If we take a non-exceptionalist view of creativity (as Kronfeldner does), translation is creative, since it has to be partially independent from the influence of the original; it cannot be a mere copy. This is why David Bellos speaks of matches rather than equivalences. "The only certainty," he writes, "is that a match cannot be the same as the thing that it matches. If you want the same thing, that's quite all right. You can read the original."[66] Finding matches is a kind of creative problem-solving. The creativity of a commissioned translation is limited, however, by the contract, which will typically contain a clause like the following: "The Translator warrants that she is the sole author of the Translation, and that said Translation shall be a faithful rendition into idiomatic English and shall neither omit anything from the original text, nor add anything to it, further than what is necessary for translation into English." What this means in practice is that creativity is exercised mainly on the micro scale. In general, the sentences of the original are taken to set up the problems that the translator must solve. Writers have to solve their own sentence-level problems, as well as larger-scale problems of character, plotting, atmosphere, and so on. In addition to which, they have to invent or find all those problems in the first place. A translator's problems are mostly ready-made and limited in scale, however difficult and numerous.

And yet a translation can enter into composition at the macro scale when it communicates meaningfully with a translator's original writing. It is significant that Queneau, Perec, and Métail all cite the translations discussed here in their "By the same author" lists. *The Palm-Wine Drinkard* resonates with Queneau's campaign for an oral literature in French, and *L'ivrogne dans la brousse* anticipates both the structure of *Zazie in the Metro* and the magical causality operating in that novel's storyworld. The example of *Tlooth* encouraged Perec to write an Oulipian novel based on a formal "mutiplex," and its digressive revenge plot foreshadows that of *Life: A User's Manual. Tlooth* also served as a source of intertextual fuel for Perec's voracious storytelling plant. Su Hui's "The Map of the Armillary Sphere" was instrumental in initiating Métail's quest for non-arbitrary forms, adapted to the peculiarities of the language of composition and anchored in the experience of a particular individual, but also reflecting a cosmology, a sense of how the whole universe works. While translation and composition remain distinct in the work of Métail, Perec, and Queneau, there are "many subtle passages" between them, as Le Lionnais said of the analytic and synthetic aspects of the Oulipo's work (OPPL 28).

Given the recent revaluation of the terms "unoriginal" and "uncreative" it may be worth concluding this chapter with a clarification.[67] It is obvious that originality cannot be absolute. Writers recombine rather than create from nothing. A literary work is usually an arrangement of words drawn from the common stock, all used countless times before. Even writers who invent new words, like Joyce in *Finnegans Wake*, usually forge them from morphemes that can, in principle, be recognized and interpreted, since they exist in a pool of natural languages. If Joyce had not recombined pre-existing elements, his lexical inventions would have been absolutely opaque rather than relatively obscure.

When originality has been exaggerated or overemphasized, the often-repeated words from Ecclesiastes, "there is no new thing under the sun," may have a corrective effect.[68] But there obviously are new things under the sun, from the molecular level up, such as the SARS-COV-2 virus, and levitating bluetooth speakers. And there obviously is such a thing as relative originality in literature because there are more and less original ways of recombining. The interest of experienced readers is sensitive to this variation.

As well as being relative, originality is always multidimensional, since the recombinations operate at many different levels on different kinds of components.[69] A work's verbal originality might be crudely gauged by measuring the frequency of its word strings on the internet. But originality is not simply or always a matter of word combination. To take an example from the work of a writer who declined an invitation to join the Oulipo, Valérie Mréjen's short film *Capri* shows a quarrel between lovers, whose lines have been collaged from movies made for television.[70] The subtle semantic incoherence of the exchange is accompanied by spectacular failures of cohesion: the names used by the couple to address each other keep changing. This effect mirrors the experience of feeling trapped in a stereotypical situation that dissolves the individuality of the antagonists.[71] The parts of the scene are all clichés; the whole is strange and unsettling.

There are many dimensions along which we might measure original-ity and no obvious way of weighting them relative to one another. This makes originality hard to agree about. Kenneth Goldsmith's campaign for uncreative writing rests on an original privileging of the conceptual over the verbal dimension of originality. Another relevant dimension, as I suggested above with respect to Perec and Métail, is that of influences. A highly original writer is often one who combines influences that others would consider incompatible or not even consider. Originality can also be measured along specifically formal dimensions. A writer who adheres strictly to an inherited pattern, such as a verse form, grants that pattern the role of an original, and is less independent with regard to it than a writer who devises a variant. Many of the Oulipo's formal inventions go beyond simple variation and attain a high degree of originality by effecting radical rearrange-ments and importing abstract structures from the field of mathematics. But the historically conditioned desire and need to be original are not the only motives for the Oulipo's inventive efforts. The Oulipians also devise new forms to enrich the meanings of their works. The following chapter explores how.

5

Meaningful Forms and Clinamen

JUDGING A TEXT BY ITS LOOK

Forms and constraints can be generative, prompting and sustaining literary production. They can also have semiotic functions, bearing meaning. In the first part of this chapter, I will discuss a range of ways in which a constraint or form can do this. The first way is superficial but plays an important role in a reader's life.

The mere use of a certain kind of visible form can signify a certain writerly "posture," to use a term conceptualized in literary studies by Jérôme Meizoz. For Meizoz, a posture is a writer's self-presentation, both in the work and in public behaviour: "A person exists as a writer only through the prism of a posture, which is historically constructed and related to the set of existing positions in the literary field."[1] For example, in the Australian poetry of the 1970s and '80s, the avoidance of capital letters, the use of ampersands, slashes, and abbreviated spellings (such as *yr* and *tho*) signified allegiance to raw American as opposed to cooked British poetics. The poet's posture, and their place in the conflictual field, could be roughly gauged simply by scanning the work for these signs. Similarly, in prose fiction since Joyce, the suppression of paragraph breaks or punctuation indicates an experimental posture, giving the reader fair warning: "Don't expect this to be easy."

For some experimental poets, the visually distinctive handed-down forms described in manuals of poetics are irremediably obsolete. Such a conviction is at the root of Christian Bök's disappointment with the Oulipo: "the poetic tastes of the group can often seem quite banal, in so far as its members seem to enjoy dickering with the gearboxes of obsolete, literary genres (like the sestina or the rondeau), revivifying these antiquary styles, yet entrenching their canonical repute" (NA 222). Here the Oulipians are imagined as vintage car enthusiasts, curating the past, as opposed to inventors of new vehicles, creating the future. The British poet Sam Riviere reacts in a similar way to one of the forms that has fascinated the Oulipo: "I dread a sestina as much as the next person."[2]

The dread and the boredom expressed by Riviere and Bök are provoked very quickly by visible features: a poem is identifiable as a sestina or a rondeau at a glance, before it has been read through. Form interpreted in this way works like the allergy-triggering postures catalogued by Javier Marías in his little "Guide to What Not to Read": it gives us a pretext to set works and authors aside, so that time spent deciding what to read does not eat excessively into reading time.[3] We all end up watching for features that signify "This is not for me," especially when faced with the task of heavy sifting. The poet and editor Don Paterson writes: "One of the grim things you learn after many years working as an editor – I hardly dare confess this – is that you can hold a poem at arm's length and, without having read a word, know there's a ninety-percent chance that it's bad." Among the "reliable pointers," he cites "centered text, colored ink, copperplate fonts."[4]

Interpreting form in this way is undeniably useful, and undeniably superficial. This is the point of a story told by Michael Robbins: "I once tried to explain my admiration for Paul Muldoon to a young poet I know, a graduate of the Iowa Writers' Workshop. I opened a book to Muldoon's poem 'Yarrow'; she immediately balked: 'I don't like poems that look like that.'"[5] There is always a chance that a centred poem will turn out to be good, and the young poet in Robbins's anecdote is surely missing out. But few readers, even among the most open-minded and sociologically aware, could honestly claim never to rely on such pre-judgments.

More or less consciously, writers make use of typographic look and feel to manage first impressions. Roubaud's frequent suppression of capitals, his use of blank spaces for punctuation, and of supplementary characters such as the at sign (@) and the tensor product sign ($\otimes$), give his poetry and much of his prose, from his first book ($\in$) onward, a decidedly experimental air, which serves to counterbalance his interest in traditional forms and forestall the categorization of his work as neoclassical.

Il

veut mettre le pied
dans un seau. O.K.
Que quelqu'un ap-
porte un seau.

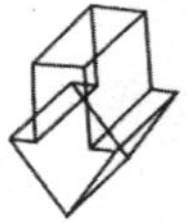

Chi chi.

La lune s'enfuit
dans une ombre
cette direction.

    Saison où les
fleurs du cerisier
tombent et tombent.

Le moi parfait

1. Nous sommes la
cavalerie.

2. Bientôt victimes des
imitateurs.

3. On s'attendait à
quoi.

marin-cowboy
cheval-piscine

Sophie était à la recherche
de sa maman qui était au
ciel. Sa carte bleue dans
l'océan était tombée dans
l'océan. Et sa harpe et
son cœur. Étaient tom-
bés dans l'océan. Dans
l'océan.

Edward est heureux

Est triste.

Est ravi.

Est furieux.

Edward est heureux.

I ♥ Pandas

À midi sur le toit une.

Banane plantée dans
le bras mon amour.

Elle est jaune.

Oh là là.

ATTENTI
ONCECIN
ESINSPIR
EPASDEFA
ITSRÉELS

Où
tu
dis
que
c'est
fi-
ni.

74

75

Figure 5.1 From Forte's *Dire ouf*

The look of a text filters its readership, especially in the domain of poetry. The third part of Frédéric Forte's *Dire ouf* (2016), "Pied-de-biche *album*," immediately declares its inventive intent, and its debt to the typographical hijinks of the avant-gardes, by dividing the space of the double page into twelve cells, which are occupied by text in different font sizes, but also by inscription-like blocks of unspaced capitals, numbered lists, geometric diagrams that often bear little relation to their captions, and verbal "fractions" (all this material is based on the lyrics of songs by the American band Deerhoof).

For the fans, the double page shown in figure 5.1 composes a new Deerhoof album by citing fragments of the following eleven songs:

"Kneil" (*The Man, The King, The Girl*, 1997)
"Itchy P-Pads" (*The Man, The King, The Girl*, 1997)
"C'Moon" (*Deerhoof vs Evil*, 2011)
"The Perfect Me" (*Friend Opportunity*, 2007)
"Mirror Monster" (*La Isla Bonita*, 2014)
"My Purple Past" (*Offend Maggie!* 2008)
"Blue Cash" (*Apple O'*, 2010)
"Panda, Panda, Panda" (*Apple O'*, 2010)
"Milk Man" (*Milk Man*, 2004)
"Secret Mobilization" (*Deerhoof vs Evil*, 2011)
"Breakup Songs" (*Breakup Song*, 2012)

But one need not be a fan of Deerhoof to be intrigued by Forte's adventures in page space and reminded that literary writing has barely begun to explore the technical possibilities open to all the users of word-processing and drawing software.[6]

IMAGES, DIAGRAMS, INDICES, AND SYMBOLS

The meaning of literary form is not only a matter of first impressions, of a text's general look and feel, or of the writer's overall posture. Forms can signify in less immediate and more specific ways, which I categorize here by adopting C.S. Peirce's threefold typology of the sign, as articulated by Roman Jakobson. Peirce divides signs into icons, indices, and symbols.

"The icon," writes Jakobson, following Peirce, "acts chiefly by a factual similarity between its signans and signatum, e.g. between the picture of an animal and the animal pictured: the former stands for

Meaningful Forms and Clinamen 131

the latter 'merely because it resembles it.'"[7] There is an ancient tradition of literary forms that set up a visual resemblance between the pattern made by a text and what the text is about. In the West, this tradition stretches back at least as far as the poems in the shape of wings, an axe, and an egg ascribed to Simias of Rhodes in the *Greek Anthology*, and dating from the third century BCE.[8] Dick Higgins, author of the study *Pattern Poetry: Guide to an Unknown Literature*, speculates that the undeciphered "Phaistos Disk," dating from roughly 1700 BCE and written in the Minoan Linear A script, is an "enigmatic forerunner" of the tradition.[9] Famous exemplars from later eras include George Herbert's "Easter Wings" (1633) and Guillaume Apollinaire's *Calligrammes* (1918). Literary forms that are iconic in this way, including pattern poems or *carmina figurata*, fall into a subcategory that Peirce dubbed "images." The signifier of an image resembles its signified by virtue of "simple qualities" such as a rapidly apprehensible overall shape.[10]

The Oulipo has made only occasional use of such forms. The "snowball" ("boule de neige") – a text in which each successive word has one letter more than the preceding word – might be regarded as a Peircian image in that its shape on the page mimics the growth of the object that gives the form its name:

I

am

the

text

which

begins

sparely,

assuming

magnitude

constantly,

perceptibly

proportional,

incorporating

unquestionable

incrementations

(OC 228)

This is a rather abstract image because its signified is a process rather than an object at a moment in time. Jouet's "Monostiques paysagers" (Landscape monostichs), discussed in chapter 2, could also be regarded as Peircian images, in that their single long line imitates the horizon. Lécroart's "Portraits en creux" (intaglio portraits) are more straight-forwardly figurative: in each case the pattern made by the text resembles its specific subject, a member of the Oulipo.

The portrait of Jacques Jouet in figure 5.2 is both a visible artwork and a readable text, but not simultaneously. To see the pattern made by the engineered "channels" of aligned spaces, the viewer must take in the whole image at once. But the reader must zoom in on a single line, and this reveals that in addition to the spacing constraint that makes the image, others are at work. This is a "kick-start" text ("texte à démarreur"), which systematically employs the figure of anaphora, beginning each line with the same negative formula: "Ce texte ne ..." ("This text" + negated verb).[11] It also contains two monovocalic lines (18 and 47). There are references to works by Jouet scattered through-out, from the direct ("This text is not constantly ending, ..., as opposed to "'Fins' [Endings], the book by Jouet," line 35) to the oblique ("This text does not discourse upon the eye, old, not old, although it does, sometimes, fix it," line 23). The second of these lines effectively "fixes" the eye, running across the face precisely at eye-level, but also alludes to Jouet's three-volume collection of poems *Navet, linge, oeil de vieux* (Turnip, cloth, pocket grid).

Within the category of icons, alongside images, Peirce identified another kind of sign: the diagram, based on a likeness between signi-fier and signified that exists "only in respect to relations of their parts."[12] Literary forms may be diagrams in this sense. Georges Perec makes the lipogram a diagram in *A Void* by thematizing disappear-ance: an element has disappeared from the set of letters used to write the novel, in which a series of characters disappear, die, or are killed. The diagrammatic relation is underlined by the surname of the first character to vanish, which is the word "vowel" stripped of the vocalic letter *e*: vowel → Vowl (in the translation); voyelle → Voyl (in the original).

In the work of Grangaud, diagrammatic signification plays an important although not obvious role. Her first three books – *Memento-fragments* (1987), *Stations* (1990), and *Renaître* (1990) – are entirely composed of anagrams, a constraint that the author internalized to the point where complete rearrangements of relatively long strings of

Meaningful Forms and Clinamen 133

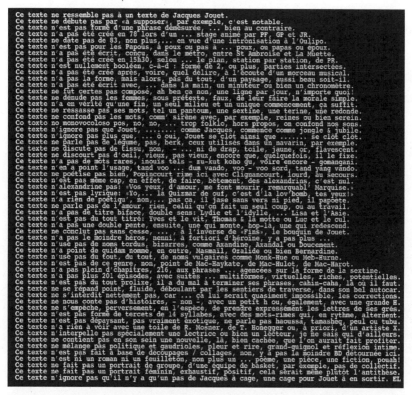

Figure 5.2 Lécroart, "Portrait en creux (Jacques Jouet)"

letters would sometimes occur to her spontaneously. In conversation with Astrid Poier-Bernhard, she has recounted how when listening to Bach's *St Matthew Passion* one day, the sentence "Mais un solo sans pitié la hante" (But a pitiless solo haunts her) came into her mind and she sensed, with a thrill, that it was an anagram of "La passion selon Matthieu." In one sitting she then wrote the twenty-nine-line anagram poem that integrates her "given" line (twice).[13] A feature of the anagram poem that particularly pleased Grangaud, as she explained to Poier-Bernhard, is the "equality" of each line with the others, since they are all composed of the same set of letters. "Equality is a concept to which I'm very attached, in every way, politically but also aesthetically."[14] Grangaud's committment to the value of equality is evident also in the form of *Geste* (Gesture), which I discuss in chapter 9. The hundreds of actions narrated in that book are each granted the same syllabic space.

The second category in Peirce's tripartite system is the index, which "acts chiefly by a factual, existential contiguity between its signans and signatum, [...] 'psychologically, the action of indices depends upon association by contiguity,' e.g. smoke is an index of a fire."[15] The writers of the Oulipo have often structured their works on numerical principles, and that structuring has sometimes been indexical. That is, the structuring numbers have been significant by virtue of particular existential contiguities, being determined, for instance, by the dates of events that are especially significant to the author.

Bernard Magné has demonstrated that the numbers eleven and forty-three play crucial roles in many of Perec's works. These numbers are associated with his mother's death. In *W or the Memory of Childhood*, Perec writes: "My mother has no grave. It was only on 13 October 1958 that she was officially declared to have died on 11 February 1943 at Drancy (France)" (WMC 41). She did not in fact die at Drancy, but was deported from there to Auschwitz with her sister. The eleventh of February 1943 is the date of her "disappearance" (the official record of her deportation is an "acte de disparition," or "certificate of disappearance").[16] Eleven and forty-three feature in two ways in Perec's work: the numbers are mentioned, and they function as structuring factors at a range of levels. What follows are just a few examples of these mentions and functions:

the apartment building described in *Life: A User's Manual*
  is located at number 11 on the imaginary street, rue
  Simon Crubellier;
Marguerite Winckler, the wife of the puzzle-maker Gaspard
  Winckler, in *Life: A User's Manual*, dies in November
  (the eleventh month) of 1943;
each poem in the collection *Alphabets* is based on a grid
  of eleven lines made up of eleven letters;
the forty-third poem in *Alphabets* seems to allude to the death
  of Perec's mother, with its funerary and mortuary vocabulary:
  ange (angel), *geint un glas* (a knell groans), *on gisait* (one lay),
  le sorti sang (the spilled blood), and its diagonal acrostic of
  Ls (homophonous with *elle*, she).[17]

Magné has coined a critical term to refer to these subtle biographical allusions: *æncrage*, a combination of the homophonic words *ancrage* (anchoring) and *encrage* (inking). Perec's *æncrages* anchor his fictions as well as his autobiographical writing in a textual space marked out in ink, which must stand in for the familial space destroyed by capital-*H* History: "To write: to try meticulously to retain something, to cause something to survive; to wrest a few precise scraps from the void as it grows, to leave somewhere a furrow, a trace, a mark, or a few signs" (ss 91–2). Not all the *æncrages* identified by Magné are manifest in constraints or forms, but the "arithmetical" examples that I have mentioned, which organize an "intimate numerology," show how patterns in a literary text can function as Peircian indices.[18]

The symbol, Peirce's third broad category of signs, differs from the index in that it "acts chiefly by imputed, learned contiguity between signans and signatum. This connection 'consists in its being a rule,' and does not depend on the presence or absence of any similarity or physical contiguity. The knowledge of this conventional rule is obligatory for the interpreter of any given symbol, and solely and simply because of this rule will the sign actually be interpreted."[19] Symbols, in other words, are conventional. In the realm of numbers, they establish a numerology that is not intimate (as in the case of Perec's attachment to eleven and forty-three) but widely shared. The unluckiness of thirteen (in the West) and of four (in East Asia) are symbolic.

Roubaud's *Some Thing Black*, a sequence of elegiac poems written after the death of his wife, Alix Cléo, is composed of nine groups of nine poems, most of which are composed of nine fragments. In a conversation with Marcel Bénabou, Florence Delay, and Francis Marmande, Roubaud explained: "There are a number of reasons for the choice of the number nine. One of those reasons is the hierarchy of the angels [...] Especially because Alix was a believer, a Catholic [...] the hierarchy of the angels was important to her."[20] Nine is not only the number of angelic orders according to Pseudo-Dionysius the Areopagite and the neo-Platonic and Scholastic traditions, it was also associated with pain and sadness by Pietro Bongo in his long-influential compendium *Numerorum mysteria* (1591), which attempted to reconcile Pythagorean doctrine with Christian theology.[21] And Dante made nine the numerical emblem of his lost love Beatrice in *La vita nuova*, whose title, repeated in Latin at the opening of the text ("Incipit vita nova"), puns on "new" and "nine."[22] The same pun is possible in French, and Roubaud builds it into the first poem of *Some Thing Black*: "Cette image se présente pour la millième fois à *neuf*" (my italics, "This image again for the thousandth time").[23] As Elvira Laskowski-Caujolle points out, in devoting a book of poems structured by the number nine to Alix Cléo, Roubaud sets her alongside Beatrice.[24]

NUMEROLOGY AND MATHEMATICS

In an interview with José Luis Reina, Roubaud said that another reason for his choice of the number nine to structure *Some Thing Black* was that a spiral permutation applied to a stanza of nine lines produces a "nine-ine," which works like the sestina: all the end-words change places from stanza to stanza, and after nine stanzas the initial order is re-established.[25] Nine, in other words, is a Queneau number: it belongs to a sequence discovered by Raymond Queneau, which is defined as follows by the *On-line Encyclopedia of Integer Sequences*: "numbers n such that the Queneau-Daniel permutation $\{1, 2, 3, ...,$ $n\} \to \{n, 1, n\text{-}1, 2, n\text{-}2, 3, ...\}$ is of order n."[26]

Initially, Roubaud planned to compose each section of *Some Thing Black* as a nine-ine, with individual poems functioning as stanzas. Formally, this would have made the book a scaled-up version of "Tombeaux de Pétrarque" (Tombs of Petrarch) in his previous collection, *Dors* (Sleep): not a single nine-ine but a suite of nine.[27] However, as Roubaud explained to Olivier Salon, the initial plan was "bombarded" by the interaction between his poems and Alix Cléo's journal, which he had transcribed for publication after her death. The result is a formal "ruin" in which the nine-ines have left lexical traces. Salon lists nine key words – *silence* (silence), *sang* (blood), *image* (image), *noir* (black), *nombre* (number), *temps* (time), *regard* (gaze), *pensée* (thought), and *espace* (space) – which are frequently repeated (especially *noir* and *image*) but their recurrence is not governed by the spiral permutation, and many poems in the book contain none of these words.[28] As in *Parc sauvage* (Wild grounds), discussed later in this chapter, the constraint yielded to the emergent demands of the material.

Roubaud's motivations for giving *Some Thing Black* its nine-cubed structure and the meanings that the structure may convey are complex. His relation to numbers is deeply but not purely mathematical, as he explains in *The Great Fire of London*: "When I *see* a number, and when I enlist it into one of my endless counting operations, or a reclusive man's absentminded mental games, it appears with all its idiosyncrasies (some mathematical, others aesthetic, and even others stemming from our personal relationships, our common adventures)"

(GFL 232). The three kinds of idiosyncrasy indicated by Roubaud are not mutually exclusive. For example, he has made extensive use of Queneau numbers in composing *The Great Fire of London* (GFL 284), both to determine the numbers of parts and to regulate the process of writing. Since seven is not a Queneau number, Roubaud decided that he could not work on the project seven days a week, but had to have at least one day of rest.[29] The "no doubt obsessive omnipresence" of Queneau numbers in *The Great Fire of London* is overdetermined: they are mathematically remarkable, and therefore attractive to Roubaud the professional mathematician, but they are also aesthetically pleasing to the neo-Pythagorean that he has confessed to being (PECH 159).[30] Roubaud attributes a kind of neo-Pythagoreanism to his mentor too when he points out that the Fibonacci numbers belong to the family of s-additive sequences, and conjectures that Queneau's mathematical investigation of that family, which led to the publication of an article in the *Journal of Combinatorial Theory*, was partly motivated by the desire to discover analogues of the golden ratio: limits approached by the quotients of successive terms in the sequences, which might turn out to have special aesthetic virtues, like those often attributed to the corresponding limit of the Fibonacci sequence: $\varphi = 1.6180339887...$ etc. (OPPL 96).[31]

The examples of *Some Thing Black*, with its ninefold structuring, and *The Great Fire of London*, with its reliance on Queneau numbers, show that Roubaud's use of numerical constraints is significant as well as generative, that his motivation for the choice of constraints is mixed (mathematical, aesthetic, personal), and that the constraints may function as indices (signifying Roubaud's affiliation to Queneau and the Oulipo) and as symbols (tying his work to a long numerological tradition). In this complexity and "impurity," Roubaud follows Queneau's example, although he has been more consistent over time in his approach to number symbolism, remaining, as he has written, "agnostic": "If I submit myself to my passion for numbers, even so it involves an unbeliever's submission; I have no blind faith in them [*je n'en ai aucune mystique*]. I'm a numbers agnostic despite everything" (GFL 104).[32] Queneau's use of numbers, by contrast, is marked by a certain mysticism, at least in certain phases of his writing life.

"Technique of the Novel" (1937), whose conclusion I quoted at the end of chapter 2, shows that indexical, symbolic, and diagrammatic uses of form were intertwined in Queneau's work from the start. He explains in the essay that his first three novels express variants of a single theme: the circularity of time. "In the first novel [*Witch Grass*], the circle closes on itself and returns to its point of departure, which is suggested, perhaps heavy-handedly, by the fact that the last sentence is identical to the first" (LNF 27). This structure makes *Witch Grass* a diagram of the eternal return. Queneau goes on to account for the numerical structuring of the novel as follows:

> I found it intolerable to leave the number of chapters in these novels to chance. For this reason, *The Bark Tree* [*Witch Grass*] is composed of 91 (7 x 13) sections, 91 being the sum of the first thirteen numbers and its own "sum" being 1; it is thus the number of the death of living things and of their return to existence, a return that at the time I conceived as the irremediable perpetuity of hopeless suffering. In those days I considered 13 a beneficent number because it denied the possibility of happiness; as for 7, I saw it, and still do see it, as a numerical image of myself, since my family name and my two given names are each composed of seven letters, and since I was born on the twenty-first (3 x 7) of the month. Thus, although apparently non autobiographical, this novel's form was determined by entirely egocentric motivations: the form expressed what the content believed it was disguising. (LNF 27)

The use of thirteen is symbolic in the Peircean sense, for it is conventionally regarded as an unlucky number in Western cultures, although the young Queneau inverted this meaning. Seven and twenty-one are used indexically: they are associated with the author by contiguity, since his names happen to be made up of seven letters, and he happened to be born on a date that is a multiple of seven.

It is not immediately clear why ninety-one symbolizes the death of beings and their return to existence. Queneau's "thus" ("donc") is somewhat elliptical. Jordan Stump provides a helpful note to explain why the "sum" of ninety-one is one: "In other words, $9 + 1 = 10$; $1 + 0 = 1$" (LNF 207). Summing the digits of ninety-one takes us back to the beginning of the series of positive whole numbers; this is a "return to existence" after the completion of the decimal cycle. Similarly, thirteen, which is the number common to the two ways of breaking down ninety-one ($91 = 7 \times 13 = 1 + 2 + 3 + 4 + 5 + 6 + 7 + 8 + 9 + 10 + 11 + 12 + 13$), symbolizes a starting again, since it transgresses the closed system of the twelve calendar months and the twelve signs of the zodiac, reinitiating the cycles.[33] As Gérard de Nerval writes in his sonnet "Artemis": "The thirteenth returns ... it is the first again."[34] The thirteenth arcanum in the Tarot stands for death and rebirth.[35] These symbolic associations have nothing to do with modern mathematics, and no doubt many mathematicians would find them silly or tiresome, as Audin is wearied by the thought of disquisitions on the golden ratio (FS 127). Nevertheless, they are pertinent to *Witch Grass*. The novel is Oulipian in its rigorous patterning, as has often been noted, but it is also strongly linked to the numerological tradition that flourished in pre-modern Western literatures and culminated in the work of Dante.

Read closely and in context (alongside Queneau's other articles for *Volontés* in the late 1930s), "Technique of the Novel" turns out to be more than a manifesto for numerical structuring or an anticipation of Oulipian writing under constraints. Certainly it rejects formlessness, but it also relativizes the value of rules or constraints, as I argued at the end of chapter 2. In addition, it gives an account of the author's changing approach to literary form. The first three novels are subtly qualified as apprentice works. They are flawed, Queneau hints, by disharmony between form and content, superstition, and lack of subtlety.

First, lack of subtlety. Queneau admits that the circular structure of *Witch Grass* is "suggested, *perhaps heavy-handedly*" (my italics) by the fact that the last sentence in the novel repeats the first (LNF 27). Second, superstition. Each chapter of *Witch Grass* contains thirteen sections, a feature which Queneau justified as follows: "In those days, I considered 13 a beneficent number because it denied the possibility of happiness" (LNF 27). This inverted superstition is reminiscent of Roland Travy's stubborn attachment to his own misery in *Odile*. With the help of his friends, and Odile above all, Travy sheds his protective carapace of pessimism. It is implied in "Technique of the Novel" that the author has undergone a similar transformation and is no longer attached to the number thirteen: "In those days ..."

The third kind of structural flaw hinted at in the essay is a disharmony between form and content. *Witch Grass* contains seven chapters since seven, as noted above, was the author's signature number. "Thus, although apparently nonautobiographical, this novel's form was determined by entirely egocentric motivations: the form expressed what the content believed it was disguising" (LNF 27). *The Last Days* (*Les derniers jours*) corrects this bad faith by making no attempt to disguise the autobiographical nature of its content: "In the case of *The Last Days*, the autobiographical element is so obvious that the numerical expression can aspire to a greater objectivity. Its number is 49 (7 x 7, or rather 6 x 8 + 1)" (LNF 37). The numerical expression as originally planned was overridden, however, by considerations of narrative tension and variety: the published text contains only thirty-eight chapters (LNF 29). The novel's emergent, intrinsic form prevailed over the rules, as Suzanne Meyer-Bagoly notes (OC 11 1516).

This emancipation with respect to pre-formulated rules is carried a step further in *Odile*, published nine months before "Technique of the Novel" but not mentioned there. *Odile* is not divided into sections or chapters and has no explicit numerical structuring, although Carol Sanders has shown that the narrative is punctuated by regular references to a man the narrator once saw beside a road in Morocco. The eight mentions constitute a symmetrical pattern.[36] Although Queneau returned to complex schemes like those of *Witch Grass* in *Children of Clay* (*Les enfants du limon*, 1938), he opted for simpler and more supple forms in subsequent novels. In an interview with Georges Charbonnier (1962), he contrasted his early numerical obsessions with a more moderate and flexible formalism: "I think I have gotten away from that arithmomania, while maintaining the concern with structure" (EGC 56).

It seems that Queneau came to regard his early preoccupation with numerology as an obsessive quirk, while maintaining an active and creative interest in mathematics until the end of his life. For the Oulipo, he proposed constraints inspired by combinatorics and matrices: the "quenina" (OC 97–9) and "x mistakes y for z" (OC 245–6).[37] But he kept these exercises in a compartment and resisted encouragement to produce the "great Oulipian novel" based on structures explored or elaborated by the group.[38] That task fell to Perec, who discharged it with *Life: A User's Manual,* published not long after Queneau's death.

Curiously, however, in his last collection of poems, *Elementary Morality* (*Morale élémentaire*, 1973), Queneau returned to numerology. The collection is divided into three parts, comprising fifty-one, sixteen, and sixty-four poems respectively. Queneau eliminated several finished poems in order to arrive at a total of 131, which he described in his journal as a "rather fitting prime number" (OC 1 1453). Métail has noted that 131 is the smallest non-trivial palindromic prime.[39] The sixty-four prose poems of part 3 correspond to the sixty-four hexagrams of the *I Ching* (OC 1 1456–8). In *Elementary Morality*, this and other intertexts (notably the *Divine*

Comedy) are related to a quest narrative, and to episodes from the author's life and work, obliquely evoked. In addition, Queneau alludes systematically to mathematical concepts and problems.

All the commentators agree: *Elementary Morality* is a deeply enigmatic book. A closer look at one of the prose poems from part 3 will indicate the density of meaning in these unassuming blocks of text, and the freedom and understated humour with which Queneau treats the *I Ching*.[40]

> Everything got going the instant the sun rose. The mare tugs
> the cart, the ox accepts the yoke, the cock resumes his song
> of departure. On the white page, only a single dot was visible,
> while the green multiplied its images. Listening out for a unique
> precedent, the stone no longer awaits the hammer and the chisel.
> We have already begun the inscription of everything. The
> geometer considers the empty set and from this deduces the
> series of integers. Irrational and transcendental numbers will
> come to nourish the uncountable weft. The grammarian
> discovers the passive conjugation. The child – it's a girl –
> creates a fairy with smooth, plastic, polychromatic wax.
> (EM 76; OC I 670–1, translation modified)

This poem is based on the "Earth" hexagram, which according to the Taoist commentaries, stands for flexible, receptive humility. The mare symbolizes these qualities because she follows the stallion, yet here the mare takes the lead, pulling the cart, followed by a (neutered) ox and a cock.[41] The wax that the child is manipulating in the final sentence exemplifies flexibility and receptiveness, but it is worth noting that this is a female child: both modeller (girl) and modelled (the fairy and the wax: *une fée, des cires*) are feminine (OC I 670). So Queneau has to some degree neutralized the gendering of the traditional symbols.

In his synoptic plan of *Elementary Morality* part 3, for this poem Queneau noted "passivity, the birth of all things" (OC I 1454). Passivity is figured by the passive voice in grammar as well as by the wax. Everything is beginning: the day, with the rising of the sun and the cry of the cock; universal inscription, with the marking of a first point on a sheet of paper; spring, with the appearance of leaves (the green multiplying its images); numbers, with the empty set, from which Gottlob Frege, Richard Dedekind, and Giuseppe Peano deduced the series of whole numbers.[42]

The whole numbers are a subset of the rational numbers, which are complemented by the irrationals, those that cannot be expressed as a ratio (or fraction). Certain irrationals are also transcendental, that is, they cannot be expressed as the root (or solution) of a non-zero polynomial equation with integer coefficients. In 1882, Ferdinand von Lindemann proved that π was transcendental. It followed that the ancient construction problem of squaring the circle was insoluble.[43] In 1874 and 1891, Georg Cantor published his two proofs that the set of real numbers is uncountable.[44] A corollary of those proofs was that the irrational numbers, including the transcendentals, are also uncountable. Two sentences in Queneau's poem ("The geometer considers the empty set and from this deduces the series of integers. Irrational and transcendental numbers will come to nourish the uncountable weft") condense this series of major mathematical discoveries.

In *Elementary Morality* part 3, the overarching structure is anchored in traditional numerology. Yet the return of numerology does not mean the eviction of mathematics. The two are closely woven together. Thus Queneau's last book adumbrates a reconciliation that is contrary to the development of Western mathematical thought, which since the seventeenth century has generally rejected the attachment of non-mathematical meanings to numbers.[45] Kepler (1571–1630) is often identified as the last important scientific thinker to have reasoned numerologically, even as his contemporaries Galileo (1564–1642) and Descartes (1596–1650) were developing a new world view in which the language of numbers – rather than indicating correspondences between the orders of nature hierarchically organized in a closed cosmos – would express the fundamental laws governing a uniform nature in an open universe.[46]

INTERESTING NUMBERS AND FORMULAE

For the modern mathematician numbers are meaningful in specifically mathematical ways: their properties make them interesting or remarkable. *Les nombres remarquables* (Remarkable numbers), which Le Lionnais published in his seventies, is based on a catalogue that he began to compile during his student days. In the introduction, he writes: "Mathematics does not have a monopoly over numbers [...] But only numbers distinguished by mathematics interested me and seemed worthy of inclusion in my anthology."[47]

Meaningful Forms and Clinamen 143

There is no formal, agreed-upon definition of mathematical interestingness or remarkability. In fact, the notion is paradoxical, as Queneau notes, because if we divide numbers into two classes, interesting and boring, the smallest boring number is interesting by virtue of that particularity and will have to be shifted to the interesting class, likewise for the new smallest boring number, and so on (B 33–4). Nevertheless, numbers are more or less interesting for mathematicians, and a famous anecdote recounted by G.H. Hardy gives some indication of what makes them so. Shortly before Srinivasa Ramanujan's death, Hardy visited him in hospital: "I remember going to see him once when he was lying ill at Putney. I had ridden in taxi-cab No. 1729 and remarked that the number seemed to me rather a dull one, and that I hoped it was not an unfavourable omen. 'No,' he replied, 'it is a very interesting number; it is the smallest number expressible as the sum of two cubes in two different ways.'"[48]

The Oulipians have been drawn to certain numbers because of their mathematically interesting properties, and have used them to design new forms. For example, Jacques Bens's "irrational sonnets" are made up of stanzas of three, one, four, one, and five lines, corresponding to the first five digits of the irrational (and transcendental) number π: 3.145 ...[49] Various members of the Oulipo have used Queneau numbers to write queninas, that is, poems with stanzas of n lines, where n is a Queneau number, whose end-words or rhymes are subject to the spiral permutation explained in chapter 2.[50] The structure of the quenina has also been used in composing prose narratives, for example Audin's *One Hundred Twenty-One Days* (*Cent vingt et un jours*), in which an *onzine* or eleven-ina ($n = 11$) regulates the appearance of characters, literary references, and other elements of the story.[51]

Numbers are mathematically interesting because of the ways in which they interact with each other, and the more mathematically sophisticated Oulipian constraints and forms mobilize patterns, configurations, and formulae rather than individual numbers. An example is Audin's Desarguesiennes constraint, based on Desargues's theorem, which states that "Two triangles are in perspective from a point (centrally) if and only if they are in perspective from a line (axially)." The triangles in figure 5.3 are in perspective in these ways.

There are ten lines and ten points in the configuration. Each of the lines passes through three of the points and each of the points is on three of the lines (PM 55). Audin has proposed two linguistic transpositions of this pattern. Replacing figure by sentence, line by word, and

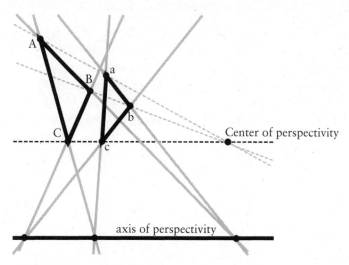

Figure 5.3 The Desargues configuration

point by letter produces an extremely difficult constraint, which she has relaxed by authorizing the use of "small" words, of one or two letters, between the ten constrained words.[52] Replacing figure by poem, line by line, and point by word allows for greater ease of composition, and Audin has applied this version of the constraint to the description of the Parisian street named after Girard Desargues (1591–1661), author of the theorem in question, and a pioneer of projective geometry. The constraint applies to the odd-numbered lines of Audin's poem, shown below, to which I have added numbers in brackets to indicate the words that correspond to the ten points in the Desargues configuration.

> Rue Desargues he looks [1] **silently** [*silencieux*] at an empty green trashcan the [2] **shutters** and [3] **tags**
>
> Rue Desargues he is sitting by the rue de l'Orillon end in front of a [4] **pink** [5] **store** with a brown [6] **grating**
>
> Rue Desargues he sees at the rue de la Fontaine-au-roi end a large blue and green [3] **tag** half concealed by a [7] **closed** [8] **van**
>
> Rue Desargues he knows that behind its brown [2] **shutters**, [9] **number** 17, protected by the parallel bars of the [6] **grating**, is empty

Rue Desargues he hears from behind the [4] **pink** [10] **buildings** the noise of the [8] **van** as it vanishes towards rue de l'Orillon

Rue Desargues perhaps he is waiting for the [7] **closed** [2] **shutters** of the [5] **store** he is sitting in front of to open over there rue de la Fontaine-au-roi is empty

Rue Desargues in front of his eyes still the trashcan and bare [10] **building** and the [1] **silent** [*silencieuse*] [6] **grating**

Rue Desargues his eyes [7] **closed** behind his [4] **pink** scarf he knows that the [9] **numbers** go up on both sides, from rue de l'Orillon to rue de la Fontaine-au-roi

Rue Desargues where he is still sitting and still [1] **silent** [*silencieux*], he observes the carry-on of the [8] **van** collecting the trashcans from the [5] **store**

Rue Desargues, the [9] **number** of the [10] **building** opposite vanishes under the parallel lines of a large [3] **tag** (PM 54–5)

The cumulative, sestina-like effect of the poem is accentuated by multiplying repetitions beyond the requirements of the constraint. As well as the name of the street, repeated ten times, and the words indicated with the numbers [1] to [10] above, there are six words that are repeated twice (*green, large, vanishes, brown, parallel, eyes*). There are also four terms repeated three times (*empty, trashcan, rue de l'Orillon, rue de la Fontaine-au-roi*), which are not integrated into the figure. If any of these words were substituted for one of the ten "point" words, there would be lines passing through too many and too few "points."

In the odd-numbered lines we learn that the anonymous observer is sitting silently in front of a store, perhaps waiting for it to open, eyes closed at first behind his scarf, then open to observe the trash van. Most of the even-numbered lines provide numerical information about the street – length, width, numbering – but the last line builds on the foregoing hints about the observer's situation: "(that day on rue Desargues one man, all alone, was sitting on the ground)" (PM 55). This man seems to be homeless.

"Rue Desargues" brings together two of the principal themes in Audin's literary writing: the history of mathematics and social inequality. It might be argued, at a stretch, that because this version of the constraint entails insistent, even monotonous, lexical repetition, it reflects the experience of the probably homeless observer. It is clear, however, that the name of the street, rather than what the author found there, determined the choice of constraint.

Numbers and mathematical structures are not purely generative in Audin's writing, but the meanings they bear are primarily mathematical. There is not a trace in her work of the Pythagorean mysticism that Roubaud diagnosed in Queneau, nor of the symbolic use of numbers that I examined in Roubaud's *Some Thing Black*. In this sense, she is the most mathematical of the Oulipo's writers. She has also written more about mathematics than the other members of the group, even Roubaud, whose *Mathematics* is largely autobiographical (and accessible to non-mathematicians, making minimal use of mathematical notation). Roubaud's book might have satisfied the editor who, having read a sample from Audin's novel *La formule de Stokes, roman* (Stokes's theorem, a novel), suggested that she say more about herself, and about her relationships with colleagues and friends (FS 155). She replied that what she wanted to do was to "tell the story of Stokes's formula, of its transformations and evolution, of those who contributed to its elaboration, in all their diversity, an emerging mathematical community" (FS 154–5). The idea was to make the theorem itself the heroine of the novel, the principle of its narrative unity. Audin held her course with an admirable firmness and included at least one formula in each chapter. Some of the formulae are highly complex, and will have to serve as decoration for readers not well versed in vector calculus and differential geometry.

Seriously mathematical fiction is a strictly limited niche because the intersection is small between the set of serious fiction readers and the set of people with an advanced education in mathematics. The paradox baldly stated by Ian Hacking may be regretted and campaigned against but should be acknowledged: "We are the mathematical animal. A few of us have made astonishing mathematical discoveries; a few more of us can understand them. Mathematical applications have turned out to be a key to unlock and discipline nature to conform to some of our wishes. But the subject repels most human beings."[53] Given this social fact, it is understandable that the editors encountered by Audin in the course of writing *La formule de Stokes,* and portrayed satirically in the novel, were worried about cost recovery, and suggested making more room for meanings of a non-mathematical kind (FS 73, 99, 124–7, 155–6, 199–200).

Meaningful Forms and Clinamen

In the first part of this chapter, I explored the various ways in which constraints and forms can be meaningful. Oulipian works (as opposed to exercises) often deviate from their constraints at certain points or exhibit formal irregularities. This phenomenon, referred to as clinamen by the members of the Oulipo, has a semantic dimension. Forms and constraints, it turns out, can signify in the breach as well as in the observance.

CLINAMEN: A SWERVING NOTION

In the second book of *De rerum natura* (*On the Nature of the Universe*), which began circulating around 55 BCE, the Roman poet Lucretius, following the teachings of Epicurus, explains that if atoms did not swerve in their fall they would never interact: "When the atoms are travelling straight down through empty space by their own weight, at quite indeterminate times and places they swerve ever so little from their course, just so much that you can call it a change of direction. If it were not for this swerve, everything would fall downwards like rain-drops through the abyss of space. No collision would take place and no impact of atom on atom would be created. Thus nature would never have created anything."[54] For Lucretius, this little swerve is the source of the "free will in living creatures all over the earth," allowing them to "snap the bonds of fate." If the mind, which is made of atoms, can bid us to depart from "the path along which we are severally led by pleasure," individual atoms must be able to move in a way not determined by weight or impact: "besides weight and impact there must be a third cause of movement, the source of this inborn power of ours, since we see that nothing can come out of nothing."[55] Will, then, must be present in the fundamental particles. Lucretius and Epicurus before him were panpsychists.[56] And will is manifest in a motion that Lucretius names with a word – *clinamen* – which occurs nowhere else in surviving Latin: "But the fact that the mind itself has no internal necessity to determine its every act and compel it to suffer in helpless passivity – this is due to the slight swerve of the atoms at no determinate time or place [*id facit exiguum clinamen principiorum / nec regione loci certa nec tempore certo*]."[57]

Warren Motte has traced the erratic career of the clinamen in modern thought, noting its appearances in the work of Alfred Jarry, Harold Bloom, Michel Serres, Ilya Prigogine, Isabelle Stengers, and Jeffrey Mehlman.[58] In each of these cases, to varying degrees, the notion itself swerves away from its previous uses. The clinamen has continued its career since the publication of Motte's article in 1986, with Stephen Greenblatt's *The Swerve: How the World Became Modern* (2011), a history of Poggio Bracciolini's rediscovery of *De rerum natura*, and Morgane Cadieu's *Marcher au hasard: Clinamen et création dans la prose du XXe siècle* (Random walks: clinamen and creation in twentieth-century prose, 2019), which maps the "disruptive actualizations" of the clinamen in theory from Henri Bergson to Quentin Meillassoux.

One of the reasons for the repeated revival of the concept of clinamen seems to be its way of lending itself to appropriation. This conceptual drift exasperates the mathematician René Thom, the founder of catastrophe theory: "I can hardly explain this fascination with the 'clinamen,' with the small fluctuation initiating large events, except by a certain literary affectation. Plunging the evolution of phenomena into a sort of 'artistic blur,' imagining oneself at the crossroads, and by an involuntary flick of the finger hurling the world into an abyss of successive catastrophes …"[59] My focus here will be relatively tight: I will be concerned with the clinamen as localizable deviation from a writing constraint. But it will become clear that even understood in this limited sense, the clinamen can work in more than one way. And one of its functions is to introduce, if not a blur, a degree of asymmetry or irregularity that many thinkers, including Immanuel Kant, Rudolf Arnheim, and Ernst Gombrich, have recognized as a positive characteristic of art.[60]

The notion of the clinamen has a prehistory in the Oulipo. The founders did not envisage constraints as absolutely rigid or all-determining. In 1961, Le Lionnais stressed the importance of choice within a system of constraints in a remark whose wording may surprise, given the Oulipo's general hostility to the idea of inspiration: "The aim of potential literature is to provide future writers with new techniques that can *leave room for their feeling-based inspiration*. Thence the necessity of a certain freedom. Nine or ten centuries ago, when a practitioner of potential literature proposed the sonnet form, he made sure that its mechanics left open the possibility of a choice" (GO 83–4). Queneau, for his part, had been consciously "syncopating" the structures of his novels since *The Last Days* (*Les derniers jours*, 1936).[61] It was Perec, however, who applied the concept of clinamen to writing under constraint and gave it currency in the Oulipo.[62] In 1978, he said: "Whenever you try to apply a system rigidly, something jams. To operate freely within it, you have to deliberately introduce a little error. It's like what Klee said: 'Genius is the error in the system'" (EC I 240–1). This is just one of a series of remarks in which Perec associates three notions:

clinamen, error, and *jeu* in the mechanical sense of looseness, give, room for manoeuvre, *Spielraum* (EC I 281; EC II 82, 166, 193, 202, 317). As I pointed out in chapter 3, error, in these contexts, means a deliberate irregularity, a choice, rather than an inadvertent action.

Jacques Roubaud insists on the freely chosen nature of the clinamen when he stipulates that for it to be properly Oulipian it must not be a cop-out: "A clinamen is an intentional violation of constraint for aesthetic purposes: a proper clinamen therefore presupposes the existence of an additional solution that respects the constraint and that has been deliberately rejected – but not because the writer is incapable of finding it" (OC 44). It is worth noting that Perec himself was not quite so strict, presenting the clinamen as a kind of cheating on at least one occasion: "I set myself rules for the construction of my book, which are often extremely difficult, and when I can't follow them, I 'cheat' and call it a *clinamen*" (EC I 281).

OPENINGS

There are two ways of "cheating" when writing under constraints. The writer can deviate either from the constraint itself or from rules of spelling, grammar, or syntax. The second kind of deviation is exemplified by the non-standard spellings that abound in Perec's monovocalic novel *The Exeter Text*. The reader is given fair warning: "Various distortions will be accepted as the text progresses" (TH 55). In fact there is a distortion in the original French title, which would normally be spelt *Les revenantes* not *Les revenentes*. A sentence from the final paragraph, as recreated by E.N. Menk (Ian Monk), illustrates how far the distortions are taken: "Then, sleyeghtlee wrecked, yet cheered, deleyeghted, Hélène, Thérèse, Estelle 'n' me resembled the three Mewsketeers" (TH 113). Similarly, in the original edition of Perec's "Ulcérations," a long poem based on isograms – in this case, permutations of the set of eleven letters most commonly used in French (ESARTINULOC) – there are various deviant spellings, such as *csar* (for *czar*), *ciclone* (for *cyclone*), *tiran* (for *tyran*) and so on.[63] Although deviations of this kind are sometimes referred to as clinamens, they are conceptually distinct from the clinamen proper, which is a departure from a freely chosen constraint.[64] For example, when Perec was composing the sequence of poems entitled "La clôture" (The enclosure), he slightly relaxed the isogram constraint that he had used in "Ulcérations" and *Alphabets* by adding a freely chosen "joker" to the set of the eleven most frequently used letters (ALP 236).

With this opening, Perec seems to have been seeking, as Christelle Reggiani notes, "a certain balance between obscurity and readability" (O II 1189). His revision of "Ulcérations" for inclusion in the volume *La clôture et autres poèmes* also favours the normative and the readable: the non-standard spellings are corrected. In the original publication, the text departs from spelling conventions; in *La clôture et autres poèmes*, it departs from the formal constraint. This orthographic normalization coincides with Perec's decision not to publish the grids of eleven-letter sequences alongside the poems derived from them, as he had done earlier in *Alphabets* and the original version of "Ulcérations."

Reflecting on this change of strategy, Perec said: "The problem when people see the constraint is that they stop seeing anything else [...] I realize that when I publish poems composed according to systems that are equally complicated but without providing a key, as I did just recently in *La clôture*, in the end the reader can receive them as a poem. Or at least that's what I would like" (O II 1189). Mireille Ribière has underlined the singular "as a poem," and taken it to refer to the whole of *La clôture et autres poèmes*.[65] She is surely right to insist on the careful composition of the volume. A striking feature of that composition is the swerve away from constraint in the book's last poem, "Un poème." The amplitude of the swerve can be measured by comparing "Un poème" with the last poem of the sequence "La clôture," quoted below, which Perec reused as back-cover copy for the collection:

Car plus en toi s'unit l'archéologue
criant son écart, plus il saigne court.

La porte s'incurve: ni sa clôture, ni
blocus à ton désir tu.

L'accalmie (ton sûr port au silence
conquis): l'art? (O II 773)

For the more the archeologist gathers himself in you
wailing his split, the shorter he bleeds.

The door curves: neither its closure, nor
blockade of your suppressed desire.

Quietude (your sure port to silence
conquered): art?[66]

Meaningful Forms and Clinamen 151

According to Bernard Magné, this poem ciphers a refusal of self-pity.[67] It is not, however, a celebration of the stiff upper lip. The archeologist of the first couplet is an ambivalent figure, as Jean-Jacques Poucel remarks: "In order to bring the dismembered fragments of his story together, to knit them into a textile that will symbolically arrest, clot, or constrain the bleeding, the archeologist must dig."[68] The constraint or binding required to stanch the flow of blood occasioned by the split (*écart*), is ambivalent too: it effects neither a total closure, nor a blocking of desire. The door curves, giving under the pressure of what it holds back. And the tension or the balance between constraint and that which it constrains seems to lead to a temporary quietude or lull in the midst of turbulence (*accalmie*), which is tentatively identified with art.

"Un poème," too, reflects on the nature of art and its relation to loss and separation. But by contrast with "La clôture," the diction of this unconstrained poem is disarmingly straightforward. With "Un poème," Perec takes up a rhetorical stance deeply rooted in the lyric tradition: apostrophizing the gone.

> *Est-ce que j'essayais d'entourer ton poignet*
> *avec mes doigts?*

> *Aujourd'hui la pluie strie l'asphalte*
> *Je n'ai pas d'autres paysages dans ma tête*
> *Je ne peux pas penser*
> *aux tiens, à ceux que tu as traversés dans le noir et dans la nuit*
> *Ni à la petite automobile rouge*
> *dans laquelle j'éclatais de rire*

> *L'ordre immuable des jours trace un chemin strict*
> *c'est aussi simple qu'une prune au fond d'un compotier*
> *ou que la progression du lierre le long de mon mur.*

> *Mes doigts ne sont plus ce bracelet trop court*
> *Mais je garde l'empreinte ronde de ton poignet*
> *Au creux de mes mains ambidextres*
> *Sur le drap noir de ma table.* (O II 800)

> *Did I try to encircle your wrist*
> *with my fingers?*

Today the rain is streaking the asphalt
There are no other landscapes in my head

I cannot think
of yours, of those you crossed in the dark, in the night
Or of the little red car
in which I burst out laughing

The immutable order of days traces its strict path
it's as simple as a plum sitting in a fruit dish
or the ivy's progress across my wall

My fingers are no longer that too-small bracelet
But I still hold the round impression of your wrist
In my ambidextrous hands
On the black cloth of my table

The "little red car" corresponds to the vehicle that figures in the description of a photograph taken in June 1940, during the invasion of France, as described in *W or the Memory of Childhood* (WMC 52; O II 697).[69] The black cloth in the last line recalls the description of Perec's writing desk in "Still Life / Style Leaf."[70] Bartlebooth uses a similar table, covered with a black cloth, for assembling his jigsaw puzzles in *Life: A User's Manual* (LUM 126; O II 150).

Given this intertextual web, and especially the allusion to *W or the Memory of Childhood*, it is hard to resist the identification of the *you* addressed in "Un poème" as Perec's mother. The landscapes of which the poem's *I* cannot think are presumably those through which Cyrla Perec passed on her journey by train from the concentration camp at Drancy to the death camp at Auschwitz. The child's fingers that could not close around the mother's wrist, and which lost their hold on her at the Gare de Lyon in autumn 1941, when Perec was sent to stay with relatives at Villard-de-Lans in the "free zone," rest now on the black cloth of the writing desk, and write, tracing the split (*l'écart*), which widens as "the immutable order of days follows its strict path."[71] Nevertheless, the hands of the orphaned adult hold the "round impression" of the vanished wrist.[72]

This sober but tender declaration of loyalty to the lost, closing *La clôture et autres poèmes*, suggests why, for many years, Perec shied away from the idea of writing poetry without constraints. In an interview with Jean-Marie Le Sidaner, he spoke of his isogram poems in the following terms: "The intense difficulty of writing in this way, and the patience required to put together, for example, eleven 'lines' of eleven letters each, that's nothing compared to what it would be like for me to write 'poetry' freely, the terror of that. But maybe I'll dare to do it one day" (EC II 99). This "terror" was not simply a variant of the "lyric shame" recently diagnosed in North American poetry by Gillian White, or the fear of being understood, which Don Paterson encouraged poets to face in his T.S. Eliot lecture: "Real danger flirts with the things we most dread as poets. Perhaps the biggest risk of all is that of being largely understood and then found to be talking a pile of garbage."[73] Perec's "lyric terror," as Reggiani has called it, is fear of opening the door too wide, and being undone by what comes through. When he writes "I cannot think / of yours, of those you traversed in the dark and the night," he is not admitting to an imaginative incapacity, but marking the limits of what, for the moment, he can bear.

In Perec's last poem, "L'éternité" (Eternity), also written without constraints, he follows the journey further, into a country where the blurring of the horizon prefigures a catastrophe that, as Reggiani suggests, is indistinguishably personal and cosmic (O II 1204):

l'horizon dans son absence
est une hésitation émoussée

la préfiguration tremblante
du *corral*
où se tapit sa catastrophe (O II 813)

the horizon in its absence
is a blunted hesitation

the trembling prefiguration
of the *corral*
where her [its] catastrophe lay hidden

The italicized *corral* is a metaphor for the destination of the freight and cattle cars used for prisoner transport to the death camps. This, the term of Perec's swerve away from constraint, is as close as he came, in print, to evoking the circumstances of his mother's death.

In *La clôture et autres poèmes*, the designed irregularity or clinamen has a range of functions and effects. It favours readability and conformity to linguistic norms; it makes the constraint less salient; and, thematically, it results in an added gravity, particularly when constraint falls away altogether in "Un poème." The clinamen, in Perec's poetry, does more than lubricate the formal machinery, it also regulates an approach to writing without constraint.

ASYMMETRIES

As mentioned in chapter 3, *Life: A User's Manual* presents itself as a description of an unfinished painting that depicts an apartment building as it might appear if the façade were removed. Each chapter corresponds to one of the rooms thus revealed. The rooms constitute a ten-by-ten grid, which the novel covers almost exhaustively by moving from one room to another as a knight does in chess. The path traced chapter by chapter is an imperfect, open "knight's tour": open because it does not end where it began, and imperfect since it does not pass through every square. In "Four figures for *Life: A User's Manual*," Perec teasingly signals the significant clinamen: "It should nevertheless be noticed that the book has not 100 chapters but 99. For this the little girl on pages 295 and 394 is solely responsible [pages 231 and 318 in the English translation]" (OC 175).

The little girl appears first in the catalogue of characters who are to figure in Valène's painting of the apartment building, then in a list of odds and ends kept by Madame Moreau's cook, Gertrude:

106. A little girl gnawing at the edges of her shortbread cookies (LUM 231)

100. La petite fille qui mord dans un coin de son petit-beurre Lu (O II 268)

an old biscuit box, made of tin, square in shape, on the lid of which you can see a little girl munching the corner of her *petit-beurre*. (LUM 318)

une vieille boîte à biscuits en fer-blanc, carrée, sur le couvercle de laquelle on voit une petite fille mordre dans un coin de son petit beurre. (O II 365)

As Magné has shown, there is a *mise-en-abyme* in these two mentions: the missing corner of the cookie corresponds to the missing room and chapter in the bottom left-hand corner of the ten-by-ten grid. The brand of the cookie is significant too: *Lu*, the past participle of the verb *lire* (to read) signals, as Magné puts it, "the metalinguistic reach of this nibbling."[74] The incomplete "read" biscuit points to the chapter that we cannot read. Similarly, the description of the biscuit tin includes a play on words that also hints at the clinamen: "fer-blanc, carré" (tin, square) suggesting "faire [un] blanc [dans le] carré" (to make a blank space in the square).[75]

The unwritten room in the novel's structure is mirrored by a gap in the compendium of characters and stories in chapter fifty-one. This compendium is highly constrained: each line contains sixty characters (including spaces, but not brackets), and the lines are grouped into three "stanzas." The first two stanzas have sixty lines, but the third has only fifty-nine. Within each stanza a letter moves back one space from the last toward the first position with each successive line. The three shifting letters in the original are *a, m*, and *e*, spelling *âme*, which means soul, spirit, or mind, but also has a range of technical senses, including the bore of a canon, the core of a magnet, the soundpost of a violin, and perhaps most pertinently, a sketch for a painting ("l'âme d'un tableau"). Valène's actual depiction of the apartment building is, in fact, the barest sketch (LUM 500).

Since a clinamen has eliminated the last line of the compendium, the letter *e* is missing from its bottom left-hand corner: *e*, the letter missing from *A Void*, and the letter that figures in the dedication of *W or the Memory of Childhood*: "For E," "Pour E," which may be read homophonically as "Pour eux," "For them." "They," in the first instance, are Perec's father, killed in action while serving in the French army in 1940, and his mother, deported to Auschwitz in 1943. Magné points out that the figure of the missing bottom left-hand corner, of which I have mentioned two occurrences in *Life: A User's Manual*, links this novel to *W or the Memory of Childhood* in yet another way, since it appears in Perec's earliest memory. In the remembered scene, the three-year old child is looking at a Yiddish newspaper, surrounded by family. He recognizes and names a "sign [...] supposedly shaped like a square with a gap in its lower left-hand corner" (WMC 13).

In an interview, Perec said that the missing chapter of *Life: A User's Manual* had to disappear "to break the symmetry" (EC 11 202). But

156   How to Do Things with Forms

the breakage is not purely formal. It produces a supplement of meaning by connecting the novel to *W or the Memory of Childhood* and *A Void* via the theme of lack and a geometrical motif. Far from being mere licenses, the missing chapter and the missing line in the compen-·dium are strategically and significantly deployed. Where the system seems to falter, it draws the patient reader into an interpretive game of a kind whose fascination and potential dangers I explore further in chapter 6.

Perec's clinamens have a range of functions: compositional (affording greater flexibility), semantic (encoding meanings), and aesthetic (masking constraints and breaking symmetry). But a functional analysis should not obscure the clinamen's potential to transcend functionality. Often it introduces *jeu* in the sense of play, as well as in the word's mechanical sense (give, room for manoeuvre). It can be a way of playing with a structure for the pleasure of it, gratuitously. To explore this link between play and clinamen I turn now to Roubaud's *Parc sauvage* (Wild grounds), in whose storyworld a constraint and the numerous deviations from it are attributed to a pair of heroically playful children.

EODERMDROMES

The constraint employed in *Parc sauvage*, known as the eodermdrome, is difficult. "Very hard. Maybe too hard," wrote Roubaud in an article published in 1997.[76] A procedure for composing eodermdromes is set out as follows by Mathews in the *Oulipo Compendium*:

1   Choose five letters.
2   Arrange the letters in a pattern corresponding to the angles of an equilateral pentagon.
3   Connect each angle of the pentagon with every other angle (ten lines in all).
4   If the letters have been properly chosen and arranged, it will be possible to obtain a meaningful sequence of eleven letters by moving progressively along the lines joining the angles of the pentagon, each segment being used once and once only.
5   The sequence necessarily ends at the point at which it began. (OC 140)

The word eodermdrome is itself an eodermdrome, as shown in figure 5.4.

Meaningful Forms and Clinamen

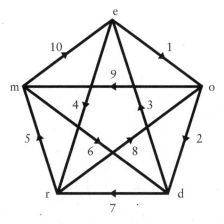

Figure 5.4 The eodermdrome

As a result of the constraint's extreme difficulty, relatively natural eodermdromes made up of letters are even rarer than relatively natural palindromes, such as "A man, a plan, a canal: Panama!" or "Was it a car or a cat I saw?" In his 1997 article, Roubaud cited the example "surtout, sors" ("above all, get out") and wrote: "At the present time (in the current state of research), this beautiful eodermdromic verse (which could be the object of a lengthy commentary) is probably the most pleasing utterance produced in conformity with the constraint."[77] This remark prefigures *Parc sauvage*, which could be construed as a lengthy narrative commentary on "Surtout, sors."

The book tells the story of two children, Dora and Jacques, sent by their respective families to stay at a property in the Corbières region of southern France in September 1942, three months before the occupation of the "free zone." It is clear that these children and their families are in danger of being arrested and deported. Plans are afoot to get them across the Pyrenees into Spain. The property at which the children stay, Sainte-Lucie, belongs to a certain Camillou, familiar to readers of Roubaud's *The Loop* (*La boucle*). The fourth chapter of that book, entitled "Parc sauvage," describes Sainte-Lucie in detail and concludes with a glimpse of a mysterious "little blonde girl," in whom the reader of *Parc sauvage* can hardly fail to see a prefiguration of Dora (L 117–37).

"Tears at rest," the eodermdrome in English that closes *Parc sauvage*, is attributed to the adult Jacques, who has immigrated to Scotland and changed his name to James Goodman. Fifty years after the events of the main story, Goodman returns to the scene of his childhood games with Dora and discovers the diary that she left there. The eodermdromes "surtout, sors" and "tears at rest," which are relatively natural, and narratively suggestive, serve as conclusions to the two parts of the story, and may also have served as points of departure for the writing, since Roubaud mentioned the first ten years before publishing *Parc sauvage*, in the article cited above, and the second was included in an article by the mathematicians Gary Bloom, John Kennedy, and Peter Wexler in 1980.[78] But these are not the only eodermdromes in *Parc sauvage*. Each chapter is followed by a short text in italics constructed according to the same principle. Instructions for use are provided by Goodman in the second part of the book. Between the pages of Dora's journal are sheets of paper on which he finds

> sequences of letters, mostly crossed out, geometrical figures with routes from one letter to another indicated by arrows. Goodman explained that it was a kind of game: letters were placed at the angles of the figure. You had to choose the letters carefully and follow the route indicated by the arrows without ever using the same line twice. That way you ended up with a bit of a sentence, or a sequence of two or three words. He and Dora played this game all the time, and they tried to find solutions which somehow recounted, in condensed form, something that had happened during the day. Since it was very difficult, they often allowed themselves to join up words rather than letters. Sometimes they didn't get anywhere. Even with this "license," the result was never very clear or explicit. But it mattered to Dora, she stuck at it. (PS 134)

This passage, which applies Roubaud's first principle ("a text written in accordance with a restrictive procedure [*contrainte*] refers to the procedure"), rewards close reading (OC 222; ALP 90).

The bits of sentences ("bouts de phrase") recount one of the day's events in condensed form. In most cases there is a clear semantic link between the short text in italics and the chapter that it concludes. The text can be read as a fragmentary summary. "They often allowed themselves to join up words rather than letters," Goodman tells us. Of the twenty-four eodermdromes in total, eleven are composed of words, eleven of letters, and two of syllables. "Sometimes they didn't get anywhere," and sometimes, it might be added, the result was imperfect or irregular. But to know this, the reader must "resolve" the little texts in italics, which is not always a simple task. First the texts must be broken down into five elements, of which four are repeated twice and one is repeated three times. Then these five elements must be placed at the vertices of a pentagon in order to verify that the path linking them is Eulerian, not passing more than once via any edge.

It turns out that of the twenty-four eodermdromes, just over half (thirteen) are regular, while the others display one or more of the following types of clinamen:

1   addition of a "joker" element not included in the basic set of five, such as the *a* in "soir, alors lis" ("evening, then read," chapter 18);
2   two elements located at the same vertex, as in "étoile, ortie" ("star, thistle," chapter 21), which superposes *l* and *r* (see figure 5.5);
3   an incomplete sequence, that is, of less than 10 steps, such as "orage" ("storm," chapter 17), which does not repeat any of the five elements;
4   the path passes via an edge more than once, as in "ai radio, dora" ("have radio, dora," chapter 22), which includes $o \rightarrow d$ and $d \rightarrow o$, as well as $r \rightarrow a$ twice (see figure 5.6).

Resolving the texts in italics reveals a tension between the mathematical structure of the constraint and narrative or poetic motivation. In chapter 22, Jacques and Dora prepare themselves for the arrival of the Germans, who they are sure will come to arrest Jim, an English airman who is staying at Sainte-Lucie and sending coded messages by radio to London. The text in italics at the end of the chapter contains two eodermdromes: "tout dur dort" ("every hard [man] sleeps"), which is regular, and "ai radio: dora" ("have radio, dora"), which, as indicated above, is not. A narrative motivation for the first eodermdrome can be found, at a stretch, by linking it to the first sentence of the chapter: "He would be captured" ("Il serait pris.") Jim is tough and well trained, but he too must sleep; he cannot be vigilant all the time. "Every hard man sleeps": no one is invulnerable. The second eodermdrome – "have radio: dora" ("ai radio: dora") – has stronger links with the content of the chapter because Jacques and Dora have taken the radio transmitter that Jim was using. In addition, the

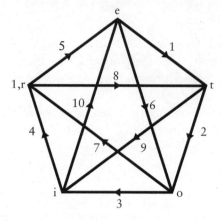

Figure 5.5 "étoile, ortie"

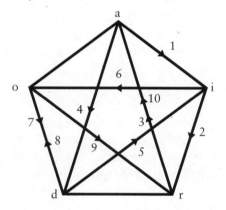

Figure 5.6 "ai radio, dora"

fragment has a telegraphic syntax, which resembles that of manually coded messages. Roubaud could have used the first eodermdrome alone, but he added a second, although it is irregular, probably because it recounts one of the day's events more effectively and transmits the atmosphere of secrecy.

Sometimes the reason for a deviation from the constraint is more poetic than narrative. In chapter 21, Jacques and Dora go to see what Jim is doing in the cabin and find him sending messages in Morse code. Night has fallen. The stars are shining. The children make their way

Meaningful Forms and Clinamen

through brambles and thistles. The chapter ends with "thistle, star" ("étoile, ortie"). As stated above, in order to construe this sequence of letters as an eodermdrome, *l* and *r* have to be placed at the same vertex of the pentagon. Stars (*étoiles*) and thistles (*orties*) figure in the chapter but only as background elements; they are not integral to the plot. In joining the stars and the thistles, the eodermdrome is not recounting one of the day's events, not even in condensed form, but bringing together two mutually remote things to make the spark of a surprising resemblance jump between them. As thistles prick the children's legs, stars prick the sky (as in the expression "un ciel piqué d'étoiles" ["a sky pricked with stars"]). Formal rigour is sacrificed here to poetic effect.

By attributing the eodermdromes in *Parc sauvage* to a pair of ten-year-olds, Roubaud excuses himself for their often approximate nature. Sometimes Jacques and Dora take a very easy way out, as at the end of chapter 16, where the eodermdrome consists of the word *Espagne* (Spain) repeated eleven times. But the attribution is also a way of placing the Oulipian constraint among a range of children's games, explicitly designated as such: sliding down a banister and jumping down stairs; discovering where the duck Bacadette has laid her daily egg; a kind of handball, which the children call "la pelote basque" (pelota); adapting and acting out stories from *The Jungle Book*; playing with grapes in the vineyard; and building a dam (PS 15–16, 48, 51, 83–4, 86, 118–20).

These games amuse the children and distract them from the anxiety of separation. But playing also prepares them for an imagined eventuality: when they sense that the Germans are approaching, they turn a secret tunnel discovered in the course of their games into a hiding place, in which they deposit blankets, sleeping bags, and supplies of food and water. Even in hiding, Dora persists in the composition of her eodermdromes, and the last one recorded in her journal gives sound advice: "surtout, sors" ("above all, get out"). Jacques and Dora abandon their hideout, and with the help of a railwayman they are able to ride a goods train to Toulouse. The moral here seems to coincide with Perec's interpretation of the first dream recorded in *La boutique obscure*: "We can save ourselves (sometimes) by playing" (BO 5), which resonates in turn with an anecdote in *A Short Treatise Inviting the Reader to Discover the Subtle Art of Go (Petit traité invitant à la découverte de l'art subtil du go)* by Perec, Roubaud, and Pierre Lusson: "The second day of the National Championship of 1945 was to have taken place in Hiroshima on 6 August. The Chief of Police, 'taken by a premonition,' insisted that the event take place a few kilometers away. Thus, not one of the 79,400 victims was a Grand Master of that time."[79] Sometimes we can save ourselves, escape or flee (*se sauver*) by playing, but only sometimes. Dora's escape is temporary. In Toulouse she is arrested with her mother, who has decided against leaving the country.

Playing is obviously not a fail-safe defence, but there is a certain heroism in obstinately continuing to play in spite of an imminent danger, or in inventing a game that is a means of survival and mental escape, as Le Lionnais did during his wartime captivity, mentally reconstituting his favourite paintings.[80] This "memory constraint," as Roubaud has called it (BW 229), served as an inward escape route, like Dora's journal in its padlocked box and the game of the eodermdromes. It is surely no accident that Roubaud's heroine in *Parc sauvage* bears the name of the camp in which Le Lionnais was imprisoned.[81]

In light of Roubaud's first principle, Dora's last eodermdrome – "above all, get out" ("surtout, sors") – can also be read as a formal injunction: Do not allow the constraint to shut you in. If Oulipians are "rats who construct the labyrinth from which they propose to escape," the clinamen may be a means to that end (OC 201; GO 49). A formal analysis of the eodermdromes in *Parc sauvage* shows that Roubaud does not hesitate to depart from his little pentagonal labyrinths when strictly respecting the constraint would limit the poetic or narrative effectiveness of the result. To paraphrase Queneau in "Technique of the Novel," there are no more rules when they have outlived their value (LNF 29).

6

Revelation and Dissimulation

BETWEEN ROUSSEAU AND ROUSSEL

In Roman Jakobson's scheme of the six functions of language, there is one that the Oulipo has obviously cultivated: the poetic function, characterized by "the set (*Einstellung*) towards the MESSAGE itself, focus on the message for its own sake."[1] This is the function that dominates when language is strongly patterned, and, as Jakobson remarked, strong patterning is to be found beyond the domains of poetry and literature, in proverbs and advertising slogans, for example. When the set is toward the addresser of a message, the emotive or expressive function comes to the fore. This function is laid bare in interjections – as when I bump my shin and curse – but it also flavours all our utterances to some extent.[2]

At first glance, the writers of the Oulipo would appear to be averse to kinds of writing in which the emotive function prevails. Le Lionnais seems to be confirming this when he opposes writing under constraints to "shriek-literature or eructative literature." Yet he adds: "This tendency has its gems, and the members of the Oulipo are not the least fervent of its admirers ... during those moments, of course, not devoted to their priestly duties" (OPPL 30). Oulipian writing is light-heartedly presented here as a sacred activity (*un sacerdoce* [AO 794]) neatly separated from the profanity of primal self-expression. But writing under Oulipian constraints or in Oulipian forms does not exclude the emotive function. And as Bénabou has shown in his essay "Entre Roussel et Rousseau, ou contrainte et confession" (Between Roussel and Rousseau, or constraint and confession), a number of the Oulipo's members have, while continuing to perform their priestly duties, ventured into a domain where the addresser is central: autobiography. In those ventures, Oulipian constraints and forms have served to frame autobiographical revelations.

Bénabou's own *Why I Have Not Written Any of My Books* (*Pourquoi je n'ai écrit aucun de mes livres,* 1986) meditates on and paradoxically overcomes a long-suffered literary sterility, systematically using homophonic variation and other kinds of word play as prompts. In "Entre Roussel et Rousseau," Bénabou follows Raymond Roussel's example in *How I Wrote Certain of My Books* (*Comment j'ai écrit certains de mes livres,* 1935) and reveals some of the method behind his first large-scale literary work. In an early draft, the opening sentence was a variation on Proust's famous incipit: "Longtemps, j'ai rêvé de vrais chefs d'œuvre" ("For a long time, I dreamed of real masterpieces") (AS 85). Having repeated this sentence over and over in his head, one day Bénabou spontaneously transformed it into: "Longtemps, j'ai ravaudé des déchets d'œuvre" ("For a long time, I repaired scraps of works"), and the idea of a book built from the remains of earlier stalled projects came to him, suggesting a method that he would use again, especially in *Jacob, Menahem, and Mimoun: A Family Epic* (*Jacob, Ménahem et Mimoun, une épopée familiale,* 1995).

On a larger scale, Jacques Roubaud's *The Great Fire of London,* which runs to over two thousand pages in the one-volume edition (*Le grand incendie de Londres,* 2009), is also a work built on ruins, in this case, the ruins of a grandiose Project which was to have combined poetry, mathematics, and a novel whose title, *The Great Fire of London,* came to the author in a dream (GFL 1). Roubaud has denied, but not categorically, that this massive prose work in six "branches" is an autobiography: "I was living at 56 rue Notre-Dame-de-Lorette, on the first floor, with Sylvia, my wife, Laurence, my daughter, Mlle Martínez (Conchita), who looked after Laurence (less than two at the time) when we were out, and Séraphin, the cat. Shall I say more? Am I writing an autobiography? I shall say no more (I am not writing an autobiography). (Or a bit, sometimes, in connection with the reason for my verbal journey [*ce qui motive mon parcours de mots*])" (P 116). That reason is clarified in *The Loop* (*La boucle*): "One could also say that, if there is indeed any autobiography here, it's an (auto)biography of the **Project** and of its double, **The Great Fire of London,** and consequently, in large measure, an <u>autobiography of no one</u> (or: <u>nobody's autobiography</u>)" (L 265).

Revelation and Dissimulation

However, as Florence Marsal has remarked, the memories that Roubaud recounts are not always clearly related to the Project, and their inclusion sometimes seems to be motivated by the pleasure of storytelling or the wish to introduce a dose of thematic variety.[3] The erotic episodes involving "Louise" and "Agnès," for example, are tangentially related to the Project in that both women were doing postgraduate research on medieval poetry at the time of the relationships, "Ronsasvals" and Layamon's "Brut," respectively (GFL 301; P 401). But neither seems to have been an important intellectual interlocutor. What drives these digressions – "for the first time in this prose, I am straying from the absolute chastity I maintained in the 'story' section of this 'branch'" (GFL 299) – is the pleasure of remembering pleasure, and specifically pleasure taken outside the context of domesticity. It is striking how Roubaud's "(auto)biography of the Project," a "large, loose, baggy monster" (to quote Henry James) if ever there was one, with space for an eight-page disquisition on the making of azarole jelly (GFL 62–9), revisits some of the author's affairs in intimate detail but barely mentions his marriages.[4]

At the end of *Pas un jour* (*Not One Day*) Anne F. Garréta thanks "J.R., to whom, although he is unaware of the debt, and would perhaps not recognize it, this book owes more than one of its features."[5] Garréta is indebted to Roubaud in her use of the concept of "memory-image" (*image-mémoire*), and more specifically in linking memory-images to portraits of lovers, for *Not One Day* is a "stammering alphabet of desire," born of the following optimistically formulated process constraint: "you will allocate five hours (the time it takes a moderately well-trained subject to compose a standard academic essay) each day, for a month, at your computer, aiming to recount the memory you have of one woman or another whom you have desired or who has desired you" (NOD 4–5). The method of writing each day without revising – "No erasures, no rewrites. Sentences as they come, without plotting them, cut off as soon as they're left hanging. Syntax matching composition" (NOD 5) – may also owe something to Roubaud and his improvisatory protocol for *The Great Fire of London*: composing "without deletions, regrets, reflection, imagination, impatience" (GFL 5).

In the end, Garréta narrates only twelve encounters, and one, she tells us in the "Post Scriptum," is a fiction (NOD 87). Since the exception is not identified, it casts the veracity of all the episodes into doubt. Garréta's plan to restrain her inclination to syntactic complexity is soon abandoned: "As for writing simple sentences ... Pious vow. Even speaking, you can't manage it" (NOD 86). What distinguishes *Not One Day* from the genre of the erotic memoir is the book's focus on desire rather than its consummation – "Who cares whether we've actually had the women we've desired?" (NOD 11) – and its critique of desire as an obligation and a ruse of capitalism, which the anecdotal content saves from any suspicion of prudery: "How we love to exaggerate the power of desire. So resistible, so often" (NOD 17).

In the "Post Scriptum," Garréta dismisses momentary worries about the effects that her book might have on readers who recognize themselves (or imagine that they do): "You'll remember to tell your loved ones to stay away from this book. It's a book that you intend only for your adversaries, or else for strangers" (NOD 90–1). Like Roubaud, Garréta is a writer energized by the existence of human and conceptual adversaries. *Not One Day* is not hobbled by fear of swelling their number, but it makes no attempt to present its author "in all the truth of nature," to quote the opening of the *Confessions*, in which Jean-Jacques Rousseau, "who invented or perfected our corruption" according to Garréta, claimed to be composing the very first complete and truthful literary self-portrait (NOD 3–4).[6] *Not One Day* is without doubt a revealing book, but what it reveals is framed by the constraints: these regulated confessions are situated between the effusions of the supposedly all-baring Rousseau and the constructions of Roussel who claimed not to draw at all on his own experience.[7]

Garréta's constraints, governing process and content, were set up to counter an intellectual distaste for the confessional: "If you aim to thwart your inclinations, you might as well go about it systematically" (NOD 4). They suspended a personal taboo. This is a virtue of constraints in general according to Bénabou, who presents them as devices for eluding self-censorship in a passage that I quoted at the end of chapter 2. Garréta's aim was also to write more quickly and reward the fidelity of her readership: "Figuring out the next novel on the horizon will take years of research, composition, writing. You pity your few readers and always take care not to exceed their patience and good will. In the meantime you would like to offer them what they expect they desire: a distraction, the illusion of revealing what they imagine to be a subject" (NOD 3). In fact, the book increased Garréta's readership significantly when it won the Prix Médicis in 2002. Even if she failed to adhere to her initial program, this would seem to be a case of constraints leading to one of the results that Freud said a patient might expect from analysis: efficiency or capacity to get work done (*Leistungsfähigkeit*).[8]

Revelation and Dissimulation

The constraint, however, is no panacea. It is not even a fail-safe cure for writer's block, as I noted in chapter 3. Given when and where the Oulipo began, it is hardly surprising that a number of its members, frustrated by their various inefficiencies, have also had recourse to the services of psychoanalysts. The analytic relationship turns out to be an important although sometimes subterranean theme in the work of Queneau and Perec, in particular.

PSYCHOANALYTIC AUTOBIOGRAPHIES

Queneau and Perec both wrote autobiographies: *Chêne et chien* (Oak and dog, 1937) and *W or the Memory of Childhood*. These anomalous examples of the genre are connected by the epigraphs that Perec used to introduce parts 1 and 2 of *W*: "That mindless mist where shadows swirl, / how could I pierce it" (WMC 1); "This mindless mist where shadows swirl, / – is this then my future?" (WMC 63). Together, the two epigraphs make up the last stanza of a poem from *Chêne et chien*, in which Queneau says that his life up to the age of five is covered by night (OC I 19). *Chêne et chien* is a psychoanalytic autobiography, the first in French according to Anne Clancier.[9] It recounts a quest for repressed childhood memories. In the second section, Queneau gives an account of his experience in analysis and evokes a primal scene (OC I 24). It emerges that his case is one of regression to the sadistic-anal stage caused by unresolved Oedipal conflict.

While *W or the Memory of Childhood* does not thematize psycho-analysis, Perec wrote the book while in treatment with Jean-Bertrand Pontalis.[10] It has often been called upon to ground interpretations of Perec's other works, and Claude Burgelin has, in turn, persuasively used "The Scene of a Stratagem" ("Les lieux d'une ruse"), Perec's essay on his experience of analysis, as a key to *W*.[11] The epigraphs quoted above indicate that, like *Chêne et chien*, *W* is an attempt to illuminate and dissipate the fog enveloping the memories of early childhood.

In both cases the quest is partly successful. *W* is organized around the ellipsis marking the division between parts 1 and 2, which corres-ponds to the separation of mother and child (WMC 61). Perec's only memory of his mother, or the only one recounted in *W*, is of their final moments together at the Gare de Lyon, before he left with a Red Cross convoy for the "free zone." Perec remembers wearing his arm in a sling and being given a comic whose cover showed Charlie Chaplin parachuting, but it emerges that he was wearing a truss, not a sling

(WMC 55). He offers an auto-analytic reading of this distorted memory – "it suggests suspension, support, almost artificial limbs. To be, I need a prop [*Pour être, besoin d'étai*]" (WMC 55; O 1 700) – and he goes on to explain how his experience of parachute jumping helped him interpret it: "Sixteen years later, in 1958, when, by chance, military service briefly made a parachutist out of me, I suddenly saw, in the very instant of jumping, one way of deciphering the text of this memory: I was plunged into nothingness; all the threads were broken; I fell, on my own, without any support. The parachute opened. The canopy unfurled, a fragile and firm suspense before the controlled descent" (WMC 55).

The ellipsis (*points de suspension*) at the centre of *W or the Memory of Childhood* is a double emblem: rupture and suture; broken threads and mending stitches; mark of discontinuity and promise of continuation (the "to be continued" of the adventure serial that makes up the book's other strand). At the end of "The Scene of a Stratagem," written shortly after *W*, Perec accentuates the second terms of these oppositions (suture, mend, continuation), sharing responsibility for the broken threads – "I had to retrace my steps, to remake the journey I had already made *all of whose threads I had broken*" (SS 172, my italics). And he gives an oblique account of the breakthrough in his analysis, which, he says, reassembled the fragments of his personal history and effected an irreversible change in his life and writing.

Similarly, Queneau's account of his analytic treatment in part 2 of *Chêne et chien* comes to a triumphant close. In the seventh poem, the mental apparatus is figured as a ship, with the passengers, crew, and captain corresponding to id, ego, and superego. The ship is hit by a storm and "more than one prisoner" (or repressed desire?) escapes. The crew disguise themselves as savages (probably an allusion to the programmatic revolt of Queneau's surrealist years), but then the ship enters calmer waters and the sailors put away their knives (OC 1 28–9). In the final poem of part 2, however, the id / ego / superego trio is replaced by a binary division: *Chêne et chien*, dog and oak, the two possible roots of Queneau's name. The poem correlates the oak / dog opposition with a series of others: gods / demons; ignoble / noble; tree of knowledge / serpent; heaven / hell. This is more Manichean than Freudian, as Alain Calame has pointed out.[12] And the poem ends with the dog descending into hell, while the oak rises and walks toward the summit of the mountain. Both Calame and Clancier have remarked that this does not match Freud's idea of sublimation.[13] From a Freudian point of view it is a kind of self-mutilation, a premature

Revelation and Dissimulation

repression of infantile wishful impulses, whose energy true sublimation would have harnessed for higher ends.[14] Nevertheless, in Queneau's poem, it is implied that the psychoanalytic cure gives access to the earthly paradise of the third part, "La fête au village" (The village fair).

"La fête au village" is not, however, Queneau's last word on the analytic treatment. In a late poem, "Le boulanger sans complexes" (The baker without complexes) from the collection *Fendre les flots* (Breaking the waves, 1968), he looks back skeptically:

Sur les égouts je naviguerai	I will navigate in the sewers
a dit le psychanalyste	said the psychoanalyst
sur les égouts je naviguerai	I will navigate in the sewers
même si cela sent mauvais	even if it smells bad
j'y pêcherai vieilles godasses	I will fish out old shoes
et je lui dirai finement	and tell him cleverly
quoi que désormais tu fasses	whatever you do from now
on tu seras chaussé vachement	you'll be neatly shod
et si je pêche une vieille boîte	and if I fish out a rusty
de thon tout rouillée	old tuna tin
je dirai que c'est dans tes rêves	I'll say it was in your dreams
que je l'ai trouvée	that I found it
l'autre au fond de la barque	the one reclining in the boat
se laisse doucement emmener	lets himself be gently led
lequel des deux est le monarque	which of the two is the monarch
lequel est le lessivé	which the one being had
mais parfois un rai de soleil	but sometimes a ray of sun
par une bouche éclate un jour	light breaks in through
	a manhole [mouth]
alors il faut le saisir pareil	then you have to seize it like
au mitron devant son four	the baker's boy at the
	oven door
cette lumière comestible	this edible light
hors la sentine attirera	will draw from the bilge
quelque tourment putrescible	some putrescible torment
transformé en harmonica	transformed into a mouth organ
(OC I 599)	

170 How to Do Things with Forms

Here the treatment is envisaged as a navigation in the sewers, with the analyst fishing out old shoes and rusty tuna tins, whereas in *Chêne et chien* part 2, the nets brought up edible fish (OC I 23). The patient allows himself to be taken for a ride (*mené en bateau*) and had, or cleaned out (*lessivé*). But the experience is redeemed by illuminations, which come from the world above through manholes (*bouches d'égout*) or the talking mouths (*bouches*) of patient and therapist, and provide a kind of nourishment – edible light – permitting the analysand to hoist himself out of the bilge-water and convert his torment into music (the poems of *Chêne et chien*). The analyst, by contrast, seems quite at home in the sewer. In *Chêne et chien*, relating a phase of negative transference, Queneau coined the portmanteau word *pyschanasouillis*, from *pyschanalyse, souiller* (to soil), and *fouillis* (jumble) (OC I 30). In "Le boulanger sans complexes" the negative judgment implicit in the earlier coinage seems to be definitive. If a cure is adumbrated, it is one that the analysand effects by extirpating himself from the psychic refuse of the subconscious rather than exploring it. The joyful scatology of "La fête au village" has given way to a disquieting eschatology, which is suggested here by the putrescible torment, and dramatized in another poem from *Fendre les flots*, "Résipiscence" (Resipiscence):

Fiel en pluie tombant sur la ville	Rain of gall falling on the city
où le chagrin hurla	where grief howled
ombre que la nuit ourla	shadow hemmed by night
n'y a-t-il plus de sentence?	is there no longer a sentence?
Vers ce qui point rouge	Toward what breaks red
blanc vert	white green
aube d'un jour neuf découverte	dawn of a new day discovered
assiste ma résipiscence (OC I 561)	[may] my resipiscence tend[s]

Resipiscence is defined in the *Oxford English Dictionary* as "repentance for misconduct; recognition of one's past misdeeds or errors" and "the action or fact of coming to one's senses, or of returning to a more acceptable opinion." The first sentence of the poem seems to be a highly compressed vision of judgment: a rain of gall, lamentation, a mysterious shadow hemmed by night. It may be worth remembering here that Queneau grew up in Le Havre, a city devastated by Allied bombing in September 1944, the effects of which he describes in the essay "The Café de la France."[15] The second sentence of the poem is hardly less enigmatic. The new day dawns in three colours: red, white, and green, the colours of the Italian flag, but also, traditionally, the colours of charity, faith, and hope, the theological virtues, as Queneau noted in a manuscript (OC I 1430).[16] This short poem seems to be recording the start of a new life, or perhaps expressing desire for a new start, since the verb *assiste* may be read as a subjunctive: "*may* my resipiscence tend or open the way" (the expression *assister quelqu'un vers quelque chose* means to help someone to achieve something).

In her notes to the Pléaide edition of Queneau's poems, Claude Debon reproduces a draft version of "Résipiscence":

Vinaigre en pluie sur la	Rain of vinegar on the
cité où le malheur hurla	city where sorrow howled
ombre que la nuit ourla	shadow hemmed by night
n'y a-t-il plus de sentence?	is there no longer a sentence?
vers le jour qui point mauve	toward the day that breaks
rouge blanc et vert	mauve red white and green
italie des sonnets, des vers	italy of sonnets, of verses
assiste ma résipiscence	[may] my resipiscence tend[s]
pénitence	penitence
incompétence (OC I 1430)	incompetence

Manuscript notes reveal that this is an acrostic: the Latin proverb *vincit omnia veritas* (truth conquers all) can be read vertically in the first syllables of each line. Calame claims that the proverb functions here as an initiatory motto (*devise initiatique*), to which André Blavier responds skeptically, pointing out that a poem written around the same time can be read as encrypting the sentence "J'aimais Suzanne. Ah!" ("I loved Suzanne. Ah!").[17]

Rather than trying to adjudicate in the debate, I would like to consider how the manuscript evidence alters our reading of the poem. The encrypted proverb reinforces the etymological meaning of the title: coming to one's senses, recognizing the truth. Yet without the manuscript, the acrostic is virtually illegible, since *vinaigre* is replaced by *fiel*, *cité* by *ville*, while *Italie*, first home of the sonnet, disappears. All that is left of the proverb is *omnia ver as*, and it is doubtful that anyone could have reconstructed it from the finished poem alone.[18] Queneau's compositional method here resembles what Roussel calls his "evolved procedure," and as Michel Foucault pointed out, had Roussel not left *How I Wrote Certain of My Books* for posthumous publication, the words and phrases subjected to that procedure would probably never have been discovered.[19]

The example of "Résipiscence" shows how the manuscripts provide support for an autobiographical reading of *Fendre les flots*. In the latter part of this late book, Queneau reassesses his life, judging certain episodes severely, while discreetly signalling the beginning of a new phase.[20] When he looks back at his experience of psychoanalysis in "Le boulanger sans complexes," he sees it as a scam which neverthe-less, accidentally or providentially, provided occasions for a different sort of illumination. *Fendre les flots* encrypts an autobiographical secret: Queneau's return to spiritual preoccupations.[21] From a Freudian point of view such a return is a relapse into illusion.[22] And it could be argued that "Le boulanger sans complexes" is eminently ill-titled, since it shows the author still working through his negative transference, thirty years after the end of the analysis.

Turning back now to Perec, I mentioned above that in "The Scene of a Stratagem" he gave an oblique account of the breakthrough in his analysis with Pontalis, which occurred in 1975, shortly after he finished writing *W or the Memory of Childhood*. Philippe Lejeune has shown how after the publication of *W*, Perec changed direction: in the summer of 1975 he abandoned two autobiographical projects: *Lieux* (Places), and *L'arbre* (The tree).[23] From then on, autobiography would intervene more obliquely in his writing. In 1969 his ambition had been to rival Leiris and Proust, organizing a totalizing work around his life story; from 1975 on it was to exhaust the field of generic possibilities: "to write all that it's possible for a man of today to write" (ss 142). In October 1976, during the week after Queneau's death, Perec launched into the composition of the long novel that he had been planning for years: *Life: A User's Manual*, which he completed in less than eighteen months.[24] Yet rather than gratefully leaving the treatment behind, he seems to have brought some analytic baggage into the new work.

Life: A User's Manual is a murder mystery of a sort. The central characters are an eccentric millionaire, Bartlebooth, and his employee, Gaspard Winckler. Bartlebooth's perfectly futile lifetime project consists of painting five hundred seascapes at ports around the world, having them converted into puzzles by Winckler, solving them one by one, and then having the reconstituted pictures treated with solvent at the sites of their painting to leave blank sheets of paper. Winckler the puzzle-cutter finally outwits Bartlebooth the puzzle-solver with the 439th puzzle. Bartlebooth dies, half blind and exhausted, with an X-shaped gap left in the puzzle, and one piece left to place, in the shape of a *W*. Throughout the book there are indications that Bartlebooth's death is not an accident and that Winckler has planned or wished it: "Gaspard Winckler is dead, but the long and meticulous, patiently laid plot of his revenge is not finished yet" (LUM 6); "And behind that ever-closed door the morbid gloom of that slow revenge, that ponderous business of two senile monomaniacs churning over their feigned histories and their wretched traps and snares" (LUM 200). It would, I think, be misguided to search for a single, definitive solution to the enigma of Winckler's motive, which seems to be a deliberately insoluble mystery: the gap or absence around which the web of stories has been woven, the unknown in the formula. The gap is, after all, a fundamental figure in Perec's work, and in *W or the Memory of Childhood* he relates it to a possible etymology of his patronym: "My family name is Peretz. It is in the Bible. In Hebrew it means 'hole'" (WMC 35).

Isabelle Dangy-Scaillierez has shown how several stories in *Life: A User's Manual* warn against yielding to the temptation of an ultimate solution: "The charm of The Solution […] is at once offered as a temptation and unmasked as a mirage."[25] Nevertheless it is precisely this temptation that sharpens the eye and enables the reader to make new conjectures, bringing out connections that had previously gone unnoticed, as Claude Burgelin showed in 1996, when he published *Les parties de dominos chez Monsieur Lefèvre* (The games of dominoes at Monsieur Lefèvre's place). Winckler and Bartlebooth, Burgelin argues, correspond to the analysand and the analyst, particularly the writer in analysis and the analyst as reader and writer, or more specifically still, Perec the autobiographer in analysis and his analyst the prolific and polyvalent author Pontalis. Burgelin's book is nuanced (and 250 pages long). At the risk of making it sound more ad hominem than it is, I identify its key points as follows: Pontalis failed to appreciate the significance of *W or the Memory of Childhood*; he betrayed Perec's trust by discussing his case in public and publishing thinly disguised accounts of it; and the treatment was less effective than Perec suggests in "The Scene of a Stratagem."

On 28 January 1975, Perec noted in his diary: "J-B P gives me back my 'heap of relics' and asks if I want a third session."[26] "Heap of relics" refers, in all probability, to the manuscript of *W*. Burgelin argues that, for the analyst, *W* was little more than a compilation of screen memories, used to construct what Donald Winnicott calls a "false self." This gives a special resonance to Winckler's revenge in *Life: A User's Manual*. Not only is the W-shaped piece the puzzle-cutter's signature, it may also be a way of symbolically imposing the book *W* on the analyst figure, who could not see that it contained the answer and insisted on continuing the search for an illusory *X*.[27] Pontalis discusses Perec's case in at least eight published texts, three of which appeared in the *Nouvelle revue de psychanalyse* while the analysis was still under way.[28] He used a series of false names, but readers of *W* would have had no trouble identifying the patient. It is more than likely that Perec felt his trust had been betrayed.[29]

One of the disguised quotations or "implicitations" (to employ Bernard Magné's expression) in *Life: A User's Manual* can be read as a coded denunciation of the analyst's indiscretion. It comes from a letter that Freud wrote to Oskar Pfister in 1910: "Discretion is incompatible with a satisfactory description of an analysis; to provide the latter one would have to be unscrupulous, give away, betray, behave like an artist who buys paints with his wife's housekeeping money or uses the furniture as firewood to warm the studio for his model. Without a trace of that kind of unscrupulousness the job cannot be done."[30] In *Life: A User's Manual* these words are put into the mouth of a decidedly shady character, a nightclub owner named Didi (the verbal overlap between the two passages is more extensive in the original, where Perec uses Marthe Robert's translation of Freud's letter):

> Didi goes in for the "artistic" pose, that is to say he justifies his stinginess and pettiness with remarks of the sort: "You can't get anything done without bending the rules," or "If you want to be up to achieving your ambitions you have to be prepared to act like a shit, expose yourself to risks, compromise yourself, go back on your word, behave like any artist taking the housekeeping money to buy paints."
> Didi doesn't expose himself to risk that much, except on stage, and compromises himself as little as possible, but he is without doubt a shit, detested both by his performers and his staff.
> (LUM 292–3; O II 339)

Burgelin suggests that Pontalis, as well as failing to appreciate the significance of *W* and betraying his patient's trust, was less than completely successful as a therapist in Perec's case. This emerges from a close examination of the dates inscribed in *Life: A User's Manual* and

Perec's unpublished papers. The novel describes an apartment building at a particular moment in history: 23 June 1975. On this date, Perec wrote in his agenda "The old man is dead," echoing St Paul's letters, where the death of the old man is necessary to make way for the birth of the new.[31] This watershed does not correspond to the last session of Perec's analysis, twenty days before, or to the earlier "break-through" event evoked in "The Scene of a Stratagem," but to the beginning of his relationship with Catherine Binet.[32] Perec followed the example of Joyce, whose "Bloomsday," 16 June 1904, was the day he started falling in love with Nora Barnacle.[33] "The old man is dead" implies a new life beginning (*incipit vita nova*) for the writer, but as Burgelin points out, it also applies proleptically to a character that Perec would later imagine: Bartlebooth, who in *Life: A User's Manual* dies on 23 June 1975. So the beginning of Perec's new life coincides with the death of a fictional character who corresponds to the analyst, while the cure, it seems, came from another quarter, as Queneau suggests with respect to his own case in "Le boulanger sans complexes."

Extending Burgelin's allegorical interpretation, there may be a further reason for Winckler's hostility. Fredric Jameson writes that *Life: A User's Manual* thematizes non-alienated labour in the form of the hobby.[34] This is true, but in order to pursue his hobby, Bartlebooth alienates the labour of Winckler, who comes to Paris as a penniless young man, signs a mysterious contract with the millionaire, and gives him the best years of his life. The contract controls Winckler's ingenuity but also destines its products to be destroyed without trace. His work is not only alienated but annulled. Here I would not agree with Gabriel Josipovici when he writes that Bartlebooth's project harms no one.[35]

The relationship between Bartlebooth and Winckler may reflect a situation in which Perec felt that he was being exploited, or "lessivé" to use Queneau's expression. He was, after all, paying to provide material for Pontalis's conference papers, articles, and book chapters, while working as a research librarian, and having to supplement his income to fund the treatment, which he had begun partly because he was unsatisfied with his literary productivity.[36]

HIDE-AND-SEEK

Life: A User's Manual and *Fendre les flots* can be read as containing supplements to the autobiographical books *W or the Memory of Childhood* and *Chêne et chien*: in different ways, they mark the beginning of a new life and cast a critical eye on the psychoanalytic institution. But these readings are not self-evident. They depend in part on posthumous paratexts: diaries and manuscripts. Rather than the framed revelations of *Why I Have Not Written Any of My Books, The Great Fire of London*, or *Not One Day*, we are dealing here with strategically dissimulated autobiographical content.

The posthumous paratexts continue a game of hide-and-seek that Queneau and Perec began playing almost as soon as they started to publish: partly revealing concealed design features and encrypted content, while indicating the partial nature of the revelations. When Queneau presented the form that he had invented for the first part of *Elementary Morality* at a meeting of the Oulipo in 1974, he spoke of "a little Chinese music." Métail took this hint and ran with it, exploring the formal and philosophical parallels between the book and certain classical Chinese poems.[37] But the full depth of Queneau's debt to the Chinese tradition in his final work did not become apparent until Debon examined his drafts and journals to prepare the Pléiade edition of his poems in the early 1980s and found that each prose poem of part 3 corresponded to one of the sixty-four hexagrams of the *I Ching*.[38]

Similarly, in a 1979 interview with Jean-Marie Le Sidaner, Perec said that two rules govern the compendium-poem in chapter 51 of *Life: A User's Manual*, then explained one of those rules but not the other. Magné scrutinized the poem in vain until, in the early 1990s, one of his graduate students, Dominique Bertelli, discovered that it contained a diagonal acrostic, spelling the word: *âme* (soul).[39] Two readers, at least, were already in on the secret: the German translator Eugen Helmlé, for whom Perec had annotated a copy of the novel, and the English translator David Bellos, with whom Helmlé had shared information.[40]

The paratexts that have prompted new ways of reading the work of Queneau and Perec have not been found accidentally. They belong to archives constituted by the writers (as well as their executors). Of course it is common to keep drafts and diaries, especially when they may have economic value for legatees. But a writer may also choose to let the final version stand alone, as Proust did, destroying the manuscripts of the early volumes of *In Search of Lost Time*.[41] Queneau and Perec, by contrast, were both careful archivists. And both liked to play with the reader. Perec admits to this inclination at the beginning of *W or the Memory of Childhood*: "Once again the snares of writing were set. Once again I was like a child playing hide-and-seek, who doesn't know what he fears or wants more: to stay hidden, or to be found" (WMC 7).

Not all the Oulipo's writers encrypt patterns and secrets in their work. Jouet believes firmly in laying his cards on the table, since knowledge of a book's "formal principle" can prompt readers to discover important aspects of its meaning (RP 63), and explaining how a work was made facilitates the reuse of the devices in question. In a programmatic preface to his rapidly growing collection of novels, *La République roman* (The novel republic), he writes: "the way I see it, a form arrived at by one or other of our great forerunners enjoins us to take it up again in order not to be original but to include ourselves in a community of the form, or as I'd rather call it, 'The Republic of Forms' (once I would have said 'the communism of forms')."[42] On the other side of what Levin Becker has called "the biggest active debate in the workshop" (MSC 77) is Mathews, who refused to be drawn in an interview with Lytle Shaw:

> LS: I don't want to lose the opportunity to ask you about your own constrictive procedures. I've never heard an account of some of the very specific mechanisms that allowed you to write some of your books.
> HM: And you never will! In the Oulipo there are two schools of thought: one – Perec, Calvino to some extent, and several other people – says that it is normal to reveal your methods. The other school – Queneau, myself, Roubaud – says that not revealing your methods makes them work better. For one thing, it takes care of the problem of readers saying "Oh that's all it is!"[43]

The separation between the schools of thought is not quite as clear as Mathews makes it seem, and the motivations for adopting one position or the other may be complex. Giving the reader a full "road map" may be more generous and community-spirited, but it may also be a way of capitalizing immediately on one's formal ingenuity. The risk of such a strategy is that it may pre-empt the reader's explorations and ultimately shorten the work's reception. On the other hand, revealing nothing about constraints and forms may mean that they go unnoticed, and few modern writers are prepared to take that chance. It is natural to hope that toil and ingenuity will be appreciated one day. The game of hide-and-seek that a writer plays is often one in which, as for a patient discussed by Winnicott, "it is joy to be hidden but disaster not to be found."[44]

FORMAL ENCODING
AND PARANOID INTERPRETATION

In chapter 5, I cited Queneau's explanation of the significant numbers in *Witch Grass*. By combining thirteen with his signature number seven, he encoded a particularly gloomy meaning in the structure of the novel: existence itself is essentially and perpetually unhappy. By publishing "Technique of the Novel" four years later, he provided a key to the code and encouraged his readers to interpret the numerical structuring in his published novels and those he would go on to write. While military and security codes are designed to restrict the number of people who can receive an encoded message, the formal encoding practised by Queneau, Perec, Roubaud, and other members of the Oulipo aims to delay full reception of the message, thus prolonging the process of interpretation.[45] As Charles Grivel has said, literary encryption aims to slow reading down.[46]

Writers might want to do this if they believe that the ideal work should be readable and rereadable, cohering in the mind when first read, but also containing certain features that readers are likely to miss if they do not read it again. Such is the model that Queneau proposes in his essay "Strange Tastes" (1938), where he compares the well-made text to three things: a marrow bone, which must be broken in order to suck out the marrow; an onion, which can be peeled layer by layer; and a bird whose flight may be hard to follow for those accustomed to looking down (LNF 67). Of these comparisons, the first two imply that the deep or difficult reading is more valuable than the superficial or easy one. The nourishment is in the marrow not the bone (this comparison is explicitly borrowed from the prologue to Rabelais's *Gargantua*), and simply to skin the onion would be to pass over its layered complexity. The bird comparison, however, suggests that a literary work should be amenable to an immediate understanding, which should provide a starting point for deeper comprehension: "In order to follow the bird in its flight, you have to have seen it take wing" (LNF 67).

In "Strange Tastes," Queneau's contemporary example is Joyce's *Ulysses*: "*Ulysses* can be read *like* a novel; and then one goes beyond" (LNF 67). When Jacques Benoist-Méchin asked to see the scheme of *Ulysses* in order to translate the final section accurately, Joyce replied: "If I gave it all up immediately, I'd lose my immortality. I've put in so many enigmas and puzzles that it will keep the professors busy for centuries arguing over what I meant, and that's the only way of insuring one's immortality."[47] This remark suggests a second and less idealistic reason for prolonging interpretation: it may be a bid to outlive one's biological self and one's contemporaries, who are also vying for the scarce attention of readers and a place in a crowded canon.

Significant constraints and forms function like Joyce's enigmas and puzzles, recruiting a certain readership and training it to read in a certain way. Only readers with a bent for puzzle-solving will have the patience to uncover the hidden patterns. Such readers are often fans and completists, collecting works and information about the author in a highly focused manner. Their reading tends to be iterative: they work through the texts repeatedly, drawn on by the ideal of an exhaustive and totalizing interpretation, motivated by a desire to crack the fundamental code of the work.[48] The results may sometimes be described as paranoid.[49]

In very general terms, a paranoid reading is one that is not acceptable in a given interpretive community because it is felt to attribute significance to too many aspects or features of the text: it foregrounds what should be left in the background in order for the work's meaning to remain clear.[50] It is a reading that is judged to make something out of nothing, to paraphrase Brian Carr, or that seems to join too many dots, as Richard Rorty puts it.[51] My main concern here will be a particular variety of paranoid interpretation induced by writers who not only employ constraints and construct elaborate forms, but also demonstrably use those features to encode specific meanings.

Some of the experts on such writers admit to paranoid tendencies. Claude Burgelin refers to his "overinterpretive skids" and to the "lively critical paranoia" induced by Perec's work.[52] Bernard Magné confesses that his rereading of the same author borders on obsessive behaviour and writes ironically of his "unanswerable demonstrations."[53] He even mounts a defence of paranoia, concluding an article on *W or the Memory of Childhood* with a citation from the Robert dictionary, according to which the condition is generally stable and not associated with any loss of intellectual capacity.[54] These characteristics of paranoia are both mentioned by Freud in his essay on the case of Daniel Paul Schreber, and both are attested by recent psychiatric research.[55]

Jonathan Culler goes a step further, arguing that a degree of paranoia is inseparable from deep understanding of communication in certain contemporary social contexts. He gives the following example in his essay "In Defence of Overinterpretation":

If I greet an acquaintance by saying as we pass on the sidewalk, "Hullo, lovely day, isn't it?", – I don't expect him to walk on muttering something like, "I wonder what on earth he meant by that? Is he so committed to undecidability that he can't tell whether it is a lovely day or not and has to seek confirmation from me? Then why didn't he wait for an answer, or does he think I can't tell what sort of day it is that he has to tell me? Is he suggesting that today, when he passed me without stopping, is a lovely day by contrast with yesterday, when we had a long conversation?" This is what Eco calls paranoid interpretation, and if our interest is in simply receiving messages that are sent, then paranoid interpretation may be counterproductive, but at least in any academic world, with things the way they are, I suspect that a little paranoia is essential to the just appreciation of things.[56]

In a discussion of the Oulipo's critical reception, Garréta has defended paranoid interpretation in somewhat different terms: "I'd be inclined to say that it's very important these days, at the present time, to be paranoid. Why? Because most of what we see and interact with is no longer natural in any way, and all our representations and our actions on the real are coded from underneath by a whole series of logico-mathematical processes."[57]

The defences of paranoia mounted by Culler and Garréta are realist in tenor. In academic worlds, Culler implies, apparently simple messages may well conceal malicious and perverse intentions. Digital media, Garréta suggests, shape our representations and actions in ways that most of us are barely aware of. Her remark, made in 2011, was prescient, foreshadowing the age, upon us now, of alternative facts and deep fakes. But whether it is important to be paranoid depends on precisely what it is that we are seeing and interacting with. Academics may sometimes be justified in their suspicious interpretations of each other's speech, and users of the internet and apps should certainly be wary of how they are being tracked and targeted, but does it follow that a dose of paranoia will benefit literary interpretation?

The realist argument can be adapted to justify paranoid readings of texts that are, it is claimed, inherently paranoid in their functioning. Slavoj Zizek and Brian McHale associate paranoid reading with modernism as opposed to postmodernism.[58] According to Zizek, the modernist text is superficially incomprehensible and remains incomplete until supplemented by an interpretation, but the process of supplementation is open-ended and can lead, with Joyce, for example, to interpretive delirium.[59] The postmodern text, by contrast, is superficially comprehensible, although it can be defamiliarized by interpretation.[60] McHale characterizes the modernist / postmodernist distinction differently. He suggests that modernist fictions often revolve around epistemological quests, searches for knowledge, which give rise to paranoid interpretation. Postmodernist fictions, by contrast, are more concerned with ontological projects of world-making or projection, for example the invention of an imaginary world by the secret society in Borges's story "Tlön, Uqbar, Orbis Tertius."[61] Such projects, according to McHale, often illustrate the dangers of paranoid reading, and prompt us to resist it.

The modernist / postmodernist distinction cannot, however, be used to limit the domain of an interpretive style. McHale does not deny that postmodernist authors like Thomas Pynchon and Don DeLillo induce as well as thematize paranoid interpretation. And interpretive delirium clearly predates modernism, as Umberto Eco shows in *Interpretation and Overinterpretation.*[62] Nevertheless one could attempt to maintain the realist position, arguing that certain texts from a broad range of historical periods solicit and so legitimate paranoid interpretation, while others do not. This is Eco's approach: "I am not assuring that it is fruitless to look for concealed messages in a poetic work: I am saying that, while it is fruitful for *De laudibus sanctae crucis* of Raban Maur, it is preposterous for Leopardi."[63] The suggestion is that we should let the text determine our interpretative style. But we cannot decide what kind of reading a text is calling for without already having interpreted it to some extent.

So is it simply up to us to choose an interpretive style? That is what Culler seems to be saying when, in his defence of overinterpretation, he abandons the realist position and argues that if interpretations are extreme, they have a better chance of bringing to light interesting connections that have so far gone unnoticed or unexamined.[64] At that point, Culler is justifying paranoid reading by appealing not to the paranoid characteristics of a context or a text but to the innovative nature of the result. It is an argument that has considerable persuasive force. In an individualistic society, who wants to be moderate, consensual, and therefore dull? What is wrong with paranoid reading anyway? Shouldn't we learn to "relax" and enjoy it? Over the last thirty-five years, a number of influential critics – notably Eco,

Eve Kosofsky Sedgwick, and Rita Felski – have replied in the negative, and made cases for restraining the tendency to overinterpret.[65]

Eco sees paranoid interpretation as a continuation of the hermetic tradition and Gnosticism, which identified truth with "what is not said or what is said obscurely and must be understood beyond or beneath the surface of a text."[66] For Eco, paranoid interpretation not only discerns hidden secrets but also, crucially, applies an obsessive method, which compels it to dispense with the criteria of economy and coherence that normally guide scientific research and forensic investigation, halting the inquiry once an explanation has been found that is relatively simple and consistent with the rest of the evidence.[67] Paranoid interpretation is guided instead by two "principles of facility": an excess of wonder, leading to an overestimation of the importance of coincidences, and the inversion of cause-effect sequences (*post hoc ergo ante hoc*).[68]

Once produced in accordance with these principles, a paranoid interpretation is liable to be ruled out by a community of "cultivated readers" who share a background of "standard encyclopedia knowledge," Eco says.[69] In *The Limits of Interpretation*, he argues with support from Peirce that even if we cannot definitively grasp the real meaning or meanings of a text, we may be able to approach them asymptotically by a process of public agreement among interpreters, and we can certainly rule out illegitimate readings.[70] This stance is open to a sociological objection: there may be various communities, each with its claims to be cultivated, and each with a differently constituted knowledge base. More philosophically, it could also be argued that since we construct what Eco calls the *intentio operis* (the "intention of the work") by interpreting it, the constructed "intention" cannot be an independent guide to interpretation.[71]

The difficulty of drawing a clear line between interpretation and overinterpretation is nicely illustrated by one of Eco's examples. He mentions an article by Giosuè Musca on his own novel *Foucault's Pendulum*, which he says is among the best analyses he has read: "He masterfully isolates many ultraviolet quotations and stylistic analogies I wanted to be discovered; he finds other connections I did not think of but that look very persuasive; and he plays the role of a paranoiac reader by finding out connections that amaze me but that I am unable to disprove – even though I know that they can mislead the reader."[72] This is not an anomalous case. The most acute readers of authors who like to play hide-and-seek end up, at some point, going "too far" in the sense that some of their interpretations end up provoking skeptical reactions, either from the author, as in this case, or, more significantly in terms of Eco's own argument, from the fellow members of the readers' interpretive communities.[73] In such cases the skeptical reactions often result from the sense that the principle of economy, rather than that of coherence, has not been respected: the paranoid part of the reading is coherent with the rest, but it seeks to explain features of the text for which there are simpler, more economical explanations.

I do not want to suggest that the most paranoid readings are the most interesting. As Culler admits, "many 'extreme' interpretations will no doubt have little impact, because they are judged unpersuasive or redundant or irrelevant or boring."[74] Queneau reached a similar conclusion after years of work collecting the forgotten texts of literary eccentrics ("fous littéraires") for an "Encyclopedia of Inexact Sciences," which he partially integrated into the novel *Children of Clay* (one half of the encyclopedia bore the subtitle "History of Paranoid France"): "Nothing much came of my search. I'd exhumed little more than a bunch of paranoid reactionaries and doddering blowhards. 'Interesting' lunacy proved hard to find" (LNF 168).[75]

What I am arguing is that if, as Eco says, a text "is a device conceived in order to produce its model reader," then a certain kind of text, which uses constraints and forms to encode meaning, tends to produce a model reader who is inclined to overread.[76] Being able to read such a text well (being able to decode the hidden meanings) means having acquired a disposition to go "too far," that is, to "decode" meanings that cannot be authenticated by the author or by critical consensus.

DEEP FORMALISM

In an analysis of Perec's "La clôture," Jean-Jacques Poucel writes that virtuoso formalism can produce a "bedazzled blindness," a "form-fascinated reading."[77] When readers sense that a constraint is at work, they are preoccupied by the attempt to identify it. Once identified, the constraint tends to obscure other features of the text, as Perec remarked (EC II 170). In prose fiction, constraints can skew interpretation toward puzzle-solving and turn attention away from dimensions of the work that would normally engage the reader affectively, such as plot development and character portrayal, which can come to be regarded as superfluities to be stripped away in pursuit of the formal structures underneath. Deep formalism of this kind operates on the assumption that if structures are difficult to discern, they must be more important than what can be easily grasped or what commands the reader's attention. For all its plumbing of putative depths, this way of reading works against the imaginative immersion that Perec defends when he expresses his wish "to write the sort of books that are devoured lying face down on your bed" (ss 142) and that Clémentine Mélois celebrates in *Dehors, la tempête* (Outside, the storm). Deep formalism may be fuelled by curiosity but it can also be driven by the fear of looking or feeling stupid if one misses a coded message. As Kosofky Sedgwick writes, "The first imperative of paranoia is 'There must be no bad surprises,'" which ends up meaning that there can be no good ones either.[78]

Another hazard of deep formalism is that it often yields progressively less interesting results. This can be illustrated by examining Perec's personal numerology. As I explained in chapter 5, the numbers eleven and forty-three feature frequently in Perec's writing and structure it in various ways. Magné's enumeration of these mentions and functions may leave some readers dubious with regard to particular cases, but it is convincing on the whole, and no one has challenged his biographical explanation of the numbers' significance. A strong case can also be made for the resonance of the palindromic pair seventy-three / thirty-seven, related to Perec's own birth date: 7 March 1936 (or 3/7/36). Since he was born in 1936 he was thirty-seven in 1973. Thirty-seven and seventy-three feature principally as functions, determining structures, and Perec justified their use in notes for an Oulipo workshop.[79]

Numerological reading becomes somewhat more speculative when Bernard Magné wonders why *La clôture* contains seventeen poems and why the number seventeen structures several other texts.[80] The poems of *La clôture* allude to the rue Vilin, the street where Perec lived as a boy with his parents, and the site of his mother's arrest. The date of the arrest, which Perec did not cite in *W or the Memory of Childhood*, but which is recorded on the *acte de disparition*, was 17 January 1943.[81] Magné writes: "Hidden in the sphere of private papers, the number seventeen would thus represent a masked, encrypted, clandestine *æncrage*, the deepest point of this 'art inscribed to the enclosed buried.'"[82]

Magné affirms that with the *æncrage* of seventeen we have reached the deepest level, but Rémi Schulz has kept digging and come up with more potentially significant numbers. In his vertiginous essay "31, maquette à démonter" ("31, Disassembly Kit": an allusion to

Cortázar's *62 A Model Kit*), Schulz writes: "Magné has noted the importance of the initials C and S in chapter 40, so it can hardly be by chance that Anne Breidel has for lunch five dishes beginning with C and for dinner five beginning with S, *but is it pure coincidence that the difference in calories between these two meals is 464, the number under which Cyrla Szulewicz was deported to Auschwitz in train 47?*"[83] (emphasis added).

C and S are the initials of Perec's mother (Cyrla Szulewicz) and of a character called Cat Spade who appears in chapter 40 of *Life: A User's Manual*. Schulz refers to Magné's fantasia on the names in that chapter, in which it is pointed out that Anne Breidel's calorie notebook contains a list of items that seems to have been composed in order to underline the initial letters C and S rather than to reflect a particular diet. We can follow Schulz so far without too many skeptical scruples. But how did he arrive at the number 464? Adding the calories for the lunch items beginning with C produces a subtotal of 532, and repeating the operation for the dinner items beginning with S gives 996. The difference between the two totals is 464. But how do we know that Perec's mother was deported under the number 464? The French police at Drancy kept entry and exit lists, and the exit list for 11 February 1943 is given in Serge Klarsfeld's *Mémorial de la déportation*, which Bellos cites in his biography of Perec.[84] Perec himself does not refer to Klarsfeld's work. If we ask whether the encryption of the number 464 is something that Perec *could* have meant, the answer will have to be yes. He could have, since we know that Perec, like his friends in the Oulipo, was given to elaborate games with numbers.

This lead can be followed further still. The *Tableau complet de la valeur énergétique des aliments habituels* (Complete table of the energy values of common foodstuffs), which Anne Breidel is said to be using in her calculations, is an actual pocket guide. Examining how Perec used this source may give us some clues to what the list encrypts. Table 6.1 correlates the entries in the notebook with the caloric values in the *Tableau*.

The fact that Perec chose items beginning with C and S over their (sometimes approximate) equivalents in the *Tableau* strongly suggests an intention to highlight these letters:

Agneau (deux petites cotelettes) → **C**ôtelette d'agneau (deux)
Fromage caillé → **C**hèvre frais
Myrtilles → **S**orbet aux myrtilles

Table 6.1
Anne Breidel's calorie notebook

Life: A User's Manual (177)	La vie mode d'emploi (O II 210)	Tableau complet de la valeur énergétique des aliments habituels	caloric value	
			Perec	Tableau
Grated carrots	Carottes râpées	Carottes crues	45	
Lamb cutlets (2)	Côtelette d'agneau (deux)	Agneau (deux petites cotelettes)	192	
Courgettes	Courgettes	Courgette	35	
Goat cheese, fresh	Chèvre frais	Fromage caillé	190	
Quinces	Coings	Coing	70	
Fish soup (without bread or garlic mayonnaise)	Soupe de poissons (sans croûtons ni rouille)	Soupe de poissons	80	90
Fresh sardines	Sardines fraîches	Sardines fraîches	240	120
Cress and lime salad	Salade de cresson au citron vert	Cresson	66	22
Saint-Nectaire	Saint-Nectaire	Cantal/Chester/ Emmenthal/ Gervais/Gruyère	400	
Blueberry sorbet	Sorbet aux myrtilles	Myrtilles	110	55

The caloric values in Anne Breidel's list are either equal to or multiples of those in the *Tableau*, with one exception: the fish soup, from which Anne has whittled ten calories, since she forwent bread and garlic mayonnaise. This subtraction, and the multiplication of the values for sardines, cress, and blueberries may reflect both Anne's precision in recording – she has "scrupulously entered all she ate at breakfast, lunch, and dinner" (LUM 177) – and her powerful appetite. Between meals she makes "forty or fifty furtive raids [...] on the fridge (LUM 177), so it is not surprising that she should dress her cress salad, prefer sorbet to plain fruit, or have a double helping of sardines. The manipulations may also have been performed to obtain a difference of exactly 464 between the items beginning with *C* and those beginning with *S*. But here it should be remembered that the difference in question does not appear in the text; it is the result of one among many possible arithmetical operations on the numbers in the table.

At this point, even a patient reader may want to ask: Is this line of inquiry worth pursuing? A law of diminishing returns seems to be operating, for the extraction of the number 464 adds little to what has already been signified more clearly (if still obliquely) by the initials C S and the recurrence of eleven and forty-three elsewhere in *Life: A User's Manual*: the deportation and killing of Perec's mother. Here interpretive paranoia might be profitably tempered with the reflexive irony that is evident in Magné's dry reference to his own "unanswerable demonstrations."[85]

A third hazard of deep formalism is that it can impoverish the context in which a work is interpreted. Formal encoding lays claim to an extra degree of attention from readers, and by rewarding that attention, it often increases their admiration for the writer. When admiration approaches idolatry, it can lead to concentration on a single author's life and work. This is one of the reasons for Foucault's vigorous attack on the author function in "What Is an Author?" If we are always reading texts to find out what they tell us about a writer's unique personality or development, we may be blind to how they are informed by wider contexts and how they participate in larger historical developments.[86]

Experts strongly focused on a single author do of course read around that author's work. Nevertheless, even such reading around can be directed by liminal texts or paratexts, such as Perec's list of authors cited in the post scriptum to *Life: A User's Manual*, or Queneau's lists of books read, which have been edited and published by Florence Géhéniau.[87] These lists could shape a lifetime's reading. They could also favour a daydream of totalization. National traditions are too big to be mastered, and institutional canons often too unstable, but it may seem possible to master the work of a single writer combined with his or her personal canon. Even if critics did, however, manage to read everything the writer had read, would that be enough? Wouldn't they also have to have all the writer's experiences in order to understand the works completely? Wouldn't critics have to be able to rewrite those works from scratch, as the hero of Borges's famous story, "Pierre Menard, Author of the Quijote," claims or pretends to have done? The "theme of total identification with the author" (to cite Novalis, cited by the story's narrator) is a phantasm.[88] As Hans-Georg Gadamer argues in *Truth and Method*, taking issue with Friedrich Schleiermacher's theory of "the divinatory act, by means of which one places oneself entirely within the writer's mind, and from there resolves all that is strange and alien about the text," understanding is not simply the reproduction of an original production, but always a productive activity as well.[89]

PARABLES OF PARANOIA

I have been claiming that the fiction of Queneau and Perec has the potential to induce a form-focused style of paranoid interpretation. But if we attend to the narrative content and not just the forms of their novels, both authors also warn against the dangers of overreading.

Chapter 31 of *Life: A User's Manual,* which Schulz puts under the microscope in "31, maquette à demonter," recounts a case in which the interpretation of signs reaches paranoid extremes. Elizabeth Breidel, working as an au pair in London, accidentally lets her employer's son drown in the bath. She panics and flees the country. The child's mother returns to find her son dead and commits suicide. The father, Sven Ericsson, discovering the bodies, reconstructs the events, and vows to avenge the deaths of his wife and son. The au pair proves very hard to track down since she was working under an assumed name. Ericsson hires an army of detectives and after years of fruitless searching begins to lose his reason.

> I awoke covered in sweat. I had just dreamt the obvious solution to my nightmare. Standing beside a huge blackboard covered in equations, a mathematician was concluding his demonstration, in front of a turbulent audience, that the celebrated "Monte Carlo theorem" was generalizable; that meant not just that a roulette player placing his stake on a random number had just as much chance of winning as a martingale player systematically doubling his stake on the same number on each loss in order to recoup eventually, but that I had as much if not more chance of finding Elizabeth by going to Rumpelmeyer's for tea next day at sixteen hours eighteen minutes precisely than by having four hundred and thirteen detectives looking for her.
>
> I was weak enough to give way to the dream. At sixteen hours eighteen minutes I went into the teashop. A tall redhead left as I entered. I had her followed, uselessly of course. Later on I told my dream to one of the investigators who was working for me: he said quite seriously that I had only made a mistake of interpretation: the number of detectives should have made me suspicious: 413 was obviously the inverse of 314, that is to say of the number π: something would have happened at eighteen hours sixteen minutes.

So then I began to appeal to the exhausting resources of the irrational. (LUM 147)

The interpretive activity recounted here is paranoid in that it makes something out of nothing, and Ericsson himself judges it to be irrational in a moment of greater lucidity. This overinterpretation is also associated with a vengeance that is both sadistic and self-destructive. Elizabeth herself informs Ericsson of her whereabouts in order to end her nightmare of persecution. After cruelly delaying his action, Ericsson murders Elizabeth and her husband, then commits suicide.

In a study that analyzes this and other stories of detection in Perec's work, Isabelle Dangy-Scaillierez notes that the detectives are often paranoid readers, and their determination to crack the code, to solve the enigma, is almost always futile and ruinous.[90] The paradigm case is the anonymous narrator in the unfinished novel *53 Days*, a professor of mathematics in the imaginary country Grianta, who is asked by the French consul to read a manuscript by Robert Serval, a famous author of detective novels. Serval entrusted the manuscript to the consul, saying that if he should ever disappear, the reason could be found in the text. And sure enough he disappears. The consul gives the manuscript to the narrator because he was at school with Serval and is fond of puzzles. The manuscript is entitled *The Crypt* and naturally the narrator tries to decrypt it: "*The Crypt*: it suggests a hidden meaning, a message encrypted. Somewhere in the book is a name, or a detail, or a *petit fait vrai*, or an invented one, a clue, or a color, or a sign, or a cipher which refers to a secret in Serval's possession, a secret for the sake of which he may even have met his death" (5 3 D 43).

As Dangy-Scaillieriez points out, this presumption is questionable. Why should the message, if there is one, have a precise and limited location in the text? Couldn't it be conveyed by the story as a whole, signifying parabolically?[91] The narrator of *53 Days*, myopically focused on details, obsessively comparing *The Crypt* to four intertexts privileged by the author, cataloguing similarities and differences, is an anti-model reader, and is finally forced to admit his error. Having supposed that *The Crypt* concealed scandalous information about the complicity of a French diplomat in the theft of a statue of the Roman emperor Diocletian, he comes to see that the theft is not the novel's secret theme but simply the source of a number of incidental details: "I thought that all these new puzzle pieces would make it easier to figure out the truth that Serval had put in *The Crypt*. In fact he only makes a brief allusion to the statue on page 32, and none of his hints points significantly toward a supposedly 'real' culprit" (53 D 91). More disturbing is the realization that the consul has in fact used the manuscript of *The Crypt* to incriminate the narrator in the murder of Serval, of which he is himself guilty. "The book contains no hidden truth, it was just a decoy, a pretext" (53D 98). The narrator is a victim of the "vertigo of explanations without end" (53D 132). The story of entrapment can be read as a cautionary tale.

In Queneau's novel *Witch Grass*, the central character, Étienne Marcel, a Parisian bank clerk, is initially a kind of automaton who hardly thinks or feels. As his adopted son says, he is "asleep on his feet" (WG 80). But gradually he begins to reflect on his existence and experience it emotionally. He notices curious aspects of his environment, such as a hat in a shop window, filled with water, in which two little rubber ducks are floating (WG 9). He comes home to find that his cat has been shot (WG 13). The curiosity he entertains and the indignation he feels have a perceptible effect on Étienne Marcel, who appeared at first to be two-dimensional, a silhouette, but now begins to thicken, acquiring volume. The psychological dimension of thought and feeling is figured as his body's third dimension. Étienne's curiosity develops into an existential and phenomenological project of affirming his freedom through gratuitous acts, such as his visit to a cheap diner at Blagny (WG 33), and of "bracketing" the objective world, as Husserl recommends: "Not to take the destination of an object into account, what a strange activity!" (WG 130).[92]

This project, however, is gradually derailed by the mysterious Pierre Le Grand, who having observed the transformation in Étienne, decides to make his acquaintance and see what fun he can have with the former silhouette. When they visit a junkyard that belongs to the significantly named Père Taupe (Old Mr Mole), they notice a blue door. Pierre Le Grand imagines that the door conceals a hidden treasure, while Étienne thinks not: "obviously he hasn't dug a cellar in the embankment [...] that door has some sort of value in his eyes perhaps it's connected with some incident in his life perhaps it revealed happiness to him" (WG 97). This spontaneous interpretation of the door's meaning turns out to be right. Taupe has treasured the door not because it hides a treasure, as Pierre and various other characters come to think, but because he carved his name and that of his sweetheart into it, before her untimely death (WG 258). Nevertheless, Étienne allows himself to be drawn into Pierre's treasure hunt, which gives rise to a great deal of paranoid speculation on the part of La Mère Cloche, a local witch-like midwife, who plans to steal the treasure and imagines that Pierre and Étienne are gangsters who will stop at nothing to achieve the same objective. The treasure hunt may also be related to the death of Ernestine, the waitress at the diner, who marries Taupe with his hypothetical riches in mind. That, in any case, is Taupe's belief: "and *because of that door*, Ernestine, that I loved, is dead" (WG 259).[93]

I would suggest that the blue door is a metaphor for the metaphor of depth. The moral of the fable seems to be that obstinately digging for buried meanings can limit the mobility and range of the interpreter's attention. In this case the digging is futile, since the door's meaning does not lie beyond or beneath it, but in a metonymic connection with another place and time. It is further suggested that such interpretation may be harmful as well as misguided, since it distracts Étienne from the adventure of thought and may have led to Ernestine's death.

By choosing to reveal only some of their formal rules and patterns, Queneau and Perec may induce interpretive paranoia, but both authors also warn against that condition, prompting us to resist the fascination of enigmatic details and free up our attention. The metaphor of depth is not always misleading, and it has recently found an eloquent defender in Joshua Landy.[94] But the kind of deep formalism that Oulipian texts tend to induce can favour a counterproductive hardening and fixing of the hermeneutic gaze. Resourceful readers need "soft eyes," as Jason Baskin has put it.[95] To literalize Baskin's metaphor somewhat, they need to be able to focus without deactivating peripheral vision, so as to increase their chances of noticing what they have not set out to look for.

In *Rereading*, Matei Călinescu writes: "The major revelation produced by rereading for the secret is simply (but also mysteriously) the value of attention, of intense concentration, of focused ingenuity, of total absorption."[96] But when we are concentrating intensely on solving a puzzle in interpretation, it is easy to forget that we are free to direct our attention to other aspects of the text. When we are totally absorbed in the attempt to discover the text's real message beneath appearances, to crack its code, we can lose sight of the fact that interpretation is always, as Gadamer writes, productive as well as reproductive, and that "understanding always involves something like applying the text to be understood to the interpreter's present situation."[97]

7

Games Gone Wrong

TAKING PLAY SERIOUSLY

The Oulipo is a ludic group. Its members tend to adopt a markedly playful posture when they collaborate to conduct writing workshops, perform in public, or compose their collective publications, such as the *Oulipo compendium* or *L'abécédaire provisoirement définitif*. This posture can serve as a refreshing corrective to others, still common in the literary field, which are characterized by solemnity, self-importance, and a sense of entitlement. Perhaps the corrective is especially salutary in France, where what Paul Bénichou called the consecration or coronation of the writer ("le sacre de l'écrivain"), beginning in the mid-eighteenth century, invested the role with a quasi-sacred mission, assumed most powerfully by Victor Hugo.[1] That mission was accompanied by a mystique, which lingers around the "great writer," or "grantécrivain" in Dominique Noguez's coinage, a figure that has metamorphosed and receded since the time of Hugo, but not disappeared.[2]

The features shared by Noguez's "great writers," from André Gide to Marguerite Duras (capacity to build fictional worlds, stylistic distinction, generic versatility, active presence on the literary scene, fluent handling of ideas, political engagement) do not include humour or playfulness. It is not that "great writers" must all and always be sternly serious, but playfulness is not a core requirement, and too much of it may prevent a writer from being taken seriously, as I remarked in chapter 1.

There is, as Jean-Jacques Poucel notes, "a general tendency to classify the members of the Oulipo as tricksters. The implication being that their work does not qualify as *serious* literature."[3] Sometimes it is more than an implication. Henri Meschonnic, one of the group's fiercest critics, uses the term "ludic" as a sledgehammer argument against its approach: "It works, potential literature. And the better it works, the better it reveals the perverse effect of the ludic: persuading others and in the end oneself that *playing* and poetic self-invention [*s'inventer poème*] are the same thing."[4] Laurent Jenny, too, sees the ludic as a limit: "The Oulipo is thus condemned to revisit the whole literary field as a game, unable to escape from the ludic in order to ground itself. Here as elsewhere, in the ideology of the times, play has become a destiny rather than the exercise of a freedom."[5] Calvin Bedient associates the group with gambling and games of chance, calling it "a literary gaming house."[6] In response to a paper given by Jean-Jacques Thomas, in which Oulipian formal play was mentioned, Gérard Genette remarked that if play there was, it was "a sad sort of play."[7]

All these objections characterize the Oulipo's playfulness as disabling rather than empowering. It is true that playfulness can be exasperating when it is a way of refusing to acknowledge matters of serious concern. It can also seem sad if it is symptomatic of a restricted emotional range or an incapacity to get down to work. Relentless playfulness reaches an extreme in the condition known as Witzelsucht or pathological joking, which goes with an insensitivity to the humour of others.[8] Queneau diagnoses something like collective Witzelsucht in the trenchant essay "Humor and its Victims" (1938), although the addiction that he deplores is self-interested rather than hapless:

> There are people who make of humor, of that sort of humor, a daily practice. I've known some myself. This is the most convenient pose imaginable, as I soon realized. Whatever they do, they have a ready excuse. If they commit a dirty trick, they do it in the spirit of humor, and of course, if it's meant in the spirit of humor, we can only bow down before it. If they commit an act of cowardice, that's also in the spirit of humor. If they do nothing at all, that's still in the spirit of humor […] Perpetual humor is truly a form of intellectual cowardice. (LNF 50–1)

The Oulipo's humour is not perpetual in this sense (always available as an excuse), but it is always close at hand in the group's collective publications and performances, which might leave an unsympathetic critic with the impression that the group can only play at writing. Such a critic might be inclined to echo the question put by the editor

Clémence Balmer to the novelist Victor Miesel in Le Tellier's *L'anomalie*: "When are you going to stop playing?"[9] But this question loses much of its pertinence and force when the critical gaze turns from exercises to a representative range of Oulipian works.

I have already shown that the writers of the Oulipo are capable of seriousness and gravity. Indeed loss and mourning are key themes in Perec's *W or the Memory of Childhood*, Roubaud's *The Great Fire of London*, and Garréta's *Sphinx,* while Jouet's *Mountain R (La montagne R)* and Audin's *One Hundred Twenty-One Days* are thoroughly preoccupied with domination and violence, at a range of scales, from the domestic to the national. Fournel's branching novel *Chamboula* is written with a light touch, but the story of modernization that it tells is also unambiguously a chronicle of colonial greed. After the arrival of multinational oil and mining companies, the African village at the centre of the narrative, "Le Village Fondamental," significantly changes its name to "Macombo," which recalls the town of Macondo in Gabriel García Márquez's *One Hundred Years of Solitude,* similarly plundered by a banana company strongly resembling United Fruit.[10]

The writers of the Oulipo rarely point to the grave themes of their works when faced with the charge of being merely playful, as if such a strategy would oblige them to adopt a self-important posture and take themselves too seriously. What they do instead is defend the value of play and challenge its separateness from the serious. This defence has taken a number of forms. For a start, play can have instrumental value. As noted in chapter 1, Queneau pointed out that "recreational mathematics" had stimulated the development of topology, number theory, probability, and game theory, implying that the Oulipo's "recreational poetics" could do the same for literary theory and practice. The benefits of playing can also be more direct. I observed in chapter 5 that the Oulipians have testified in their lives and their fictions to the protective powers of play as a psychological defence mechanism. What Ishion Hutchinson has said of poetry, that it is "an inner armor available to anyone," applies also to the Oulipo's playful devices, emblematized by the children's eodermdromes in Roubaud's *Parc sauvage.*[11]

As well as leading to extrinsic benefits, playing can be intrinsically valuable. In his manifestos, Le Lionnais argues that "when they are the work of poets, entertainments, pranks, and hoaxes still fall within the domain of poetry. Potential literature remains thus the most serious thing in the world" (OPPL 28). For Le Lionnais, this transmutation of play into poetry is not effected simply by adding something that play

Games Gone Wrong   195

lacks, such as emotion or sincerity, for virtuosity in play can be an independent source of aesthetic value: "People are a little too quick to sneer at acrobatics. Breaking a record in one of these extremely constraining structures can in itself serve to justify the work; the emotion that derives from its semantic aspect constitutes a value which should certainly not be overlooked, but which remains nonetheless secondary" (OPPL 30). I believe that the Oulipians would agree with W.H. Auden when he writes in *The Dyer's Hand* that "among the half dozen or so things for which a man of honor should be prepared, if necessary, to die, the right to play, the right to frivolity, is not the least."[12]

The Oulipo takes play seriously, then, as a potential source of long-term cognitive benefits, a defensive strategy, a space for the production of aesthetic value, and perhaps even a fundamental right. But this valuing does not entail an idealization of play. In fact I will be arguing that if we read the works of the Oulipo writers attentively, we will see that they have explored the darker margins of games, play, and sport. The fictions of Roubaud, Perec, and Garréta, in particular, illustrate a possibility discussed by psychologists and ethologists, although more rarely noted by philosophers: real play can be perverted or corrupted by the aggression that it ideally serves to sublimate. In registering the ambiguity of play, Roubaud, Perec, and Garréta are, for all their artifice, realists.

DECEPTION

Roubaud's short and apparently simple narrative texts *La dernière balle perdue* (1997) and *Parc sauvage* (2008), subtitled *roman* (novel) and *récit* (narrative) respectively, mirror each other intriguingly and offer complementary perspectives on play, dramatizing its potential uses for protection and for harm. Both are stories of childhood friendships during the Second World War in the so-called free zone south of the Loire. In both, the friendships are cemented by games – or so it seems initially at least.

In *Parc sauvage*, which was discussed in chapter 5, the child protagonists Jacques and Dora play at a series of games, which the novel imagines or reconstructs in fond detail. These include adapting and acting out stories from *The Jungle Book* and dam building (PS 83–4, 118–20), as well as the more sophisticated mathematical and verbal game of composing eodermdromes. In *La dernière balle perdue*, Laurent Akapo and his friend Norbert Couarat (nicknamed NO) also build dams and play-act, but their favourite games are competitive rather than co-operative: racing paper boats, playing marbles, and collecting lost golf balls (DBP 20–1, 23, 37, 50).

In both narratives, while the children play, the Occupation is closing in on them and their parents. In *Parc sauvage*, Dora's mother, who is Jewish, having planned to cross the border into Spain, finally decides against flight, as Perec's mother did (WMC 33). Denounced by a neighbour in Toulouse, she is deported with her daughter. Both die in the camps (PS 133). In *La derniere balle perdue*, Laurent's father, John, who is working for the Resistance, is arrested in Lyon and sent to Buchenwald. He survives until the liberation of the camp but dies there of typhoid, like Robert Desnos at Terezín (DBP 67).

Both books recount irremediably tragic stories, which end about fifty years after the war, in 1992 (*Parc sauvage*) and 1995 (*La dernière balle perdue*), but the endings have very different tones. In *Parc sauvage*, the adult Jacques, now known as James Goodman, finds a kind of peace, epitomized by the final eodermdrome in English: "tears at rest" (PS 135). The loss of his parents and his country is not repaired but is in some way eased by the preservation of Dora's journal, which records both her short life and the game that she and Jacques played together right up until their escape from Sainte-Lucie. A kind of peace is found also at the beautiful conclusion of Roubaud's *Ciel et terre et ciel et terre, et ciel* (Sky and earth and sky and earth, and sky, 1997) – Proustian in its movement and music even as it argues with Proust – where Goodman's visit to Constable Country in Suffolk opens the way back "to the center of his memory" and offers the possibility of reconciliation with the past.[13]

By contrast, the end of *La dernière balle perdue* is utterly bleak, principally because the plot hinges on a betrayal that differs in two respects from the denunciation of Dora's mother in *Parc sauvage*: it is committed by an intimate, and it is not a one-off act confined to wartime, but plays out over the half-century that follows. During the war, Laurent's parents John and Éléonore help get refugees across the border into Spain (DBP 59). One day in 1944, John says goodbye to his family and leaves for an "important, dangerous, and secret" meeting (DBP 62). Laurent is to come to the meeting place, on a cliff near a lighthouse, after his day's work as a caddy on the golf links. Caddying for the Gestapo commander Geideherr – whose name is a metathesis of Heidegger – and the leader of the local militia, he overhears their conversation and realizes that they have been informed of the secret meeting. Since he cannot leave the links without arousing suspicion, he implores his friend Norbert (NO) to go and warn his father. NO asks what Laurent will give him in return. "Whatever you want," says Laurent, and swears that he will keep this open promise (DBP 62).

John eludes the ambush, alerts his network, and escapes to England. He is parachuted into France and establishes contact with the Resistance command in Lyon, which has been "decimated by the arrest of Marc Bloch" (DBP 109). Afterwards, he is followed by a Gestapo agent. A cinematic chase through the *traboules* (covered passageways) ensues. But John's apparently providential familiarity with the labyrinthine ins and outs of the neighbourhood serves only to delay his capture. The German officer waiting for him in the train that he finally boards says: "Do come in, Monsieur Akapo [...] We were waiting for you" (DBP 113).

At the end of the novel, NO reveals:

> I didn't warn your father, that day, about the trap the Germans had set; I went home and took it easy. What happened was, at the last minute your father got suspicious and didn't go to meet the contact from London, a double agent,
> my father. (DBP 133)

Having fraudulently extracted an open promise from Laurent on the day of the ambush, and then discovering that John has escaped, NO avenges the failure of his betrayal by demanding that Laurent give him 55,555 golf balls lost on the links:

> "But it will take me years!"
> "I know, but you promised."
> "I promised. I will keep my word." (DBP 64)

Laurent commits a tragic error by respecting, in this exceptional case, the principle stressed by his father, in English: "A gentleman always keeps his word," and forgetting the paternal caveats added in relation to truth-telling: "a gentleman never lies [...] except to his enemies"; and "in wartime, one has to conceal the truth. Only then can exceptions be made to the absolute rule that forbids a gentleman to lie" (DBP 29, 57). Laurent fails to recognize his enemy and to see that on a personal level wartime may continue beyond a declaration of peace between nations.

Is he naïve? Or a victim of his Kantian adhesion to the Categorical Imperative? Both, no doubt, but there is more going on here. This novel, published in a series for young readers, is haunted by the tradition of the *conte*, the folk tale, which clearly informs Laurent's love for the ethereal, princess-like Marie-Ange, who eventually marries NO. In folk tales the hero is often charged with a "difficult task." What NO demands of Laurent belongs to the category that Vladimir Propp calls "tasks of supply."[14] As A.E. Stallings writes in her poem "Fairy-Tale Logic," these tasks are actually more than difficult in the old tales: they are impossible without the aid of magic.[15] In Roubaud's modern tale, Laurent's task is not quite impossible but calculated to consume and alienate a whole life, and in the end NO intervenes to slow Laurent's approach to the limit and make it asymptotic by collecting the stray balls himself (DBP 132). Thus he deprives Laurent of the formal satisfaction of keeping his word, before revealing that the promise was invalidated from the start by his deception.[16] The significance of NO's nickname is by this point abundantly clear: he embodies the spirit of negation. And the portmanteau of his family name (Couarat) unpacks itself irresistibly to produce *couard* (coward) and *rat* (rat).

It would be reductive, however, to consider Laurent simply as a passive victim and to see the task as succeeding completely in its alienating intent. The collecting of the balls has uses and meanings for him, too, and these he protects by refusing to allow NO to come and check on his progress (DBP 84–5). In attempting to keep his word, he is paying tribute to the memory of his father as well obeying his injunction ("a gentleman always keeps his word"). And rather than simply accumulating the balls, he invents an installation for their display, disposing them at first on the wall of his bedroom, beginning in the top left-hand corner, the number of each ball painted in blue and the date of its collection in black (DBP 69–70). Laurent lives in a villa composed of two symmetrical halves; he and his mother in the half named *Voici*, his aunt Jeanne in the *Voilà* half. After the deaths of his mother and aunt, he moves the collection of golf balls through the looking glass, as it were, to the room corresponding to his bedroom in the other half of the building, so as "to completely separate activities related to survival (eating, sleeping, reading …) from those required for the fulfillment of his promise" (DBP 84).

He survives, he keeps himself alive, in order to keep his promise, to pursue his "work in progress," which gradually covers wall after wall (DBP 124). The numbers of the balls are not written as numerals but as words in Basque, and Laurent says each one aloud as he paints it. The dates are inscribed and pronounced in English. "In 1968, after coming back from Scotland and Lyons, he decided to gradually whiten the numbers and the dates; from blue and black, they would shade into white; and the last inscription would be as white as the white of the last ball. He would speak the numbers more and more quietly, until his voice was absolutely silent" (DBP 126).

Here a striking similarity appears between Laurent's installation and Roman Opalka's OPALKA 1965/1–∞, which is the subject of an essay by Roubaud.[17] Beginning in 1965, Opalka began painting the sequence of whole numbers in white on black canvases, which he called *détails*. The idea – at once admirable and rather terrifying – was to continue for as long as he physically could. In 1968, he changed the backgrounds to grey, began recording his voice pronouncing each number in Polish, and started taking passport-like photographs of himself in front of the canvas after each day's work. On passing the million mark in 1972, he decided to add an extra percent of white paint to the grey that he used for the background of each new canvas, anticipating the moment when he would be painting white on white, invisibly.[18] The last number that he painted was 5,607,249, on 6 August 2011, the last day of his life.

The slow accumulation of the integers in order, the pronunciation of their names (in Polish or in Basque), the whitening (of the background in one case, of the numbers and dates in the other), the exhaustion of a life in the accomplishment of a single task: these common features strongly link the real and the fictional practices, and the relation is further underlined by Laurent's name. Akapo is a real Basque family name, but L. Akapo is also an anagram of Opalka.

And yet, there is a crucial difference. Laurent is not executing an aesthetic project; indeed, he uses the task as an anaesthetic, to numb the pain of loss. He is not intending to produce a lasting work: "When he was finished, he would destroy this strange and complicated decoration. He would remove the balls one by one in reverse numerical order, working backwards from the last to the first. He would put them into one-hundred-and-fifty-liter garbage bags, hire a truck [...], dump the lot on the lawn of NO's magnificent residence, and tell him to count them, to check that they were all there" (DBP 126). Like Percival Bartlebooth's project in *Life: A User's Manual*, Laurent's is destined to come to nothing in material terms. Bartlebooth's task is built around puzzle-solving, and Laurent's originates in a game. During the war, having given up their other games for golf, NO and Laurent begin to count the lost balls that each boy finds (DBP 31). Laurent keeps his booty in a "war chest," and looks after NO's collection as well. He is the score-keeper of this "new and exciting competition" (DBP 49–50).

The competition conforms to Bernard Suits's persuasive account of what it is to play a game: "to attempt to achieve a specific state of affairs [prelusory goal], using only means permitted by rules [lusory means], where the rules prohibit use of more efficient in favour of less efficient means [constitutive rules], and where the rules are accepted just because they make possible such activity [lusory attitude]."[19] In a game of golf, the prelusory goal is to put the ball into all the holes on the course. The constitutive rules stipulate that this may be done only by striking the ball with one of a series of clubs (rather than carrying it to the hole and dropping it in, for example). The lusory attitude of the players consists in accepting these highly inefficient means because they set up an interesting game, the winner being the one who makes the best of the inefficiency and requires the smallest number of strokes.

In the game that NO and Laurent invent, the prelusory goal is to collect more balls than one's competitor, and the lusory means are limited by a constitutive rule specifying that the balls must be officially lost; it is prohibited to keep any others (DBP 50). In the task that perverts the game, the means and the rules are preserved, but the prelusory goal is altered: now it is to reach a total of 55,555. The crucial change, however, is in the attitude of the "player," Laurent, who no longer accepts the rules just because they make the game possible, but because he has promised to do whatever NO asks. This dissolves the game. As Colas Duflo writes, following Johan Huizinga: "there is no play under duress."[20] As soon as one is obliged to play, one is no longer truly playing.[21]

Before the war, from the first day of school, Laurent and NO are inseparable friends and seem to form a complementary pair. As one of their teachers says: "The two of them made one excellent student" (DBP 19–20). When they are mocked at school for wearing golf pants, they blend into a formidable agent: "the combination – NO + Laurent – constituted a single and very effective fighter, with two hard pairs of fists and faultless coordination" (DBP 52). But this perfect unity is an illusion. The war has already come between them, and the task that NO imposes on Laurent is a continuation of war by other means. The novel's punning title – a translator's nightmare or sleepless night – makes this point very neatly. The last lost ball (*balle perdue*), lost to

Laurent for good when NO snatches it from under his nose in the final scene, is also the last stray bullet (*balle perdue*) in that Laurent is a casualty of the conflict, fifty years after the declaration of peace. The ludic object is also a weapon. The playmate turns out to have been the worst enemy, not content to win and dominate but determined to negate and destroy the life of his opponent. In game-theoretical terms, he wins by monstrously dilating a single move so that it occupies the best part of a life, converting his struggle with Laurent into a one-shot game.

It might be objected that the reading proposed above gives too much weight to the material continuity between the competitive golf-ball collecting and the task of supply, and not enough to the different functions of the balls before and after Laurent's fateful promise. Is it really fair to implicate play in NO's destructive scheme? To answer this question, we need to return to Laurent and NO's childhood games, to see if there is also strategic and psychological continuity between them and the later pact.

Laurent tends to win the boat races because he folds the paper more skillfully: "Laurent's boats were better built, more robust that NO's. He often won. Sometimes, going round a corner, NO cheated" (DBP 22). Laurent is also better at marbles: "Laurent won more often. His marbles didn't go as far as NO's, but they rarely went out of bounds. He could have gone on playing like that for weeks, but NO got impatient" (DBP 23). NO loses patience with losing, and when they move on to collecting lost golf balls, he cheats again, "a bit" (DBP 31). Similarly, in class, he is "a bit of a copier" (DBP 19).

Rereading the novel, it is hard not to see these instances of cheating as early warning signs. The worm, it would appear, was in the fruit from early on if not from the start; and the occasional, minor cheating seems to have been practice for the long, systematic deception. Here the novel lends support to the psychoanalyst André Green when he nuances Donald Winnicott's assertion that "play belongs to health": "I think the activity of play can sometimes become distorted, corrupted and perverted, in society as well as in individuals."[22] This will strike many as obvious, parents and primary schoolteachers in particular.[23] Rather than speaking of a primal purity corrupted, Sergio and Vivien Pellis, authors of *The Playful Brain*, point to human play's roots in the developmental rough-and-tumble that we, as a species, have in common with many mammals and birds, and which is, they argue, fundamentally ambiguous.[24]

I do not want to suggest that *La dernière balle perdue* reveals the hidden nature of play in general, only that it points to a possible continuity between playing and domination and shows how far real play can be from the ideals of thinkers as different as Donald Winnicott, Bernard Suits, and Friedrich Nietzsche. Amia Srinivasan provides an elegant formulation of Nietzsche's utopian conception of play (expressed in *The Gay Science* and *Beyond Good and Evil*): "Play creates its own value and makes its own meaning. It needs nothing outside itself. Play can't properly be considered a project: it has no purpose apart from its disruption of purposiveness."[25] This idea of play is what Suits calls "radical autotelism," and it rules out all professional players, for a start.[26] But it also excludes all those who play for their health, or to socialize, or to turn their minds away from a source of anxiety. Without being a project, play can accomplish extra-lusory purposes such as these.[27]

In *Parc sauvage*, as I argued in chapter 5, Jacques and Dora's eodermdrome game is a means of psychological resistance. Even as they hide from the German soldiers who are searching Sainte-Lucie to find a radio transmitter and its operator, Dora insists on continuing the game: "it mattered to Dora, she stuck at it" (PS 134). And they are able to follow the prompting of their last eodermdrome: "Surtout, sors" ("Above all, get out") (PS 128). Tragically, as I mentioned above, Dora's mother fails to heed the oracle that speaks through the children's game.

The separation of play from everyday life, on which Johan Huizinga, Roger Caillois, Émile Benveniste, Bernard Suits, Colas Duflo, and other theorists in the field have insisted (Guy Debord is a characteristically bold exception), cannot be absolute.[28] Because the membrane that bounds play is permeable to aggression, a degree of circumspection in choosing playmates is generally warranted, even if there can be no guarantee against betrayal of trust. This was clear to Le Lionnais and Queneau when, in later middle age, they instituted cautious procedures for recruitment to the Oulipo.

COMPETITION

La dernière balle perdue tells the story of a victorious cheat and his honourable victim. In Perec's *W or the Memory of Childhood*, the account of the extinct society that inhabited the island of W tells a similar story of pseudo-ludic conflict, not between singular individuals but between classes. Kimberly Bohman-Kalaja has aptly described **W** as a "parable of corrupted play."[29] I argue in this section that its parabolic or allegorical significance has a very broad reach.

The book's autobiographical strand, to which I referred in chapter 6, alternates with another, printed in italics, which begins as an adventure story. In part 1 the narrator of this story is living in Germany under the name Gaspard Winckler, having deserted from the French Foreign Legion. One day he receives a letter summoning him to a meeting with a certain Otto Apfelstahl, who reveals that when the narrator was helped to desert by a Swiss organization, he was given the papers of a deaf-mute boy named Gaspard Winckler, who later disappeared when the yacht on which he was travelling with his mother was wrecked off the Chilean coast. The crew and passengers, with the exception of Gaspard, were all found dead in the wrecked vessel. Apfelstahl persuades the narrator to set out in search of the missing boy. His departure is imminent at the end of part 1, but we know from the first chapter of the book that he reached the island of W, near the location of the wreck, and found it deserted, the towns and facilities in ruins: "the lianas had unseated the foundations, the forest had consumed the houses; sand overran the stadiums" (WMC 4).

The relation between Winckler's narration in part 1 and the "continuation" of the adventure strand in part 2 is far from clear. The italic font common to both cannot mask the ruptures: the tense shifts from past to present, the narration from first person to third, the content from the story of a single life to quasi-ethnographic description of a society centred on competitive sport. At first, that society seems to be a realization of the ideals of Pierre de Coubertin, founder of the International Olympic Committee. But its fundamental cruelty soon begins to show.

The almost exclusively North European ancestral background of the population (WMC 67) is slightly disquieting for a start, given the existence on Chilean soil of an infamous commune of German emigrants formerly known as Colonia Dignidad (1961–2005), where the sexual abuse of children was systematic, and political prisoners were tortured during Pinochet's dictatorship. Chile was also a host country for Nazi fugitives, including the SS officer Walter Rauff, who was responsible for the deployment of mobile gas chambers during World War Two.[30]

The island of W has a rigid class system, with a hierarchy of administrative functions and sporting disciplines (WMC 72, 147). There is little mobility between disciplines, relegation to the pentathlon or the decathlon being "one of the very rare instances of changing team" (WMC 86). The complex rules governing the transition from Athlete to Official might seem liberal, but they are subject to the whims of the Hierarchy (WMC 154), and the impression given by the "Laws of W" that all the island's inhabitants belong "to the same Race" is misleading. Athletes, for example, are never chosen as members of the government, which is made up exclusively of Organizers, Judges, and Referees (WMC 72). Women have access to none of these functions.

Although all the Athletes represent one of the four villages, there is no real teamwork. Relay races are unknown: "here they would have no meaning, would not be understood by spectators: an individual win is always a win for the team, so a 'team win' means nothing" (WMC 82–3). The alliances that emerge when Athletes are competing for women in the so-called Atlantiads are unstable because they can be formed on the basis of two kinds of loyalty – to the village or to the discipline – which are in constant tension, and neither kind is robust, since both are undermined by the rest of the island's social arrangements (WMC 131–2).

In a kind of sporting Taylorism, Athletes are obliged to specialize in one kind of event. The history of the Olympic Games, with its multiple medal winners, like Jesse Owens at the Berlin Olympics (1936), shows that this policy is a mutilation of human possibilities (WMC 83–6). On W, the pentathlon and the decathlon, which require versatility, are transformed into joke events that mock the very idea of the multi-talented athlete (WMC 85–6). Winning is simply all that matters: "it is not Sport for Sport's sake, achievement for the sake of achievement, which motivates the men of W, but thirst for victory, victory at any price [...] victory at every level" (WMC 89). Athletes are nothing more than their victories, and therefore are known not by their own proper names but by those of the men who first achieved their most recent results (WMC 98–9).

In order to "heighten competitiveness" (WMC 89), losers are deprived of their evening meal. The consequent risk of creating a self-reinforcing "vicious circle" is obviated by encouraging the winners to overeat at the feasts held to honour them (WMC 92). The Organizers "put their trust in what they call, laughingly, nature" (WMC 92), but the system is engineered to exploit an artificially maintained hunger: "Sugar-starved, they usually bolt their food, stuff themselves like pigs" (WMC 92). The games on W are negative-sum: the privileges of the victors are more than balanced by the punishments inflicted on the vanquished. In the "noblest" event of all, the hundred-metre sprint in the Olympiad, the Athlete who comes last may be executed (WMC 110). The society of W has systematized infanticide: one in five female children is allowed to survive. Sexual violence is ritualized: in the Atlantiads, presumably fertile women are released in the stadium with half a lap's head start and pursued by Athletes who eventually rape them in public (WMC 124–5). Novice Athletes are used by their "protectors" as servants and catamites (WMC 146–7).

As in Kafka's *The Castle,* the Law is implacable but also unpredictable (WMC 117). The Officials may decide at any point to invert the results, granting victory to the athlete who came last (WMC 117). They see this as a reminder that sport is a "school of modesty" (WMC 120), but it is principally a reminder of their absolute power over the competitors. The Officials organize injustice, which they believe to be "the most effective stimulus [*le ferment le plus efficace de la lutte*]" (WMC 112; O I 740). "Permanent strife [*cette lutte permanente*]" is one of the great "Laws of W life" (WMC 132; O I 755). Curiously, however, the strife does not begin until adolescence: up to the age of fifteen, the children enjoy an idyllic existence, boys and girls "mixing quite freely and happily" (WMC 137–8). They are then separated and brutally initiated into "real life," to which "there is no alternative," as the narrator says, anticipating Margaret Thatcher (WMC 140). And yet a whole adult life of brutal exploitation is not enough to kill hope definitively: "even the most senior Athletes, even the doddery veterans who clown on the track in between races and are fed rotten vegetable stalks by the hilarious crowd, even they still believe that there is something else, that the sky can be bluer, the soup better, the Law less harsh; they believe that merit will be rewarded, that victory will smile on them, and be wonderful" (WMC 140). They are not wrong to believe that there is something else. Their mistake is to believe that luck or minor reforms will bring it about, when the objectives of the system to which they are subjected are "conscious, organized, structured oppression" and "the systematic annihilation of men" (WMC 161).

Perec's account of life on W has often been read as allegorizing the Nazi concentration and extermination camps, and this reading is irresistible, especially but not only in the final chapters.[31] The "Chief Trainer" is known as the Oberschrittmacher because the first person to hold the post was a German (WMC 102). But the term also recalls the use of the *Ober-* prefix in the naming of SS ranks, as Claude

Burgelin notes (O I 1090). The Officials give orders in German: "Raus! Raus! [...] Schnell! Schnell!" (WMC 154–5). In the penultimate chapter, the Athletes wear striped uniforms (WMC 161), and the future discoverer of the ruins of W will find remains very similar to those exhibited at the memorials and museums established on the sites of former Nazi camps: "piles of gold teeth, rings and spectacles, thousands and thousands of clothes in heaps" (WMC 162). The account of the games on W given in the penultimate chapter is mirrored in the final chapter by a long quotation from David Rousset's *L'Univers concentrationnaire* (*A World Apart: Life in a Nazi Concentration Camp*), which describes a sadistic parody of athletics inflicted by the SS on prisoners at Neue Bremm.[32]

Although W and the Nazi camps converge indisputably at the end of *W or the Memory of Childhood*, particular historical atrocities do not exhaust the meaning of the allegory, as indicated by the fact that the systematic femicide practised on W was not a feature of the camp system. The book's final sentence couples Nazi Germany with Chile in 1974: "Pinochet's Fascists have provided my fantasy with a final echo: several of the islands in that area are today deportation camps" (WMC 164). And Perec's imaginary ethnography suggests that the camps, under Pinochet or Hitler, are the clearest historical illustration of a more general phenomenon, which he named in a review of Stanley Kubrick's film adaptation of *A Clockwork Orange*: "violence is the continuation of exploitation, not 'by other means' [...] but by its own means, finally revealed, one might say: violence is the only truth of capital, its only instrument, its only resort [...] the camps are not and never were an exception, an illness, a defect, a disgrace, a monstrosity, but capitalism's only truth, its only coherent response."[33] Maryline Heck and Mireille Ribière observe that this passage is inspired by Henri Lefebvre's assertion in *Critique of Everyday Life* that fascism is the limit case of capitalism, and by Robert Antelme's characterization of the prisoner's lot in the Nazi concentration camps as an extreme of the proletarian condition.[34] The tone of Perec's review is unusually strident, as Alison James remarks, and might be thought to reflect a "rather peremptory leftism" ("un gauchisme assez crispé") in Burgelin's phrase.[35] The rhetorical effect derives largely from the very broad use of the term "capitalism" as shorthand for all forms of organized domination, going back to ancient social systems based on slavery, long before the rise of what Marx calls the "capitalist mode of production" in the fifteenth and sixteenth centuries.[36]

Capitalism is not mentioned in *W or the Memory of Childhood*, but the political critique implicit in the book is clear and forceful: exalting competition and struggle legitimates domination and leads via a slippery slope to atrocity. Incidentally, the book also suggests that an ideology of competitiveness can fail on its own very limited terms. The society of W has adopted the Olympic motto *Citius, Altius, Fortius* (Faster, Higher, Stronger) but significantly reversed the order of the terms (WMC 67, 111) to privilege strength, the capacity most directly related to physical domination, and downplay speed, which serves for flight as well as pursuit. Reversed or not, the motto is an exhortation to continual improvement of performance. But the starved and humiliated Athletes of W cannot excel: "it should come as no great surprise that the performances put up are utterly mediocre: the 100 meters is run in 23.4", the 200 meters in 51"; the best high jumper has never exceeded 1.30 meters" (WMC 161). These results reveal the hypocrisy of a motto that masks the society's real operative values. Here Perec's allegory resonates with research in education and economics that shows how an ideology of competitiveness can produce significant inefficiencies, as well as social harms, from the level of the individual learner or worker to that of the nation.[37]

A key sentence in the penultimate chapter clarifies the politically radical nature of *W or the Memory of Childhood*: "Submerged in a world unchecked, with no knowledge of the Laws that crush him, a torturer or a victim of his co-villagers, under the scornful and sarcastic eyes of the Judges, the W Athlete does not know who his real enemies are, does not know that he could beat them or that such a win would be the only true Victory he could score, the only one which would liberate him" (WMC 159–60). Like Laurent in *La dernière balle perdue*, the W Athletes fail to recognize their real enemies. But here they cannot be standing for the prisoners in the Nazi camps. The use of *kapos* or prisoner functionaries by the SS did lead to hostility among the incarcerated, but it cannot have been unclear to most of them who their real enemies were. Certainly it was clear to writers such as Robert Antelme, Primo Levi, David Rousset, Germaine Tillion, and many other former prisoners who have borne witness.[38] Once under arrest, the prisoners had very little chance of beating their enemies, at least until the administration of the camps began to collapse with the approach of Allied forces. Uprisings did occur, notably at Treblinka, Sobibor, and Auschwitz, and some prisoners did escape, but most of those involved did not survive.[39]

By contrast, it seems that the W Athletes need only become conscious of their oppression and band together to stand a fair chance of "true Victory." On W, there are two worlds: the world of the masters and that of the slaves (WMC 160). But a successful slave revolt seems to be a real possibility. It is perhaps significant that the humblest of the games on W, for unseeded Athletes, are known as the Spartakiads, recalling the international events sponsored by the USSR from 1928 to 1937, but also the historical figure for whom they were named: Spartacus, one of the leaders of a major slave uprising in the Roman Republic (73–71 BC), which began with a breakout from a *ludus* or gladiatorial school near Capua.[40]

Claude Burgelin suggests that the society of W has collapsed as a result of the progressive degradation narrated in the book: "The world of rules and customs that is supposed to regulate society on W falls apart at an accelerating rate; law is transformed into a negation of law, eventually bringing down even those who had engineered its hellish mechanisms" (O 1 1076). It is true that the contradictions and perversities of W's social system are progressively revealed, but this does not necessarily mean that they are progressing in the society described. The account of life on W is given in a relentless present tense right up to the penultimate paragraph of the penultimate chapter, which is followed by an ellipse marked by an asterisk and then by a paragraph imagining the future discovery of W. The system detailed up to the ellipse appears to be both atrociously stable and not entirely invulnerable to overthrow from within. Perhaps it is a revolution that has led to the downfall of the barbaric civilization of W. Perhaps the Athletes have escaped from their island prison. This possibility, discreetly left open, slightly mitigates the grimness of the book's ending.

In *La dernière balle perdue*, what begins as a game between the boyhood friends is perverted by NO and transformed into an unfulfillable and life-consuming obligation. When Laurent accepts the task, he is no longer playing the game of collecting lost golf balls because he has abandoned what Suits calls the "lusory attitude," that is, the attitude of a player who accepts the rules just because they make the game possible. Laurent feels bound by the promise that he made to NO. In Perec's account of life on W, the corruption of play is due to a dominant class of Officials who have abolished the lusory attitude by raising the stakes of competition to the point where the Athletes are literally competing for survival like gladiators in ancient Rome. The events for which they are trained from adolescence on are starkly opposed to the games they freely invent as children, and there is a bitter dramatic irony to their prospective imaginings: "They sometimes hear far-off shouting, thunderclaps, trumpet blasts; they see thousands of colored balloons floating by overhead, or magnificent flocks of doves. They know these are the signs of great celebrations which they will be allowed to join in one day. Sometimes they act them out in great joyful round dances, or else, at night, brandishing flaming torches, they rampage around in wild processions until they fall on top of each other in a heap, breathless and drunk with gaiety" (WMC 138). This turbulent, vertigo-inducing play, falling into the category that Roger Caillois calls *ilinx* (from the Greek for whirlpool), while founded on an illusion, is a reminder that competitive games (*agon* in Caillois's typology) are not the only kind. Perhaps it is also a prefiguration of what play could be for the Athletes were they to recognize and defeat their real enemies.

GAMIFICATION

In *La dernière balle perdue* and *W or the Memory of Childhood*, play is corrupted from without by a cheat and a class of oppressors respectively. In both books it is denatured by suppression of the lusory attitude. In Garréta's novel *La décomposition* (1999), the narrator-protagonist maintains a lusory attitude to a game that is both criminal and technically flawed. Falling victim to his own gamification of crime, he loses his grip on the distinction between the world of the game and the world that contains it.

In his introduction to the English translation of Garréta's *Sphinx*, Levin Becker writes that her later novels *Ciels liquides* (Liquid skies) and *La décomposition* are "excellent examples of the class of modern French novel or film that sounds charming or fun when you hear its synopsis but turns out to be sort of existentially upsetting when you actually read or watch it."[41] The novel is indeed existentially upsetting when read, but even hearing the synopsis of *La décomposition* might upset a Proustian and would certainly offend a member of what Christopher Prendergast has called the "Proust cult."[42] The narrator-protagonist has devised a plan for executing perfect crimes, murders that are not humanly motivated but determined by the rigorous impersonality of a constraint (D 23).

The player of this murder game counts off the sentences of *In Search of Lost Time* (*À la recherche du temps perdu*) until he finds one containing a proper name. Madame de Saint Loup, for instance, appears in sentence number thirty-seven. The player then chooses a busy public place:

> Now, take up a position one afternoon at some strategic location in any metropolis (station waiting room, subway turnstiles, café terrace at the corner of two avenues ...). Count the bodies. The thirty-seventh to pass in front of your chosen focal point is the one. Agreement in number. Now, look closely: is the passer-by a man or a woman? It's a man? You [...] give up on murder for today. It's a woman? Bingo! Agreement in gender. [...] Now you are obliged to execute the amphibious entity that has sprung up at the interface between fiction and the world [...] by stabbing, by shooting ... all of this determined in advance by the work's supplementary constraints. (D 29)

These supplementary constraints are never explained, and the principle constraints leave the murderer ample latitude for choice: no rule is given for determining the place, the time, or where precisely in the visual field to begin counting.

Having killed the stranger corresponding to a character from Proust, the player is required to go home and remove from an electronic copy of *In Search of Lost Time* all the sentences containing the name of that character or a pronoun referring back to it: "The idea, realized by the at once fortuitous and inevitable way in which the victim has been found, is to deny subjectivity as a criminal method in the decomposition of the novel and the depopulation of the world" (D 31). The denial, however, is not entirely convincing. The unregulated choices required of the killer are so many windows through which subjectivity, kicked out the front door, may easily return.

This is not a criticism of the novel. It is soon apparent that the narrator-protagonist is a well-read psychopath rather than a criminal mastermind: he has rhetorical and stylistic gifts but is not committed to coherent reasoning. And this becomes progressively clearer. On page 125, for example, he replies to the imagined objection that an "eliminated" character might reappear in a new work of fiction: "What does it matter to me, reader, what does it matter to me since, by virtue of my murder, she [Françoise] is effectively missing from her origin." But in fact she is missing only from the copy of *In Search of Lost Time* on the protagonist's hard drive (D 31), not from the numerous other copies, and certainly not from her historical origin in the mind of Marcel Proust. Even if the protagonist *is* the super-hacker he later claims to be, secretly performing his expurgations in online databases containing copies of *In Search of Lost Time* (D 233), and even if, as he argues, libraries containing paper books will soon be deserted (D 234), his enterprise has a fatally piecemeal character.

The projected decomposition of *In Search of Lost Time* does not aim to strip it of all characters. The historical figures François I and Charles Quint, who appear in sentence three, are spared, as are Eve and Adam from sentence twenty. The narrator justifies this clemency by arguing that the names of historical figures are already attached to a body (be it dead and buried), while the fictional characters native to the work should be "smothered in the cradle" (D 125). As to Proust's narrator, Garréta's narrator does momentarily envisage obliterating him as well, but this remains a daydream, contrary to the murderer's "principles of parsimony" (D 133). The named targets, then, are: "Swann," "Madame de Saint Loup," "Françoise," "Cottard," "Norpois," "Gilberte," "Berma," "Bergotte," "Bloch," "Verdurin," "Madame Blatin," and "Albertine."

Not all of these are effectively taken out. Distracted by imagining the murder in advance, the protagonist allows "Madame de Saint Loup" to escape (D 101), while "Bloch" eludes him by slipping into a backroom at a nightclub (D 217). The individuals corresponding to Gilberte and La Berma, a man and a woman, change places in a cinema, which leads to a conundrum: should the identifications be determined by temporal or spatial factors? Since the man arrived first, should he correspond to Gilberte (Gilberte's name appears before La Berma's in the relevant sentence). Or should the identifications be reversed, since the man and the woman swapped seats: "Shall we maintain that no conclusion should be drawn from chronology, and that the attribution of a name to each body should rather be determined by physical positions, the order of the seats read from left to right, like a sentence?" (D 192) This is the first mention of a spatial system for associating bodies with names. Without having resolved the conundrum, the narrator shoots the woman: "I have just killed a woman without knowing whether she is Gilberte or Berma. It's sloppy [*Ce n'est pas sérieux*]" (D 193).

From the narrator's formalist point of view, his error is one of imprecision. The impersonal rigour claimed for the constraint at the outset is by now seriously compromised. When the constraint dictates that the narrator must murder a friend, Monsieur de Cadillac, he fails to follow the designated target, knowing where to find him, and lapses into Wittgensteinian doubts about what it means to follow a rule: "If I contravened the procedure, which is what the rule comes down to in the end, wouldn't I be fooling myself and, believing that I was still following my rule, wouldn't I be already in the process of interpreting it, that is, on the point of pretending to follow it?" (D 206).[43]

Perhaps he does merely pretend to follow his rule. The murder of "Bergotte" (Monsieur de Cadillac) is narrated in the future and conditional (D 210–11), and that of "Verdurin" in the imperative (D 220–2), which casts some doubt on the accomplishment of these acts in the world of the story (although mention is made of the "late M. de Cadillac" on page 225). Similarly, the narrator's remark that he has seen nothing in the papers about the earlier deaths of "Swann" and "Françoise" may raise a doubt in the reader's mind (D 161). The narrator has told us that he shot "Swann," whose body fell from a window into the street (D 16), and that he cut "Françoise's" throat in her apartment (D 116). No attempt was made to hide either body. So it is strange indeed that there should be no trace of these crimes in the news.

The hypothesis that the narrator-protagonist is thoroughly delusional finds further support in the final chapter, entitled "[–   –]," where he addresses himself as *vous*. Travelling in a train, he sees a woman sleeping in the next compartment and dubs her Albertine. From this point on, it is not possible to say with certainty what happens in the storyworld and what the narrator imagines or dreams. It is as if the narrator had encountered a glitch in his murderous game, that is, a place where the coded model fails to mirror the world familiar from everyday life. So-called speedrunners are adept at exploiting glitches in videogames to advance quickly to the next level, but Garréta's narrator is confronted with a "game over" scenario.

He seems to fall asleep and wake again. "You must have fallen asleep, in the first moment you don't know where or who you are". (D 241), he says to himself, echoing the beginning of *Combray*.[44] Then he witnesses an erotic scene framed by a window, involving what seem to be the hand and face of "Albertine" and another woman's naked back, but as he says: "you no longer know if you are dreaming or awake" (D 242). The scene then begins to slide into the darkness, at which point another train comes flying past, and the protagonist shoots at his putative victim. But what he has shot is a reflection, as we are promptly told: "You want to get up, be done with it, go and find the woman you thought was sleeping in the next compartment, the woman you thought you had torn up with all the bullets you fired at a mirage in the night, at a mirror, find her and kill her sleep, flee in the night, *sleep no more* ..." (D 244). Firing repeatedly at a mirror, a mirage, the "perfect" criminal has missed his target and given himself away.

Reality breaks in finally "when a knock on the partition wall, then a second, perturb your heart, and the terror of a third knock resounding sets it beating in your skull till it bursts your eardrums with its dull, syncopated blows" (D 244). This loss of nerve is explicitly linked by means of citations in English to Macbeth's panic after murdering Duncan: "sleep no more" in the passage cited above, and "How is't with you, when every noise appals you" (D 244).[45] There is also an implicit allusion to Thomas De Quincey's famous essay "On the Knocking at the Gate in Macbeth." (Earlier, Garréta's narrator presented himself as a successor to De Quincey, delivering, like him, the fictional Williams's Lecture on Murder, considered as one of the Fine Arts [D 17]).[46]

In the essay on the knocking at the gate, De Quincey explains the powerful effect of this dramatic device by showing how it announces the return of normal human thought and feeling after the commission of a fiendish act: "the pulses of life are beginning to beat again: and the re-establishment of the goings-on of the world in which we live first makes us profoundly sensible of the awful parenthesis that had suspended them."[47] Ironically, however, in Garréta's novel, reality and ordinary life reassert themselves with a knocking that flaunts its fictional status. The protagonist's panic indicates that his fantasy world has shattered like the glass at which he fired, but the knocking is unlikely to affect the reader in the way described by De Quincey: it is difficult to inhabit the storyworld of *La décomposition* as one might be drawn into a performance of *Macbeth*, because the novel foregrounds its own and its borrowed styles so insistently, as Montserrat Cots Vicente and María Dolores Vivero García have shown.[48] The action is in the discourse at least as much as in the story.

The narrator's project unravels, leaving us uncertain as to what he has effectively done. It is clear, however, that he has been playing a game according to Suits's definition. His prelusory goal is to commit murders in a systematic and non-subjective way while eliminating the characters imagined by Proust. The highly inefficient lusory means are determined by the pseudo-Oulipian constitutive rules explained above.

Had he wanted simply to kill without a personal motive and "decompose" Proust's novel, he could have proceeded more efficiently. He rejects the surrealist method of depopulating the world by firing blindly into a crowd, as imagined by André Breton in the "Second Surrealist Manifesto," because it "stinks of inspiration" (D 19).[49] But a range of automatic randomization techniques might have guarded against selection bias in the designation of victims. And he claims to possess already a "little name-killing program," which he can introduce into online databases (D 233).

Although the narrator's game is flawed by the vagueness of the constitutive rules and the unattainability of the prelusory goal's literary component (Proust's characters are disseminated too widely and variously to be eradicated even by a super-hacker), he maintains a lusory attitude until the final scene, providing evidence, were any required, that playing games can be destructive. This applies to purely literary games as well. The clastic experimentalism discussed in chapter 2, which breaks down conventional forms and structures, is often playful in nature. The Oulipo's N + 7 procedure destroys the semantic coherence of the source text, usually producing comic effects. It might seem that Garréta is performing a similarly clastic operation on *In Search of Lost Time*. But unlike her narrator, she recomposes the text of Proust's novel as well as decomposing it.

Reviewing the English translation of *Sphinx*, Adam Mars-Jones wrote of *La décomposition*: "The novel contains various deformations of Proust's famous opening sentence – such as 'longtemps je me suis consumé de bonheur au récits de duels, de massacres, de tueries' – but they seem to be straightforward desecrations, rather than mechanical transformations in the approved Oulipo mode."[50] It is true that the transformations are not mechanical in that they have not been regulated by an algorithm like the N + 7 procedure. But are they straightforward desecrations? Stereoscopic close reading is the only way to tell. But first I should point out that *La décomposition* cites very widely indeed. It contains unsignalled borrowings of two kinds. First, brief citations of well-known phrases, lines, or sentences from a range of canonical authors: novelists (Kafka and Melville, notably, in the chapter entitled "Mortel K," which mashes up *The Castle*, *Moby-Dick*, and the violent video game *Mortal Kombat*), but also romantic and post-romantic poets (Wordsworth, Lamartine, Heine, Nerval, Baudelaire, Mallarmé, Rimbaud, Valéry, Eliot, Breton), and analytic philosophers of language (Frege, Wittgenstein, Quine, Kripke).

These brief citations belong to the category of intertextuality as Genette defines it in *Palimpsests*, as opposed to hypertextuality, which links a whole text to the pre-existing text from which it is derived (that is, its hypotext).[51] The question of when a privileged intertext becomes a hypotext may be delicate in some cases, but it is clear that *In Search of Lost Time* is the key work behind *La décomposition*, not only because it plays an instrumental role in the plot but also because it is massively cited and manipulated. A characteristic example is shown in table 7.1, first in the original, then in a version drawing on published translations of *In Search of Lost Time*.

In *La décomposition*, the narrator is waiting for his first victim ("Swann") to appear. In the passages from Proust, (1) the narrator is meditating on intermediate states between sleep and waking (in "Combray"); (2) Swann is approaching the shuttered window behind which he imagines Odette with her lover Forcheville (in "Swann in Love"); (3) the narrator is returning to his apartment after the Verdurins' party and looking at the light in Albertine's room (in *The Fugitive*). The substituted words at the beginning of the passage – *rues, croisées, songes* (streets, windows, dreams) – rhyme roughly with the words that they replace: *heures, années, monde* (hours, years, world). Garréta's description of the windows blends expressions from two passages that are very far apart in Proust, although designed to correspond to one another. This is a cunning, intricate verbal marquetry, which conserves the sensuous texture of the plundered material. To call it straightforward desecration would be to simplify. Here we can see desecration and homage going hand in hand, as in Octavio Paz's dismembering variations on a sonnet by Francisco de Quevedo in "Homage and Desecrations."[52]

Sometimes the altered citation argues with the original, as in the passage translated in table 7.2. The word "chimera" may refer to the chimerical combination of a fictional name and a real person (the victim), with whom the narrator has a murderous appointment. If so, the biological meaning of chimera is in play: a composite organism containing a mixture of genetically different tissues.[53] But Garréta's italicization of the word suggests a second reading: the self itself, Proust's "true self" ("moi véritable"), is a chimera, in one of two possible senses: an illusion, or, again, a composite.[54] A later passage supports this second possibility: "What does it matter if personal identity [...] is nothing but a procession [*théorie*] of identifications, and each of us is several in Time, both successively and

Table 7.1
Garréta's "decomposition" of Proust

Garréta	*Proust*
Sur le trottoir opposé j'attends, <u>tenant en cercle autour de moi le fil des rues, l'ordre des croisées et des songes.</u> Dans le jour s'amuïssant, <u>parmi toutes les fenêtres éteintes</u> au fond desquelles fuient et tombent en cendre les derniers ambres du crépuscule, je regarde sourdre <u>entre les volets qui en pressent la pulpe</u> d'abord pâle puis dorée toujours plus, <u>entre les lames obliques</u> qui en segmentent en <u>barres d'or parallèles, la matière translucide et chaude,</u> de la lumière. (D 12–13)	(1) Un homme qui dort, <u>tient en cercle autour de lui le fil des heures, l'ordre des années et des mondes.</u>[1]
	(2a) <u>Parmi l'obscurité de toutes les fenêtres éteintes</u> depuis longtemps dans la rue, il en vit une seule d'où débordait – <u>entre les volets qui en pressaient la pulpe</u> mystérieuse et dorée – la lumière qui remplissait la chambre[2]
	(2b) il se glissa le long du mur jusqu'à la fenêtre, mais <u>entre les lames obliques</u> des volets il ne pouvait rien voir[3]
	(3) je voyais la fenêtre de la chambre d'Albertine, cette fenêtre, autrefois toujours noire, le soir, quand elle n'habitait pas la maison, que la lumière électrique de l'intérieur, <u>segmentée par les pleins des volets, striait</u> de haut en bas de barres d'or parallèles.[4]
	(2c) Il éprouvait une volupté à connaître la vérité qui le passionnait dans cet exemplaire unique, éphémère et précieux, d'une <u>matière translucide si chaude</u> et si belle.[5]
I wait on the opposite sidewalk, <u>holding in a circle around me the sequence of the streets, the order of the windows and dreams.</u> In the day as it falls silent, <u>amid all the windows in which the lights have been put out,</u> in the depths of which flee and fall to ash the last ambers of dusk, I watch <u>between shutters which press its mysterious golden pulp, between the oblique slats</u> that <u>section it into parallel golden bars,</u> pale at first then ever more golden, the welling up of light's <u>warm, translucid substance.</u>	(1) A sleeping man <u>holds in a circle around him the sequence of the hours, the order of the years and worlds.</u>[6]
	(2a) <u>Amid the blackness of all the windows</u> in the street <u>in which the lights had</u> long since <u>been put out,</u> he saw just one from which there spilled out – <u>between shutters which pressed its mysterious golden pulp</u> – the light which filled the bedroom[7]
	(2b) he slipped along the wall as far as the window, but <u>between the oblique slats</u> of the shutters he could see nothing[8]
	(3) I could see the window of Albertine's bedroom, that window which had always been dark in the evening when she did not yet live in the house, and which the electric light from the inside, <u>sectioned by the slats of the shutters, now striped with parallel golden bars.</u>[9]
	(2c) He felt a delicious pleasure in learning the truth that so impassioned him from this unique, ephemeral, and precious transcript, made of a <u>translucid substance so warm</u> and so beautiful.[10]

1 Proust, *Du côté de chez Swann*, 5.
2 Ibid., 268.
3 Ibid.
4 Proust, *La prisonnière*, 218.
5 Proust, *Du côté de chez Swann*, 270.
6 Proust, *Swann's Way*, 5.
7 Ibid., 282–3.
8 Ibid., 283.
9 Proust, *The Prisoner*, 305.
10 Proust, *Swann's Way*, 284–5.

Table 7.2
Garréta's "corrective citation"

Garréta	Proust
Mais j'aurais le courage de répondre à celles qui viendraient s'insinuer ou m'assaillir que j'avais, pour des choses essentielles qu'il fallait que je manifestasse, un rendez-vous urgent, capital, avec une *chimère*. (106)	Mais j'aurais le courage de répondre à ceux qui viendraient me voir ou me feraient chercher, que j'avais pour des choses essentielles au courant desquelles il fallait que je fusse mis sans retard, un rendez-vous urgent, capital, avec moi même.[1]
But I would have the courage to reply to those who might come to worm their way in or attack me that I have, for essential matters that I must manifest, an urgent, a crucially important meeting with a *chimera*.	But I would have the courage to reply to those who came to see me, or who sent for me, that, because of essential matters that I needed to get abreast of immediately, I had an urgent, a crucially important meeting with myself.[2]

1 Proust, *Le temps retrouvé*, 367.
2 Proust, *Finding Time Again*, 295.

simultaneously" (188). The word *théorie* in the original can also be understood non-etymologically as theory.

This arguing with *In Search of Lost Time* depends on the phantom presence of Proust's wording, and differs significantly from the correction-by-inversion that Isidore Ducasse undertakes in his *Poésies*, an example of which is given in table 7.3. Ducasse's parody of a famous sentence from Blaise Pascal's *Pensées* is an intuitive "anticipatory plagiarism" of the Oulipo's practice of antonymic translation. But Garréta is doing something more complex in the example cited above, because "chimera" (*chimère*) is not an antonym of "myself" (*moi-même*); it is a one-word critique of the notion of the self. Rather than replacing the term with an opposite, Garréta impugns its pertinence. To grasp this, one needs to read stereoscopically, keeping both texts in view; it is not enough simply to recognize the intertext and identify the procedure.

Genette has described Oulipian intertextuality as mechanical: "Chance is at the helm; no semantic intention is at work, nothing 'tendentious' or premeditated."[55] In a similar vein, Tiphaine Samoyault has remarked that the Oulipian approach to intertextuality tends toward a writing without memory.[56] A clear semantic intention does, however, preside over Garréta's manipulations of Proust, and their richest effects depend precisely on memory, both spontaneous and

Table 7.3
Ducasse inverting Pascal

Ducasse	Pascal
L'homme est un chêne. La nature n'en compte pas de plus robuste. Il ne faut pas que l'univers s'arme pour le défendre. Une goutte d'eau ne suffit pas à sa préservation.[1]	L'homme n'est qu'un roseau, le plus faible de la nature: mais c'est un roseau pensant. Il ne faut pas que l'univers entier s'arme pour l'écraser; une vapeur, une goutte d'eau suffit pour le tuer.[2]
Man is an oak. The most robust in all of nature. It is not necessary that the universe take up arms to defend him. A drop of water is not sufficient for his preservation.[3]	Man is but a reed, the most feeble thing in nature, but he is a thinking reed. The entire Universe need not arm itself to crush him. A vapor, a drop of water suffices to kill him.[4]

1 Lautréamont, *Œuvres complètes*, 338.
2 Pascal, *Pensées*, 121–2.
3 Lautréamont, *Maldoror*, 321 (translation modified).
4 Pascal, *Pensées*, trans. W.F. Trotter, 97.

mechanically assisted. Discussing her treatment of *In Search of Lost Time* in an interview, Garréta said: "I ground it up on my computer."[57] But *La décomposition* is far from being the product of a purely mechanical procedure, in spite of the narrator's fantasy of a depopulated world in which a machine reads Heinrich Heine's "Die Lorelei" over and over (D 134–6).

Garréta's semantic intention is not simply to take Proust down, and her deformations are not symptomatic of what Shirley Hazzard, in an appreciative essay on Scott Moncrieff's translations, has called a "distrust of stature."[58] They do, however, imply a revisionary understanding of what constitutes the true stature of Proust: style more than doctrine, to put it abruptly. The narrator of *La décomposition* caresses the dream of a totally dehumanized version of *In Search of Lost Time*, which would nevertheless retain "that intangible asset of the business, its brand: the style" (D 166). It would be unwise to take anything this narrator says on trust, but his valuation of Proust as a stylist above all is shared by Garréta in her essay for *The Proust Project*: "Who knows ... Those stilts of time could still very well be stilts or thin threads holding together a tattered harlequin's coat; we would have mistaken for a cathedral a great circus, and the acrobat juggling the rings of style for a high priest."[59] The "rings of style" here allude to the "necessary rings of a beautiful style" from *Finding Time Again*, but instead of enclosing two different objects linked by a metaphorical relation, securing a truth beyond enumerative description, as in Proust, the rings are being juggled: they serve to display a virtuosic skill, and seem to have lost their necessity. Balls or skittles might do just as well.[60]

To take "the high priest" at his word, to adhere to his metaphysical doctrine, would be a mistake from Garréta's point of view, and a number of eminent readers of Proust – Leo Bersani, Vincent Descombes, and Christopher Prendergast among them – have adopted similarly skeptical approaches, particularly in relation to *Finding Time Again*.[61] But it would be hasty to read Garréta's circus allegory as implying that the achievement of *In Search of Lost Time* is a display of mere skill, for it prompts the question: what is so mere about skill, or style? In revaluing the exercise of literary virtuosity, Garréta follows Le Lionnais, who writes in the "Second Manifesto": "People are a little too quick to sneer at acrobatics" (OPPL 30).[62]

In saying that it would be unwise to trust Garréta's narrator, I do not mean to imply that he is never lucid, for he is *thoroughly* unreliable, that is, not even reliably wrong. Perhaps this is why Garréta's novel is, as Levin Becker writes, "sort of existentially upsetting": since there is no assigning the narrator to a stable place or status, each of his claims or flourishes must be assessed on its own merits. If, as Terence Cave claims, fiction demands especially acute epistemic vigilance, *La décomposition* takes this demand to an extreme.[63]

There are moments at which Garréta seems to use her narrator as a mouthpiece: particularly when he makes savage fun of "literary consumerism," as Lucy O'Meara puts it, and of the highly selective fetishization of *In Search of Lost Time*, a target that Thomas Baldwin has emphasized in his reading of the novel.[64] But the narrator slides without any kind of warning from this congruence and connivance with the author to positions that should alert our critical faculties. Often those positions are outrageous, but sometimes they are apparently commonsensical.

For example, near the end of the novel, the narrator complains about a slow internet connection: "ultimate irony, the transport of incorporeal information is subject to the limits of the physical substrate [...] the physical substrate, always the physical substrate ... Who will free us from it?" (D 235). Ironically, the "ultimate irony" is not ironic, since to call information incorporeal is to employ a misleading metaphor. The information that the narrator is referring to is a micro-organization of matter, invisibly small but still physical and subject to physical limits. Some philosophers – so-called expansive Platonists – might argue that the information in question can exist as a string of abstract entities (specifically zeroes and ones).[65] But to be manifest in space-time, it must take a concrete, physical form.

Consequently I think it would be misguided to hear the narrator-protagonist's question "Who will free us from it?" as a cry from the heart, or a version of the cyberpunk dream of "leaving the meat behind."[66] The question is better read as rhetorical, eliciting a simple answer: Nobody. The body, as the narrator says himself, is "that obtuse thing before which and with which all the logical creations of intelligence expire" (D 229). Garréta's most recent novel *In Concrete* (*Dans l'béton*), makes this point allegorically, as Annabel Kim shows: there is no deliverance from intractable materiality, figured in the narrative as the concrete and excrement in which the characters are mired, but which they also employ as materials of resistance.[67]

In casting a critical eye on the longing for disembodiment, whether it rests on religious belief or technophilia, Garréta's narrator is responding to the intellectual climate of the years in which *La décomposition* was written and published: the "flesh-eating 90s" as Arthur and Marilouise Kroker called them.[68] But he is also an uncanny prefiguration of the terrorists who took their first-person shooter games into the real world twenty years later in Christchurch, New Zealand; El Paso, Texas; and Halle, Germany, live-streaming their attacks. He would have nothing but disdain for the all-too-human motives that those killers made abundantly clear, but like them he gamifies murder.[69]

La décomposition, like *W of the Memory of Childhood* and *La dernière balle perdue*, shows that the writers of the Oulipo, for all their famous playfulness, are very much alive to the possibility of games going wrong. This is realistic, not contradictory. Games and play can be instrumentalized for harm, like kitchen knives. But such abuses do not reveal an essence; rather, they are realizations of a potential or a power, requiring the intervention of a malevolent agency.

8

Potentiality, Uptake, and Spread

TWO KINDS OF POTENTIALITY

At a meeting of the Oulipo on 5 May 1961, Queneau reminded his colleagues: "We have approved the qualification *potential* rather than *experimental*. Now, the potential is that which does not yet exist" (GO 57). From the early days of the Oulipo, however, "potential" has served to qualify not only the as yet inexistent literature of the future but also its harbingers in the literature of the present. Existing works are said and felt to be more or less endowed with potentiality.[1] What these judgments mean can be approached by considering two texts that the early Oulipo regarded as beacons.

For Le Lionnais, writing before the group had decided to adopt the term "potential," Queneau's *Cent mille milliards de poèmes* and *Exercises in Style* were the works with which experimental literature had finally emerged in a fully self-conscious form. The two books exemplify two different kinds of potentiality, which can be distinguished using a pair of expressions proposed by Jacques Roubaud: "predisposed potentiality" ("potentialité prédisposée") and "potentiality in actuality" ("potentialité en acte").[2] Predisposed potentiality resides in a constraint or form and precedes the composition of texts, while potentiality in actuality is manifested in texts that actualize a constraint or form and transform it by means of variations and mutations, producing a "family" that evolves over time.[3] According to Roubaud, it is with the Oulipian works of Perec, from *A Void* on, that potentiality in actuality comes to the fore, thus revealing the potentiality of the Oulipo itself.[4]

The paradigmatic example of predisposed potentiality, says Roubaud, is *Cent mille milliards de poèmes*, whose ten "parent sonnets" potentially contain the 10^{14}-10 other poems that can be derived from them. The immensity of this combinatory potentiality actually discourages reading: since exhausting the combinations is well beyond the capacity of any individual, the reading of the book is not oriented by an attainable goal, and readers are generally satisfied with a few samples once they have grasped the principle. *Cent mille milliards de poèmes* is largely conceptual in that the explanations given in the preface and the postface make even a brief sampling of the virtual contents optional. There is a certain irony to the quotation from Lautréamont in Queneau's preface ("Poetry should be made by all, not by one" [OC 1 334]), since the making to which the readers are invited is purely mechanical.[5]

Although *Cent mille milliards de poèmes* is often cited as a founding text, the Oulipo never limited itself to combinatory literature. From the start, the members of the group also attempted to foster the potentiality of what Queneau in his interviews with Georges Charbonnier called "empty structures." Charbonnier asked it if was really possible to separate form and content so cleanly. With his characteristic reserve, Queneau answered: "Probably" (EGC 154–5). It is indeed possible to propose empty structures, as Le Lionnais did in his "Idea Box" (AES 34–9). But an empty structure may be pleasing as a concept without working well for writers. Preliminary testing in exercises is required to filter out false good ideas.

The potentiality of an empty structure is not as specifically predisposed as that of a combinatorial system, but both are distinct from what Roubaud calls potentiality in actuality, which relates to the way in which a filled or realized structure "harbours the seeds of *variations* and *extensions*."[6] Following Roubaud, I have used Queneau's *Cent mille milliards de poèmes* to exemplify predisposed potentiality, but this work has been varied and extended. The Spanish poet Sofía Rhei has written nineteen superposable sonnets using the rhymes of Quevedo's "Amor constante, más allá de la muerte" (Constant love, beyond death) to produce far more potential combinations than Queneau's hundred thousand billion.[7] Also under the influence of Queneau, the Uruguayan songwriter Jorge Drexler has written a combinatorial set of ten *décimas* (ten-line lyrics), which have been recorded by ten different singers. Each of the hundred lines has a different melody as well as different words. Drexler's application *n* allows listeners to combine their own *décimas* in real time by tapping on the names of the singers, extracting combinations from the ten thousand million possibilities.[8]

Queneau's combinatory system of "parent" and "child" sonnets suggests an intriguing possibility: what if each of the "parents" contained one or two lines from a preceding "grandparent," a hidden but reconstructible urtext? No evidence of such an urtext has been produced in the case of *Cent mille milliards de poèmes*, but there is nothing, apart from the technical difficulties of the task, to stop a poet from writing a set of combinatory poems based on a single "grandparent." The reader's patience or luck might then be rewarded with a suite of lines that would be more rather than less semantically coherent than the poems from which it was derived. If *Cent mille milliards de poèmes* has a predisposed potentiality that is practically inexhaustible, it also has a potentiality in actuality that is yet to be exhausted.

The expression "potentiality in actuality" has a strong Aristotelian resonance, and recalls in particular Aristotle's arguments against the Megarians in book Theta (9) of his *Metaphysics*: "There are some – such as the Megarians – who say that something is capable only when it is acting, and when it is not acting it is not capable. For example, someone who is not building is not capable of building, but someone who is building is capable when he is building; and likewise too in other cases."[9] According to Aristotle, the Megarians conflated potentiality or capacity (*dynamis*) and actuality (*energeia*), and therefore did away with movement and becoming, which led to such absurd conclusions as "what is standing will always stand, and what is seated will always be seated":

> So if these things cannot be said it is plain that capacity and actuality are different (for those arguments make capacity and actuality the same, and so it is no small thing that they try to abolish), so that it can be possible to be something and yet not be that and possible not to be something and yet be that, and likewise too in the case of the other categories – it is possible for something not walking to walk, and possible for something walking not to walk.
>
> And this is what is possible – that for which, if the actuality of which it is said to have the capacity obtains, there will be nothing impossible.[10]

At first glance, the last sentence appears to be a tautology. Giorgio Agamben, however, reads it as advancing a subtle argument: "if a potentiality to not-be originally belongs to all potentiality, then there is truly potentiality only where the potentiality to not-be does not lag behind actuality but passes fully into it as such."[11]

At the risk of simplifying Agamben's thought, this interpretation can illuminate both "predisposed potentiality" and "potentiality in actuality" by reminding us that they are also and always potentialities to not-be. An empty structure has potential in that it can guide the composition of a multiplicity of texts, or remain an abstract formula. A constrained text has a different kind of potential, according Roubaud: it may provoke variations and mutations of the constraint. Or not. For a potential to be realized it must encounter what Stephen Mumford and Rani Lill Anjum, following C.B. Martin, call mutual manifestation partners.[12] To take one of Mumford and Anjum's examples, sugar will only realize its potential to be dissolved if it is plunged into a liquid. The final effect, the sweet solution, is produced by the sugar and the liquid together.

Certain literary forms and constraints have the potential to spread and participate in the composition of numerous works, but to do so they must meet appropriate manifestation partners: specific writers, mechanisms of diffusion, and communities of readers. A form, like an idea or a body of work, may lie dormant for decades or even centuries before the conditions required for its flourishing obtain. The sestina was introduced into English poetry by Philip Sidney and Edmund Spenser in the late 1570s, but was little used until the late nineteenth century. The form began to find wide favour from the 1930s on and is now commonly employed by poets who are not traditional formalists. The online version of *McSweeney's* ran a poetry section that published only sestinas from 2003 to 2007.[13] For the English sestina to realize its potential in this way, a range of manifestation partners had to come together: a revival of interest in romance-language verse forms in 1870s England; the commitment of prestigious poets, including Algernon Charles Swinburne, W.H. Auden, Elizabeth Bishop, and John Ashbery; the spread of the writing workshop with its hunger for exercises; and a taste for apparently arbitrary constraints among experimental poets at the end of the twentieth century.[14] The potential of a form emerges over time but is not simply revealed by time's passing.

PROOFS OF POTENTIAL

Christelle Reggiani has underlined the way in which the Oulipo insistently uses biological metaphors to discuss the fortunes of constraints and structures, imagining them as organisms capable of reproduction, spread, and evolution.[15] In this metaphorical network, potentiality is identified with fecundity: certain structures give birth to a large number of texts, while others "refuse to engender," as Arnaud puts it.[16] It is also in terms of fecundity that Jouet ruminates on potentiality, dividing the generative process into a phase of abstraction and a phase of concretization: "it's an abstract or theoretical method pregnant with concrete (for example, literary) things, a concrete thing being, in turn, not a final outcome but a possible new start, from which a further abstract or theoretical method pregnant with concrete things may be deduced."[17] Jouet is describing an ideal case here. Few of the Oulipo's numerous inventions have demonstrated a strong generative capacity of this kind.[18]

The N + 7 method is one of the few. It has turned out to be durably productive and lent itself to multiple variations.[19] The generalized sestina or quenina, and the so-called nonina, which applies the sestina's spiral permutation to stanzas with non-Queneau numbers of lines, have also continued to throw up new possibilities.[20] The spiral permutation has proved its viability for structuring narratives as well as poems, for example in Roubaud's three Hortense novels, Le Tellier's *The Sextine Chapel,* Jouet's *Fins,* Fournel's *Dear Reader* (*La liseuse*), Audin's *One Hundred Twenty-One Days,* and Berti's "Mañana se anuncia mejor" (Better weather forecast for tomorrow).[21] In *Tuyo es el mañana* (Tomorrow is yours), Martín Sánchez reverses the spiral permutation to reorder the monologues of his six main characters (including a greyhound and a painted portrait). This has the advantage of spacing the monologues more widely: at least two other characters always intervene before a character speaks again:

```
a b c d e f
b d f e c a
d e a c f b
e c b f a d
c f d a b e
f a e b d c
```

In the two cases just mentioned (N + 7 and the spiral permutations), an Oulipian's formal proposal gave rise to a family of constraints and multiple realizations: the process began with "an abstract or theoretical method" (even if that method was inspired by the existing form of the sestina in the second case). This validates Queneau's cautious optimism in his conversation with Georges Charbonnier: structures conceived abstractly may prove to be practically fruitful. But the Oulipo's inventions have not always worked in this way. In other cases, the process has been initiated by "concrete things," that is, finished texts or works, which have proved to have "potentiality in actuality," and in some cases functioned "epidemically," triggering imitations and variations within the group and beyond.[22] So far, the largest networks of uptake and spread have been initiated by four texts: Queneau's *Exercises in Style* and the first section of his *Elementary Morality*; Perec's *I Remember* and his story "The Winter Journey." Before looking in detail at the special case of *Elementary Morality*, I would like to underline three features that the other texts have in common: they are substantially inspired by previous works; they invite the reader to write a continuation; and they do not impose tight constraints on the reader-and-writer who takes up that invitation.

In the draft of a preface to *Exercises in Style*, Queneau wrote: "It was after having heard variations by Bach at a concert that I set out to come up with a literary equivalent" (OC III 1383). I argued in chapter 1 that *Exercises in Style* also talks back to a literary precursor: the banal coincidence recounted over and over is a deflationary response to Breton's doctrine of "objective chance," and perhaps more specifically to his brief text "The New Spirit." At the beginning of *I Remember*, Perec signals a debt of capital importance: "The title, the form, and to a certain extent, the spirit of these texts are inspired by *I Remember* by Joe Brainard" (IR 24).

The antecedents of "The Winter Journey" are multiple and not so clearly announced. The story's protagonist is Vincent Degraël, a young literature teacher, who, staying in a friend's country house on the eve of the Second World War, discovers a book entitled *The Winter Journey* by an author unknown to him, Hugo Vernier. This book starts ringing bells for Degraël; many of its turns of phrase resemble moments in the work of authors he knows well from his research in nineteenth-century French literature. At first he thinks that Vernier is a plagiarist and compiler, but then he checks the date of publication and sees that *The Winter Journey* was published in 1864, *before* all

Potentiality, Uptake, and Spread

the works that he had thought it was drawing on. The copy of the *Winter Journey* that Degraël has consulted is destroyed in the war, and he is never able to find another or even prove the existence of its author.

Perec's story gives an impression of familiarity analogous to the "already-read" effect of *The Winter Journey* on Vincent Degraël. In both cases, the effects depend on intertextual links that range from precise echoes to vague family resemblances. The old couple who take Vernier's anonymous hero by the elbows clearly mimic the "tenth-rate old actors" sent to finish off K in the final chapter of Kafka's *The Trial*, and this link is indirectly reinforced by a citation of the same passage in Perec's *A Man Asleep*.[23] According to Jouet, writing under the pseudonym Mikhaïl Gorliouk, the verbal overlap between the original titles of "The Winter Journey" and *If on a Winter's Night a Traveller* (*hiver – inverno, voyage – viaggiatore*) is not a mere coincidence. Both texts were published in 1979, and Gorliouk reads them as the first fruits of a project mentioned by Perec at a writing workshop in 1978: to collaborate with Harry Mathews, Italo Calvino, and Julio Cortázar on a novel in four languages.[24]

Likenesses that are more diffuse situate Perec's story in the wake of Gérard de Nerval's "Angélique" and Marcel Proust's "L'affaire Lemoine," as the intertextual sleuthing of Jean-Louis Jeannelle and Maxime Decout has shown.[25] And "The Winter Journey" is, in Bernard Magné's words, "a sort of Borgesian variation on the reversibility of time."[26] More specifically, it is a variation on the essay "Kafka and His Precursors," in which Borges collects passages from disparate texts that anticipate various aspects of Kafka's later work, with its "sombre myths and atrocious institutions."[27]

For Borges, the fact that Kafka's precursors do not all resemble each other is more significant than their resemblance to Kafka. It could be argued that having such dissimilar antecedents is part of what gives Kafka's work its high degree of relative originality. "The Winter Journey" reverses the temporal scheme of "Kafka and His Precursors": where Kafka brings together traits discernible in a heterogeneous group of earlier thinkers and writers (Zeno, Han Yu, Søren Kierkegaard, Robert Browning, Lord Dunsany), the combination of features in Vernier's *Winter Journey* is dispersed among his later imitators or plagiarists. It is worth noting that there is nothing in Perec's "The Winter Journey" to confirm the relative originality or literary quality of Vernier's book. Degraël is fascinated exclusively by its external relations with other works, not by what it is in itself and how its parts are interrelated.

The disjunction between the two main parts of the book seems to be repeated within the fragmented second part, "a long confession of an exaggerated lyricism, mixed in with poems, with enigmatic maxims, with blasphemous incantations" (ss 280).[28] The sample of borrowed or stolen fragments given in the story – five out of almost three-hundred and fifty such passages – does not provide conclusive support for Degraël's hypothesis that the writers concerned "used *The Winter Journey* as a bible from which they had extracted the best of themselves" (ss 283). There are almost thirty plagiarists, and assuming that the appropriation was evenly distributed, this means they each took eleven or twelve phrases or sentences: a very limited "best." In addition, although some of the material supposedly taken from Vernier is well known, none of it corresponds to the best-known moments in the work of the supposed plagiarists. Rimbaud allegedly stole "I readily could see a mosque in place of a factory, a drum school built by angels" (ss 281), not "I is someone else" or "A black, E white, I red, U green, O blue."[29] In Mallarmé's case, the common line is "the lucid winter, the season of serene art" (ss 281), not "A throw of the dice will never abolish chance."[30] And Lautréamont is supposed to have copied, "I gazed in a mirror at that mouth bruised by my own volition" (ss 281), not "Beautiful [...] as the fortuitous encounter upon a dissecting-table of a sewing-machine and an umbrella."[31]

Is Hugo Vernier a wronged and secret genius or a sponge for the zeitgeist with no gift for composition? The story does not give us firm grounds on which to settle the question. Vernier is an ambiguous figure by design, just as Vincent Degraël is shown to be less than objective in his quest for the Grail of the lost masterpiece.[32] In a textbook instance of confirmation bias, he leaps to the conclusion that mentions of "Hugo" and "V.H." in late nineteenth-century correspondence "definitely" do not refer to the most famous French author of the day, Victor Hugo, but to his phantom double Hugo Vernier (ss 284). Is Degraël absurdly unlucky or thoroughly delusional? This question too remains open. The ambiguities of "The Winter Journey" have played a key part in stimulating writerly responses to the story.

Exercises in Style, *I Remember*, and *The Winter Journey* all substantially draw on and respond to previous works, but they also project themselves into the future by signalling their own incompleteness and

Potentiality, Uptake, and Spread

calling for continuation. The call is explicit in the prospectus for *Exercises in Style* that was published in the *Nouvelle revue française*: "The book has neither a preface nor a conclusion. And readers will easily be able to imagine further tricks to play, should they be so inclined" (OC III 1385). As opposed to *Cent mille milliards de poèmes*, which is framed by a preface and a postface, and delivers the components of a practically inexhaustible but finite set of poems, *Exercises in Style* presents a set of texts that is easy to read right through but intended to be open, stopping before the round number of one hundred as if to hold out the baton.[33] The extraordinary potentiality of this text – its capacity to stimulate adaptations, variations, and mutations – shows no sign of approaching exhaustion, and the following survey is far from exhaustive.

Le Tellier's *Joconde jusqu'à 100* (1998) and *Joconde sur votre indulgence* (2002), whose punning titles might be translated as "I count up to a hundred" and "I count on your indulgence," each approach the Mona Lisa (la Joconde) from a hundred different points of view. The first piece in the series underlines the evident debt to Queneau by adopting the point of view of his character Zazie. The Oulipo's *Cher Père Noël* applies the principle of stylistic variation to a series of letters to Father Christmas, with senders ranging from Ulysses to Greta Thunberg.

The expanded New Directions edition of *Exercises in Style* (2012) includes a series of homages by contemporary writers including Jonathan Lethem, Lynne Tillman, and Enrique Vila-Matas. Ryan O'Neill's *The Drover's Wives* (2018), dedicated "to Henry Lawson and Raymond Queneau," lines up ninety-nine versions of Lawson's iconic Australian short story "The Drover's Wife" (1892). Many of O'Neill's new variations have a strong visual component, for example "Lecture Slides," "A 1980s Computer Game," "Cosmo Quiz," "Emojis," "Scratch and Sniff," and "Paint Swatches." While O'Neill's transposition is rich in satire, Berti's *Por* (2019) takes a more recent cultural icon and treats it more analytically. Berti offers forty-seven rewritings of the song "Por" by Luis Alberto Spinetta, from his album *Artaud* (1973), a landmark in Argentine rock music. The number of rewritings was determined by the number of words in the lyric. Berti's variations are preceded by a meticulous essay in forty-seven sections, and followed by a set of forty-seven cards on which are printed lines or extracts from other songs by Spinetta, designed to be shuffled so as to extract new combinations from the songwriter's corpus.

As O'Neill and Berti's responses suggest, *Exercises in Style* lends itself to transmedial treatment. This began shortly after the book's initial publication, with Yves Robert's theatrical version performed by the Frères Jacques in 1949, and the editions illustrated by Pierre Faucheux (1956), Gabriel Paris (1961), and Robert Massin and Jacques Carelman (1963) (OC III 1564–5). The adaptations have continued, in theatre, radio, advertising, and on the internet. For the growing series of hip-hop versions available on the site of the double-neuf project, Queneau's theme has been slightly modified: the action of the first part takes place in the metro instead of on a bus, and in the second part, the young man is telling his friend not to add a button to his coat but to put some cheese on his French fries.[34] In the graphic domain, Matt Madden's *99 Ways to Tell a Story* (2005) subjects a minimalist action sequence to a riot of visual styles, making it clear that "what appear to be merely 'stylistic' choices are in fact an essential part of the story."[35]

Queneau's *Exercises* have also inspired three mathematical adaptations, which appeared within a ten-year period: Ludmila Duchêne and Agnès Leblanc's *Rationnel mon Q* (Rational my ass / Q), which offers sixty-five demonstrations of the irrationality of the square root of two; John McCleary's *Exercises in (Mathematical) Style*, which tells ninety-nine "stories of binomial coefficients"; and Philip Ording's *99 Variations on a Proof* (the theorem in question is: "If $x^3 - 6x^2 + 11x - 6 = 2x - 2$, then $x = 1$ or $x = 4$"). In his preface, Ording writes: "While there is necessarily some overlap between these books, it is surprising that studies of style could themselves vary in style so much. This in and of itself further confirms the potential of the basic premise of Queneau's original."[36]

Perec's *I Remember* is also a text that invites the reader to continue the series. The book ends with the following note: "At the request of the author, a number of blank pages have been left for readers to write their own 'I remembers' which the reading of these ones will hopefully have inspired" (IR 133). The subtitle of the original was "Les choses communes I" ("Things in common I"). Perec planned two further volumes in the series: *Lieux où j'ai dormi* (Places where I have slept) and *Notes de chevet* (Bedside notes), a pillow book, modelled on that of Sei Shonagon.[37] But the things evoked in *I Remember* are common only to a generation of French people, and more specifically Parisians. For readers from subsequent generations and other places, the book has become almost hermetic, as Christelle

Reggiani remarks in the Pléiade edition, which, like Philip Terry and David Bellos's English translation, provides explanatory notes for most of the 480 micro-memories (o 1 1100). The opacity that results from the programmed obsolescence of these evocations contributes to the text's promptive power. The best way to gauge the effect that the book must have had on Perec's Parisian contemporaries is to fill the blank pages at the end, recovering memories of one's own. Many have taken up this invitation, both members of the Oulipo (Mathews, Jouet, Bens, Garréta, Valérie Beaudouin, Berti), and writers outside the group, including Nicolas Pages, Christian de Montrichard, Christophe Quillien, Lydia Flem, Mathieu Lindon, and Martín Kohan, who have all produced book-length collections.[38] Kohan's *Me acuerdo* acknowledges and exploits its own belatedness by omitting the anaphoric formula "I Remember" except in the title and at the beginning of one memory.[39]

The invitations to continue *Exercises in Style* and *I Remember* are located in paratexts and liminal texts, as well as in the deliberately incomplete overall structures of the works. In "The Winter Journey" the invitation is in the story itself. Vincent Degraël's former students find among his documents and manuscripts "a thick register, bound in black cloth whose label bore, carefully and ornamentally inscribed, *The Winter Journey*. The first eight pages retraced the history of his fruitless researches, the other 392 pages were blank" (ss 285). Faithful to the memory of Perec, and stimulated by his story's finely balanced ambiguities, the members of the Oulipo have metaphorically filled the blank space by proposing continuations that together make up a volume of over four hundred pages.[40]

As far back as 1984, before the first continuation was published, Claudette Oriol-Boyer underlined the text's invitation to "take up the pen in the dead man's place."[41] The invitation was addressed in the first instance to Roubaud, via an onomastic wink signalled by Christophe Reig: the friend at whose parents' house Degraël discovers *The Winter Journey* is named Denis Borrade, a paragram of Jacques Denis Roubaud.[42] And Roubaud's "Yesterday's Journey" ("Le voyage d'hier") inaugurated the series of Oulipian responses that has given rise to a collective novel in progress. Since the publication of *Winter Journeys (Expanded Edition)* (*Le voyage d'hiver et ses suites*) in 2013, two further instalments by Audin and Berti have appeared in the bibliothèque oulipienne.[43] And Ryan O'Neill's *Their Brilliant Careers* (2016) contains a prequel to "The Winter Journey" in which it is revealed that the Australian writer Wilhelmina Campbell, married to

232 How to Do Things with Forms

the Frenchman Victor Vernier, published *The Winter Journey* under the name of her dead son Hugo. This explains the mentions of kangaroos and a billabong, which had perplexed Degraël.[44]

The invitations issued by the three works that I have been discussing do not oblige the reader-turned-writer to adopt exacting formal constraints. Queneau's *Exercises in Style* is a virtuoso work, certainly, but its principle is simple: executing variations on the same minimal story. For a writer intending to continue the series, proficiency in the freely chosen styles is the chief requirement. Filling the blank pages at the end of Perec's *I Remember* does not call for any "special training or command of language," as Bellos remarks (IR 9). This is what Ron Padgett meant when he wrote in an afterword to Brainard's *I Remember* that it employs "one of the few literary forms that even non-literary people can use."[45] In describing his preparatory process, Perec explained that the recuperation of micro-memories was more like a spiritual than a stylistic exercise: "I think there's something not unlike meditation, a wanting to create a void" (ss 131). As to "The Winter Journey," Reig remarks that it does not seem to have been written under any Oulipian constraint.[46] Coming up with a sequel (or a prequel) requires imaginative resourcefulness rather than formal acrobatics, even if most of the continuers have played on Perec's title and multiplied proper names beginning with V and H. "The Winter Journey," writes Alison James, is "less a constrained work, in strictly formal terms, than an illustration of literary potentiality as such."[47]

ELEMENTARY MORALITIES

The poems in the first part of Queneau's *Elementary Morality*, which inaugurate the most reused of all Oulipian forms according to Marc Lapprand, might seem to present a very different case from the three texts that I have been considering.[48] Philip Terry translates the opening poem as follows:

Dark Isis	Green fruit	Spotted animal
	Clear neologisms	
Red flower	Transparent attitude	Orange-coloured star
	Clear springs	
Brown forest	Russet boar	Bleating flock
	Sparse tree	

A boat
on the water
soleabrious
follows the current
A crocodile
bites the keel
in vain

Ochre Isis   Crumbly statue   Apricot totem
                  Clear neologisms (EM 3)

Philippe Moret has pointed to the irony in the expression "clear neologisms," particularly as it refers to the word translated above as "soleabrious."[49] Terry seems to have interpreted Queneau's *seulabre* (OC I 611) as a portmanteau combining *seul* and *salubre*, and put together the English words "sole" (or "solitary") and "salubrious." In an earlier translation, Mathews opts simply for "solo" (OC 143), and this could be justified by pointing out that the word *seulabre* is not a neologism forged by Queneau but an argot word meaning "alone." In this context, however, and given Queneau's fondness for invented words, it may function as a portmanteau and pack together more than two components. Elaborating on Claude Debon's reading of the poem as alluding to the loss of Queneau's wife Janine, Moret suggests that the word *seulabre* compresses the idea of a lone (*seul*) subject who is falling apart (*qui se délabre*), having been cut off from his other half as if by the stroke of a sabre (*sabre*). If this poem has clarity, it is clearly of the kind defended by Proust in "Against Obscurity," his mini-polemic with Mallarmé: the kind that gives onto mysterious depths.[50]

On first looking into *Elementary Morality*, the poems in part 1 do not seem to share the three features that I discerned in *Exercises in Style, I Remember*, and "The Winter Journey": responding to specific previous works, inviting the reader to write a continuation, and the absence of strict formal constraints. In fact, one might be tempted to say that the form appears from nowhere, that the poems look hermetically inward (as suggested by the glossing of *seulabre* above), and that they are evidently constrained. But this curious case merits a more patient examination.

Minutes of the Oulipo's meeting on 12 January 1976 record how Queneau presented the form:

RQ [Raymond Queneau]: Explains the genesis of a new form (that of the opening of *Elementary Morality*). Poem heard as Chinese music: the words corresponding to gong notes.
PB [Paul Braffort]: Will poets "follow" this fixed form?
RQ: Reminds the meeting that troubadours were required to create ten to fifteen fixed forms each. Confesses that he is not musical and never listens to music, but for this form the sensations are auditory. Two mountains separated by a stream, with gong notes and flashes of light. Pimpaneau has just published a collection of twelfth-century Chinese poems that is particularly popular among the hippies. The book gives the Chinese text, a word-for-word translation, and a reworked version. There are six or seven different translations for certain poems at the beginning. Title of the book: The DHARMA Bum by Han Shan.[51]

The mention of Han Shan is significant. Métail, who was an active member of the Oulipo in 1976 and wrote her doctoral thesis on Chinese poetry under the supervision of Jacques Pimpaneau, has shown how the "Chinese music" of *Elementary Morality*'s first part has roots in the *I Ching* and in *lushi* (eight-line regulated verse), a key form in Chinese classical poetry, practised notably by Li Po (Li Bai) and Han Shan.[52]

In January 1974, the *Nouvelle revue française* published nineteen specimens of the new form, along with the following note:

The reader will have noticed that a fixed form has been used. First three sets of three-plus-one groups, each group made up of a noun and an adjective (or participle), with some repetitions, rhymes, alliterations, and echoes (*ad libitum*); then a kind of interlude of seven lines of one to five syllables; finally a conclusion: three-plus-one noun-and-adjective groups, which reprise, more or less, some of the twenty-four words used in the first part.

Purely internal "reasons" determined this form, which was not preceded by any explainable mathematical or rhythmic investigation. The first of the poems written in this way was genuinely "inspired"; some reflections (the mother bear licking the baby bear) and a certain amount of practice led to modifications, which gave rise to the form finally adopted. The fact that the body of the poem, minus the interlude, contains thirty-two words, and that there are fifteen lines in all (one more than in a sonnet) did not result from any preliminary decision. (OC I 1466)

If the word "inspired" is distanced with scare quotes, it is also reinforced by "genuinely" (*proprement*). The "genuinely 'inspired,'" Queneau suggests, has its "reasons" that reason does not know, to adapt a thought from Pascal.[53] Reflection and practice intervened after the initial determination, in order to refine the form of what had been given, like the mother bear licking her formless baby into shape, according to the ancient and medieval belief.[54] This reclaiming of inspiration, even in inverted commas, was bound to surprise and even shock the other members of the Oulipo. According to Mathews in the *Oulipo Compendium*, Queneau's note on the genesis of the form "would seem to place it squarely outside the domain of the Oulipo, and while the point is theoretically granted, virtually all the active members of the group have used it to write poems, sometimes adding their own supplementary restrictions to the form" (OC 142).

Mathews passes quickly over the simultaneously practical and theoretical difference that Queneau was at pains to make clear. When Le Lionnais asked all the members of the Oulipo in 1970 if they were currently considering "personal Oulipian projects," Queneau's response was terse: "Frankly: no."[55] This does not mean that he had given up on formal invention, and his note in the *Nouvelle revue française* indicates that starting with Oulipian constraints is not the only way to invent. There is also the messier and more intuitive process of feeling one's way toward a new configuration, and coming upon it suddenly, followed by what Jouet calls "tinkering" (*bidouillage*) (AS 34).

During the composition of the first part of *Elementary Morality*, Queneau noted in his journal: "While continuing to write poems of this kind, I discover that I can use the new structure to do Oulipism [*pour faire de l'oulipisme*]. You just have to take noun + adjective pairs from poems (or prose texts) [...] and write a *ritornello* inspired by the context. It produces good results" (OC 1 1452). He did not, however, judge the results sufficiently good to be included in *Elementary Morality*. If the new structure could serve for the writing of poems and doing Oulipism, the difference between the two ways of using it remained pertinent for Queneau.

For Perec, on the contrary, poetry and Oulipism overlapped almost entirely. He ventured onto the terrain of poetry armed with hard constraints, and it was only after a long campaign that he set them aside to write "Un poème" and "L'éternité," discussed in chapter 5. His response to Le Lionnais's question about personal Oulipian projects was the polar opposite of Queneau's: "That's all I'm doing."[56] In his collection *La clôture et autres poèmes*, he included two elementary moralities, the first of which clearly contradicts the form's inventor:

Roubaud's Principle

Noticed reader	Formed poem	Fixed first
	Grouped nouns	
Grouped adjectives	Grouped participles	Rhymed repetitions
	Alliterated echoes	
Versified interludes	Concluding syllables	Grouped nouns

three times three
plus one
one to five
three plus one
twenty-four
thirty-two
fifteen

Written poem	Inspired reflection	Preliminary decision
	Explainable research	

Le principe de Roubaud

Lecteur remarqué	Poème formé	Abord fixe
	Substantifs groupés	
Adjectifs groupés	Participes groupés	Répétitions rimées
	Échos allitérés	
Interludes versifiés	Syllabes concluantes	Substantifs groupés

trois fois trois
plus un
un à cinq
trois plus un
vingt-quatre
trente-deux
quinze

Poème écrit	Réflexion inspirée	Décision préalable
	Recherche explicitable	
	(O II 794)	

All the semantic material in this poem is drawn from Queneau's note explaining the form, although some words have undergone a change of class, *groupes* becoming *groupés*, and *conclusion concluantes*, for example. The shading below shows how Perec has mined the note:

Le lecteur aurait remarqué qu'il s'agit de formes fixes.
D'abord trois fois trois plus un groupe substantif plus adjectif
(ou participe) avec quelques répétitions, rimes, allitérations,
échos *ad libitum*; puis une sorte d'interlude de sept vers de une
à cinq syllabes; enfin une conclusion de trois plus un groupe
substantif plus adjectif (ou participe) reprenant plus ou moins
quelques-uns des vingt-quatre mots utilisés dans la première
partie.

Des "raisons" purement internes ont déterminé cette forme
qui n'a été précédée d'aucune recherche mathématique ou
rythmique explicitable. Le premier des poèmes ainsi écrit a
été proprement "inspiré"; quelques réflexions (l'ourse léchant
l'ourson) et une certaine pratique ont provoqué des modifications
procurant la forme finalement adoptée. Que le corps du poème
(moins l'interlude) comporte trente-deux mots et que l'ensemble
présente quinze vers (un de plus que le sonnet) ne résulte
d'aucune décision préalable.

As Jean-Jacques Poucel has pointed out, the poem contains a clinamen: the twelfth word pair is missing.[57] So most of the numbers given in the interlude do not apply to the modified form.[58]

Perec's mining of lexical material is also an undermining. His poem is a tit-for-tat response to Queneau's note: "une réponse du berger au berger" as Jouet has put it. This becomes especially clear with the inversion of Queneau's meanings in the last two lines.[59] Instead of a "genuinely 'inspired'" poem, we are offered an "inspired reflection," which suggests a quite different approach. Then, by omitting the negative adjective *aucune* (no), Perec's poem lays claim to what Queneau's note explicitly sets aside: "aucune décision préalable" ("no preliminary decision") becomes "Decision préalable" ("Preliminary decision"); likewise for "no explainable research." While contradicting Queneau, the poem demonstrates solidarity with Roubaud by illustrating his "first principle" – "A text written in accordance with a restrictive procedure refers to the procedure" (OC 222) – even if the self-reference is inexact in this case, as noted. "Roubaud's Principle" is thus an

Oulipian mini-manifesto and a declaration of independence with regard to a figure whom Perec had not always held in high regard.[60] If Queneau's explanatory note was intended as a reminder that literary invention may be achieved by means other than explicit research and preliminary decisions, if he wanted to show another way, be it the way of "inspiration" or more modestly of tinkering, Perec replied with a firm negative.

Nevertheless, Queneau's provocative presentation succeeded in launching the form. Perec's vigorous response, after the more respectful homages of Jean Queval and Paul Fournel, opened a breach into which other Oulipians have stepped.[61] The elementary morality easily accommodates supplementary constraints: homonymic or homophonic word pairs, lipograms, threnodials (*ulcérations*), synonymic drift, concatenation, anadiplosis, and more.[62] Jouet has grafted the form onto the Renaissance genre of the anatomical *blason*.[63] Forte has miniaturized it to make a "portable mini elementary morality," which conserves and concentrates the form's flavour.[64] But the most ambitious response to Queneau's last book has come from Grangaud.

In *Les temps traversés* (Times traversed, 2010), Grangaud proposes a poetic history of the French language from 1501 to 1968. Working from a large file in which she arranged words and word pairs by order of their dates of attestation in Alain Rey's *Dictionnaire historique de la langue française*, she composed elementary moralities by taking all the lexical words in each poem from a set whose use was first attested within a short period, ranging from a year to a decade.[65] These samplings subtly capture social history. In her preface, Grangaud writes: "What emerges most clearly from this chronological arrangement is a parallel between the rise of a democratic ideal and the development of the language" (TT 7). A philosophy of history akin to Jules Michelet's – a vision of liberty's long struggle against fatality – underlies the project. This does not imply a blind optimism. The following poem, corresponding to the year 1793, takes word pairs from the title of the book that Nicolas de Condorcet wrote while in hiding from the Revolutionary authorities: *Esquisse d'un tableau historique des progrès de l'esprit humain* (*Sketch for a Historical Picture of the Progress of the Human Mind*).[66] The book was published posthumously in 1795, after Condorcet's death in prison on 28 March 1794.

General picture	Revolutionary measures Revolutionary tribunal	Sympathetic illness
Native soil	Poste restante Provisional government	Historical picture
Soft tissue	Pectineal muscle Eyebrow arch	Red heel [aristocrat]
	The levelling of fortunes is the watch- word for appreciating the drama of life	
Historical picture	Revolutionary measures Human mind	Republican calendar
Tableau général	Mesures révolutionnaires Tribunal révolutionnaire	Maladie sympathique
Sol natal	Poste restante Gouvernement provisoire	Tableau historique
Tissu spongieux	Muscle pectiné Arcade sourcilière	Talon rouge
	Le nivellement des fortunes c'est le mot d'ordre pour apprécier le drame de la vie	
Tableau historique	Mesures révolutionnaires Esprit humain (TT 64)	Calendrier républicain

By signalling the source of the word pairs "Historical picture" and "Human mind," and associating them with the "Revolutionary measures" taken by the "Revolutionary tribunal," which included convicting Condorcet of the capital offence of treason for having dared to criticize the new constitution drafted by Marie-Jean Hérault de Séchelles, Grangaud suggests, without lapsing into anti-revolutionary rhetoric, that the progress of the human mind is not irreversible. Condorcet himself held a more sanguine view in his *Sketch*, asserting that the Enlightenment was too widespread by the time of the first French Republic to suffer any real setbacks.[67]

As well as flourishing within the Oulipo, the elementary morality has demonstrated its productivity beyond the group. Philip Terry, translator of the work that gave the form its name, composed a sequence based on the adventures of Sherlock Holmes, entitled "Elementary, My Dear Watson," before writing a whole book of *Quennets*, as they are also sometimes known. The book takes Queneau's invention for walks around estuaries in Essex, along the line of the Berlin Wall, and in the footsteps of W.G. Sebald in Suffolk, renovating the tradition of the topographic poem.[68] Along the way, the form is reshaped in response to the land- and cityscapes the poet encounters. Following the Mauerweg in Berlin, Terry suppresses the line breaks in the opening and closing sections to produce "a wall-like block of prose." In Suffolk, he multiplies the line breaks, to make tall, thin poems with ragged right-hand margins that mirror "the eroding effects of the sea on the Suffolk coastline."[69]

In 1964, Queneau reflected on the exceptional fate of the sonnet form. "Why has the sonnet alone survived? This is perhaps a problem for literary sociology, or rather, a problem for mathematics and linguistics, the sonnet furnishing an optimal solution to the poet's demand for a well-defined form that responds to conscious or unconscious aesthetic exigencies" (OPPL 54). It would be rash to claim as much for the elementary morality, which is still less than fifty years old, but it is worth asking what has permitted the form to respond to the exigencies of a considerable number of writers, to the point where it is the best candidate for the status of "new Oulipian sonnet."

From a formal point of view, the elementary morality is not, in the end, especially complex. In its repeated employment of two fundamental linguistic operations (nomination and qualification), and in its enumerative structure, it is truly elementary. It is not governed by strong or hard constraints. For a fixed form, it is flexible, as

Astrid Poier-Bernhard has remarked.[70] The repetitions, rhymes, alliterations, and echoes are, as Queneau put it, *ad libitum*, at the poet's discretion, and if regularities can be detected among them in part 1 of *Elementary Morality*, these are statistical tendencies, not constraints in the strict sense.[71] The lines of the interlude are of variable length, from one to five syllables, although Queneau himself does not always respect the upper limit (OC 1 618). This flexibility leaves ample room for the addition of supplementary constraints. So the elementary morality allows writers to leave their mark on the form, or co-sign it, as Jouet, Forte, Grangaud, and Terry have done.

For a contemporary writer, to take up a form invented recently by an identifiable individual and use it without modification is to submit symbolically to the form's inventor. Assuming such a posture is not a simple matter. The modern injunction to be original is felt by all writers today, even those who, like Jouet, would like to "bring modernity into line."[72] A "fixed" form that leaves a margin for individual invention may furnish an optimal solution to the problem of reconciling the demand for originality with the desire to belong to a tradition.

On close inspection, it emerges that part 1 of *Elementary Morality* is not so different from the other three outstanding exemplars of potentiality in actuality: *Exercises in Style*, *I Remember*, and "The Winter Journey." Queneau's new form is more the result of adaptation, "inspiration," and tinkering than of preliminary decisions and explainable research. It was launched by a paratext that projected it toward the future by provoking responses (including Perec's provocative quasi-rebuttal). And because of its relative simplicity and suppleness, the form is easy to adapt.

It may be that the most productive Oulipian forms and constraints, those that reproduce themselves most abundantly within and beyond the group, are neither the most complex nor the most interesting from a mathematical point of view. Regarding complexity, Roubaud writes: "A good Oulipian constraint is a simple constraint" (OPPL 86). And transposing mathematically interesting patterns into literature is not at all straightforward, as Queneau showed indirectly at the very end of his life.

LITERATURE AND GEOMETRY

"The Foundations of Literature (after David Hilbert)" (OL 3–15), Queneau's last published text, has often been treated as a 'Pataphysical diversion.[73] Its irony is certainly amusing, but the text also makes a serious point about the obstacles to what Le Lionnais called "the amalgam of mathematics and literature" (OPPL 74–8). Queneau begins by recounting an anecdote concerning the German mathematician David Hilbert: "After attending a lecture in Halle by Wiener (not Norbert, obviously) on the theorems of Desargues and Pappus, David Hilbert waiting in the Berlin station for the train to Koenigsberg, murmured pensively: 'Instead of points, straight lines, and planes, it would be perfectly possible to use the words tables, chairs, and tankards.' This reflection gave birth to a work that appeared in 1899, *The Foundations of Geometry*, in which the author established in definitive (or provisionally definitive) fashion the axiomatic system of Euclidean geometry (and of several others besides)" (OL 2).

Queneau goes on to take Hilbert at his word, extracting the axioms from *The Foundations of Geometry* and replacing *points* with *words*, *lines* with *sentences,* and *planes* with *paragraphs.* In this transposition, Hilbert's geometric spaces correspond to texts.[74]

The first axiom of connection translates smoothly into literary terms:

I, 1 – *A sentence exists containing two given words.*

COMMENT: Obvious. (OL 5)

But already, with the second axiom, problems arise:

I, 2 – *No more than one sentence exists containing two given words.*

COMMENT: This, on the other hand, may occasion surprise. Nevertheless, if one considers the words "years" and "early," once the following sentence containing them has been written, namely "For years I went to bed early," clearly all other sentences such as "For years I went to bed right after supper" or "For years I did not go to bed late" are merely pseudo-sentences that should be rejected by virtue of the above axiom.

SCHOLIUM: Naturally, if "For years I went to bed right after supper" is the sentence written originally, "For years I went to bed early" becomes the sentence to be excluded by virtue of axiom I, 2. In other words, no one can write *À la recherche du temps perdu* twice. (OL 5–6)

As Alice Bamford has noted, "Queneau's system breaks down almost immediately."[75] Axioms I, 2 and I, 1 are contradictory since both are sentences containing the words *sentence* and *words*, and according to I, 2 there should be only one sentence containing a given pair of words. This leads to a "metaliterary axiom" ironically proposed to save the consistency of the system: "Axioms are not governed by axioms" (OL 7).

Nevertheless, the translation from geometry to literature continues to throw up counterintuitive results. When considering these, it should be remembered that Queneau's text is entitled "The Foundations of *Literature*" not "The Foundations of Natural Language." Robert Tubbs writes: "Queneau does not imagine that all of his axioms would hold for any particular piece; rather, his thinking is that by adopting particular axioms, an author imparts a particular style (or, to use geometric language, certain properties) to a text."[76] In other words, translating Hilbert's axioms could be a way of generating constraints, or of formulating constraints applied intuitively by writers of the past. It follows from the first group of axioms and Theorem I, for example, that "The repetition of a word already used in a preceding paragraph requires the repetition of the entire sentence – a crushing obligation. It is just as well – and far more prudent – to avoid any repetition of the word. Flaubert complies with this axiom scrupulously" (OL 10). The fun here is in the absurdly roundabout route taken to arrive at Flaubert's rule proscribing close repetition of lexical words, and in the absurdly arbitrary stylistic precepts laid down along the way.

Queneau concludes: "The process of transposition might be pursued still further. Curiously enough, once the domain of conic sections is reached, there is no more need of transposition. We find ourselves immersed in rhetoric. There is no talk of anything but ellipses, parabolas, and hyperbolas, all figures of speech well known to writers, even if in our day ellipsis is rare, the parable has been neglected (for nearly two thousand years), and hyperbole is common coin" (OL 15). The names of the geometrical and the rhetorical figures coincide, but their referents are very far apart, and by saying, tongue-in-cheek, that there is no need of transposition, Queneau is staging "a confrontation between the axiomatic method and the particularities of literature" as Bamford puts it, or at least indicating a deep gap.[77]

In 1899, Hilbert wrote to Gottlob Frege, defending his axiomatic system: "But it is surely obvious that every theory is only a scaffolding or schema of concepts together with their necessary relations to one another, and that the basic elements can be thought of in any way one likes. [...] In other words: any theory can always be applied to infinitely many systems of basic elements."[78] This was not obvious to Frege, for whom, as Patricia Blanchette explains, "the sentences we use in mathematics are important only because of the nonlinguistic propositions (or, as he puts it, the 'thoughts') they express," and "each thought is about a determinate subject-matter."[79] Nor was it obvious to Queneau, who seems to have agreed at the end of his life with Roland Travy's vigorous rejection of mathematical formalism in *Odile*:

> You must be familiar with this idea, it's a popular theory that your own philosophy teacher must have had. A building, they see mathematics as a building! You make sure the foundations are solid before you build the first floor, and when you've built the first floor, you move on to the second floor, and then the third, and so on, and it just goes on and on. But things aren't actually like that; you shouldn't compare geometry and calculus to building houses or walls, but to botany, to geography or even to the physical sciences. It's about describing a world, discovering it, not about constructing or inventing it, because it exists outside the human mind and independently of it. (O 16)

"The Foundations of Literature (after David Hilbert)" was first published as number three of the bibliothèque oulipienne, after Perec's "Ulcérations" (Ulcerations) and Roubaud's "La Princesse Hoppy ou le conte du Labrador" ("Princess Hoppy or the Tale of Labrador"). In a journal entry dating from 10 January 1974, the day of an Oulipo meeting, Queneau wrote: "Perec has brought forth another monstrous work, a performance equal to his palindrome."[80] According to Roubaud this work was "Ulcérations" (MO 22). Queneau added: "something that I've been thinking about is the danger of the Oulipo for young writers."[81] As well as being a diversion, "The Foundations of Literature (after David Hilbert)" is a deflationary gesture, a reduction to absurdity of the hyperbolic "amalgamation" of literature and mathematics, a warning against taking the Oulipian approach too far or too seriously. But the gesture has been largely ignored within and beyond the Oulipo. Queneau had no sovereignty over the group, as Perec showed with his poem "Roubaud's Principle." The ground rules that Le Lionnais and Queneau laid down in 1960 guarded the Oulipo against domination by any single member, and gradual renewal by co-optation has diluted the influence of the founders, as I explain in the concluding chapter.

9

What Has Become of the Oulipo?

TAKING STOCK

Many movements and -isms have come and gone since 1960, but the Oulipo is as active and productive as ever. Over this unusually long lifetime, the group's notoriety and influence have grown steadily. Its name is now routinely associated with literary works that have acquired canonical status, such as Perec's *Life: A User's Manual* and Calvino's *If on a Winter's Night a Traveller*. In France, the adjective *oulipien* is applied to playful formalism in general. Oulipian exercises are widely used in schools, and the Oulipo's public readings have a large and faithful following. In 2020, the current president of the Oulipo Hervé Le Tellier was the first Oulipian to win the Prix Goncourt, with his novel *L'anomalie*.

In the English-speaking world, the Oulipo is recognized as an important feature in the landscape of contemporary writing, as indicated by Jan Baetens's chapter on "Oulipo and Proceduralism" in *The Routledge Guide to Experimental Literature* (2012) and Hélène Aji's chapter on "Poems that Count: Procedural Poetry" in the Wiley-Blackwell *Companion to Poetic Genre* (2012). Special numbers of the web journals *Drunken Boat* (2006), *Eleksographia* (2009), *Words without Borders* (2013), and *Anomalous* (2015) also testify to this recognition and uptake.

One of the most widely discussed books in North American poetry around the turn of the millennium, Christian Bök's *Eunoia* (2001), which won the Griffin Prize for Excellence in Poetry, was directly and avowedly inspired by Perec's exercises in monovocalic writing. Perec's emblematic Oulipian novel *A Void* has been translated into German,

Italian, Spanish, Swedish, Russian, Turkish, Japanese, Croatian, and Portuguese, as well as English, respecting or adapting the formal rule in each case.[1] As this list of languages indicates, the Oulipo's influence has not been limited to Western Europe and North America. When the South Korean novelist Han Yujoo, an admirer of Calvino and Perec, set up a micropress devoted to experimental writing, she named it Oulipo Press.[2] According to an official but not entirely reliable history, in 2014, Ryan O'Neill and Julie Koh founded "Kanganoulipo, a writing collective which would showcase the best experimental writing in Australia, and which would hopefully also be tax deductible."[3] In 2020, the Turkish architect Levent Şentürk and his colleagues published a collection of 199 exercises in architectural style, proudly declaring their debt to the Oulipo by including translations of Le Lionnais's two manifestos and Queneau's "Foundations of Literature (after David Hilbert)."[4] What began discreetly with a group of friends meeting for monthly lunches and discussions has become an international phenomenon, whose effects have rippled out from literature into a range of artistic domains.

After more than sixty years, it is legitimate for critics to take stock and measure the success of the Oulipo's enterprise. That is the aim of Lauren Elkin and Veronica Esposito's *The End of Oulipo? An Attempt to Exhaust a Movement*, which focuses on "the most significant latter-day Oulipians to be published in English – Jacques Jouet and Hervé Le Tellier," and concludes that they "have not been able to match the seriousness of purpose characteristic of earlier Oulipian work."[5] Elkin and Esposito's approach is far from exhaustive, but they formulate a widely held impression: that the group's glory days have passed.[6] Kenneth Goldsmith has described the Oulipo as a "mid-century movement," and Susan Sontag corrected herself significantly in the sentence quoted on the back cover of the *Oulipo Compendium*: "The Oulipo was – is – a seedbed, a grimace, a carnival."[7] "Today, as the group enters its sixth decade of existence," write Elkin and Esposito, "its relevance and its future are in question."[8]

Dennis Duncan, too, raises the question of relevance, proposing a cross-media comparison: "The Oulipo are still going strong, but I sometimes wonder whether they don't have something in common with another creative entity formed at the start of the sixties, a sort of Rolling Stones paradox where a group that's been around for nearly sixty years can be globally bigger and more profitable than ever, yet their greatest hits – and their *relevance* – are many years behind them."[9] It is true that the greatest Oulipian "hit" so far, *Life: A User's Manual*, dates from 1978, but it is not so clear that the group has lost its relevance. In 2015, Duncan himself quoted a remark made by Stephanie Burt in 2012: "US and Canadian writers seem to be on an Oulipo kick."[10] A few years earlier, Simon Turner welcomed "the Oulipian invasion of British literature."[11] Two hearty recent anthologies – *The Penguin Book of Oulipo* (2019) and *All That is Evident is Suspect* (2018) – testify to ongoing interest in the group among English-speaking readers. What I suggest in this chapter is not that the Oulipo has become irrelevant but that its influence, in spreading, has become more diffuse.

Unlike the Rolling Stones, the Oulipo has lost all of its original line-up, and many of its later recruits. When a group has counted among its members three writers of the stature of Queneau, Perec, and Calvino, it is almost certain to seem decadent after their passing. But it is worth remembering that the Oulipo's future has been in question since 1970, when Le Lionnais attempted to rally the troops with a questionnaire entitled "How to unblock the horizon?" The first question is indicative of the group's condition in the late 1960s: "Do you want the Oulipo to continue its activities?"[12] Writing to Valérie Guidoux in 1984, Stanley Chapman was thoroughly dismissive of the Oulipo after Queneau's death: "I must say that at the beginning it was far more interesting than it is now [...] The two (?) small volumes that have come out are quite useless – there are a thousand English literary games that are a thousand times more amusing and experimental and productive than the little ideas of certain members of the OuLiPo" (AES 67). It is never too early to be nostalgic, and the Oulipo has had its own declinists, from Bens in his correspondence to Roubaud in *Peut-être ou la nuit de dimanche.*[13]

Any global assessment of the Oulipo's achievements must, however, be provisional. Garréta has said that the Oulipo functions as an irritant in the literary system because it is mutagenic (that is, it causes genetic mutations).[14] I would add that the Oulipo is itself a mutant entity: the membership, the concerns, and the methods of the group are in constant metamorphosis. This makes predictions about its future hazardous. Thanks in part to its recruitment of highly productive writers and artists in the decade 2010–20 (Étienne Lécroart, Eduardo Berti, Pablo Martín Sánchez, and Clémentine Mélois), the Oulipo is still a space to watch. It still has a range of potentials:

1   Much of what the Oulipo has published is still waiting to be read closely, appreciated, and translated.

2   Many of the constraints invented by the group have yet to
    be tried out in fully fledged works.
3   There are kinds of constraints and structures that the Oulipo
    has not yet explored extensively.
4   The Oulipo's verbal inventions continue to produce diverse
    and unpredictable effects on writing beyond the group.
5   Finally, the Oulipo as a social invention has potential to
    stimulate and influence the collective practice of writing and
    art-making in other groups.

In what follows, I explore these five kinds of potential in turn.

As Hermes Salceda has pointed out, an ambivalent advantage of
the Oulipo's partly conceptual approach is that the group's ideas can
circulate without the works of its members being read.[15] As a result,
the Oulipo is both widely known and underknown. A small set of
constraints and works are often taken to be to be emblematic of its
practice: the N + 7 method, the lipogram, *A Hundred Thousand Billion
Poems*, *A Void*, *Life: A User's Manual*. This can give a false impression
of familiarity and manageability. The Oulipian corpus is very large by
now and growing so rapidly that it is difficult even for the group's
own members to keep up. Nothing that has joined the corpus since
the early 1980s has achieved as much critical recognition as *Life: A
User's Manual*, although Roubaud's *Le grand incendie de Londres*
(The great fire of London) was widely saluted as a major work when
it was published in one volume in 2009. Recognition, however, is a
scarce commodity, and few would regard its spectacularly uneven
distribution as just.[16]

There are certainly Oulipian works that deserve to be better known.
I have already discussed some of these: Perec's *La clôture et autres
poèmes* (The enclosure and other poems), Garréta's *La décomposition*
(Decomposition), and Roubaud's *Parc sauvage* (Wild grounds), none of
which has yet been translated into English. Here, toward the end
of what is already a long book, I have space to examine only one
more of these underknown works: Michelle Grangaud's *Geste* (Gesture).

THE UNDERKNOWN OULIPO

In an essay on contemporary short narrative, after mentioning various
uses of what Perec called the infraordinary, Pierre Alféri writes: "A
little more recently, an undervalued book by Michelle Grangaud sewed

What Has Become of the Oulipo? 249

together several hundred moving micro-events, gestures [*des gestes*] which became a *chanson de geste* [*une Geste*], an epic of the everyday. But it has remained a hapax."[17] The reading of *Geste* that follows is essentially an unfolding of these sentences.

Geste is a series of one thousand three-line stanzas, with lines of five, five, and eleven syllables. In these modest spaces, slightly larger than that of the haiku, Grangaud describes, for the most part, human actions or gestures – thence the title (or one of its senses). She has explained that the form emerged from her attempts to reappropriate the resources of the sentence after years of writing syntactically fragmented anagram poems: "I set myself a sort of re-education exercise: writing sentences that describe a gesture, one sentence per gesture and one gesture per sentence."[18]

It is worth noting that the form employed in *Geste* was not invented a priori. In an interview with John Stout, Grangaud says that she began by accumulating about two thousand sentences of variable length, and then found herself unable to arrange them to her satisfaction:

> Then there was a night when [...] I went to bed very sad, thinking:
> "Oh well. It was a good exercise, but I won't be able to get
> anything out of it. That's it." I lay down. I switched off my lamp,
> and just then a sentence came to me, with a very pleasant rhythm.
> I thought: "That's a good one!" So I switched the lamp back
> on and wrote it down. Then I switched the lamp off again, lay
> down, and another sentence came, with the same rhythm. That
> was when I counted and realized that it was five syllables, five
> syllables, eleven syllables. Several more came to me, in fact, that
> night. Sometimes they were sentences that came spontaneously,
> sometimes it was a sentence that I'd already written, without any
> special rhythm, which I retranslated. So I rewrote my sentences.
> The amazing thing is that after that, once I'd rewritten them
> (in any old order), [...] I had practically no trouble sequencing
> them; at that point I saw how they had to be sequenced.[19]

In another interview (with Astrid Poier-Bernhard), Grangaud stressed the apparent autonomy of the rhythm, which she was able to ride, as it were: "I was amazed to find this rhythm suggesting images and 'gestures' that I had never thought of before; it was as if the rhythm were already full of words."[20] Form in this case, as in *Elementary Morality*, is an emergent principle of organization: "at once daughter and mother to all the elements that it polarizes," as Queneau writes in "Technique of the Novel" (LNF 29).

The initial brief of "one sentence per gesture and one gesture per sentence" was relaxed once the form emerged. The first tercet contains two sentences, both of which describe states rather than actions:

> La salle d'attente
> est tout à fait vide.
> Curieusement, les fauteuils sont très présents. (G 7)

> The waiting room
> is completely empty.
> Oddly, the armchairs are very present.

No agent appears, but there is an implied perceiver for whom the marked presence of the armchairs does not go without saying. Humans intervene in most of the tercets that follow, as here in the second:

> Quand le réveil sonne
> il détend le bras,
> presse le bouton avant d'ouvrir les yeux. (G 7)

> When the alarm goes off;
> he reaches out,
> hits the button before opening his eyes.

The verbs in *Geste* are almost all in the third person and the present tense, as in the first two tercets. Male and female subject pronouns alternate in a quasi-systematic fashion. Grangaud has said that she adopted this principle in order to resist facility and egocentrism.[21]

The gestures and actions are performed by unnamed people, with the exception of the child who appears in the very last tercet:

> Il apprend à é-
> crire son prénom:
> Joseph. C'est à la fin que c'est difficile. (G 131)

> He is learning to
> write his first name:
> Joseph. It's at the end that it gets hard.

What Has Become of the Oulipo?

In spite of their general anonymity, Grangaud's agents are not seen from a distance. They are portrayed as subjects of experience, the tercets registering their perceptions and states of mind. Peter Consenstein has shown that the material of *Geste* consists largely of qualia, which Michael Tye defines as "the introspectively accessible, phenomenal aspects of our mental lives."[22]

Grangaud's language in *Geste* is simple and, with a few exceptions, literal. Yet it affirms its literariness by literalizing and thereby awakening dead metaphors:

> Les feuilles des arbres
> palpitent. Le vent
> s'envoie en l'air avec du papier journal. (G 10)

> The leaves on the trees
> quiver. The wind
> gets off with sheets of newspaper.

> L'enfant est giflé,
> la trace des doigts
> une giroflée, reste marquée aux tempes. (G 17)

> The child is slapped,
> the mark of the fingers,
> a wallflower, remains on the temple.

The first of these tercets revives the metaphor in the expression "s'envoyer en l'air," literally "to send oneself into the air," figuratively "to have sex." The metaphoric idiom implicit in the second is "une giroflée à cinq feuilles" ("a five-leafed wallflower"), meaning a slap in the face.

The often prosaic content of *Geste* is also set off by Grangaud's use of a traditional resource in French versification, the so-called mute *e*, whose articulation gives her lines a certain elasticity:

> Ell<u>e</u> coup<u>e</u> la
> poire en gros morceau
> qu'ell<u>e</u> met à pocher dans de l'eau sucrée. (G 9)

> She cuts the
> pear into big chunks
> which she puts on to poach in sugar water.

252 How to Do Things with Forms

There are hard enjambments throughout the book, but the division of words across line breaks begins toward the end, with tercet 824 (G 109), and then increases in frequency, along with grammatical incompletion, as if the form itself were wearing out and beginning to break down:

En mangeant son ar-
tichaut, elle effeuille
un peu beaucoup précipitamment passionn (G 127)

Eating her arti-
choke, she counts off the leaves
a little a lot suddenly passiona

Behind this tercet is the counting game that consists of plucking the petals off a daisy while saying "un peu, beaucoup, passionnément, à la folie, pas du tout" ("a little, a lot, passionately, madly, not at all") to divine how much one is loved. Here the game is applied with a twist to the consumption of a chunkier flower belonging to the same family. The interpolation of *précipitamment* ("suddenly") suggests a play on the expression "avoir un cœur d'artichaut" (literally, "to have an artichoke heart," meaning to be quick to fall in love).

Initially it might seem that each stanza is self-contained, and the agent a different person every time. The world built by the book might appear to be thoroughly atomized. But gradually and subtly sequences begin to appear, for example in the following non-consecutive tercets:

Il n'est pas rentré.
Elle commence à
s'inquiéter. La pendule marque huit heures. (G 22)

He hasn't come home.
She starts to get
worried. The clock strikes eight.

Elle n'ose plus
regarder sa montre.
La nuit est tombée, il n'est pas revenu. (G 23)

She doesn't dare look
at her watch now.
Night has fallen, he hasn't come home.

Il n'est pas rentré.
Elle se demande
quand, raisonnablement, appeler les flics. (G 46)

He hasn't come home.
She's wondering when
it would be reasonable to call the cops.

Elle téléphone
au commissariat.
Elle dit mon fils n'est toujours pas rentré. (G 67)

She calls
the police station.
She says my son still hasn't come home.

On sonne à la porte.
Elle va ouvrir,
le coeur battant. Mais ce n'est rien. La voisine. (G 68)

There's a knock at the door.
She goes to open it,
heart pounding, but it's nothing. A neighbor.

These tercets seem to belong to one thread, but as Raluca Manea writes, "Notwithstanding overt similarities in diction, one can never be certain that events evoked are part of the same narrative, involving the same characters and plot."[23] Perhaps the connections here are thematic rather than causal, paradigmatic rather than syntagmatic, as seems to be the case in the sequences that are linked by setting (barracks, bedroom, factory) or kind of action (accident, dream, excretion).

Once the reader has noticed the presence of these two kinds of sequences, which cannot be sharply distinguished, no stanza is evidently self-contained or free-standing, and links can be found or made over large textual distances. For example, stanza 840:

Serrés peau à peau,
le désir fou de
franchir la barrière de peau, d'être l'autre. (G 111)

Clasped together, skin
to skin, the mad desire
to cross the skin barrier, be the other.

seems to echo stanza 283:

Les vêtements volent,
le désir les presse
de se trouver nus, se prendre l'un dans l'autre. (G 42)

Clothes fly, they are
rushed by the desire
to be naked, to fit into each other.

Whether the connection here is made or found, whether we are reading about the same pair of lovers or two similar situations, such links tend to multiply as one rereads *Geste*. Thus Grangaud exploits uncertainties relating to what linguists call participant tracking, with the effect of stimulating the reader's narrative and poetic imagination.

In spite of its systematic fragmentariness, *Geste* is immersive and eminently rereadable. The small cells of the tercets afford glimpses into the lives of strangers, as if from a passing train, except that they often give access to a point of view as well as a living space. The rapid succession has a powerful cumulative effect, to which Poier-Bernhard bears witness when she writes that it procures an experience of totality, prompting the reader to perceive herself as part of a whole.[24] It is this effect that justifies Pierre Alféri's description of *Geste* as an "epic of the everyday," a contemporary *chanson de geste*, in spite of the absence of heroes.

In its horizontality, its refusal to privilege a small number of protagonists, *Geste* radicalizes the strategies of literary simultaneism, as practised in the first half of the twentieth century by Alfred Döblin, John Dos Passos, and Jules Romains, among others.[25] A historically closer model is Perec's *Life: A User's Manual*. Perec said in an interview that his ambition when he began work on the novel was to design a machine for producing "entanglements of concomitant stories, somewhat in the style of Dos Passos, the father of 'simultaneism'" (EC I 228). But the decisive influence on *Geste*, according to Grangaud herself, came from another quarter. In 1989, she attended a conference on the work of the North American Objectivist poets organized by Emmanuel Hocquard, at which Carl Rakosi was present: "I came out of there saying to myself: 'That's exactly what I want to do.' I wasn't intending to efface myself or hide, at all. It seemed like the best way to make what I felt, personally, as strong as possible. Via that (apparently) maximal objectivity."[26]

In *Geste*, as in the work of the Objectivists, avoiding direct self-expression by no means excludes commitment or implies a chimerical neutrality of worldview. This is clear from the kinds of actions and situations that Grangaud chooses to include and exclude. The experience described in *Geste* is remarkably diverse: from the banal to the dramatic, from the everyday to the once-in-a-lifetime, from the infra- to the extraordinary. Like Perec, Grangaud is unafraid of insignificance:

Une cigarette
roule sur le quai,
encore allumée, n'est fumée qu'à moitié. (G 34)

A cigarette
rolls on the platform,
still alight, only half smoked.

But she is also unafraid of the dramatic and the wrenching:

Elle ouvre la porte,
entre dans la chambre,
allume la lumière, aperçoit les corps. (G 12)

She opens the door,
goes into the room,
switches on the light, notices the bodies.

Hôpital cardio.
Entre eux, les enfants
nomment le lit roulant "chariot de la mort." (G 130)

Cardiac ward. Amongst
themselves the children
call the gurney the "cart of death."

Tercets such as these, which deliver their impact with the last word,
give *Geste* an emotional range and a capacity to shock that Perec's
deliberately flat on-site logging of everyday life (discussed in chapter 2)
eschews. Grangaud's book is attuned to the "tears at the heart of
things," to quote Seamus Heaney's version of a famous phrase from
the *Aeneid*.[27]

There are moments of joy and pleasure in *Geste*, but most of the
lives glimpsed in the book are hard-bitten, whether by limited means,
exhausting work, illness, domestic tensions, or solitude. The following
still life is symptomatic:

Les plantes en pot
sont pâlottes. Seule,
la misère pousse drue et florissante. (G 106)

The pot plants
are pallid. Only
the spiderwort is thick and flourishing.

La misère in the original is ambiguous: as well as naming a species of
spiderwort (*tradescantia zebrina*) it may also refer to misery, wretched-
ness, or destitution.

Some of the anonymous agents in the book may be rich and powerful, but none are conspicuously so. Or rather, as with anonymity, there
is a single exception to this rule:

Casquette à la main,
il ouvre la porte
de la voiture où le président s'installe. (G 112)

Cap in hand,
he opens the door
of the car for the president to get in.

And here it is significant that the president is grammatically subordinate to his chauffeur. By declining to privilege certain agents or patients

over others, by treating the everyday and the once-in-a-lifetime equally, by alternating between male and female subject pronouns, and by legislating for these kinds of equality in the form of her sequence, Grangaud makes a strong if implicit axiological statement.

One of many underknown Oulipian works, *Geste* is now partly accessible in English, thanks to Levin Becker's translation of a selection of tercets in *All that is Evident is Suspect* (127–32). Grangaud's book has surely not exhausted its potential to reach and touch readers, but it may have another kind of potential too. According to Pierre Alféri, *Geste* has remained a "hapax," a one-off. This may not be its destiny. The combination of simple syllabic template and minimal thematic brief has a power that other writers might actualize anew and turn to their own ends. Even now that social media allow authors to hover over their published work like helicopter parents, there really is no knowing what a book will get up to in the world.

SOUNDS AND VISIBLE SIGNS

Many of the constraints and structures proposed by the Oulipo still await serious testing. For example, in Le Lionnais's "Idea Box," originally published in the group's first collective book in 1973 (LP 289–99) and recently translated into English for *All that is Evident is Suspect*, the co-founder of the Oulipo floats the idea of antirhymes: "Linguists and phoneticians have proposed several different procedures to characterize and distinguish phonemes. Such a procedure could be taken up if it allows a phoneme *A'* to be defined in relation to the complementary (or opposite, or symmetric) characteristics of another phoneme *A*. By definition, *A'* would be the antiphoneme of *A*. From this the notion of antirhyme follows naturally" (AES 35). Antirhymes were discussed at meetings of the Oulipo in 1963 (GO 229, 262), and they figure in the list of constraints on the Oulipo's website, but as far as I have been able to ascertain they have not been employed by any of the group's members in a series of exercises or a work.

A phoneme could have various antiphonemes, depending on the parameter considered. The antiphoneme of the English vowel /i/ with respect to lip position and place of articulation is the rounded back vowel /u/ (if you say *beat* then *boot,* your tongue moves back in your mouth and your lips pucker). With respect to tenseness, the antiphoneme of /i/ is /ɪ/ (say *beat* then *bit*: your jaw drops slightly). The classification of the consonants is more complex: phoneticians

258 How to Do Things with Forms

identify seven places and four manners of articulation in the English system. And the total phonemic inventory of English is relatively modest compared to that of many languages.

This complexity does not invalidate the idea of antirhyme, which in fact exists as a feature of vowel harmony in Turkish verse traditions.[28] Turkey, as it happens, is the source of another sound-related "anticipatory plagiarism." For its first public reading at the Avignon Festival in 1978, the Oulipo invented a constraint that obliged the writer and speaker to avoid the labial and labio-dental consonants (/b/, /m/, /p/, /v/, /f/), which involve a closing of the mouth. This was known in the group as the ventriloquist's constraint, since it makes the resulting text easier to read aloud without moving one's lips. As Roubaud tells the story, after the reading, a Turkish novelist who had been in the audience came to congratulate the members of the Oulipo on their performance, and said: "But you know, in my village in Anatolia, we have been doing that for centuries," before adding, "and of course, it's much harder in Turkish."[29] The ongoing Turkish tradition of *Lebdeğmez* (un-touched lips) is a kind of verse duelling or flyting: *Âşıks* or minstrels criticize each other by turns in verses that contain no labial or labiodental consonants, while using a pin to hold their lips open, and playing the saz.[30]

Since this incident, the members of the Oulipo have often referred to the ventriloquist's constraint as "vers turcs" (Turkish verses) (AO 732–3). Turkish verses and antirhymes are somewhat atypical in the catalogue of Oulipian constraints in that they are based on sounds. In the first classification of the group's inventions, "Queneleyev's Table," prepared by Queneau in 1974, there was no row for phonemes or for any sound-based unit (OC 217–19; ALP 74). Bénabou addressed this lack in the table that accompanies his article "Rule and Constraint" (1983), where the row shown in table 9.1 appears (OPPL 44).

Of the examples given, two are clearly linked to Oulipian inventions: Luc Étienne's phonetic palindromes (OC 77), recordings of which are available in *Drunken Boat*'s Oulipo feature, and Jean Lescure's "Poèmes pour bègues" (Poems for stutterers) (OC 230; AO 746–9).[31] The category of the lipophoneme includes Turkish verses. The other examples in this row are either anticipatory plagiarisms (by Robert Desnos and Michel Leiris) or traditional figures and techniques. Even if the row were updated by adding the newer sound-based constraints listed on the oulipo.net site (which are mainly kinds of rhyme), it would be more sparsely populated than the row for letters. The phoneme is

What Has Become of the Oulipo?

Table 9.1
Phonemes in Bénabou's classification of constraints

	Displacement	Substitution	Addition	Soustraction	Multiplication
Phoneme	phonetic palindrome spoonerism Rrose sélavy (Desnos) glossary (Leiris)	à peu-près alphabetical drama	stuttering	lipophoneme	alliteration rhyme homeoteleuton

not absent from Oulipian practice, but it is clearly subordinate to the letter, as indicated by the fact that the lipogram is an emblematic constraint, while the lipophoneme is rarely mentioned.

This may be due in part to practical difficulties. In order to apply a constraint to phonemes in a language with complex letter-sound correspondences like French or English, most writers would need to use a phonetic alphabet. When the difficulty of translating into and out of an additional code is added to the difficulty of the constraint itself, the sum may be discouraging. A second explanation for the subordination of the phoneme is that it is relatively difficult for a reader to perceive a phonemic constraint. The Oulipians, and Perec in particular, have trained us to look at their work carefully. "Look with all your eyes, look," reads the epigraph to *Life: A User's Manual*, from Jules Verne's *Michel Strogoff* (LUM xiii). Roubaud writes that the Oulipian constraint is "visible, necessarily."[32] If this were not the case, the reader might not notice it at all. To take the example of the anaphone (the phonic analogue of the anagram), it is by no means certain that a reader coming to the following lines without forewarning would notice that they are made up of the same set of twenty-two phonemes, and verifying this would require phonetic transcription:

> midnight calm, a lake of tea, the south
> the inner life makes a dark mouth eat
> this line came out of the dark at me

A third reason for the relative neglect of the phoneme is more theoretical. According to Roubaud, constraints cannot bear on "'invisible' data" like phonemes (PECH 222). This is hard to square with the phoneme-based constraints mentioned above. The assertion is made in the course of explaining that the Oulipo has avoided the error of trying to offer a systematic presentation of its constraints as Bourbaki did with its structures. The basis of any such presentation, Roubaud writes, would have been vulnerable to theoretical upheaval: "It [the Oulipo] has not sought to provide an overview of constraints, an organization based on the hidden parameters of a theory of linguistics (for which it has been criticized, by the way, though this criticism is based both on the analogue of the Bourbakist error (the choice of one theory rather than another, which is even more subject to collapse in linguistics), and on ignorance of the way in which literary constraints function, since they cannot be based on 'invisible' data, such as phonemes, for example)" (PECH 222; PEM 213, translation modified).

A long philosophical tradition, going back to Plato and Aristotle, has placed sight at the top of a hierarchy of the senses.[33] And there is a widespread pre-reflexive tendency to consider sounds heard less real than things seen because of their evanescence and impalpability. But it would be simplistic to attribute Roubaud's remark about "'invisible' data" to a graphocentric prejudice that privileges the visible over the audible, since it can be supported by practical and theoretical considerations.

Practically, constraints have better purchase on the written code, which is more stable and uniform than the oral code. We pronounce phones, which are the concrete realizations of phonemes, and a phoneme may be realized by various phones. The French /R/ for example may be occlusive or constrictive, and occlusive /R/s may be trilled (*roulés*) or tapped (*battus*). Moreover, a word may correspond to different sequences of phonemes, depending on the accent of the speaker. So a constraint that bears on phonemes is not guaranteed to work in the same way for everyone everywhere. All readers and writers of English share the same alphabet, but speakers of English do not all have exactly the same repertoire of phonemes and phones. Accents and pronunciations vary in time as well as in space: a lipophoneme written today, omitting a particular vowel, could at some point in the future be infected by the initially banished sound.

From a theoretical point of view, the validity of the phoneme as a unit of analysis may be challenged. Dominic W. Massaro and others have argued that the operative units of speech perception are larger than phonemes: syllables and demi-syllables.[34] Other linguists, in the wake of Noam Chomsky and Morris Halle, regard phonemes as too coarse rather than too fine, and treat them merely as convenient labels for bundles of distinctive features.[35]

In response to the practical issues, it could be replied that the instability of the oral code affects rhyme too. Certain rhymes are complete for some speakers and incomplete for others at a given moment. And as pronunciations shift, some rhymes fall into the category of eye-rhyme. Turning to the theoretical difficulty and Roubaud's skepticism regarding phonemes as constructs, it is true that their "psychological reality," affirmed by Edward Sapir in 1933, has been contested since the 1960s, but the debate is ongoing.[36] As labels they continue to be eminently convenient. And even if a new phonology were to sweep aside phonemes altogether, it is not clear that this would be a fatal blow to the literary value of a work written under a phonemic constraint. Must a literary work share the fortunes of a theory that has informed it? For those who, like Jerome Stolnitz, are convinced of the "cognitive triviality of art," the answer is clearly no, because the aesthetic value of an artwork has nothing to do with the knowledge that it communicates or embodies.[37] And those who defend the cognitive value of art are not obliged to situate that value in what an artwork has borrowed from science, history, philosophy, or another discipline. Like Hilary Putnam, they may trace it instead to a non-propositional kind of knowledge, specific to the artist.[38]

Given the complications that I have been discussing, the Oulipo might simply have left sound to the writer's intuition, and perhaps that was what Queneau was recommending implicitly by not including phonemes in his classification. But if anyone was averse to limiting aims in that way, it was the group's primary founder, Le Lionnais, for whom the Oulipian approach was potentially universal. His idea of antirhymes suggests a range of further phonemic constraints. On the model of the Oulipo's Turkish verses, a writer could compose with restricted sets of phonemes, using only voiceless consonants, for example, or only rounded vowels. Smooth vowel-to-vowel pathways could be arranged, progressively modulating the degree of aperture. Or acrobatic courses might be set up, constantly shifting the place of articulation from lips to pharynx and back. Onomatopoeic possibilities naturally spring to mind: using only voiceless consonants, one could write a text whose content must be whispered, while the rounded vowels might suit particularly affected characters, constantly puckering their lips. But nothing would oblige writers to pursue naïve or clichéd mimetic effects; they could just as well create sound shapes independent of, or even contrary to, the text's semantic content.

The phonemic repertoires of two languages could be compared, and writers could choose to use only the phonemes that are more or less common to both, writing for example in an anglophone-friendly French, without nasal vowels, /u/ or /R/. Or those sounds could be deliberately multiplied. Constraints could be used to put into practice an intriguing and questionable theory proposed by Don Paterson: what distinguishes the sound of poetry from that of prose is more variation in the vowels and less in the consonants.[39] In collaboration with phoneticians, writers might conduct experiments to determine which phonemic structures are most effective in casting what Roman Jakobson and Linda Waugh call the "spell of the pure sound of words."[40] Thus they might arrive at empty "magic" formulae, waiting for content but already endowed with aesthetic potential. The complexity of phoneme systems need not be discouraging. Their multi-dimensionality offers ludic opportunities that the linear sequence of the alphabet cannot afford.

I have been trying to indicate how much remains to be done by applying an Oulipian approach to the patterning of linguistic sounds. But it would be unjust not to mention a project recently launched in this space by one of the Oulipo's most prolific inventors. Frédéric Forte has imagined a system of equivalence between the vowel sounds of French and the notes of the diatonic scale, numbered 1 to 7, as in the Chinese system of simplified notation ("jiǎnpǔ"). Families of vowel sounds are attributed to notes, for example /a/, /ɑ/, and /ɑ̃/ correspond to C (do), /y/ corresponds to D (ré), and so on. By Forte's admission, these associations are "totally arbitrary," but they are governed by a complex set of principles. The oral vowels, for example, correspond to natural notes, and the nasal vowels to sharps. With this system in place, a series of compositional possibilities opens up. Taking Perec's isograms and Schönberg's twelve-tone serialism as models, Forte has written poems in which no note may be repeated until the sequence of seven has been exhausted (sharps and flats being assimilated to the natural note). These texts provide composers with melodic lines to be used as they see fit. As Forte points out, existing melodies can also be used to generate sequences of vowel sounds in accordance with his system. One could even re-vowel an existing lyric to make it correspond to the setting, performing a "jiǎnpǔ translation." The "jiǎnpǔ system" is still sounding its first notes.

What Has Become of the Oulipo?

TABLES AND CELLS

When Dmitri Mendeleyev published his periodic table of the known elements in 1869, he predicted the properties of four elements that were unknown at the time: germanium, gallium, scandium, and technetium, isolated in 1886, 1875, 1879, and 1937 respectively.[41] According to Mathews, Queneau had a similar aim in drawing up his classificatory table: "to direct Oulipian research to areas as yet unexplored" (OC 219).

The table has four columns, corresponding to aspects of the unit manipulated: length, number, order, nature. The rows are divided into two sections. In the first, there are rows for letters, syllables, words, sentences, and paragraphs. In the second, under the heading "semantic constraints," there are rows for characters, objects, events, feelings, place, and duration (OC 218; ALP 74–6). A glance reveals that the first section is much more densely populated than the second. In fact it contains only one empty cell, for constraints that would regulate the length of syllables. The Oulipo has not explored this kind of rule, which is hard to apply to languages without distinctive vowel length like French or English, but fundamental to quantitative meter in ancient Greek, Latin, Sanskrit, and classical Arabic.

The second section of Queneau's table was mostly empty when he presented it to the Oulipo, and the group has produced little to fill it. Jean-Jacques Thomas describes this inattention to semantic constraints as a "blind spot."[42] But some Oulipians have been aware of the gap, especially Le Lionnais, who laments it in the "Second Manifesto": "On the other hand, semantic aspects were not dealt with, meaning having been left to the discretion of each author and excluded from our structural preoccupations. It seemed desirable to take a step forward, to try to broach the question of semantics and try to tame concepts, ideas, images, feelings, and emotions. The task is arduous, bold, and (precisely because of this) worthy of consideration. If Jean Lescure's history of the Oulipo portrayed us as we are (and as we were), the ambition described above portrays us as we should be" (OPPL 29). Striking a similar note in a companionable farewell to the Oulipo, "Prolégomènes à une occultation" (Prolegomena to an occultation, 1998), Paul Braffort writes: "Beyond the alphabet, the lexicon and even syntax, semantics awaits us still."[43]

It is worth considering why the Oulipo's progress in this direction has been halting. Looking at Queneleyev's Table, it is hard to see what could or should fill certain cells in the second section. Is the length of a character a length of life in the story or an amount of textual space occupied? In order to constrain the nature of characters, objects, events, feelings, places, or durations, one would first have to establish taxonomies for each. How many natures can a character have, and what are they? Ever the enterprising optimist, Le Lionnais did not shy away from these difficulties. In his "Idea Box," he suggests compiling a dictionary of "significant elements" such as "Ideas (I), Sentiments (St), Sensations (Ss), Objects (O), Actions (A), Phenomena (P), etc" (AES 39). Any such dictionary would presuppose a metaphysical account of what there is. Are objects fundamentally distinct from phenomena, or sentiments from sensations? And how should Le Lionnais's brief list of categories be completed?

A quicker way to get down to work with semantic constraints is to derive them from an existing theory, as Calvino did in *If on a Winter's Night a Traveller*. In "How I Wrote One of My Books," originally published in French in 1982 and included in *Oulipo Laboratory* (OL 1–20) and *All that is Evident is Suspect* (AES 48–63), Calvino presents, with minimal explanation, a series of semiotic squares, which the title of the piece invites us to read as generative devices underlying the numbered chapters of his best-known novel.

The semiotic square, proposed by Algirdas Julien Greimas as the elementary structure of meaning, connects a seme (semantic term) to three others by relations of contradiction, contrariety, and implication. It has been used to analyze all manner of semiotic objects in studies that are often austerely technical and abstract. But a note at the end of "How I Wrote One of My Books" indicates that "the model square is a personal adaptation" of Greimas's structure (AES 63). And introducing Calvino's essay in *Actes sémiotiques*, Greimas himself wrote: "Nothing would be more false than to try, for example, to validate the squares of his presentation by reference to a theory of the semiotic square, whether standard or post-standard."[44] In a letter written in 1984, Calvino described the essay as "just a diversion" ("solo un divertimento") and said that it had nothing to do with semiology.[45]

Natalie Berkman has assembled reasons to be skeptical about the generative function of the squares, which she sees rather as providing a method of a posteriori interpretation.[46] Nevertheless, they are present, as Berkman admits, in the manuscripts shown in a BBC interview recorded shortly before Calvino's death. Pointing to a square whose terms are "the reader," "the not-reader," "writing as life," and "writing as mystification," which incidentally does not figure in "How I Wrote One of My Books," Calvino says: "I don't remember what I meant with my little drawings. Sometimes I get crazy when I am writing."[47] Whatever the precise function of the squares in the genesis of the work, and the degree of mystification in Calvino's later presentation of them, one thing is clear: his approach to Greimas's semiotic theory was playful, not scientifically rigorous.

It is not surprising that in the 1970s and '80s Calvino's fellow Oulipians did not follow his example of playing with the theories of structural semiotics, given the reservations that most of them had about structuralism in general. In the "Second Manifesto," Le Lionnais coins the word "structurElist" and begs the reader not to confuse it with "structurAlist, a term that many of us consider with circumspection" (OPPL 29). But were Le Lionnais alive today, he might be encouraging the members of the group to investigate the "Natural Semantic Metalanguage" (NSM) proposed by Anna Wierzbicka and her colleagues. Wierzbicka's contemporary version of Leibniz's "alphabet of human thoughts" is made up of simple semantic primes, atoms of meaning.[48] Cliff Goddard describes it as "the intersection of all human languages."[49] Such an alphabet would seem to lend itself to Oulipian exploitation. And perhaps a very austere kind of poetry could be written using the semantic primes of NSM, whose sixty-five English exponents include SMALL, WORDS, MOVE, IF, and TRUE. This would be comparable to the Algol poetry proposed by Le Lionnais (OC 47), which, in its strict version, employs only the twenty-four words of the Algorithmic Oriented Language, as in the following example:

Table

Begin: to make format,
go down to comment
while channel not false
    (if not true). End. (OC 47)

But the poetic potential of a set of highly abstract semantic terms may be quickly exhausted.[50] This is what Arnaud seems to have found in testing out the idea of Algol poetry. He decided to break up the words of the programming language and freely recombine their syllables and letters. In a preface to Arnaud's plaquette *Algol*, Le Lionnais writes: "freed from those wretched fetters, the poverty of the vocabulary was transformed into richness, and its dryness into a lyricism capable of great expressive variety" (LP 221).

Powerful poetry has been written using small if not strictly limited vocabularies. And proscribing abstraction across the board (not only as an antidote to vagueness and cliché in beginners' work) infantilizes poets, suggesting that they should leave thinking to those with real capacities for it.[51] Nevertheless, there are extremes of abstraction that clearly have a desiccating effect on literary writing, as Le Lionnais readily admits. And in the most successful poetic uses of small vocabularies, the key terms (such as Yves Bonnefoy's stones or Alejandra Pizarnik's shadows) are concrete enough to stimulate the production of mental images as few terms in Algol or NSM can ("table" and "channel" in Algol are exceptions).

In any case, the Oulipo has not drawn substantially on recent work in semantics, and it was a different kind of linguistic expertise that the group recruited in 1995 with Bernard Cerquiglini, a historian of philology and orthography, as well as a language policy-maker and consultant. Le Lionnais acknowledged a certain reluctance to regiment meaning in his interviews with Jean-Marc Lévy-Leblond and Jean-Baptiste Grasset (1976): "there's a tendency within the Oulipo, to which I don't subscribe – after a while, within a church, dissidents and schisms are bound to appear – I mean the tendency, represented by my dear friend Jacques Roubaud, to concentrate exclusively on form."[52] In line with this tendency, Bénabou dropped semantic constraints from his classificatory table (OPPL 44–5), although he did retain an intermediate circle of semantic objects in the accompanying diagram of "The Three Circles of Lipo" (OPPL 47; OC 230).

Instead of heeding Le Lionnais's and Braffort's calls to explore the semantic domain, the Oulipo has, in the twenty-first century, advanced in other directions. Interviewed by Camille Bloomfield in 2011, Jouet said: "In my opinion, semantics has never been a real lead for constraints [*piste de contrainte*]," and pointed out that the notion of constraint had been enlarged to encompass the process of a text's production.[53] As I explained in chapter 2, constraints have also been applied to the performance and publication of texts. In addition, cross-media collaboration has intensified, thanks in particular to Forte's work with musicians, and the recruitment of the visual artists Lécroart and Mélois. Recent examples of this collaboration include Mélois's illustrations for Berti's *L'Ivresse sans fin des portes tournantes* (The endless drunkenness of revolving doors), a collection of *greguerías* or

What Has Become of the Oulipo?

imagistic aphorisms, and Forte's ongoing combinatorial song project with Greg Saunier of the US band Deerhoof.[54]

In his notes for a third Oulipian manifesto, Le Lionnais mentions a "GRAND TABLEAU," which would be "a double-entry grid, each column corresponding to a mathematical structure, each row to a literary object" (AO 799). Replacing Queneau's aspects and Bénabou's operations with structures, Le Lionnais envisages a very large table indeed. But the "GRAND TABLEAU" has not seen the light. And Bénabou's table has not been updated. Drawing up a new table or revising the old ones would require theoretical debate, a "cleaning of the paradigms," which not all members of the Oulipo are keen to undertake, to judge from the minutes of the meeting held on 21 December 2004 (AO 809).[55]

What the group has done instead is to continue inventing constraints in an obstinately artisanal fashion, one by one. This is not just an easy way out; it also a way of enabling collaboration among people who may not be able to agree on theoretical positions. Allies may approach a common goal from different starting points, as Le Lionnais explained when discussing his Resistance activities, which included sabotage:

> Jean-Marc Lévy-Leblond: So what's more important in a discussion: knowing that you share a point of departure or reaching a common point of arrival?
>
> François Le Lionnais: The axioms of my sensibility are only points of departure; in a sense, I'm more a man of sensibility than a man of intelligence. For example, why did I choose action during the war, performing acts of "terrorism" that were contrary to my sensibility? It's not something I reasoned out; it's what the people who were on the same side as me were doing. I get behind causes that matter to me; I'm part of a certain coalition, but then I realize that within the coalition, no one else shares my point of view. Every time. How could I have explained to my friends in the Resistance that I wasn't a patriot?[56]

If agents always had to agree on their reasons for acting together, many collective efforts would never get off the ground. Similarly, insisting on theoretical guarantees of an action's feasibility can lead to indefinite delays. For Le Lionnais, the Oulipo was in a position comparable to that of the scientific researcher: the more ambitious and fundamental the research, the greater the risk of wasting time in attempts that turn out to be fruitless. That risk, he felt, must be assumed. Comparing the search for viable artificial literary forms to the synthesis of living matter in the laboratory, he comments: "That no one has ever succeeded in doing this doesn't prove a priori that it's impossible. [...] Further discussion of this point would seem to be otiose. The Oulipo has preferred to put its shoulder to the wheel" (OPPL 31).

As Le Lionnais saw it, the Oulipo's project involved a hope-based wager and a commitment to the open-ended adventure of invention: "I don't believe in progress or in decline, I believe that we're in the midst of an adventure [...] I join a struggle without knowing whether or not it has a chance of succeeding."[57] In this respect, he and the Oulipo as a whole stand in stark opposition to the formal fatalism represented by Michel Houellebecq: "Don't feel obliged to invent a new form. New forms are rare. One a century is already good going. And they're not necessarily invented by the greatest poets."[58]

OULIPISM OUTSIDE THE OULIPO

The Oulipo's classificatory attempts, even in their abandoned state, sketch out a vast research program that exceeds the executive capacities of a single group, however energetic. In his notes for the third manifesto, Le Lionnais divides the program into three phases. The first – drawing up the table and filling in the cells – is far from simple, as I have already suggested. "The second phase, which is also theoretical, aims to extract structures of demonstrable efficacy from this accumulation. The third and essentially practical phase sets itself the goal of leading to the Threshold of the Work" (AO 799). These phases are successive for particular constraints, but in the Oulipo's collective endeavour, all three have been under way simultaneously at least since Perec began to write *A Void* in 1967.[59] And literary invention in the spirit of the Oulipo has spread beyond the well-marked confines of the group.

A discreet sign of this is the presence of constraints invented by non-members of the Oulipo in the list on the group's official website: for example, the Brivadois acrostic and Delmas's method (OC 139). A more striking sign is the inclusion of work by non-members in the *Oulipo Compendium* and *The Penguin Book of Oulipo*. Both volumes sample the work of anticipatory plagiarists but also gather texts by contemporary writers in an Oulipian vein. The *Compendium* has entries for Walter Abish, Richard Beard, Herbert Schuldt, Gilbert Sorrentino, and Stefan Themerson, as well as examples from the writing of John Ashbery, Lynn Crawford, Richard Curtis, Jerome Sala, and Keith Waldrop. *The Penguin Book of Oulipo* ranges more widely still, taking in the following writers, grouped here according to the tags applied by the editor, Philip Terry:

> *After Oulipo*: Gilbert Adair, Richard Beard, Christine Brooke-Rose, Inger Christensen, Paul Griffiths, Lyn Hejinian, Tom Jenks, Édouard Levé, Jackson Mac Low, Christopher Middleton, M. NourbeSe Philip, Alice Oswald, Jeremy Over, Dan Rhodes, René Van Valckenborch.

> *Noulipo*: Christian Bök, Lee Ann Brown, Bernadette Mayer, Harryette Mullen.

> *Foulipo*: Juliana Spahr.

> *Outranspo*: Lily Robert-Foley, Philip Terry.

Terry does not claim that all the writers tagged as "After Oulipo" have been directly influenced by the group. Alice Oswald's approach, for example, is very different from the Oulipo's, but for Terry, her book *Memorial* "is a perfect illustration of Oulipo's concept of slenderizing" (PBO xxxii–xxxiii). According to the *Oulipo Compendium*, slenderizing is the operation that consists of removing all instances of a particular letter from a text to leave another text that makes sense. To cite an example provided by Mathews, "He could not erase the raging borne in dearth" can be slenderized to "He could not ease the aging bone in death" by removing the letter *r* (OC 228). This letter-based constraint can stand for all the Oulipian reductions of existing texts, such as Queneau's "Redundancy in Phane Armé" (PBO 141–5). Oswald's *Memorial*, subtitled *An Excavation of the* Iliad, radically "slenderizes" Homer's epic by stripping out the narrative to leave only similes and short biographies of soldiers, thus eliminating seven-eighths of the poem's bulk.[60]

The Noulipo tag refers to a conference hosted by the California Institute of the Arts in 2005, bringing together North American writers who had affinities with the Oulipo's project. Paul Fournel and Ian Monk of the Oulipo also participated. The conference gave rise to a book – *The* n*oulipian Analects* – which is a crucial document for understanding the transatlantic reception of the Oulipo. The *n* in the name of the conference "echoes the English *new*, the French *nous*, and the Yiddish *nu*, which means *so?* or *well?* and can be used by itself to mean *what's new?*" (NA 103). In their intervention, Juliana Spahr and Stephanie Young, while undressing and dressing again, performed a slenderized text that meditated on the body art of the 1970s and how it revealed what was missing from the Oulipo's work: "We instead wondeed if thee could be a new goup fomation, a sot of feminist Oulipo, something we jokingly began calling 'foulipo' because we didn't want it to be women only, we didn't want oulipuss. We just wanted something that engaged the elation between fomalism and body at and saw both as pat of a tadition that was complicated and inteconnected" (NA 11–12). This is the origin of the "foulipo" tag.[61]

Some para-Oulipian writing is highly orthodox in that it is based on precisely pre-formulated rules, which are adhered to rigorously. Most of the inventions shared on the long-running Oulipo mailing list are of this kind.[62] Gilles Esposito-Farèse's archive of his posts gives a sense of the verbal dexterity and restless inventiveness deployed there.[63] The list's contributors devote most of their energy to phases one and two of Le Lionnais's program: inventing new constraints and structures, and testing their efficacy in short exercises. Following Queneau's example, they have often used Gérard de Nerval's sonnet "El Desdichado" as a test bed for their inventions.[64] Over six hundred rewritings of the poem are to be found on Nicolas Graner's website Avatars de Nerval, and a hundred and one were published in the anthology *Je suis le ténébreux*.[65]

In the English-speaking world, Doug Nufer has taken similarly Oulipian devices through to stage three of Le Lionnais's program, writing fully blown works. His novel *Never Again* employs the simple constraint of forbidding word repetition in a narrative of more than two hundred pages. The protagonist is a gambler who tries to correct the mistakes of his past by doing (and saying) nothing he has ever done (or said) before: "No more gambling, horseplay, poker. Hyperordered strictures posit antipredictability, perhaps."[66] The constraint does, however, predictably starve the prose of grammatical words (articles, pronouns, conjunctions) and commonly used verbs. Nufer eases the strictures somewhat by employing contracted forms of the verb "to be," calling on other languages (Spanish, French, German), inventing words, varying names, and taking some liberties with spelling. Even so, the considerable opacity of the result shows just how crucial repetition and redundancy are to reading comprehension. The following passage contains the only instance of the word "are": "Loyalty's double-edged lacerating proficiency imperils indifferent conversing's noncommittality. Mexicans are infamous, puritans warn: admitting slightest kindnesses indebtedly obliges receiver; exhaustion customarily terminates reciprocity's rally. Puritan bookkeepers're indisposed, nonloyalty's warners overrule" (89).

Never Again stands at a radical extreme even within Nufer's body of work.[67] Oulipo-inspired writing need not be so restrictive. It can play more freely with constraints, as in Harryette Mullen's *Sleeping with the Dictionary*:

> My Mickey Mouse ears are nothing like sonar. Colorado is far
> less rusty than Walt's lyric riddles. If sorrow is wintergreen, well
> then Walt's breakdancers are dunderheads. If hoecakes are Wonder
> Bras, blond Wonder Bras grow on Walt's hornytoad. I have seen
> roadkill damaged, riddled and wintergreen, but no such roadkill
> see I in Walt's checkbook. And in some purchases there is more
> deliberation than in the bargains that my Mickey Mouse redeems.
> I love to herd Walt's sheep, yet well I know that muskrats have
> a far more platonic sonogram. I grant I never saw a googolplex
> groan. My Mickey Mouse, when Walt waddles, trips on
> garbanzos. And yet, by halogen-light, I think my loneliness
> as reckless as any souvenir bought with free coupons.[68]

The source text – Shakespeare's sonnet 130: "My mistress' eyes are nothing like the sun" – has been subjected to a variant of the N + 7 procedure: the nouns have been replaced by others beginning with the same letter, although some of the substitutes precede the original nouns in the dictionary. Presumably prompted by the Theme → Theme Park → Mickey Mouse → Disney World chain of associations, Mullen has replaced "she" with "Walt." But this Walt is ambiguous: with his rusty lyric riddles, he may also bring Whitman, author of "A Riddle Song," to mind. Whitman's America as theme park? One thing is certain: Mullen is having her way with both the source and the procedure, making a strategic choice for each noun slot.

Discussing *Sleeping with the Dictionary* at the Noulipo conference, Mullen said: "Not one of those poems is written strictly according to the S + 7 formula. For me, the constraints, procedures, and language games are just ways to get past a block or impasse in the process of writing" (NA 203). "I'm not," Mullen also said, "an Oulipian, but I'm proof that their ideas have far reaching influence among poets and writers" (NA 202). That influence has passed through her to younger poets. Mullen speculates that Terrance Hayes's anagram poems in *Hip Logic* may have been prompted by her presentation of the Oulipo's devices in a workshop, and goes on to quote "Segregate" from the sequence entitled "A Gram of &s" (NA 206). In an explanatory note on the sequence, Hayes writes: "The poems are based on the daily word game found in the puzzle section of many syndicated newspapers. I end each line with one of the eleven words derived from the title word, while abiding by the other rules of the game: 1. Words must be derived from four or more letters. 2. Words that acquire four letters by the addition of 's,' such as 'bats' or 'dies' are not used. 3. Only one form of a verb is used."[69]

Oulipo or newspaper puzzle? It would be rash to identify a single key influence on Hayes's invention in "A Gram of &s" (the title is a paronym of "anagrams"). It would also be to underestimate his originality, his "partial independence from the causal influence of an original," in Maria Kronfeldner's formulation.[70] For many writers of Hayes's generation, the Oulipo is there somewhere in the mix, without necessarily being a privileged model, and its most important function may be to authorize or legitimate play. Michael Leong makes this point when he suggests that the question asked by Marjorie Perloff of Charles Bernstein's *Shadowtime* – "How Oulipo is it?" – has little pertinence when it comes to North American constraint-based or procedural writing by Jackson Mac Low, M. NourbeSe Philip, Mónica de la Torre, K. Silem Mohammad, and others, given the thoroughly "synthetic and syncretic" nature of the works in question.[71] The same could be said of contemporary Québécois authors such as Anne Archet, Nicolas Dickner, Dominique Fortier, Marc-Antoine K. Phaneuf, and Steve Savage, whose formal affinities with the Oulipo have been explored by Dominique Raymond.[72]

Now that the Oulipo has become a common resource, like surrealism and Dada, it is fully exposed to misunderstandings. The group itself is often bemused by loose uses of its name. But misunderstandings need not all be regrettable. In creative responses, they can be productive, as César Aira suggests in his essay "The Incomprehensible": "Books move in space, they leave the neighborhood, the city, the society that produced them, and end up in other languages, other

What Has Become of the Oulipo? 273

worlds, in an endless voyage toward the incomprehensible. The ship that transports them is misunderstanding. [...] When books are stripped of over-understanding, all we can do is love them. The phrase, 'to love for the wrong reasons' is what logicians call a nonsensical proposition; anyone who has loved knows that."[73] This is an attractive conclusion, but we can, of course, do something other than love a book that comes from elsewhere. We can, for example, be disappointed, or feel that it fails to fulfill its promise. And this too may impel creative effort. The New Zealand novelist Eleanor Catton found a crucial negative stimulus in Italo Calvino's *The Castle of Crossed Destinies* when writing her novel *The Luminaries*:

> I found the book a terrible struggle, despite it being very slim, and, while struggling through it, I wondered why it was that novels of high structural complexity were so often inert, and why it was that structural patterning so often stood in the way of the reader's entertainment and pleasure. Did structure have to come at the expense of plot? Or could it be possible for a novel to be structurally ornate and actively plotted at the same time? I thought about the novel that I wished *The Castle of Crossed Destinies* had been – and this, at last, was my negative-charge influence, defiant rather than imitative, longed-for rather than loved.[74]

The range of effects that the Oulipo continues to produce on writing around the world is evidence that the group has not outlived its relevance. For the fans, whose numbers are continually replenished as young writers enthusiastically discover the group, it is a source of refreshment and delight. For many others, it is a diffuse influence, providing techniques to be occasionally adopted or adapted, and a precedent legitimating literary play. For some, it serves as a foil, a pointer to unrealized potentials.

THE OULIPO AS SOCIAL INVENTION

The Oulipo's effects are not due solely to what its members have written and published. The group itself is an influential social invention. Its original statutes, discussed in chapter 1, have helped sustain its unusually long life. Over the course of that life, the group has served as an incubator for fruitful collaborations in small cells of two or three members, which have often combined specialized mathematical knowledge with literary expertise. Claude Berge supplied Perec with a crucial component of the system of constraints underlying *Life: A User's Manual*: the graeco-latin bi-square of order ten that had been published by R.C. Bose, E.T. Parker, and S.S. Shrikhande in 1960.[75] Similarly, at the request of Jouet, Pierre Rosenstiehl determined an optimized itinerary passing through every station in the Paris metro while minimizing the number of segments travelled twice and the number of line-changes. Jouet then used this itinerary to write his two "Poems of the Paris Metro," in accordance with the procedure explained in chapter 2. The marathon stints of composition lasted more than fifteen hours.[76]

More recently, Monk and Audin have collaborated in exploring the world of noninas, that is, applications of the sestina's spiral permutation to groups whose numbers of elements are not Queneau numbers.[77] And Valérie Beaudouin has used the "métromètre" tool that she developed for her doctoral research on meter, rhythm, and rhyme in classic verse drama to analyze 130,000 alexandrines from the work of Pierre Corneille, Molière, Jean Racine, Victor Hugo, Charles Baudelaire, and Stéphane Mallarmé in terms of Forte's "jiǎnpǔ system." It turns out that not one line in the corpus is "dodecaphonic," containing all twelve vocalic "notes." Only thirteen lines use eleven different notes, and the most common number of notes is seven.[78] This confirms the originality of the phonemic texture in Forte's deliberately dodecaphonic lines.

In each of these cases, it would have been difficult if not impossible for one member of the group working alone to arrive at comparable results. The diverse capacities that make such collaborations fruitful have also made the Oulipo a rather odd and unlikely group, in spite of its relative homogeneity along the dimensions of gender and ethnic background. In chapter 1, I quoted Fournel recalling a conversation with Roubaud in which they accounted for the group's oddness by formulating the hypothesis that the Oulipo is "an unwritten novel by Queneau." As Roubaud points out, this hypothesis is more persuasive for the early Oulipo, all of whose members had been chosen by the founders themselves.[79] Since their deaths, the unwritten novel has morphed into something new.

Noting the way in which Perec's *I Remember* and "The Winter Journey" have prompted the Oulipians to respond with imitations and continuations, to the point where writing a sequel to "The Winter Journey" has almost become an initiation rite for a new recruit, Alison

James has proposed an update: "perhaps, rather, the members of the group are now characters in an open-ended, infinitely extensible Perec novel."[80] And perhaps at some point in the future it will make sense to think of them as characters in another kind of novel altogether, for the Oulipo itself, like certain constraints and forms, "harbours the seeds of variations and extensions." It too manifests "potentiality in actuality."[81] This is what Forte suggests when he writes: "In a sense, every Oulipian is a preparatory note" (AES 222).

Rather than spreading to become a broad movement, the Oulipo has "sporulated," inspiring the creation of separate but related groups. The Italian Oplepo (Opificio di Letteratura Potenziale), founded on Capri in 1990, is homologous with the Oulipo in its constitution and functioning.[82] The Frankfurter Werkstatt für potenzielle Literatur was established under the patronage of Roubaud in 2011, and has a more pedagogical orientation. It has published a user's guide to potential literature and a graphic epistolary novel in collaboration with the Ougrapo (Ouvroir de design graphique potentiel), also based in the German state of Hesse.[83]

These groups, like a number of the Ou-x-pos mentioned in chapter 1, are close satellites. In other cases, the affinities are more diffuse and personal links non-existent. What the currently dormant Australian group Kanganoulipo has in common with its French elder is above all a spirit of fun and a fondness for biographical fictions of the kind that proliferate in *Winter Journeys* and Le Tellier's *Atlas inutilis*.[84] There is a more technical debt, however, in the case of Ryan O'Neill's *The Drover's Wives*, mentioned in chapter 9, and in the poetry of Dave Drayton, who brings rigorously Oulipian constraints to bear on matters of concern far from Paris.

In *P(oe)Ms*, Drayton portrays all the Australian prime ministers using only the letters of their names. This constraint – beautiful in-law or *beau présent* – is combined in each case with a structure suggested by the minister in question. Anthony John "Tony" Abbott, for example, is remembered in a "villainelle" with the refrain "A boat, not a bath-toy," which alludes to his government's determination to turn back all boats carrying asylum-seekers, a policy that Abbott recommended to European leaders in the second annual Margaret Thatcher lecture in 2015, while admitting that "it will gnaw at our consciences."[85]

There is no necessary relationship between the *beau présent* and a particular political stance. Perec wrote beautiful in-laws to celebrate marriages, and in the unlikely event that anyone should be so inclined, the constraint could also be used to write in praise of Tony Abbott. Bök is right to point out that "the conceptual foundation of *contrainte* [...] might lend itself easily to political agitation" (NA 157). But this is a potential, not an essence, and may be realized on behalf of diverse causes.

The Oulipo's general approach to writing does, however, have an important metapolitical dimension, although the group itself has rarely made it explicit. In 1987, Mathews and Roubaud collaborated with the collective Invisible Seattle in an event at which members of the public were invited to rewrite constitutions according to Oulipian procedures. The handbill for this event, entitled Constitutions Unlimited, included a questionnaire which began as follows:

Delegate yourself
Design your own constitution with
THE CUSTOM CONSTITUTION QUESTIONNAIRE
It's easy! It's fun! It's binding!

1. I want my constitution to claim to derive its authority from:
a) The People
b) God
c) Male Landowners
d) Myself and few friends in the military
e) Any suitable capitalized noun[86]

This was meant to be fun, but also something more: imagining how we might be bound by a different set of social arrangements is a first step away from fatalism and resignation. In a way, what the Oulipo has done is to realize this program at the micro-level, establishing a small community in which, as in Charles Fourier's phalansteries, work is libidinized by play.[87]

Both in literary composition and in composing a new kind of artistic group, the Oulipo has shown that the alternative between adhering to traditional conventions and rejecting them in a revolutionary clean sweep does not exhaust the possibilities. We can also invent and institute new rules, which may build on or conflict with those already in force. The new rules may have limited domains of application, but they can take effect here and now. We can use them to restructure our language use and social lives, perhaps even to establish utopian enclaves in those domains. Monk put it in a nutshell: "One definition of freedom might be the ability to choose your own rules" (NA 142). The rules of a game, as C. Thi Nguyen has shown, sculpt the ways in which a player can act, so the Oulipo, as a group of inventors and as a social invention, works not on language alone but also on human agency, loosening the grip of convention and habit.[88]

For more than sixty years now, the Oulipo has been a force for the democratization of literature, proposing constraints and forms that writers of all levels of experience can take up and start to use straight away. The group is an invitation to do it yourself. "It" can be writing in accordance with an existing rule or inventing a new rule of your own or forming a new group. This invitation to play, invent, and build is open to all, and we are, of course, all free to decline it. As the poet Anthony Madrid has written, dispensing what he only half-ironically calls "Golden Advice": "They are right not to play at games who are certain to get no pleasure."[89]

Notes

INTRODUCTION

1 For narrative accounts of how the Oulipo was launched, see Lescure, "Brief History of the Oulipo" (OPPL 32–9), and Duchateau's preface to GO (11–21).
2 Bloomfield, *Raconter l'Oulipo*, 78.
3 See De Bary, *Une nouvelle pratique*, 12.
4 Cited in Lapprand, "Jacques Jouet: Un oulipien métrologue," 65. See also "Annexe III: Entretien avec Jacques Jouet du 9 mai 2011," in Tahar, *La fabrique oulipienne du récit*, 648, where Jouet explains that the formula is a variation on a sentence from Henri Maldiney ("Le classicisme n'est que la corde la plus tendue du baroque": "Classicism is but the tautest string of the baroque"), borrowed by Francis Ponge in *Pour un Malherbe*, 238.

CHAPTER ONE

1 See Bénabou, Garréta et al., "L'Oulipo et sa critique," 232.
2 See the Deep Vellum site at www.deepvellum.org.
3 See Andrews, "Surrealism and Pseudo-Initiation."
4 Vrydaghs, "Le surréalisme fictif."
5 *Archives du Surréalisme* 2, 91.
6 "À Suivre …," ix.
7 On Naville's break with Breton, see Naville, *Le temps du surréel*, 344–5.
8 See Daumal and Gilbert-Lecomte, *Theory of the Great Game*.
9 Polizzotti, *Revolution of the Mind*, 315.
10 Ibid., 679, note 315. See also Nadeau, *The History of Surrealism*, 172–4.
11 Bourdieu, *The Rules of Art*, 267.

12 Bourdieu cites Joseph Jurt's mimeographed *Symbolistes et décadents, deux groupes littéraires parallèles* (1982), and Bertrand, Dubois, and Durand, "Approche institutionnelle du premier surréalisme." See also Jurt, "Les mécanismes de constitution de groupes littéraires," 20–33. For an application of Bourdieu's model to the case of the situationists, see Brun, *Les situationnistes*.

13 See Bloomfield, *Raconter l'Oulipo*, 466–80.

14 Lapprand, *Pourquoi l'Oulipo?*, 102.

15 Ibid., 102–3; Coquelle-Rhoëm, "De l'Oulipo à 'L'Appentis de Science plausible'"; Tahar, "Les oulipiennes," 224–6.

16 Bloomfield, *Raconter l'Oulipo*, 100.

17 Lapprand, *Pourquoi l'Oulipo?*, 124.

18 Bloomfield, *Raconter l'Oulipo*, 113.

19 Elkin, "Tied Down," *Times Literary Supplement*, 19 October 2012.

20 Bourdieu, *The Rules of Art*, 268–9.

21 On Métail's withdrawal from the group's activities see Bloomfield, *Raconter l'Oulipo*, 413–14; Tahar, "Les oulipiennes," 223–4; and chapter 2 of this book. Due to declining health, Grangaud was not an active member in the final years of her life (Tahar, "Les oulipiennes," 226), but in *Moments oulipiens* she writes that the Oulipo broke her heart for the last time (MO 124–5). In 2016, Garréta told the Spanish journalist Alex Vicente that she had distanced herself from the Oulipo, having failed to reform it from within, and that if the group is to survive it must decide whether it wants to favour parity or go on being a male monoculture, and whether it wants to concentrate on reflection or on entertainment. Alex Vicente, "Internet no inventó la literatura experimental," *El País* (Spain), 19 November 2016. On the difficulty of being a female Oulipian, see Reggiani, "Être oulipienne."

22 Bloomfield, *Raconter l'Oulipo*, 184.

23 Levin Becker, "Question your Teaspoons: An Interview with Oulipian Daniel Levin Becker," interview by Stephen Sparks, *Writers No One Reads* (blog), 2013, accessed 29 July 2021, http://writersnoonereads.tumblr.com/post/34989467768/question-your-teaspoons-an-interview-with.

24 Nugent, *American Nerd*, 6.

25 Aira, "Rendez à César," interview with Philippe Lançon, *Libération*, 1 September 2005.

26 Quoted in Bellos, *Georges Perec*, 430.

27 See *Archives du Surréalisme 3*, 13–14; and Nadeau, *The History of Surrealism*, particularly "The Naville Crisis" (139–44), "Au grand jour" (145–55), and "The Aragon Affair" (191–8).

Notes to pages 22–6

28 Roubaud, "Racontez-moi l'Oulipo," 204. The UMP, Union pour un mouvement populaire, was the right-wing party led by Nicolas Sarkozy from 2004 to 2012.

29 Arnaud, *Noël Arnaud, chef d'orchestre de l'Oulipo*, 191.

30 Bürger, *Theory of the Avant-Garde*, 83.

31 See Hewitt, *Fascist Modernism*, which focuses on Filippo Tommaso Marinetti and Italian Futurism.

32 Pettit and List, *Group Agency*, 48.

33 Faye et al., "Liminaire," 4.

34 Roubaud, "Rancontez-moi l'Oulipo," 205.

35 See Vidal-Naquet, *L'affaire Audin*; and Audin, *Une vie brève*.

36 Poucel, "Family Vocation," 36.

37 See also Calvino, "Political Autobiography of a Young Man" (140–3) and "Where I was on 25th of April 1945" (176–9) in *Hermit in Paris*.

38 Le Lionnais, *La Peinture à Dora*, originally published in *Confluences* 10 (1946), 58–65. Levi, *If This is a Man*, 115–21. For a polyphonic account of Le Lionnais's Resistance activities, captivity, and time as self-appointed mayor of the German village of Seesen, see Salon, *Le disparate, François Le Lionnais*, 125–96.

39 On Le Lionnais's activities in the Marco Polo network, see Salon, *Le disparate, François Le Lionnais*, 118.

40 Queneau, *Journaux 1914–1965*, 513–19.

41 See Arnaud, "Un Queneau honteux?" 187–9.

42 Wichner, "Interview with Ernest Wichner," 43.

43 See Wichner, "Die späte Entdeckung des IM 'Otto Stein'" *Frankfurter Allgemeine Zeitung*, 18 September 2010; Müller, "Die Akte zeigt Oskar Pastior umzingelt," interview by Felicitas von Lovenberg, *Frankfurter Allgemeine Zeitung*, 17 September 2010; Wichner, "Interview with Ernest Wichner," 51. For an overview of the revelations and reactions to them, comparing Pastior's case with those of East German writers who collaborated with the Stasi, see Heath, "Slinging Mud?"

44 Müller, *The Hunger Angel*, 221–8.

45 Poucel, "Family Vocation," 37.

46 Ibid., 36.

47 See Salon, *Le disparate, François Le Lionnais*, 188.

48 In an "Autobiographical note" (1940), George Orwell wrote: "What I saw in Spain, and what I have since seen of the inner workings of left-wing political parties, have given me a horror of politics." *The Collected Essays*, 23.

49 Viala, "L'éloquence galante," 181.

Notes to pages 26–32

50 Queneau, "Erutarettil," 604.

51 Fournel, "Queneau et l'Oulipo," 178. On the origins of the idea that the Oulipo is an unwritten novel by Queneau, see Bloomfield, *Raconter l'Oulipo*, 71–2.

52 Bloomfield, *Raconter l'Oulipo*, 471.

53 Paul Braffort and Walter Henry, "Crise(s) d'Oulipo. Quelques fragments épars d'une histoire modèle," Les travaux et les jours (website), accessed 29 July 2021, http://paulbraffort.free.fr/litterature/oulipo/crises.pdf.

54 A list of Le Lionnais's membership cards is printed on the front and back flaps of Salon's *Le disparate, François Le Lionnais*. On the notion of "the disparate" see pages 340–50.

55 Roubaud, "What is Oulipo?" paper given at Western Sydney University, 23 May 2014. This list of rules closely resembles section 8 of "The Oulipo and Combinatorial Art" (oc 38).

56 Métail explains why she broke with the Oulipo in "Femme, Oulipo, poésie sonore, musique," 118–19. Braffort gives an account of his "self-occultation" in "Crise(s) d'Oulipo" (see 282n53). Roubaud provides a key to the roman à clef in *Peut-être ou la nuit de dimanche* when he explains that he took leave of the Oulipo after a reading in memory of Harry Mathews (151).

57 Bloomfield, *Raconter l'Oulipo*, 57.

58 Nehamas, *On Friendship*, 135.

59 Ponge, *Entretiens de Francis Ponge avec Philippe Sollers*, 73–6.

60 On Le Lionnais's "messianic" vision of the constraint, see Roubaud, bw, 233.

61 Some of the Oulipo's members, of course, have made mathematical discoveries, including Queneau, who published the results of his work on s-additive sequences in "Sur les suites s-additives." This article has been regularly cited by later researchers in the field.

62 Arnaud, *Noël Arnaud, chef d'orchestre de l'Oulipo*, 171.

63 See Kojève, "Les romans de la sagesse"; and Calame, *L'Esprit farouche*.

64 On the origin of this often misattributed aphorism, see Noguez, *La véritable origine des plus beaux aphorismes*, 97–102.

65 Bibliothèque nationale de France, Fonds Oulipo, Dossiers mensuels de réunion (1960–2010), août 1971, http://gallica.bnf.fr/ark:/12148/btv1b100101296/f6.image.

66 James, "Aleatory Poetics," 32.

67 See *Archives du surréalisme 5*.

68 Breton, *Mad Love*, 23.

69 See Bens, "Queneau Oulipien," alp 25; Roubaud, "Mathematics in the Method of Raymond Queneau," oppl 87; Arnaud, "Twenty Questions

for Noël Arnaud," 300; Bénabou, "Quarante siècles d'Oulipo," 21; Mathews, OC 123.

70 James's translation, *Constraining Chance*, 110; GO 146.
71 Breton, *The Lost Steps*, 72–3.
72 Queneau, "Chansons d'écrivains," 169.
73 James, "Aleatory Poetics," 33.
74 See Queneau, *Journaux 1914–1965*, 980.
75 Hartje, "Préface," 8.
76 Bense, "The Projects of Generative Aesthetics," 60.
77 Kant, *Critique of Judgment*, 175 (part 1, section 46).
78 Birkhoff, *A Mathematical Theory of Aesthetics*.
79 Birkhoff, *Aesthetic Measure*, 13.
80 Klütsch, "Information Aesthetics and the Stuttgart School," 68.
81 Nake, "Information Aesthetics: An Heroic Experiment," 61.
82 See Watkin, "The Pantasm: Heraclitus, Michel Serres, and the Changeux-Ricœur Exchange. On Naming the Human," Christopher Watkin (blog), 7 October 2013, http://christopherwatkin.com/2013/10/07/the-pantasm-heraclitus-michel-serres-and-the-changeux-ricoeur-exchange-on-naming-the-human; and Watkin, *French Philosophy Today*, 204.
83 Serres, *Hominescence*, 133.
84 Watkin, "The Pantasm."
85 Bibliothèque nationale de France, Fonds Oulipo, Dossiers mensuels de réunion (1960–2010), août 1971, http://gallica.bnf.fr/ark:/12148/btv1b100101296/f6.image.
86 See Nake's "Information Aesthetics": "The excitement brought about by Bense's way of doing philosophy came from his total presence and absolute immersion in the process of thinking. Aided only by some scribbles on the back of a package of cigarettes, he lived and demonstrated the mind in action. Things and ideas were all happening right here and now. Everything was authentic and exciting, and even if students did not understand a single argument, they knew they had witnessed philosophy as performance. At a time when C.P. Snow's *Two Cultures* were still stirring up controversy, Bense was demonstrating that you could almost single-handedly bridge the gap between mathematics and poetry. You did not need much more for this than your own dedication plus semiotics and information theory" (62).
87 See Queneau's formalization of the constraints for the haiku, the chimera, and stanzas of alexandrines in the minutes of the meeting held on 28 November 1974 (transcribed in Bloomfield, *Raconter l'Oulipo*, 454–5).

284   Notes to pages 39–46

CHAPTER TWO

1 On the complex origins of "make it new," see North, *Novelty*, 162–9.
2 Pound, *The Cantos*, 518. See Eastman, "Breaking the Pentameter," 159–60.
3 Mallarmé, *Correspondance*, 348–9.
4 Durand, "'La destruction fut ma Béatrice,'" 373–89.
5 Mallarmé, *Correspondance*, 350.
6 Barthes, *Writing Degree Zero*, 5.
7 Mallarmé, *Divagations*, 201–11.
8 Apollinaire, *Œuvres poétiques*, 1030.
9 Cruse, "Language, Meaning, and Sense: Semantics," 88.
10 Halliday and Hasan, *Cohesion in English*, 24.
11 Isou, *Introduction à une nouvelle poésie*, 11–18.
12 Marinetti, *Critical Writings*, 15.
13 Queneau, "Erutarettil," 605.
14 "Liquidation," 1–7.
15 Marinetti, *Critical Writings*, 82.
16 Bloomfield, "L'Oulipo dans l'histoire des groupes et mouvements littéraires," 40.
17 Breton, *Manifestoes of Surrealism*, 30.
18 Perec chose this sentence from *The Exeter Text: Jewels, Secrets, Sex (Les Revenentes)* (TH 102; O I 531–2) as the epigraph to the penultimate chapter of *Life: A User's Manual (La vie mode d'emploi)* (LUM 493; O II 557), and said in an interview that it was "perhaps what I like best of everything I have written" (EC I 187). See Reggiani, *L'éternelle et l'éphémère*, 9–10.
19 On the Literary Center of the Constructivists, see Webber, "Constructivism and Soviet Literature," 294–310; and Możejko, "Constructivism," 18–20.
20 Roxanne Lapidus translates this expression as "organized manipulation." Jouet, "With (and Without) Constraints," 4. I have attempted to preserve the familiar register of *bidouillage* and its implication of improvisation.
21 Bénabou, "Le mouvement," 226; Lapprand, *Pourquoi l'Oulipo?*, 101.
22 Reggiani, "Contrainte et littérarité," 15.
23 Roubaud, "L'auteur oulipien," 85.
24 Ibid., 85–6.
25 Ziff, *Semantic Analysis*, 36.
26 Quine, "Methodological Reflections on Current Linguistic Theory," 442.
27 At the meeting of the Oulipo on 28 August 1961, the following statement by Latis met with general approbation: "I would like to make it clear, at

Notes to pages 46–9

the outset, that the work presented is of no interest unless the method used is perfectly defined in advance" (G O 80). On the inference of generic conventions, see Genette, *The Architext*, 66.

28 Combe, *Les genres littéraires*, 46; Margolis, "Genres, Laws, Canons, Principles," 136.

29 Dorsch, "Introduction," 18; A. Fowler, *Kinds of Literature*, 26–7.

30 It is worth noting that all the constraints previously identified as having been proposed by Jacques Roubaud, including those co-signed with Marcel Bénabou and Olivier Salon, have been removed from the official list on the Oulipo.net website following Roubaud's withdrawal from the group: *acrostiche syllabique caché, alexandrin greffé, baobab, co-rime, émir, érim, joséphine, mongine, mots perecquiens,* Q S S D, *rimes de début, sardinosaure, sollicitudes, terine à trois voyelles, térine syllabique, variation sur S + 7* (site consulted September 2019 and December 2014).

31 A. Fowler, *Kinds of Literature*, 153–5.

32 Ibid., 43.

33 "Experience has shown that, with constraints, it's not the really complicated ones that work" (Jouet, "Entretien de Jacques Jouet avec Camille Bloomfield," 295).

34 Fabb, "Metrical Rules and the Notion of 'Maximum,'" 73.

35 Attridge, "Maxima and Beats," 81; and Attridge, *The Rhythms of English Poetry*, 42.

36 On Browning's double offbeats, see Attridge, *The Rhythms of English Poetry*, 191.

37 Colie, *The Resources of Kind*, 30; Todorov, *Genres in Discourse*, 20.

38 A. Fowler, *Kinds of Literature*, 55; Genette, *The Architext*, 73; Frow, *Genre*, 74–6.

39 A. Fowler, *Kinds of Literature*, 40.

40 Wittgenstein, *Philosophical Investigations*, 31–2, paragraphs 65–7; Hough, *An Essay on Criticism*, 86; A. Fowler, *Kinds of Literature*, 41; Roubaud, P 154.

41 Roubaud has commented on the limitations of the double analogy axiom/constraint, theorem/text in "Mathematics in the Method of Raymond Queneau" (O P P L 89); and "The Oulipo and Combinatorial Art" (O C 41–2).

42 See Millikan, *Language: A Biological Model*, 3–6.

43 Ibid., 7–9.

44 Ibid., 86.

45 Bénabou, "Quarante siècles d'Oulipo," 25; Bénabou, "Le mouvement," 218.

Notes to pages 50–60

46 Martial: "It is absurd to make trifling poetry difficult, and hard work on frivolities is foolish" ("turpe est difficiles habere nugas / et stultus labor est ineptiarum"), *Epigrams Book II*, 260. Calvin Bedient, "Against Conceptualism," *Boston Review*, 24 July 2013. http://bostonreview.net/poetry/against-conceptualism. On the Oulipo's relation to the Grands Rhétoriqueurs, see Desbois-Ientile and Tahar, "Des grands rhétoriqueurs à l'Oulipo."

47 Salceda, *Clés pour* La disparition, 65–75.

48 Auden, *Collected Poems*, 148.

49 Grangaud, *Poèmes fondus*.

50 Jouet, "Subway Poems," 64.

51 Bellos, *Georges Perec*, 417–18.

52 Monk, *Writings for the Oulipo*, 4.

53 "Eunoia is directly inspired by the exploits of Oulipo." Bök, *Eunoia*, 103.

54 Oulipo, *Oulipo*, 50.

55 Jouet, "PPP, le poème adressé du jour," Oulipo (website), accessed 29 July 2021, https://oulipo.net/fr/ppp-le-poeme-adresse-du-jour.

56 Jouet, "Monostique paysager," Oulipo (website), accessed 29 July 2021, https://www.oulipo.net/fr/contraintes/monostique-paysager.

57 Lapprand and Moncond'huy, "Avant-propos," 10.

58 Roubaud, *Description d'un projet*, 27.

59 Bellos, *Georges Perec*, 436–54; Lejeune, *La mémoire et l'oblique*, 98–121.

60 Perec, "Tentative de description d'un programme de travail pour les années à venir"; Bellos, *Georges Perec*, 579. On Perec's rhetoric of the project see Chassain, "Perec et la rhétorique du projet."

61 Lejeune, *La mémoire et l'oblique*, 149.

62 Perec, "Lieux, un projet."

63 Ibid.

64 Ibid.

65 Aira, *Birthday*, 60.

66 Lasky, *Poetry Is Not a Project*.

67 Forte, "99 notes préparatoires à ma vie avec Raymond Queneau," 27.

68 Jouet, *Poèmes de métro*, 261.

69 Poiana, "The Hyperbolic Logic of Constraint," 75.

70 Jouet, "De la lumière pour les navets," 45.

71 Poiana, "The Hyperbolic Logic of Constraint," 75.

72 Jouet, "La République préface," Oulipo (website), accessed 26 August 2021, https://www.oulipo.net/fr/la-republique-preface.

73 Bloomfield, *Raconter l'Oulipo*, 435.

Notes to pages 60–7

74 Tahar, "Usages du chapitre dans les experimentations narratives oulipiennes," Seminar, University of Paris III, 19 October 2016, https://chapitres.hypotheses.org/559.

75 Naukkarinen and Saito, "Introduction."

76 Goldsmith, *Uncreative Writing*, 195–200.

77 Similarly, in *Species of Spaces*, an idealized, composite landscape ("there are cows in the pasture, winegrowers in the vineyards, lumberjacks in the forests") is subtly undermined by a reminder of historical violence that disappears in translation: "There are little gingham curtains in the windows": "Il y a des petits rideaux de vichy aux fenetres" (SS 14, O I 562).

78 See Perec, *An Attempt at Exhausting a Place in Paris*; "Tentative de description de choses vues au carrefour Mabillon le 19 mai 1978."

79 Magné, "Carrefour Mabillon," 62. See also Phillips, "Georges Perec's Experimental Fieldwork."

80 Goldsmith, *Soliloquy*, Electronic Literature Collection, vol. 1, https://collection.eliterature.org/1/works/goldsmith__soliloquy.html.

81 Strawson, *Selves*, 9–12.

82 For an account of a "memory test" along these lines, see Madrid, "A Conversation with Anthony Madrid," interview by Michael Robbins, The Best American Poetry (blog), 15 February 2012, https://blog.bestamericanpoetry.com/the_best_american_poetry/2012/02/a-conversation-with-anthony-madrid-by-michael-robbins.html.

83 Descombes, *Le raisonnement de l'ours*, 226.

84 Stokes, "Incubated Cognition and Creativity."

85 Bénabou, "La règle et la contrainte," 103.

86 Perec, *Dialogue avec Georges Perec*, 26.

87 Roubaud, *La dissolution*, 264.

88 Leighton, *On Form*, 1–29.

89 Levine, *Forms*, 16.

90 Ibid., 2.

91 Queneau formulated the permutation algebraically as follows, generalizing it to poems with stanzas of any length. Let p be the position of an end-word in a stanza, and n be the number of positions (that is, the number of lines per stanza). A word at position p where $p \leq n/2$ moves to position $2p$; a word at position p where $p > n/2$ moves to position $2n + 1 - 2p$ (ALP 243).

92 Jouet, *Fins*, 119–21.

93 Reggiani, "De la contrainte à la forme," 540.

94 Perec, *A Void*, 101–9; *La disparition*, 118–25.

288 Notes to pages 67–76

95 Beardsley, *Aesthetics,* 165–209; Caille, "Approche de la texture."
96 Roubaud, *Quasi-cristaux,* chapitre 2, "L'invenzione del sonetto."
97 Ladha, "From Bayt to Stanza."
98 Roubaud, *Quasi-cristaux,* chapitre 1, "Préliminaires."
99 Roubaud, "L'auteur oulipien," 85–6.
100 Métail, "Femme, Oulipo, poésie sonore, musique," 119.
101 Coleridge, *Shakespeare, Ben Jonson, Beaumont and Fletcher,* 54–5; Orsini, "Coleridge and Schlegel Reconsidered."
102 Berrigan, *The Sonnets;* Roubaud, ∈; Mayer, *Sonnets;* Coleman, *American Sonnets;* Hocquard, *Un test de solitude;* Hayes, *American Sonnets for My Past and Future Assassin.* See also Hilson, *The Reality Street Book of Sonnets.*
103 Tahar, *La fabrique oulipienne du récit,* 650–1.
104 Simonnet, *Queneau déchiffré,* 143; Calame, *L'esprit farouche,* 30–1; Debon, *Doukiplèdonktan,* 206–7; James, *Constraining Chance,* 124–5.

CHAPTER THREE

1 Aira, "La nueva escritura," *La jornada semanal,* 12 April 1998.
2 Grangaud, *Souvenirs de ma vie collective,* 136 (for the translation and the original that follows).
3 Goldie and Schellekens, "Introduction," xiii.
4 Cited by Dworkin, "The Fate of Echo," xxv.
5 Aira, *Ghosts,* 56–7.
6 Dworkin, "The Fate of Echo," xliv.
7 Goldsmith, "Why Conceptual Writing? Why Now?" xvii–xx. In chapter 9 of *The Work of Art,* Gérard Genette considers Perec's *A Void* as a conceptual literary work, reducible to its concept (a novel written without using the letter *e*) with a moderate loss of singularity, as opposed to the near total loss occasioned by reducing *The Charterhouse of Parma* to the concept "novel" (135–55). For a critique of Genette's association of writing under constraints and conceptual art, see Mougin, "Littérature conceptuelle."
8 Bloomfield, *Raconter l'Oulipo,* 241. Martín Sánchez points out that automatizing the combinations of *Cent mille milliards de poèmes* reduced its interactivity: "Where, before, reading *itineraries* were chosen, now the choice is among *results* of reading." *El arte de combinar fragmentos,* 331.
9 Martín Sánchez, *El arte de combinar fragmentos,* 178; ALP 299.
10 Braffort, Chaty, and Joncquel-Patris, "Historique"; De Bary, *Une nouvelle pratique,* 29.

Notes to pages 76–83 289

11 Laird and Schwartz's Bot or Not website is discontinued. On the evidence of Bot or Not, humans were better at imitating computers in 2020 than the other way around. The most computer-like human poem in September 2020 was Deanna Ferguson's "Cut Opinions" with 75 per cent of testees attributing it to a computer, followed by Gertrude Stein's "Red Faces" with 70 per cent, while the most human-like computer poem was the very short "#6" generated by Janus node, with 61 per cent of testees attributing it to a human. See Caitlin Dewey, "Can You Tell the Difference Between a Human Writer and a Robot?" *Washington Post*, 4 March 2014.

12 Ross Goodwin (@rossgoodwin), Twitter, 6 May 2019 (account suspended).

13 Oscar Schwartz (@scarschwartz), Twitter, 7 May 2019, https://twitter.com/scarschwartz/status/1125568944553771008.

14 Bloomfield, *Raconter l'Oulipo*, 248.

15 See Braffort, Chaty, Joncquel-Patris, "Historique"; Bloomfield, *Raconter l'Oulipo*, 236.

16 Bloomfield, *Raconter l'Oulipo*, 250.

17 Knuth, "Algorithmic Thinking and Mathematical Thinking," 180.

18 Berkman, "Digital Oulipo," 13.

19 Colton, "Computational Discovery in Pure Mathematics," 25.

20 Gowers, *Mathematics*, 134.

21 See Hacking, *Why Is There a Philosophy of Mathematics at All?*, 63–6.

22 Quassim Cassam, "Understanding Adoption Resistance: The View from Philosophy, Cognitive Psychology, and Implementation Science (DRAFT)," Academia (website), accessed 29 July 2021, https://www.academia.edu/20058598/Understanding_Adoption_Resistance_the_view_from_Philosophy_Cognitive_Psychology_and_Implementation_Science_DRAFT, 1.

23 Poe, "Von Kempelen and His Discovery."

24 Breton, *Manifestoes of Surrealism*, 26.

25 On Bénabou's friendship with Jacques Lacan, see Duncan, *The Oulipo and Modern Thought*, 4.

26 See the Littré dictionary online at http://littre.reverso.net/dictionnaire-francais.

27 Lapprand observes that Bénabou and Perec seem to have been more interested in the procedure than in its products (*Poétique de l'Oulipo*, 114).

28 On the collaboration between Perec and Helmlé in the composition and translation of *Die Maschine*, see Bellos, *Georges Perec*, 375–85.

29 Perec, *Die Maschine*, 17.

30 Perec, "The Machine," 45.

31 Ibid., 49.

32 J. White, "Goethe in the Machine," 123–4.

33 Quoted in Bellos, *Georges Perec*, 380.

34 Perec, *Die Maschine*, 75.

35 Perec, "The Machine," 88.

36 Ibid., 33.

37 In a recent paper, Valérie Beaudouin reviews a series of "writing or reading machines whose only existence is fictional," which could be seen as anticipatory plagiarisms of Perec's machine. "Les machines autrices en littérature," IA Fictions, online conference, 3–5 June 2021, https://ia-fictions.net/fr/participants/valerie-beaudouin.

38 See Bellos, *Georges Perec*, 379–85.

39 Le Tellier, *Esthétique de l'Oulipo*, 232.

40 Calvino, *The Literature Machine*, 15.

41 Fournel, "Les ateliers de l'Oulipo," 26.

42 Gaut, "The Philosophy of Creativity," 1039.

43 Plato, *Phaedrus*, 27.

44 Murray, "Introduction," 11.

45 Ibid., 11–22.

46 On the internalization of inspiration, see Ruthven, *Critical Assumptions*, 64–5.

47 Similarly, Paul Valéry writes that he would far rather write something weak in a fully conscious and lucid way than give birth in a trance to an extraordinary masterpiece. *Œuvres complètes I*, 640.

48 Clark, *The Theory of Inspiration*, 1.

49 Ibid., 1–11.

50 Roubaud, *La dissolution*, 159.

51 Le Tellier, *Esthétique de l'Oulipo*, 11.

52 Duncan, *The Oulipo and Modern Thought*, 84–5.

53 Hart, "Eugenio Montale and 'The Other Truth,'" 172.

54 Queneau, *Pounding the Pavements, Beating the Bushes, and Other Pataphysical Poems*, 47 (translation modified).

55 Queneau, "Chansons d'écrivains," 169.

56 Seiffert, Myer, Davidson, Patalano, and Yaniv, "Demystification of Cognitive Insight."

57 Dourish, *Where the Action Is*, 139.

58 Hunter, *Critical Moments in Classical Literature*, 109.

59 Longinus, "On the Sublime," 119 (chapter 13, paragraph 2).

60 Ibid., 119 (chapter 13, paragraph 3); Hunter, *Critical Moments in Classical Literature*, 110.

Notes to pages 95–103

61 Lederer, "Préface," 12.
62 On eclectic imitation, see Hunter, *Critical Moments in Classical Literature*, 113, 125; and Ruthven, *Critical Assumptions*, 102–6.
63 Seneca, *Epistulae Morale*, 279 (Epistle 84.6).

CHAPTER FOUR

1 Jakobson, "On Linguistic Aspects of Translation," 139.
2 Perec, Mathews, Pastior, Eruli, and López Gallego, *35 variations*, 8.
3 Genette, *Palimpsests*, 7.
4 Ibid., 40.
5 Arnaud, "Gérard Genette et l'Oulipo" in BO 5, 14.
6 Genette, *Palimpsests*, 44 and 42.
7 See Genette, *Palimpsests*, 397; and Genette, *Palimpsestes*, 449. In the English translation, Queneau's name has been left out of the list.
8 Bedient, "Against Conceptualism."
9 Genette, *Palimpsests*, 400.
10 Ibid.
11 Bloomfield and Salceda, "La traduction comme pratique oulipienne," 249.
12 See Bloomfield, *Raconter l'Oulipo*, 517–36.
13 Université de Bourgogne, Fonds Queneau, manuscript of *L'Ivrogne dans la brousse*, http://www.queneau.fr/static/pdf/numerise/D60_4.pdf, 2.
14 Thomas, "Blithe Spirits," 7.
15 See in particular "Written in 1937" (LNF 17–27); "Academic Language" (LNF 133–44); and "People Are Talking" (LNF 155–56). The originals of these essays are to be found in the first section of *Bâtons, chiffres et lettres*, which contains three further pieces in the same vein: "Connaissez-vous le chinook?," "Il pourrait sembler qu'en France ...," and "Écrit en 1955" (57–94).
16 "Portrait: A Life in the Bush of Ghosts," 26.
17 Translated by and cited in Bush, "Le monde s'effondre?" 517 (translation modified).
18 Bellos, *Is That a Fish in Your Ear?*, 201.
19 Ibid.
20 Schleiermacher, "On the Different Methods of Translating," 50.
21 Cited in Lindfors, "Amos Tutuola's Search for a Publisher," 96.
22 Ibid.
23 Tutuola, *The Palm-Wine Drinkard*, 24–5.
24 Tutuola, *L'ivrogne dans la brousse* 25, and manuscript of the translation, 14.

25 Manuscript of the translation, 2.

26 Ibid.

27 See Chancé, "Une traduction postcoloniale d'Amos Tutuola?" 55–6; Jullien, "Zazie dans la brousse," 278; Elsa Veret, "Queneau, lecteur et traducteur du 'néo-anglais' de Tutuola," *Malfini: Publication exploratoire des espaces francophones*, February 2009, http://malfini.ens-lyon.fr/document.php?id=134.

28 Tutuola, "My Vernacular," 26.

29 Bellos, *Georges Perec*, 467.

30 Ibid., 487.

31 Mancarella, "Harry Mathews traduttore," 267.

32 Perec, "Avez-vous lu Harry Mathews?" 82.

33 Mathews, *Le verger*, 19.

34 Jetubhai and Ghosal, "Ungendered Narrative," 272.

35 Kim, *Unbecoming Language*, 129–46.

36 Vanderschelden, "Perec traducteur," 18; see also Magné, "L'estampille," 297.

37 Magné, *Georges Perec*, 82–94.

38 See Eco, *Mouse or Rat?*

39 Aira, *Evasión y otros ensayos*, 72–3. Bellos makes a similar point in "Appropriation-imitation-traduction," 5.

40 Métail, "Poésie avec Michèle Métail."

41 Cheng, *L'écriture poétique chinoise*, 56–7.

42 Sun and Saussy, *Women Writers of Traditional China*, 675–7.

43 See Bénabou, "Las obras del obrador," 13.

44 The figure of 14,005 is given by Li Wei, quoted in *Ancient and Early Medieval Chinese Literature*, 1034–5.

45 Da, "It Is Useless to Live," *Times Literary Supplement*, 1 August 2018.

46 See Hinton's website, accessed 13 July 2021, https://www.davidhinton.net/classical-chinese-poetry-an-an.

47 Pollock, "Future Philology?" 934.

48 Jullien, "Zazie dans la brousse," 266.

49 Ibid., 271.

50 Borges, "Narrative Art and Magic," 82.

51 Benjamin, "The Storyteller," 102.

52 Coetzee, *Elizabeth Costello*, 47.

53 Quayson, *Strategic Transformations in Nigerian Writing*, 45–55.

54 Coetzee, *Elizabeth Costello*, 53.

55 Ibid.

56 Géhéniau, *Queneau analphabète*, 975, 301.

Notes to pages 118–32

57 A Tangiers brothel known as the "Pension Macadam" in *Tlooth* (150; VCM 158) becomes a louche Paris nightclub, "La Villa d'Ouest," *in Life: A User's Manual* (LUM 488; O II 552).

58 Michel Butor, "La critique et l'invention," 8.

59 Plato, *The Dialogues of Plato*, 483–84; Levin, *The Philosopher's Gaze*, 11.

60 Métail, "Poésie avec Michèle Métail."

61 On the notion of scriptworlds, see Park, "Scriptworlds."

62 See Hinton's website, accessed 13 July 2021, https://www.davidhinton.net/classical-chinese-poetry-an-an.

63 Métail, "Infinity, Minus Forty Yearly Instalments: Noun Complements (1972–2012)," trans. Tom La Farge, *Words without Borders*, December 2013, https://www.wordswithoutborders.org/article/infinity-minus-forty-yearly-installments-noun-complements-1972-2012.

64 Eco, *Mouse or Rat?*, 170.

65 Kronfeldner, "Explaining Creativity," 217.

66 Bellos, *Is That a Fish in Your Ear?*, 312.

67 See Perloff, *Unoriginal Genius*; and Kenneth Goldsmith, *Uncreative Writing*.

68 Ecclesiastes 1:9, King James Version.

69 David Novitz sketches out a "Recombination Theory of Creativity" in Novitz, "Creativity and Constraint," 76–80.

70 Valérie Mréjen was invited to join the Oulipo after being a guest of honour at a meeting in 2001. See Bloomfield, *L'Oulipo*, volume 2: Annexes, 78.

71 Mréjen, *Ping-Pong*, 78–87.

CHAPTER FIVE

1 Meizoz, "Ce que l'on fait dire au silence," 2.

2 Riviere, "Sam Riviere on Christopher Reid's *Six Bad Poets*," 78.

3 Marías, "Guía para descartar lecturas," 303–5.

4 Paterson, *The Poem*, 53.

5 Robbins, "Ripostes."

6 See also Forte, *Minute-Operas*, excerpted in PBO 311–22.

7 Jakobson, "Quest for the Essence of Language," 347.

8 Guichard, "Simias' Pattern Poems."

9 Higgins, *Pattern Poetry*, 4–5.

10 Jakobson, "Quest for the Essence of Language," 350; Peirce, *Collected Papers*, 277.

11 On "kick-starts," see Philip Terry, "Introduction," PBO xxiv–xxv.

294 Notes to pages 132–42

12 Jakobson, "Quest for the Essence of Language," 350.
13 Poier-Bernhard, *Texte nach Bauplan*, 273; Grangaud, *Memento-fragments*, 25.
14 Poier-Bernhard, *Texte nach Bauplan*, 375.
15 Jakobson, "Quest for the Essence of Language," 347.
16 This certificate is reproduced in Bellos, *Georges Perec*, photograph 12.
17 For a detailed but admittedly not exhaustive treatment of the mentions and functions of eleven and forty-three, see Magné, *Georges Perec*, 58–68.
18 Ibid., 31.
19 Ibid.
20 Bénabou, Delay et al., "Table ronde," 183.
21 Schimmel, *The Mystery of Numbers*, 115.
22 Dante, *La vita nuova*, 80–1, chapter 29; Holloway, "The 'Vita nuova,'" 107.
23 Roubaud, *Quelque chose noir*, 11; Roubaud, *Some Thing Black*, 9.
24 Laskowski-Caujolle, *Die Macht der Vier*, 62.
25 Reina, "Entretien," 39.
26 "A054639: Queneau numbers," *The On-line Encyclopedia of Integer Sequences*, https://oeis.org/A054639.
27 See Salon, "Traces et abandons oulipiens," 180.
28 Ibid.
29 Roubaud, *La dissolution*, 158.
30 Ibid., 160. And see Montémont, "*Quelque chose noir:* Le point de fracture."
31 Queneau, "Sur les suites s-additives."
32 Roubaud, *Le grand incendie de Londres*, 141.
33 Schimmel, *The Mystery of Numbers*, 204.
34 Nerval, *Poésies*, 12.
35 Ibid., 240; Calame, "*Le chiendent*," 53.
36 Sanders, *Raymond Queneau*, 32–7.
37 See Queneau, "L'analyse matricielle de la phrase en français"; and Queneau, "Meccano."
38 See Roubaud, "Mathematics in the Method of Raymond Queneau," OPPL 93.
39 Métail, "Une petite musique chinoise," 72.
40 See Debon, *Doukiplèdonktan*, 169–71.
41 For the Taoist interpretation of the hexagram, see Cleary, *The Taoist I Ching*, 43.
42 Calame, "La place des mathématiques," 114–15; Dummett, *Frege*, 12–13.
43 Hobson, *Squaring the Circle*, 51–7.
44 Gray, "Georg Cantor and Transcendental Numbers"; Aczel, *The Mystery of the Aleph*, 114–17.

Notes to pages 142–9

45 Bell, *The Magic of Numbers*, 3.
46 Butler, "Numerological Thought," 20; Koyré, *Études d'histoire de la pensée scientifique*, 196–212.
47 Le Lionnais, *Les nombres remarquables*, 16.
48 Hardy, *Ramanujan*, 12.
49 OC 163–4; Bens, *De l'Oulipo et de la chandelle verte*, 115–69; Jacques Bens, "Seven Irrational Sonnets," trans. Rachel Galvin, *Words without Borders*, December 2013, https://www.wordswithoutborders.org/article/from-41-irrational-sonnets.
50 See Saclolo, "How a Medieval Troubadour," 682–7.
51 Audin, "Michèle Audin, Mathematician and Writer," 761–2.
52 Michèle Audin, "Désarguesienne," Oulipo (website), accessed 17 July 2021, https://www.oulipo.net/fr/contraintes/desarguesienne.
53 Hacking, *Why Is There a Philosophy of Mathematics at All?*, 86.
54 Lucretius, *On the Nature of the Universe*, 66.
55 Ibid., 67–8.
56 Skrbina, *Panpsychism in the West*, 59–62. Although there is no explicit reference to the doctrine of the clinamen or swerve in the extant writings of Epicurus, Don Fowler argues that "if Epicurus really wanted to break the chain of necessity, there must be some phenomenon like the clinamen at atomic level." *Lucretius on Atomic Motion*, 306. Likewise, Walter G. Englert concludes: "From the evidence we have, it is certain that the theory of the swerve was Epicurus', and it is probable that he introduced it into his system after he wrote the works which we possess." *Epicurus on the Swerve and Voluntary Action*, 11.
57 Lucretius, *On the Nature of the Universe*, 68; Lucretius, *De Rerum Natura*, 118 (book 2, lines 292–3); Fratantuono, *A Reading of Lucretius' De Rerum Natura*, 105.
58 Motte, "Clinamen Redux."
59 Thom, "Stop Chance! Silence Noise," 17 (cited in Motte, "Clinamen Redux," 279).
60 "Everything that [shows] stiff regularity (close to mathematical regularity) runs counter to taste because it does not allow us to be entertained for long by our contemplation of it; instead it bores us, unless it is expressly intended either for cognition or for a determinate practical purpose." Kant, *Critique of Judgment*, 93. See McManus, "Symmetry and Asymmetry in Aesthetics and the Arts."
61 Reggiani, *Poétiques oulipiennes*, 21.
62 Ibid., 42.
63 Perec, "Ulcérations," BO 1, 1–15; Magné, "Quelques considérations," 12.

64 I will be anglicizing the plural of clinamen, rather than using the latinate *clinamina*.

65 Ribière, "La poésie en question," 8.

66 The English version given here draws substantially on a partial translation in Poucel, "The Arc of Reading," 137, 141.

67 Magné, "La figure de l'orphelin," 306.

68 Poucel, "The Arc of Reading," 141.

69 See Bertharion, *Poétique de Georges Perec*, 195–6.

70 Perec, "Still Life / Style Leaf," 299; O II 1200.

71 See Bellos, *Georges Perec*, 57.

72 In Perec's *W or the Memory of Childhood*, the hands of mother and child are linked by wounding and scars: "She signed on as a worker in a factory making alarm clocks. I seem to remember she injured herself one day and her hand was pierced through" (12); "However, I still have on most of the fingers of both my hands, on the second knuckle joints, the marks of an accident I must have had when I was a few months old: apparently an earthenware hot-water bottle, which my mother had made up, leaked or broke, completely scalding both my hands" (40).

73 See G. White, *Lyric Shame*; and Don Paterson, "The Dark Art of Poetry," T.S. Eliot lecture, delivered as part of Poetry International at the Southbank Center, London, 30 October 2004.

74 Magné, *Georges Perec*, 45.

75 Ibid.

76 Roubaud, "Préparation d'une famille de contraintes," 204.

77 Ibid.

78 Bloom, Kennedy, and Wexler, "Ensnaring the Elusive Eodermdrome," 131.

79 Lusson, Perec, and Roubaud, *A Short Treatise*, 18.

80 See Le Lionnais, *La peinture à Dora*.

81 On François Le Lionnais's deportation, imprisonment, and escape, see Salon, *Le disparate, François Le Lionnais*, 142–96.

CHAPTER SIX

1 Jakobson, "Closing Statement," 356.

2 Ibid., 354.

3 Marsal, *Jacques Roubaud*, chapter 2, paragraph 23.

4 H. James, *The Art of the Novel*, 84.

5 Garréta, *Pas un jour*, 160. The list of thanks does not appear in the English translation *Not One Day*.

6 Rousseau, *The Collected Writings*, 5.

Notes to pages 166–75   297

7   Roussel, *How I Wrote Certain of My Books*, 20.

8   See "Freud's Psycho-Analytic Procedure": "the aim of the treatment will never be anything else but the practical recovery of the patient, the restoration of his ability to lead an active life and of his capacity for enjoyment [*die Herstellung seiner Leistungs- und Genußfähigkeit*]" (252); Freud, "Die Freudsche psychoanalytische Methode," 6.

9   Clancier, *Raymond Queneau et la psychanalyse*, 35.

10   Sheringham, *Devices and Desires*, 320.

11   See Burgelin, *Les parties de dominos*.

12   Calame, "*Chêne et chien* et *La Divine Comédie*," 19.

13   Ibid., 24; Clancier in the discussion following Calame's paper, 27–8.

14   See Freud, *Two Short Accounts*, 85–6.

15   Queneau, *Stories and Remarks*, 82–7.

16   These associations explain why Beatrice wears red, white, and green in Dante's *Divine Comedy* (Purgatorio canto 30, lines 31–3), and his *La vita nuova* (sections 2 and 3).

17   Calame, *L'esprit farouche*, 5; Blavier, "Notes," 6.

18   Latin phrases are similarly encrypted in the poems "La mer des Sargasses" (Sargasso Sea) and "Bois flottés" (Driftwood), from which, without manuscript evidence, it is similarly difficult to extract "corruptio optimi pessima" ("the corruption of the best is the worst of all") and "post tenebras lux ordo ab ch[a]o" ("after darkness light order from chaos") (OC I 548–50, 1424–5).

19   Roussel, *How I Wrote Certain of My Books*, 12–13; Foucault, "Archéologie d'une passion," 604.

20   See Debon's "Notice" in OC I, 1409–13.

21   See Sheringham, "Raymond Queneau: The Lure of the Spiritual."

22   See Freud, *The Future of an Illusion*, 212–15.

23   Lejeune, *La mémoire et l'oblique*, 37.

24   Perec, EC I 247; Bellos, *Georges Perec*, 623.

25   Dangy-Scaillierez, *L'énigme criminelle*, 384.

26   Lejeune, *La mémoire et l'oblique*, 138; Burgelin, *Les parties de dominos*, 113.

27   Burgelin, ibid., 116.

28   Ibid., 96.

29   Ibid., 196.

30   Ibid.; Freud and Pfister, *Psychoanalysis and Faith*, 38.

31   Burgelin, *Les parties de dominos*, 170; Ephesians 4:22–24; Colossians 3:9–10, King James Version.

32   Burgelin, *Les parties de dominos*, 10.

33   Ibid., 170; Ellmann, *James Joyce*, 155.

34 Jameson, *Postmodernism*, 148.

35 Josipovici, "Georges Perec's Homage," 180.

36 Bellos, *Georges Perec*, 478.

37 Métail, "Une petite musique chinoise," 69.

38 Debon, *Doukiplèdonktan?*, 155.

39 Magné, *Georges Perec*, 45; O 11 1084.

40 Bellos, *Georges Perec*, 603; Bellos, "Perec and Translation," 30.

41 Carter, *Marcel Proust*, 693.

42 Jacques Jouet, "La République préface," Oulipo (website), accessed 20 July, 2021, https://www.oulipo.net/fr/la-republique-preface.

43 Mathews, "An Interview with Harry Mathews," 41–2.

44 Winnicott, "Communicating and Not Communicating," 186.

45 On Roubaud's strategies of dissimulation, see Montémont, "JR007."

46 Bénabou, Grivel et al., "Vers une théorie de la lecture," 205.

47 Ellman, *James Joyce*, 521.

48 Rorty, "The Pragmatist's Progress," 89, 108.

49 Eco, "Overinterpreting Texts"; Eco, "Between Author and Text," 48, 83; Culler, "In Defence of Overinterpretation," 113; and Nicol, "Reading Paranoia," 44–62.

50 On the concept of the interpretive community, see Fish, *Is There a Text in This Class?*, 147–74.

51 Nicol, "Reading Paranoia," 282; Rorty, "The Pragmatist's Progress," 97.

52 Burgelin, *Les parties de dominos*, 129–30.

53 Magné, *Georges Perec*, 25, 108.

54 Magné, "A propos de *W*," 28.

55 Freud, "A Case of Paranoia," 393; Kantor, *Understanding Paranoia*, 15.

56 Culler, "In Defence of Overinterpretation," 113.

57 Bénabou, Garréta et al., "L'Oulipo et sa critique," 231.

58 Nicol, "Reading Paranoia," 50–2.

59 Zizek, *Everything You Always Wanted to Know*, 1–2; and Zizek, "The Limits of the Semiotic Approach to Psychoanalysis," 109.

60 Zizek, *Everything You Always Wanted to Know*, 1–2.

61 McHale, *Constructing Postmodernism*, 186.

62 Eco, "Overinterpreting Texts," 45–60.

63 Eco, "Between Author and Text," 72.

64 Culler, "In Defence of Overinterpretation," 110.

65 Eco, "Interpretation and History"; Eco, "Overinterpreting Texts"; Eco, "Between Author and Text"; Kosofsky Sedgwick, "Paranoid Reading and Reparative Reading"; and Felski, *The Limits of Critique*, 14–51.

66 Eco, "Interpretation and History," 30.

Notes to pages 182–91

67 Eco, "Overinterpreting Texts," 48–9.
68 Ibid., 50–1.
69 Eco, "Between Author and Text," 82.
70 Eco, *The Limits of Intepretation*, 40–1.
71 Ibid., 50–1.
72 Ibid., 83.
73 See, for example, Bénabou's skeptical (but appreciative) remarks on Magné's interpretations of Perec in Bénabou, Grivel et al., "Vers une théorie de la lecture," 210.
74 Culler, "In Defence of Overinterpretation," 110.
75 Queneau, *Aux confins des ténèbres*, 12.
76 Eco, "Overinterpreting Texts," 64.
77 Poucel, "The Arc of Reading," 129.
78 Kosofsky Sedgwick, "Paranoid Reading and Reparative Reading," 9.
79 Magné, *Georges Perec*, 69.
80 Ibid., 72.
81 Ibid., 73; and Bellos, *Georges Perec*, figure 12.
82 Magné, *Georges Perec*, 73.
83 Rémi Schulz, "31, Maquette à démonter," Perecqation (website), accessed 20 July 2021, http://perecqation.blogspot.com/2016/10/31-maquette-demonter.html.
84 Bellos, *Georges Perec*, 61.
85 Magné, *Georges Perec*, 108.
86 Foucault, "What Is an Author?" 113–20.
87 Géhéniau, *Queneau analphabète*.
88 Borges, *Collected Fictions*, 90. The narrator of Borges's story, presented in the opening paragraph as an embittered anti-Semite (88), is far from reliable, and when he speculates that his enemy Mme Henri Bachelier has misheard or misunderstood one of Menard's jokes (90), it is entirely possible that he is also unwittingly describing his own case.
89 Gadamer, *Truth and Method*, 293, 296.
90 Dangy-Scaillierez, *L'énigme criminelle*, 92–109.
91 Ibid., 132.
92 See Husserl, "Pure Phenomenology," 15. The influence of Husserl's phenomenology on *Witch Grass* was first pointed out by Simonnet in *Queneau déchiffré*, 95–101.
93 The italics in Barbara Wright's English translation reproduce the emphasis in the original (OC II 206). The account of the treasure hunt is considerably enriched by manuscript material eliminated from the published version of the novel, as Stump shows in *The Other Book*, 94–7.

300 Notes to pages 191–9

94 Landy, "In Praise of Depth."
95 Baskin, "Soft Eyes."
96 Călinescu, *Rereading*, 272.
97 Gadamer, *Truth and Method*, 296–307.

CHAPTER SEVEN

1 Bénichou, *The Consecration of the Writer*.
2 Noguez suggests that since the 1970s, the mantle of the *grantécrivain* has passed from the omnipresent and the voluble (André Gide, Jean-Paul Sartre) to discreet and even inaccessible authors (Samuel Beckett, Maurice Blanchot, Guy Debord). See Noguez, "Le grantécrivain." Johan Faerber's *Le grand écrivain, cette névrose national*, takes a series of more visible aspirants to task: Emmanuel Carrère, Marie Darrieussecq, Virginie Despentes, Michel Houellebecq, Leila Slimani, Sylvain Tesson.
3 Poucel, "Oulipo: Explore, Expose, X-Po," curator's note, *Drunken Boat* 8 (2006), Oulipo feature, accessed 21 July 2021, http://d7.drunkenboat. com/db8/oulipo/feature-oulipo/curator/poucel/intro.html.
4 Meschonnic, *Célébration de la poésie*, 139.
5 Jenny, *La Parole singulière*, 158.
6 Bedient, "Against Conceptualism: Defending the Poetry of Affect," *Boston Review*, 24 July 2103, http://bostonreview.net/poetry/ against-conceptualism.
7 Thomas, *La langue, la poésie*, 165.
8 Granadillo and Mendez, "Pathological Joking," 162–7.
9 Le Tellier, *L'anomalie*, 322.
10 Fournel, *Chamboula*, 255.
11 Hutchinson, interview with Emily Berry, 22 November 2017, The Poetry Review Podcast, 33:00, https://soundcloud.com/poetrysociety/ ishion-hutchinson.
12 Auden, *The Dyer's Hand*, 89.
13 Roubaud, *Ciel et terre*, 83–4. See Sheringham, "Les vies anglaises de Jacques Roubaud," 241–2.
14 Propp, *The Morphology of the Folktale*, 61.
15 Stallings, *Olives*, 50.
16 On the invalidation of promises by fraud or deception, see Raz, "Promises in Morality and Law," 926; and Owens, "Duress, Deception, and the Validity of a Promise."
17 Roubaud, "Le nombre d'Opalka."
18 Savinel, "Opalka ou l'éthique de l'assignation," 6.

Notes to pages 200–7

19 Suits, *The Grasshopper*, 43.

20 Duflo, *Jouer et philosopher*, 70.

21 See Caillois, *Man, Play, and Games*, 6.

22 Green, *Play and Reflection*, 11.

23 See Sutton-Smith, *The Ambiguity of Play*, 28.

24 Pellis and Pellis, *The Playful Brain*, 138–56.

25 Srinivasan, "After the Meteor Strike," *London Review of Books*, 25 September 2014. See Nietzsche, *The Gay Science*, 80 (paragraph 107); and Nietzsche, *Beyond Good and Evil*, 62 (part 4, aphorism 94).

26 Suits, *The Grasshopper*, 158.

27 Ibid., 156.

28 See Huizinga, *Homo Ludens*, 9; Caillois, *Man, Play, and Games*, 6; Benveniste, "Le jeu comme structure," 161; Suits, *The Grasshopper*, 41; Duflo, *Jouer et philosopher*, 204; Debord, "Contribution à une définition situationniste du jeu," *Internationale situationniste* 1 (1958), accessed 21 July 2021, http://debordiana.chez.com/francais/is1.htm#contribution.

29 Bohman-Kalaja, *Reading Games*, 202, 219.

30 On Colonia Dignidad and its relations with the DINA, Pinochet's secret police, see Basso, *El último secreto de Colonia Dignidad*, 44–56. On the Nazi presence in Chile, the regime's plans for colonization of Patagonia and Antarctica, and the case of Walter Rauff, see Farías, *Los nazis en Chile*, particularly 351–9 and 447–53.

31 See, for example, Astro, "Allegory in Georges Perec's *W ou le souvenir d'enfance*," 867–76; and W. Marx, *L'adieu à la littérature*, 151.

32 Rousset, *L'univers concentrationnaire*, 49.

33 Perec, *Entretiens, conférences*, 894.

34 Heck, "Pour un Perec politique," 87; Lefebvre, *Critique de la vie quotidienne* I, 252; Ribière in Perec, *Entretiens, conférences*, 894n3; Antelme, *L'espèce humaine*, 101.

35 A. James, *Constraining Chance*, 270; Burgelin in Perec, O I 1077.

36 On the difference between the "capitalist mode of production" and previous modes, see K. Marx, *Grundrisse*, 462–8.

37 Krugman, "Competitiveness: A Dangerous Obsession," 43–4; Allouch, *La société du concours*.

38 See Antelme, *The Human Race*; Levi, *If This Is A Man*; Rousset, *A World Apart*; Tillion, *Ravensbrück*.

39 Maher, "Threat, Resistance, and Collective Action." When, in an interview with Eugen Helmlé, Perec compared competition among the W athletes and the use of *kapos* in the Nazi camps, saying "In fact, it was exactly the same in the camps," he was simplifying considerably (EC I 197).

40 Plutarch, *The Parallel Lives*, 337.

41 Levin Becker, "Introduction," v.

42 Prendergast, *Mirages and Mad Beliefs*, 1.

43 Monsieur de Cadillac's name alludes to the make of car, but also to the jeweller Cardillac in E.T.A. Hoffman's tale of murder, "Mademoiselle de Scudéri" (1819).

44 Proust, *Swann's Way*, 5.

45 Cf. Shakespeare, *Macbeth*, II.ii.26 and II.ii.58.

46 See De Quincey, "On Murder Considered as One of the Fine Arts," 9.

47 De Quincey, "On the Knocking at the Gate," 6–7.

48 Cots Vicente and Vivero García, "El juego de la parodia," 90.

49 Breton, *Manifestoes of Surrealism*, 125.

50 Mars-Jones, "The Love Object," *London Review of Books*, 30 July 2015.

51 Genette, *Palimpsests*, 5. In addition to the brief citations of well-known lines or sentences and the systematic recycling of Proustian material, Virginie Tahar signals a substantial parallel between a passage in *Life: A User's Manual*, which describes Bartlebooth's project (chapter 26, O II 141), and the narrator's description of his method in *La décomposition* (D 204). Tahar, *La fabrique oulipienne du récit*, 476.

52 Paz, *The Collected Poems of Octavio Paz*, 82–91.

53 The Oulipian constraint known as the *chimère* or "chimera" is a textual analogue of the biological phenomenon. The following instructions are given in the *Oulipo Compendium*: "Having chosen a text for treatment, remove its nouns, verbs, and adjectives. Replace the nouns with those taken in order from a different work, the verbs with those from a second work, the adjectives with those from a third" (OC 124).

54 On the "true self" in Proust, see Landy, *Philosophy as Fiction*, 111–16.

55 Genette, *Palimpsests*, 48, translation modified to take account of a probable misprint in the original, where it seems that *lucidité* has taken the place of the much rarer but also much more pertinent word *ludicité*: "Le garant de lucidité [*sic*] est ici le caractère purement 'machinal' du principe transformateur, et donc fortuit du résultat." *Palimpsestes*, 67.

56 Samoyault, *L'intertextualité*, 63.

57 Garréta, interview with Frédéric Grolleau, 1 September 1999, accessed 21 July 2021, http://cosmogonie.free.fr/paru.html.

58 Hazzard, "I Felt that this Last Sentence," 180.

59 Garréta, "A Feeling of Vertigo," 213.

60 Proust, *Le temps retrouvé*, 250. Ian Patterson translates "les anneaux nécessaires d'un beau style" as "the necessary armature of a beautiful style" (Proust, *Finding Time Again*, 198).

Notes to pages 219–25

61 See Bersani, *The Culture of Redemption*, 2; Descombes, *Proust: Philosophy of the Novel*, 7–8; Prendergast, *Mirages and Mad Beliefs*, 3.
62 For a philosophical examination of works that take the skill required to produce them as their subject, see Mark, "On Works of Virtuosity."
63 Cave, *Thinking with Literature*, 73. The notion of epistemic vigilance was developed by Sperber et al., in "Epistemic Vigilance."
64 O'Meara, "Georges Perec and Anne Garréta," 44; Baldwin, "On Garréta on Proust," 34.
65 Cowling, *Abstract Entities*, 4–6.
66 Lupton, "The Embodied Computer/User," 100.
67 Kim, "Dans l'béton, dans la merde."
68 Kroker and Kroker, *Hacking the Future*.
69 Linda Schlegel, "Can You Hear Your Call of Duty? The Gamification of Radicalization and Extremist Violence," *European Eye on Radicalization*, 19 March 2020, accessed 21 July 2021, https://eeradicalization.com/can-you-hear-your-call-of-duty-the-gamification-of-radicalization-and-extremist-violence.

CHAPTER EIGHT

1 See Lapprand, *Pourquoi l'Oulipo?*, 54–5.
2 Roubaud, "Perecquian Oulipo," 108. The French original of this article has not been published, but the terms "potentialité prédisposé" and "potentialité en acte" are cited by Poucel in "Chiquenaude," 24.
3 Roubaud, "Perecquian Oulipo," 108–9.
4 Ibid., 103.
5 See Claude Debon's note in Queneau, OC I 1321.
6 Roubaud, "Perecquian Oulipo," 109.
7 *Textos potentes*, 290.
8 Ezequiel Zaindenwerg, "Drexler a la enésima potencia," *Letras libres*, 6 June 2013, https://www.letraslibres.com/mexico/drexler-la-enesima-potencia.
9 Aristotle, *Metaphysics Theta*, 3 (1046b).
10 Ibid., 4 (1047a).
11 Agamben, *Potentialities*, 183.
12 Mumford and Anjum, "Powers and Potentiality," 269–72.
13 Burt, "Sestina!" 218; McSweeney's Internet Tendency, "Sestinas," accessed 23 July 2021, https://www.mcsweeneys.net/columns/sestinas.
14 Burt, "Sestina!" 220–2; Pagani, "Potentielle et actuelle," 5–9.
15 Reggiani, *Poétiques oulipiennes*, 65–7.

16 Ibid., 47; Arnaud, GO 11.

17 Jouet, *Ruminations du potentiel*, 73.

18 See Reggiani's comments on the Oulipo's "impossible vitalism," in *Poétiques oulipiennes*, 69–70.

19 See Oulipo, "S + 7, le retour," in BO 4, 29–54.

20 See OC 96–8; Monk and Audin, "Le monde des nonines," Oulipo (website), accessed 23 July 2021, https://oulipo.net/fr/le-monde-des-nonines. On the Oulipo's queninas, see Lapprand, *Pourquoi L'Oulipo?* 59–60.

21 Roubaud, *Our Beautiful Heroine, Hortense is Abducted*, and *Hortense in Exile*; Berti, *Círculo de lectores*, 153–212. On Roubaud's uses of the spiral permutation at a range of levels, see Reig, *Mimer, miner, rimer*, 367–76. On the narrative sestinas in Fournel's *Dear Reader* and Michèle Audin's *Mai quai Conti*, see Pagani, "Potentielle et actuelle," 10–19.

22 Bénabou, "Petit complément à l'adresse présidentielle," 307.

23 Perec, SS 279; Kafka, *The Trial*, 245; Perec, *Things*, 322.

24 Perec/Oulipo, *Le voyage d'hiver*, 201; Beaudouin, "Incontro da due iper-romanzi," 69.

25 Jeannelle, "Perec et le divers de l'histoire littéraire," 187–9; Decout, "Qui a éliminé 'Le voyage d'hiver'?" 160–2.

26 Magné, Preface," 9.

27 Borges, *Labyrinths*, 234–6.

28 Burgelin, "Le silence de Perec," 19–20.

29 Rimbaud, *Collected Poems*, 6, 171.

30 Mallarmé, *Collected Poems*, 264.

31 Lautréamont, *Les chants de Maldoror*, 263.

32 Alison James points out that Degraël's name, like that of Percival Bartlebooth in *Life: A User's Manual*, resonates with the legend of the Holy Grail. A. James, "Perec and the Politics of Constraint," 165.

33 Sanders, *Raymond Queneau*, 92.

34 Doubleneuf exercices, accessed 23 July 2021, http://doubleneuf.fr/exercices.

35 Madden, *99 ways to tell a story*, 1.

36 Ording, *99 Variations on a Proof*, x.

37 Perec, "Tentative de description d'un programme de travail," 328–9.

38 Mathews, *Le verger*; Jouet, *Exercice de la mémoire*, BO 6, 225–36; Bens, *J'ai oublié …. Mais je me souviens*, BO 7, 51–64; Garréta and Beaudouin, *Tu te souviens …?*; Jouet, *Je me souvins*; Berti, *Funes se souvient – Funes se acuerda*; Pages, *Les choses communes*; De Montrichard, *Vous souvenez-vous?*; Quillien, *Je me souviens des années 70*; Flem, *Je me souviens de l'imperméable rouge*; Lindon, *Je ne me souviens pas*; Kohan, *Me acuerdo*.

39 Kohan, *Me acuerdo*, 59.

Notes to pages 231–8

40 Perec/Oulipo, *Le voyage d'hiver et ses suites*; Oulipo, *Winter Journeys (Expanded Edition)*.

41 Oriol-Boyer, "'Le voyage d'hiver,'" 168.

42 Reig, "Nomen est (h)omen," 120.

43 Audin, *La vérité sur "Le voyage d'hiver"*; Berti, *Les voyages dispersent*.

44 O'Neill, *Their Brilliant Careers*, 129–38.

45 Brainard, *I Remember*, 143.

46 Reig, "Nomen est (h)omen," 119.

47 James, "Perec and the Politics of Constraint," 167.

48 Lapprand, *Poétique de l'Oulipo*, 138.

49 Moret, "Discontinuité du recueil," 223–4.

50 Proust, *Against Sainte-Beuve*, 135–9.

51 Bibliothèque nationale de France, Fonds Oulipo, Dossiers mensuels de réunion (1960–2010), janvier 1976, accessed 23 July 2012, http://gallica.bnf.fr/ark:/12148/btv1b100101813.

52 Métail, "Une petite musique chinoise," 69–74.

53 Pascal, *Pensées,* trans. W.F. Trotter, 78.

54 See Pliny the Elder, *Naturalis Historia*, 91 (book 8, chapter 36).

55 Queneau, "Réponse de Raymond Queneau au questionnaire 1970," Oulipo (website), accessed 23 July 2021, http://oulipo.net/fr/reponse-de-raymond-queneau-au-questionnaire-1970.

56 Perec, "Réponse de Georges Perec au questionnaire 1970," Oulipo (website), accessed 23 July 2021, http://oulipo.net/fr/reponse-de-georges-perec-au-questionnaire-1970.

57 Poucel, "Chiquenaude," 22–3.

58 See Reggiani's note 1 in Perec, O II 1199.

59 Jouet, "De la morale élémentaire," 10.

60 "We don't give a shit about Nadeauesque authenticity, because it's a pretty sloppy criterion for a start […] and then because we're all too familiar with the way he has used it. Just to take an example: as far as I know, Nadeau has never taken down Queneau. He has even allowed people to praise him in the two papers he edits." Perec, *56 lettres à un ami*, 68. Letter dated 3 October 1959.

61 Queval, "Morale élémentaire (avec un clinamen)," in BO 1, 72; Fournel, "Élémentaire moral," in BO 1, 139–63.

62 All these variants are to be found in BO 4, 57–91; and *La Morale élémentaire. Aventures d'une forme poétique*.

63 Jouet, "Blason" and "Mouvements élémentaires de déshabillage," in BO 4, 67–71, and 79.

64 Forte, "Petite morale élémentaire portative."

Notes to pages 238–46

65 Grangaud, "Les temps traversés," interview, YouTube (video), 10:01, posted 7 June 2010, https://www.youtube.com/watch?v=DjoD_oBojNc.

66 Schama, *Citizens*, 856.

67 Condorcet, *Esquisse d'un tableau historique*, 189.

68 Terry, *Oulipoems*, 26–35; and Terry, *Quennets*.

69 Terry, *Quennets*, 142–3.

70 Poier-Bernhard, *Texte nach Bauplan*, 60–3.

71 See Bories, "Échographies," 215–27.

72 Jouet, *Ruminations du potentiel*, 66. See Descombes, *Le raisonnement de l'ours*, 226.

73 For a 'Pataphysical reading, see Bök, *'Pataphysics*, 69–70.

74 Tubbs, *Mathematics in Twentieth-Century Literature and Art*, 25.

75 Bamford, "Chalk and the Architrave," 8.

76 Tubbs, *Mathematics in Twentieth-Century Literature and Art*, 26.

77 Bamford, "Chalk and the Architrave," 8.

78 Frege, *Philosophical and Mathematical Correspondence*, 39, cited in Bamford, "Chalk and the Architrave," 7.

79 Blanchette, "The Frege-Hilbert Controversy," *Stanford Encyclopedia of Philosophy,* Stanford University, 1997–, article published 23 September 2007, last modified 9 August 2018, https://plato.stanford.edu/entries/frege-hilbert/index.html#ref-7.

80 Roubaud, "Two Oulipian Moments," trans. Anne F. Garréta and Virginia M. VanderJagt, *Drunken Boat* 8 (2006), Oulipo feature, accessed 23 July 2021, http://d7.drunkenboat.com/db8/oulipo/feature-oulipo/oulipo/texts/roubaud/moments.html. Queneau's journal is cited in A. Queneau, *Album Queneau*, 263.

81 Cited in A. Queneau, *Album Queneau*, 264.

CHAPTER NINE

1 Bloomfield, "Traduire *La Disparition* de Perec," round table discussion at Assises de la Traduction Littéraire, Arles, 13 November 2011, https://www.academia.edu/2645162/Traduire_La_Disparition_de_Georges_Perec, 3.

2 "The Impossible Fairy Tale: Korean Author Han Yujoo in Conversation with Veronica Scott Esposito," 27 April 2017, accessed 23 July 2021, https://www.catranslation.org/event/the-impossible-fairy-tale-korean-author-han-yujoo-in-conversation-with-scott-esposito.

3 O'Neill, "The Official History of Kanganoulipo," Kanganoulipo (website), accessed 23 July 2021, https://www.kanganoulipo.com/about-us#_ftn1.

4 Şentürk, *199+*.

5 Elkin and Esposito, *The End of Oulipo?*, 8.

Notes to pages 246–56   307

6 See Leong, "Rats Build their Labyrinth: Oulipo in the 21st Century," *Hyperallergic*, 17 May 2015, https://hyperallergic.com/206802/rats-build-their-labyrinth-oulipo-in-the-21st-century.

7 Goldsmith, "A Response to Foulipo," Electronic Poetry Center (website), accessed 17 February 2022, http://writing.upenn.edu/epc/authors/goldsmith/goldsmith_foulipo.html.

8 Elkin and Esposito, *The End of Oulipo?*, 6.

9 Duncan, *The Oulipo and Modern Thought*, 146.

10 Duncan, "At the BnF," *LRB Blog*, 3 February 2015, https://www.lrb.co.uk/blog/2015/february/at-the-bnf; Burt, "Must Poets Write?" *London Review of Books*, 10 May 2012, https://www.lrb.co.uk/the-paper/v34/n09/stephanie-burt/must-poets-write.

11 Turner, "Arranging Excursions to Disparate Worlds," 130.

12 Bloomfield, *Raconter l'Oulipo*, 369.

13 See the letter from Jacques Bens to Paul Fournel (1983), quoted by Lapprand in *Pourquoi l'Oulipo?*, 103.

14 Bénabou, Garréta et al., "L'Oulipo et sa critique," 240.

15 Salceda, "La réception de l'Oulipo en Catalogne et en Espagne," 4.

16 One evident cause of the unevenness is "the self-reinforcing dynamic which transforms the success of a few artists into both an effect and a cause of the quality attributed to their work by consumers." Menger, *The Economics of Creativity*, 180.

17 Alféri, *Brefs*, 174.

18 Cited in Manea, "Michelle Grangaud's *Geste*," 69.

19 Grangaud, "Entretien avec Michelle Grangaud," in John Stout, *L'Énigme-poésie*, 219.

20 Grangaud, "Entretien avec Michelle Grangaud: L'Écriture sous contrainte," 376.

21 Ibid., 376.

22 Michael Tye, "Qualia," *Stanford Encyclopedia of Philosophy* (1997, revised 2017), https://plato.stanford.edu/entries/qualia; Consenstein, "Michelle Grangaud's Qualia Poems."

23 Manea, "Michelle Grangaud's *Geste*," 75.

24 Poier-Bernhard, "Michelle Grangaud," 128.

25 See *Jules Romains et les écritures de la simultanéité*; and Bibbò, "Characters as Social Document."

26 Grangaud, "Entretien avec Michelle Grangaud," in John C. Stout, *L'Énigme-poésie*, 82.

27 Seamus Heaney, "Virgil's Poetic Influence," an essay broadcast on BBC Radio 3, Greek and Latin Voices series, 15 July 2008.

308 Notes to pages 258–66

28 Manaster Ramer, "Turkish Rhymes and Antirhymes."

29 Roubaud, "Jacques Roubaud: Writer, Mathematician, Oulipian," interview with Chris Andrews, Sydney Writers's Festival, 22 May 2014.

30 Dubreuil, *Poetry and Mind*, 18.

31 Luc Étienne, "Syllabic Palindromes," *Drunken Boat 8* (2006), Oulipo feature, http://d7.drunkenboat.com/db8/oulipo/feature-oulipo/oulipo/texts/etienne/etienne.html.

32 Roubaud, "Compose, Condense, Constrain," 645.

33 Jonas, "The Nobility of Sight."

34 Kazanina, Bowers, and Idsardi, "Phonemes: Lexical Access and Beyond," 565–7.

35 Chomsky and Halle, "Some Controversial Questions."

36 Sapir, "The Psychological Reality of Phonemes"; Kazanina, Bowers, and Idsardi, "Phonemes: Lexical Access and Beyond."

37 Stolnitz, "On the Cognitive Triviality of Art."

38 Putnam, "Literature, Science, and Reflection"; Bouveresse, *La connaissance de l'écrivain*, 59–60.

39 Paterson, *The Poem*, 55–6. For a challenge to this generalization, see Attridge, *Moving Words*, 83–4.

40 Jakobson and Waugh, *The Sound Shape of Language*, 234.

41 Emsley, *Nature's Building Blocks*, 198, 192, 467, 527.

42 Thomas, *Oulipo: Chroniques des années héroïques*, 35, 101.

43 Braffort, "Prolégomènes à une occultation," Les travaux et les jours (website), accessed 26 July 2021, http://paulbraffort.free.fr/litterature/pataphysique/prolegomenes.html.

44 Greimas, prefatory note to Calvino, "Comment j'ai écrit un de mes livres," 3.

45 Calvino, *Lettere*, 1516.

46 Berkman, "*Comment j'ai écrit un de mes livres*," 190.

47 "Calvino Bookmark Interview 1985," interview with Italo Calvino, YouTube, video, 25:18, posted 24 June 2019, https://www.youtube.com/watch?v=w2UUhi3vs7g. No complete manuscript of the novel was found in the author's house after his death. Calvino, *Romanzi e Racconti*, 1400.

48 Wierzbicka, "The Alphabet of Human Thoughts," 24–7.

49 Wierzbicka, *Semantics: Primes and Universals*; Goddard, *Ten Lectures*, 1.

50 See Lapprand, *Pourquoi l'Oulipo?*, 78.

51 For defences of the role of abstraction in poetry, see Rowe, "Poetry and Abstraction"; and Lamarque, "Poetry and Abstract Thought."

52 Le Lionnais, *Un certain disparate*, interviews with Jean-Marc Levy-Leblond et Jean-Baptiste Grasset (1976), section 15, "Troisième secteur,"

Notes to pages 266–73

accessed 29 July 2021, https://www.oulipo.net/fr/un-certain-disparate/15-troisieme-secteur.

53 Bloomfield, *L'Oulipo*, volume 2: Annexes, 165–6.

54 Berti, *L'Ivresse sans fin des portes tournantes*; Forte, "Distancing #18: Future Teenage Cave Artists," *The Believer*, 3 July 2020, https://believermag.com/logger/distancing-18-future-teenage-cave-artists.

55 In 2019, Paul Fournel remarked to Marc Lapprand that the Oulipo had passed through a series of phases – secret, theoretical, public, international – and voiced his hope for a second theoretical phase. Lapprand, *Pourquoi l'Oulipo?*, 105.

56 Le Lionnais, "Un certain disparate," section 63, "Logique de l'engagement," accessed 29 July 2021, http://www.oulipo.net/fr/un-certain-disparate/63-logique-de-lengagement.

57 Le Lionnais, "Un certain disparate," section 124, "Grisements progressistes du plaisir," accessed 29 July 2021, https://www.oulipo.net/fr/un-certain-disparate/124-grisements-progressistes-du-plaisir.

58 Houellebecq, *Rester vivant*, 15.

59 Bellos, *Georges Perec*, 395.

60 Oswald, *Memorial*, 1–2.

61 Outranspo (Ouvroir de translation potencial) is an Ou-x-po or Oulipo analogue, founded in 2012, and devoted to potential translation. See the group's official website, accessed 25 July 2021: http://www.outranspo.com.

62 For information on the Oulipo mailing list, see the following URL, accessed 26 July 2021: https://groupes.renater.fr/sympa/info/oulipo.

63 Esposito-Farèse, Gef's contributions to the Oulipo mailing list (website), accessed 26 July 2021, http://www.gef.free.fr/ouliposito.html.

64 LP 153–4; Lapprand, *Poétique de l'Oulipo*, 101–5.

65 Graner, Avatars de Nerval (website), accessed 26 July 2021, http://graner.net/nicolas/desdi/index.html; Abaclar, *Je suis le ténébreux*.

66 Nufer, *Never Again*, 3, 203.

67 Nufer, "(Reciting – not Dancing) An Interview with Doug Nufer," interview by Tom Beauchamp, *Hobart*, 1 December 2011, https://www.hobartpulp.com/web_features/reciting-not-dancing-an-interview-with-doug-nufer.

68 Mullen, *Sleeping with the Dictionary*, 75.

69 Hayes, *Hip Logic*, 91.

70 Kronfeldner, "Explaining Creativity," 217.

71 Leong, "Rats Build their Labyrinth."

72 Raymond, *Échafaudages*, 112–18, 132–8, 140–2.

73 Aira, "Lo incomprensible," 232.

74 Catton, "Eleanor Catton on How She Wrote *The Luminaries*," *Guardian*, 11 April 2014, https://www.theguardian.com/books/2014/apr/11/eleanor-catton-luminaries-how-she-wrote-booker-prize.

75 Berge and Beaumatin, "Georges Perec et la combinatoire," 86; Perec, *Cahier des charges*, 21–2; OC 176.

76 Jouet, *Poèmes de métro*, 263–5; Jouet and Rosenstiehl, "Frise du métro parisien" in BO 7, 223–52.

77 Audin and Monk, "Le monde des nonines," Oulipo (website), accessed 26 July 2021, https://www.oulipo.net/fr/le-monde-des-nonines.

78 Forte, "Système jiǎnpǔ."

79 Roubaud, "L'auteur oulipien," 83. See also BW 233.

80 James, "Perec and the Politics of Constraint," 158.

81 Roubaud, "Perecquian Oulipo," 109.

82 See the Oplepo website, accessed 26 July 2021, https://www.oplepo.com/cos-e-l-oplepo.

83 Frankfurter Werkstatt für potenzielle Literatur (website), accessed 26 July 2021, https://www.oulipo-frankfurt.de; Ougrapo: Ouvroir de design graphique potentiel (website), accessed 26 July 2021, http://www.ougrapo.de. The Frankfurter Werkstatt's books are: Boehncke, Dobrigkeit, Gauder, Hohmann, and Ortwein, *Oulipo – Ougrapo Eine Gebrauchsanweisung*, and Dobrigkeit, Gauder, Hauff, and Ortwein, *Mme Perreq*.

84 Kanganoulipo (website), accessed 26 July 2021, https://www.kanganoulipo.com.

85 Drayton, *P(oe)Ms*, 49. See Melissa Clarke, "Tony Abbott tells European leaders to turn back asylum seekers or risk 'catastrophic error,'" ABC News, 28 October 2015, https://www.abc.net.au/news/2015-10-28/tony-abbott-urges-european-leaders-to-turn-back-asylum-seekers/6890886.

86 Wittig, *Invisible Rendezvous*, 159.

87 On the Oulipo as a community and an ironic avatar of the historical avant-gardes, see Kaufmann, *Poétique des groupes littéraires*, 48–53. On Calvino's interest in Charles Fourier, see Marie Fabre, "Calvino et l'utopie, de Fourier aux *Villes invisibles*: Pour une réflexion sur les fonctions de la littérature," *Colloque littérature et "temps des révoltes"* (Italie, 1967–1980), website accessed 26 July 2021, http://colloque-temps-revoltes.ens-lyon.fr/spip.php?article131.

88 Nguyen, "Games and the Art of Agency."

89 Madrid, *I Am Your Slave*, 5.

Bibliography

ARCHIVAL SOURCES

Bibliothèque nationale de France. Fonds Oulipo. https://archivesetmanuscrits.bnf.fr/ark:/12148/cc98168h.

Université de Bourgogne. Fonds Queneau. http://www.queneau.fr.

PRINTED SOURCES

Abaclar, Camille. *Je suis le ténébreux*. Paris: Quintette, 2002.

Aczel, Amir D. *The Mystery of the Aleph*. New York: Four Walls Eight Windows, 2000.

Agamben, Giorgio. *Potentialities*. Translated by Daniel Heller-Roazen. Stanford: Stanford University Press, 1999.

Aira, César. *Birthday*. Translated by Chris Andrews. New York: New Directions, 2019.

– *Evasión y otros ensayos*. Barcelona: Penguin Random House, 2017.

– *Ghosts*. Translated by Chris Andrews. New York: New Directions, 2008.

– "Lo incomprensible." In *La ola que lee: Artículos y reseñas 1981–2010*, edited by María Belén Riveiro, 226–33. Barcelona: Penguin Random House, 2021.

Alféri, Pierre. *Brefs: Discours*. Paris: POL, 2016.

Allouch, Annabelle. *La société du concours: L'empire des classements scolaires*. Paris: Seuil, 2017.

Ancient and Early Medieval Chinese Literature. A Reference Guide. Edited by David R. Knechtges and Taiping Chang. Leiden: Brill, 2014.

Andrews, Chris. "Surrealism and Pseudo-Initiation: Raymond Queneau's *Odile*." *Modern Language Review* 94, no. 2 (1999): 377–94.

Antelme, Robert. *L'espèce humaine*. Paris: Gallimard, 1957.

- *The Human Race*. Translated by Jeffrey Haight and Annie Mahler. Evanston, IL: Marlboro Press, 1998.
An Anthology of Chance Operations ... Edited by La Monte Young. New York: privately published by Jackson Mac Low, 1963.
Apollinaire, Guillaume. *Œuvres poétiques*. Edited by Michel Décaudin. Paris: Gallimard, 1956.
Archives du surréalisme 2: Vers l'action politique. Edited by Marguerite Bonnet. Paris: Gallimard, 1988.
Archives du surréalisme 3: Adhérer au Parti communiste. Edited by Marguerite Bonnet. Paris: Gallimard, 1992.
Archives du surréalisme 5: Les jeux surréalistes. Edited by Emmanuel Garrigues. Paris: Gallimard, 1995.
Aristotle. *Metaphysics Theta*. Edited and translated by Stephen Makin. Oxford: Oxford University Press, 2006.
Arnaud, Noël. *Noël Arnaud, chef d'orchestre de l'Oulipo: Correspondance 1961–1998*. Edited by Marc Lapprand and Christophe Reig. Paris: Honoré Champion, 2018.
- "Un Queneau honteux?" *Europe* 888 (2003): 180–9.
- "Twenty Questions for Noël Arnaud." Interview by Warren F. Motte, Jr. *Studies in 20th Century Literature* 10, no. 2 (1986): 289–306.
Astro, Alan. "Allegory in Georges Perec's *W ou le souvenir d'enfance*." *MLN* 102, no. 4 (1987): 867–76.
"À Suivre ... Petite contribution au dossier de certains intellectuels à tendances révolutionnaires (Paris 1929)." *Variétés*, June 1929, i–xxxxii.
Attridge, Derek. "Maxima and Beats: A Response to Nigel Fabb's Reply." *Language and Literature* 12, no. 1 (2003): 81–2.
- *Moving Words: Forms of English Poetry*. Oxford: Oxford University Press, 2013.
- *The Rhythms of English Poetry*. London: Longman, 1982.
Auden, W.H. *Collected Poems*. Edited by Edward Mendelson. London: Faber and Faber, 1976.
- *The Dyer's Hand and Other Essays*. London: Faber and Faber, 1975.
Audin, Michèle. *La formule de Stokes, roman*. Paris: Cassini, 2016. [FS]
- "Michèle Audin, Mathematician and Writer." Interview by Allyn Jackson. *Notices of the American Mathematical Society* 64, no. 7 (2017): 761–2. http://dx.doi.org/10.1090/noti1545.
- *One Hundred Twenty-One Days*. Translated by Christiana Hills. Dallas: Deep Vellum Publishing, 2016.
- *La vérité sur "Le voyage d'hiver."* La bibliothèque oulipienne no. 216. Paris: printed by the Oulipo, 2014.

– *Une vie brève*. Paris: Gallimard, 2013.

Baetens, Jan. "Oulipo and Proceduralism." In *The Routledge Companion to Experimental Literature*, edited by Joe Bray, Alison Gibbons, and Brian McHale, 115–27. London: Routledge, 2012.

Baldwin, Thomas. "On Garréta on Proust." *French Studies* 70, no. 1 (2016): 33–43.

Bamford, Alice. "Chalk and the Architrave: Mathematics and Modern Literature." PhD diss., University of Cambridge, 2015.

Barthes, Roland. *Writing Degree Zero*. Translated by Annette Lavers and Colin Smith. New York: Hill and Wang, 1968.

Baskin, Jason. "Soft Eyes: Marxism, Surface, and Depth." *Mediations: Journal of the Marxist Literary Group* 28, no. 2 (2015): 5–18.

Basso, Carlos. *El último secreto de Colonia Dignidad*. Santiago: Mare Nostrum, 2002.

Beardsley, Monroe C. *Aesthetics: Problems in the Philosophy of Criticism*. Indianapolis, IN: Hackett, 1981.

Beaudouin, Valérie. "Incontro da due iper-romanzi: *Se una notte d'inverno* ... e i 'Voyages d'hiver.'" In *Italo Calvino. Percorsi potenziali*, edited by Raffaele Aragona, 63–71. San Cesari di Lecce: Manni, 2008.

– *Mètre et rythmes du vers classique. Corneille et Racine*. Paris: Honoré Champion, 2002.

Bedient, Calvin. "Against Conceptualism." *Boston Review*, 24 July 2013. http://bostonreview.net/poetry/against-conceptualism.

Bell, E.T. *The Magic of Numbers*. New York: Whittlesey House, 1947.

Bellos, David. "Appropriation-imitation-traduction: Réflexions sur la version anglaise de *La Vie mode d'emploi* de Georges Perec." *Littérature* 4 (1992): 4–12.

– *Georges Perec: A Life in Words*. Boston: Godine, 1993.

– *Is That a Fish in your Ear? Translation and the Meaning of Everything*. London: Particular Books, 2011.

– "Perec and Translation." *Formules* 16: *Oulipo @ 50 / L'Oulipo à 50 ans*, edited by Camille Bloomfield, Marc Lapprand, and Jean-Jacques Thomas (2012): 27–32.

Bénabou, Marcel. *Jacob, Menahem, and Mimoun: A Family Epic*. Translated by Steven Rendall. Lincoln, NE: University of Nebraska Press, 1998.

– "Le mouvement." *Medium* 20–21 (2009): 232–49.

– "Las obras del obrador." Interview by Cécile de Bary. *Quimera* 244 (2004): 12–17.

– "Petit complément à l'adresse présidentielle." *50 ans d'Oulipo. De la contrainte à l'œuvre* (*La Licorne* 100), edited by Carole

Bisenius-Penin and André Petitjean, 21–7. Rennes: Presses universitaires de Rennes, 2012.

- "Quarante siècles d'Oulipo." *Magazine Littéraire* 398 (2001): 20–6.
- "La règle et la contrainte." *Pratiques* 39 (1983): 101–6.
- *Why I Have Not Written Any of My Books*. Translated by David Kornacker. Lincoln, NE: Bison Books, 1996.

Bénabou, Marcel, Florence Delay, Francis Marmande, and Jacques Roubaud. "Table ronde du 8 décembre 2007." *Textuel* 55 (2008): 181–94.

Bénabou, Marcel, Anne F. Garréta, Jacques Jouet, and Marc Lapprand. "L'Oulipo et sa critique." In *Formules 16: Oulipo @ 50 / L'Oulipo à 50 ans*, edited by Camille Bloomfield, Marc Lapprand, and Jean-Jacques Thomas (2012): 229–46.

Bénabou, Marcel, Charles Grivel, et al. "Vers une théorie de la lecture du texte oulipien – Fragments d'un débat." In *Oulipo Poétiques*, edited by Peter Kuon, 199–222. Tubingen: Gunter Narr Verlag, 1997.

Bénabou, Marcel, Jacques Jouet, Harry Mathews, and Jacques Roubaud. *Un art simple et tout d'exécution*. Lyon: Circé, 2001. [AS]

Bénabou, Marcel, and Georges Perec. *Presbytère et prolétaires: Le dossier PALF* Cahiers Georges Perec 3. Paris: Éditions du Limon, 1989. [PP]

Bénichou, Paul. *The Consecration of the Writer, 1750–1830*. Translated by Mark K. Jensen. Lincoln, NE: University of Nebraska Press, 1999.

Benjamin, Walter. "The Storyteller." In *Illuminations*, translated by Harry Zohn, 83–109. London: Fontana, 1973.

Bens, Jacques. *De l'Oulipo et de la chandelle verte*. Paris: Gallimard, 2004.

- *Genèse de l'Oulipo 1960–1963*. Bordeaux: Le Castor Astral, 2005. [GO]

Bense, Max. "The Projects of Generative Aesthetics." In *Cybernetics, Art, and Ideas*, edited by Jasia Reichardt, 57–60. London: Studio Vista, 1971.

Benveniste, Émile. "Le jeu comme structure." *Deucalion* 2 (1947): 161–7.

Berge, Claude, and Éric Beaumatin. "Georges Perec et la combinatoire." In *Mélanges*, Cahiers Georges Perec 4, 83–96. Paris: Éditions du Limon, 1990.

Berkman, Natalie. "*Comment j'ai écrit un de mes livres*: La double genèse de *Si par une nuit d'hiver un voyageur* d'Italo Calvino." *Genesis* 45 (2017): 181–92.

- "Digital Oulipo: Programming Potential Literature." *DHQ: Digital Humanities Quarterly* 11, no. 3 (2017). http://digitalhumanities.org/dhq/vol/11/3/000325/000325.html.

Berrigan, Ted. *The Sonnets*. London: Penguin, 2000.

Bibliography

Bertharion, Jacques-Denis. *Poétique de Georges Perec*. Saint Genouph: Nizet, 1998.

Berti, Eduardo. *Círculo de lectores*. Madrid: Páginas de espuma, 2020.

– *Funes se souvient – Funes se acuerda*. La bibliothèque oulipienne no. 206. Paris: printed by the Oulipo, 2014.

– *L'ivresse sans fin des portes tournantes*. Bordeaux: Le Castor Astral, 2019.

– *Por. Lecturas y reescrituras de una canción de Luis Alberto Spinetta*. Buenos Aires: Gourmet musical, 2019.

– *Les voyages dispersent. Appendice final*. La bibliothèque oulipienne no. 228. Paris: printed by the Oulipo, 2017.

Bertrand, Jean-Pierre, Jacques Dubois, and Pascal Durand. "Approche institutionnelle du premier surréalisme (1919–1924)." *Pratiques* 38 (1983): 27–53.

Bersani, Leo. *The Culture of Redemption*. Cambridge, MA: Harvard University Press, 1990.

Bibbò, Antonio. "Characters as Social Document in Modernist Collective Novels: The Case of *Manhattan Transfer*." In *Literature as Document: Generic Boundaries in 1930s Western Literature*. Edited by Carmen Van den Bergh, Sarah Bonciarelli, and Anne Reverseau, 53–77. Leiden: Brill, 2019.

Birkhoff, George D. *Aesthetic Measure*. Cambridge, MA: Harvard University Press, 1933.

– *A Mathematical Theory of Aesthetics and Its Application to Poetry and Music*. Houston: Rice Institute, 1932.

Blavier, André. "Notes." *Temps mêlés: Documents Queneau* 45–46 (1990): 6–81.

Bloom, Gary, John Kennedy, and Peter Wexler. "Ensnaring the Elusive Eodermdrome." *Word Ways* 13 (1980): 131–40.

Bloomfield, Camille. "L'Oulipo dans l'histoire des groupes et mouvements littéraires: Une mise en perspective." In *50 ans d'Oulipo. De la contrainte à l'œuvre* (*La Licorne* 100), edited by Carole Bisenius-Penin and André Petitjean, 29–42. Rennes: Presses universitaires de Rennes, 2012.

– "L'Oulipo: Histoire et sociologie d'un groupe-monde." PhD diss., l'Université Paris 8 Vincennes-Saint Denis, 2011.

– *Raconter l'Oulipo (1960–2000). Histoire et sociologie d'un groupe*. Paris: Honoré Champion, 2017.

Bloomfield, Camille, and Hermes Salceda. "La traduction comme pratique oulipienne: Par-delà le texte 'original.'" In *Oulipo mode d'emploi*, edited by Christelle Reggiani and Alain Schaffner, 249–62. Paris: Honoré Champion, 2016.

Boehncke, Heiner, Sophie Dobrigkeit, Ulrike Gauder, Michael Hohmann, and Sigrid Ortwein. *Oulipo – Ougrapo Eine Gebrauchsanweisung*. Heidelberg: Verlag Das Wunderhorn, 2014.

Bohman-Kalaja, Kimberly. *Reading Games: An Aesthetics of Play in Flann O'Brien, Samuel Beckett, and Georges Perec*. Urbana-Champaign, IL: Dalkey Archive, 2007.

Bök, Christian. *Eunoia*. Toronto: Coach House Books, 2001.

– *'Pataphysics: The Poetics of an Imaginary Science*. Evanston, IL: Northwestern University Press, 2002.

Bolton Holloway, Julia. "The 'Vita nuova': Paradigms of Pilgrimage." *Dante Studies* 103 (1985): 103–24.

Borges, Jorge Luis. *Collected Fictions*. Translated by Andrew Hurley. New York: Penguin, 1998.

– *Labyrinths*. Translated by Donald A. Yates and James E. Irby. Harmondsworth: Penguin, 1970.

– "Narrative Art and Magic." Translated by Suzanne Jill Levine. In *Selected Non-Fictions*, edited by Eliot Weinberger, 75–82. New York: Penguin, 1999.

Bories, Anne-Sophie. "Échographies (niveau de résonance dans *Morale élémentaire* I)." In *Formules 16: Oulipo @ 50 / L'Oulipo à 50 ans*, edited by Camille Bloomfield, Marc Lapprand, and Jean-Jacques Thomas (2012): 215–27.

Bourdieu, Pierre. *The Rules of Art: Genesis and Structure of the Literary Field*. Translated by Susan Emanuel. Stanford: Stanford University Press, 1995.

Bouveresse, Jacques. *La connaissance de l'écrivain. Sur la littérature, la vérité et la vie*. Marseille: Agone, 2008.

– *Prodiges et vertiges de l'analogie*. Paris: Raisons d'agir, 1999.

Brainard, Joe. *I Remember*. New York: Penguin, 1995.

Braffort, Paul, Guy Chaty, and Josiane Joncquel-Patris. "Historique." Alamo (website), accessed 10 July 2021, http://www.alamo.free.fr/pmwiki.php?n=Alamo.Historique.

Breton, André. *The Lost Steps*. Translated by Mark Polizzotti. Lincoln, NE: University of Nebraska Press, 2009.

– *Mad Love*. Translated by Mary Ann Caws. Lincoln, NE: University of Nebraska Press, 1987.

– *Manifestoes of Surrealism*. Translated by Helen R. Lane and Richard Seaver. Ann Arbor, MI: University of Michigan Press, 1972.

Brun, Eric. *Les situationnistes. Une avant-garde totale (1950–1972)*. Paris: CNRS Éditions, 2014.

Bibliography

Burgelin, Claude. *Les parties de dominos chez Monsieur Lefèvre: Perec avec Freud, Perec contre Freud.* Lyon: Circe, 1996.

– "Le silence de Perec." In *Relire Perec* (*La Licorne 12*), edited by Christelle Reggiani, 15–26. Rennes: Presses universitaires de Rennes, 2016.

Bürger, Peter. *Theory of the Avant-Garde.* Translated by Michael Shaw. Minneapolis: University of Minnesota Press, 1984.

Burt, Stephanie. "Sestina! or, The Fate of the Idea of Form." *Modern Philology* 105, no. 1 (2007): 218–41.

Bush, Ruth. "Le monde s'effondre? Translating Anglophone African Literature in the World Republic of Letters." *Journal of Postcolonial Writing* 48, no. 5 (2012): 512–25.

Butler, Christopher. "Numerological Thought." In *Silent Poetry: Essays in Numerological Analysis*, edited by Alastair Fowler, 1–31. London: Routledge and Kegan Paul, 1970.

Butor, Michel. "La critique et l'invention." In *Repertoire III*, 7–20. Paris: Minuit, 1968.

Cadieu, Morgane. *Marcher au hasard: Clinamen et création dans la prose du XXe siècle.* Paris: Classiques Garnier, 2019.

Caille, Antoine Constantin. "Approche de la texture: D'un sens des formes au niveau infrastructurel." *Formules 20: Ce que les formes veulent dire / What Forms Mean*, edited by Chris Andrews (2016): 11–30.

Caillois, Roger. *Man, Play, and Games.* Translated by Meyer Barash. Urbana, IL: University of Illinois Press, 2001.

Calame, Alain. "*Chêne et chien* et la *Divine Comédie.*" *Les Temps mêlés* 150 + 25-26-27-28 (1985): 15–27.

– "*Le chiendent*: Des mythes à la structure." In *Queneau aujourd'hui*, edited by Georges-Emmanuel Clancier, 29–64. Paris: Clancier-Guenaud, 1985.

– *L'esprit farouche.* Limoges: Sixtus, 1989.

– "La place des mathématiques dans *Morale élémentaire.*" *Lectures de Raymond Queneau. Trames, Lectures de Raymond Queneau, no. 1 Morale élémentaire* (1987): 93–117.

Călinescu, Matei. *Rereading.* New Haven: Yale University Press, 1993.

Calvino, Italo. "Comment j'ai écrit un de mes livres." *Actes sémiotiques* 6, no. 51 (1984): 1–21.

– *Hermit in Paris.* Translated by Martin McLaughlin. London: Cape, 2003.

– *If on a Winter's Night a Traveller.* Translated by William Weaver. London: Picador, 1982.

– *Lettere.* Edited by Luca Baranelli. Milan: Arnoldo Mondadori, 2000.

– *The Literature Machine.* Translated by Patrick Creagh. London: Picador, 1989.

- *Romanzi e Racconti*, vol. 2, edited by Claudio Milanini, Mario Barenghi, and Bruno Falcetto. Milan: Arnoldo Mondadori, 1992.

Carter, William C. *Marcel Proust: A Life*. New Haven: Yale University Press, 2000.

Cave, Terence. *Thinking with Literature: Towards a Cognitive Criticism*. Oxford: Oxford University Press, 2016.

Chancé, Dominique. "Une traduction postcoloniale d'Amos Tutuola?" *Traductions postcoloniales* 34 (2012): 55–6.

Chassain, Adrien. "Perec et la rhétorique du projet." In *Relire Perec (La Licorne 12)*, edited by Christelle Reggiani, 27–39. Rennes: Presses universitaires de Rennes, 2016.

Cheng, François. *L'écriture poétique chinoise*. Paris: Seuil, 1996.

Chomsky, Noam, and Morris Halle. "Some Controversial Questions in Phonological Theory." *Journal of Linguistics* 1, no. 2 (1965): 97–138.

Clancier, Anne. *Raymond Queneau et la psychanalyse*. Paris: Éditions du Limon, 1994.

Clark, Timothy. *The Theory of Inspiration*. Manchester: Manchester University Press, 1997.

Cleary, Thomas. *The Taoist I Ching*. Boston: Shambhala, 1986.

Coetzee, J.M. *Elizabeth Costello*. Sydney: Random House, 2003.

Coleman, Wanda. *American Sonnets*. Milwaukee: Woodland Pattern Book Center/Kenosha: Light and Dust, 1994.

Coleridge, Samuel Taylor. *Shakespeare, Ben Jonson, Beaumont and Fletcher*. Liverpool: Edward Howell, 1874.

Colie, Rosalie. *The Resources of Kind: Genre-Theory in the Renaissance*. Berkeley: University of California Press, 1973.

Colton, Simon. "Computational Discovery in Pure Mathematics." In *Computational Discovery of Scientific Knowledge*, edited by Sašo Džeroski and Ljupčo Todorovski, 175–201. Berlin: Springer-Verlag, 2007.

Combe, Dominique. *Les genres littéraires*. Paris: Hachette, 1992.

Condorcet, Nicolas de. *Esquisse d'un tableau historique des progrès de l'esprit humain*. Paris: Vrin, 1970.

Conort, Benoît. "Le chiffre du deuil." *Textuel* 55 (2008): 145–67.

Consenstein, Peter. "Michelle Grangaud's Qualia Poems – Geste." *L'Esprit Créateur* 49, no. 2 (2009): 21–33.

Coquelle-Rhoëm, Margaux. "De l'Oulipo à 'L'APpentis de Science PLAusible' dans *Peut-être ou la Nuit de dimanche*," *Sites* 25, no. 5: 585–93.

Cots Vicente, Montserrat, and María Dolores Vivero García. "El juego de la parodia en la escritura de Anne F. Garréta." *Çedille: Revista de estudios franceses* 9 (2013): 83–92.

Bibliography

Cowling, Sam. *Abstract Entities*. New York: Routledge, 2017.

Critical Perspectives on Amos Tutuola. Edited by Bernth Lindfors. London: Heinemann, 1980.

Cruse, D.A. "Language, Meaning, and Sense: Semantics." In *An Encyclopedia of Language*, edited by N.E. Collinge, 76–93. London: Routledge, 1990.

Culler, Jonathan. "In Defence of Overinterpretation." In *Interpretation and Overinterpretation*, edited by Stefan Collini, 109–23 Cambridge: Cambridge University Press, 1992.

Dangy-Scaillierez, Isabelle. *L'énigme criminelle dans les romans de Georges Perec*. Paris: Honoré Champion, 2002.

Dante Alighieri. *The Divine Comedy, 2: Purgatorio*. Translated by John D. Sinclair. Oxford: Oxford University Press, 1961.

– *La vita nuova*. Translated by Barbara Reynolds. Harmondsworth: Penguin, 1969.

Daumal, René, and Roger Gilbert-Lecomte. *Theory of the Great Game: Writings from Le Grand Jeu*. Edited and translated by Dennis Duncan. London: Atlas Press, 2015.

De Bary, Cécile. *Une nouvelle pratique littéraire en France. Histoire du groupe Oulipo de 1960 à nos jours*. Lewiston, NY: The Edwin Mellen Press, 2014.

Debon, Claude. *Doukiplèdonktan: Études sur Raymond Queneau*. Paris: Presses de la Sorbonne nouvelle, 1998.

Decout, Maxime. "Qui a éliminé 'Le voyage d'hiver'? Contre-enquête sur un récit de Georges Perec." In *Entre jeu et contrainte: Pratiques et expériences oulipiennes*, 153–64. Zagreb: Meandarmedia, 2016.

De Montrichard, Christian. *Vous souvenez-vous?* Paris: Fayard, 2003.

De Quincey, Thomas. "On Murder Considered as One of the Fine Arts." In *On Murder*, edited by Robert Morrison, 8–34. Oxford: Oxford University Press, 2006.

– "On the Knocking at the Gate in *Macbeth*." In *On Murder*, edited by Robert Morrison, 3–7. Oxford: Oxford University Press, 2006.

Desbois-Ientile, Adeline, and Virginie Tahar. "Des grands rhétoriqueurs à l'Oulipo. Mythe et réalité d'un plagiat par anticipation." In *Renaissance imaginaire. La réception de la Renaissance dans la culture contemporaine*, edited by Sandra Provini and Mélanie Bost-Fievet, 219–40. Paris: Classiques Garnier, 2019.

Descombes, Vincent. *Proust: Philosophy of the Novel*. Translated by Catherine Chance Macksey. Stanford: Stanford University Press, 1992.

– *Le raisonnement de l'ours*. Paris, Seuil, 2007.

Bibliography

Dobrigkeit, Sophie, Ulrike Gauder, Peter Hauff, and Sigrid Ortwein. *Mme Perreq*. Heidelberg: Verlag Das Wunderhorn, 2020.

Dorsch, T.S. "Introduction." In *Aristotle, Horace, Longinus: Classical Literary Criticism*, 7–27. Harmondsworth: Penguin, 1965.

Dourish, Paul. *Where the Action Is: The Foundations of Embodied Interaction*. Cambridge, MA: MIT Press, 2001.

Drayton, Dave. *P(oe)Ms*. Melbourne: Rabbit Poets, 2017.

Dubreuil, Laurent. *Poetry and Mind: Tractatus Poetico-Philosophicus*. New York: Fordham University Press, 2018.

Duchêne, Ludmila, and Agnès Leblanc. *Rationnel mon Q*. Paris: Hermann, 2010.

Duflo, Colas. *Jouer et philosopher*. Paris: Presses universitaires de France, 1997.

Dummett, Michael. *Frege: Philosophy of Mathematics*. Cambridge, MA: Harvard University Press, 1991.

Duncan, Dennis. *The Oulipo and Modern Thought*. Oxford: Oxford University Press, 2019.

Durand, Pascal. "'La destruction fut ma Béatrice': Mallarmé ou l'implosion poétique." *Revue d'histoire littéraire de la France* 99, no. 3 (1999): 373–89.

Dworkin, Craig. "The Fate of Echo." In *Against Expression: An Anthology of Conceptual Writing*, edited by Craig Dworkin and Kenneth Goldsmith. xxiii–liv. Evanston, IL: Northwestern University Press, 2011.

Eastman, Andrew. "Breaking the Pentameter: Speech Rhythms, Stress Clash, and Authenticity in Modern English-language Poetry." In *Ranam (recherches anglaises et nord-américaines)* 47 (2014): 159–71.

Eco, Umberto. "Between Author and Text." In *Interpretation and Overinterpretation*, edited by Stefan Collini, 67–88. Cambridge: Cambridge University Press, 1992.

– "Interpretation and History." In *Interpretation and Overinterpretation*, edited by Stefan Collini, 23–43. Cambridge: Cambridge University Press, 1992.

– *The Limits of Interpretation*. Bloomington, IN: Indiana University Press, 1990.

– *Mouse or Rat? Translation as Negotiation*. London: Phoenix, 2003.

– "Overinterpreting Texts." In *Interpretation and Overinterpretation*, edited by Stefan Collini, 45–66. Cambridge: Cambridge University Press, 1992.

Elkin, Lauren, and Veronica Esposito. *The End of Oulipo? An Attempt to Exhaust a Movement*. Winchester, UK: Zero Books, 2013.

Bibliography

Ellmann, Richard. *James Joyce*. New York: Oxford University Press, 1983.

Emsley, John. *Nature's Building Blocks*. Oxford: Oxford University Press, 2011.

Englert, Walter G. *Epicurus on the Swerve and Voluntary Action*. Atlanta, GA: Scholars Press, 1987.

Fabb, Nigel. "Metrical Rules and the Notion of 'Maximum': A Reply to Derek Attridge." *Language and Literature* 12, no. 1 (2003): 73–80.

Faerber, Johan. *Le grand écrivain, cette névrose national*. Paris: Pauvert, 2021.

Farías, Victor. *Los nazis en Chile*. Barcelona: Seix Barral, 2000.

Faye, Jean-Pierre, Jean-Claude Montel, Jean Paris, Léon Robel, Maurice Roche, Jacques Roubaud, and Jean-Noël Vuarnet, "Liminaire," *Change* 1 (1968): 4

Felski, Rita. *The Limits of Critique*. Chicago: Chicago University Press, 2015.

Fish, Stanley. *Is There a Text in This Class?* Cambridge, MA: Harvard University Press, 1980.

Flem, Lydia. *Je me souviens de l'imperméable rouge que je portais l'été de mes vingt ans*. Paris: Seuil, 2016.

Forte, Frédéric. "99 notes préparatoires à ma vie avec Raymond Queneau" *Cahiers Raymond Queneau* 1 (2011): 26–30.

– *Dire ouf*. Paris: POL, 2016.

– *Minute-Operas*. Translated by Daniel Levin Becker, Ian Monk, Michelle Noteboom, and Jean-Jacques Poucel. Providence, RI: Burning Deck, 2015.

– "Petite morale élémentaire portative." In *La morale élémentaire. Aventures d'une forme poétique, Queneau, Oulipo, etc. (La Licorne 81)*, edited by Jacques Jouet, Pierre Martin, and Dominique Moncond'huy, 173–78. Rennes: Presses universitaires de Rennes, 2007.

– *Système jiǎnpǔ: Premières notes*. La bibliothèque oulipienne no. 236. Paris: printed by the Oulipo, 2019.

Forte, Frédéric, Paul Fournel, and Hervé Le Tellier. "Généalogies oulipiennes." In *Formules 16: Oulipo @ 50 / L'Oulipo à 50 ans*, edited by Camille Bloomfield, Marc Lapprand, and Jean-Jacques Thomas (2012):115–36.

Foucault, Michel. "Archéologie d'une passion." In *Dits et écrits 1954–1988*, vol. 4, *1980–1988*, edited by Daniel Defert and François Ewald, 599–608. Paris: Gallimard, 1994.

– "What Is an Author?" In *Language, Counter-Memory, Practice*, edited by Donald F. Bouchard, translated by Donald F. Bouchard and Sherry Simon, 113–20. Ithaca: Cornell University Press, 1977.

Fournel, Paul. "Les ateliers de l'Oulipo: Écrire ici et maintenant."
   Le magazine littéraire 398 (2001): 26–7.
– *Chamboula*. Paris: Seuil, 2007.
– "Queneau et l'Oulipo." *Europe* 888 (2003): 177–9.
Fowler, Alastair. *Kinds of Literature: An Introduction to the Theory of
   Genres and Modes*. Cambridge, MA: Harvard University Press, 1982.
Fowler, Don. *Lucretius on Atomic Motion: A Commentary on De Rerum
   Natura, Book Two, Lines 1–332*. Oxford: Oxford University Press, 2002.
Fratantuono, Lee. *A Reading of Lucretius' De Rerum Natura*.
   Lanham, MD: Lexington Books, 2015.
Frege, Gottlob. *Philosophical and Mathematical Correspondence*. Edited
   by Gottfried Gabriel, translated by Hans Kaal. Oxford: Blackwell, 1980.
Freud, Sigmund. "A Case of Paranoia (Dementia Paranoides)." In
   Collected Papers, vol. 3, translated by Alix and James Strachey,
   390–416. London: The Hogarth Press, 1957.
– "Die Freudsche psychoanalytische Methode." In *Gesammelte Werke*,
   vol. 5, 3–10. London: Imago, 1942.
– "Freud's Psycho-Analytic Procedure." In *The Standard Edition of
   the Complete Psychological Works of Sigmund Freud, Volume VII
   (1901–1905): A Case of Hysteria, Three Essays on Sexuality and Other
   Works*, translated by James Strachey, 247–54. London: Hogarth
   Press, 1953.
– *The Future of an Illusion*. In *Civilization, Society, and Religion*, edited
   by Albert Dickson, translated by James Strachey, 212–15.
   Harmondsworth: Penguin, 1985.
– *Letters*. Edited by Ernst L. Freud. Translated by Tania and James Stern.
   New York: Basic Books, 1960.
– *Two Short Accounts of Psycho-Analysis*. Translated by James Strachey.
   Harmondsworth: Pelican, 1962.
Freud, Sigmund, and Oskar Pfister. *Psychoanalysis and Faith: The Letters
   of Sigmund Freud and Oskar Pfister*. Edited by Heinrich Meng and
   Ernst L. Freud. Translated by Eric Mosbacher. London: Hogarth
   Press, 1963.
Frow, John. *Genre*. London: Routledge, 2006.
Gadamer, Hans-Georg. *Truth and Method*. Translated by W. Glen-Doepel.
   London: Continuum, 1989.
Garréta, Anne F. *La décomposition*. Paris: Grasset, 1999. [D]
– "A Feeling of Vertigo Seized Me as I Looked Down." In *The Proust
   Project*, edited by André Aciman, 210–213. New York: Farrar, Straus
   and Giroux, 2004.

Bibliography

- *Not One Day*. Translated by Emma Ramadan and the author. Dallas: Deep Vellum, 2013. [NOD]
- *Sphinx*. Translated by Emma Ramadan. Dallas: Deep Vellum, 2015.

Garréta, Anne F., and Valérie Beaudouin. *Tu te souviens …?* La bibliothèque oulipienne no. 160. Paris: printed by the Oulipo, 2007.

Gaut, Berys. "The Philosophy of Creativity." *Philosophy Compass* 5, no. 12 (2010): 1034–46.

Géhéniau, Florence. *Queneau analphabète: Répertoire alphabétique de ses lectures de 1917 à 1976*. Verviers: La plume ballon, 1992.

Genette, Gérard. *The Architext: An Introduction*. Translated by Jane E. Lewin. Berkeley: University of California Press, 1992.
- *Palimpsestes: La littérature au second degré*. Paris: Seuil, 1982.
- *Palimpsests: Literature in the Second Degree*. Translated by Channa Newman and Claude Doubinsky. Lincoln, NE: University of Nebraska Press, 1997.
- *The Work of Art*. Translated by G.M. Goshgarian. Ithaca: Cornell University Press, 1997.

Godard, Henri. "Queneau et les problèmes de la construction du roman." *Europe* 888 (2003): 22–33.

Goddard, Cliff. *Ten Lectures on Natural Semantic Metalanguage*. Leiden: Brill, 2018.

Goldie, Peter, and Elisabeth Schellekens. "Introduction." In *Philosophy and Conceptual Art*, edited by Peter Goldie and Elisabeth Schellekens, ix–xxi. Oxford: Oxford University Press, 2007.

Goldsmith, Kenneth. *Uncreative Writing*. New York: Columbia University Press, 2011.
- "Why Conceptual Writing? Why Now?" In *Against Expression: An Anthology of Conceptual Writing*, edited by Craig Dworkin and Kenneth Goldsmith, xvii–xxii. Evanston, IL: Northwestern University Press, 2011.

Gowers, Timothy. *Mathematics: A Very Short Introduction*. Oxford: Oxford University Press, 2002.

Granadillo, Elias D., and Mario F. Mendez. "Pathological Joking or Witzelsucht Revisited." *Journal of Neuropsychiatry and Clinical Neuroscience* 28 (2016): 162–7. http://doi.org/10.1176/appi. neuropsych.15090238.

Grangaud, Michelle. "Entretien avec Michelle Grangaud." In John Stout, *L'énigme-poésie: Entretiens avec 21 poètes françaises*, 217–24. Rodopi: Amsterdam, 2010.

Bibliography

- "Entretien avec Michelle Grangaud: L'écriture sous contrainte." In Astrid Poier-Bernhard, *Texte nach Bauplan*, 373–380. Heidelberg: Universitätsverlag Winter, 2012.
- *Geste*. Paris: POL, 1991. [G]
- *Memento-fragments*. Paris: POL, 1987.
- *Poèmes fondus*. Paris: POL, 1997.
- *Souvenirs de ma vie collective. Sujets de tableaux sans tableaux.* Paris: POL, 2000.
- *Les temps traversés*. Paris: POL, 2010. [TT]

Gray, Robert. "Georg Cantor and Transcendental Numbers." *American Mathematical Monthly* 101, no. 9 (1994): 819–32.

Green, André. *Play and Reflection in Donald Winnicott's Writings*. London: Karnac Books, 2005.

Greenblatt, Stephen. *The Swerve: How the World Became Modern*. New York: W.W. Norton, 2011.

Guichard, Luis Arturo. "Simias' Pattern Poems. The Margins of the Canon." *Beyond the Canon* 11 (2006): 83–103.

Hacking, Ian. *Why is there a Philosophy of Mathematics at All?* Cambridge: Cambridge University Press, 2014.

Halliday, Michael A.K., and Ruqaiya Hasan. *Cohesion in English*. London: Longman, 1976.

Hardy, G.H. *Ramanujan*. New York: Cambridge University Press, 1940.

Hart, Kevin. "Eugenio Montale and 'The Other Truth.'" *Heat* 14 (2000): 166–82.

Hartje, Hans. "Préface." In Max Bense, *Aesthetica: Introduction à la nouvelle esthétique*, translated by Judith Yacar, 7–8. Paris: Éditions du Cerf, 2007.

Hayes, Terrance. *American Sonnets for my Past and Future Assassin*. London: Penguin, 2018.

- *Hip Logic*. New York: Penguin, 2002.

Hazzard, Shirley. "I Felt that this Last Sentence Was Merely Phrase-Making." In *The Proust Project*, edited by André Aciman, 174–81. New York: Farrar, Straus and Giroux, 2004.

Heath, John. "Slinging Mud? Public Discussion of the Case of Oskar Pastior: A German-Romanian Comparison." *Central Europe* 12, no. 1 (2014): 69–81.

Heck, Maryline. "Pour un Perec politique." In *Relire Perec (La Licorne 12)*, edited by Christelle Reggiani, 73–88. Rennes: Presses universitaires de Rennes, 2016.

Bibliography

Hewitt, Andrew. *Fascist Modernism: Aesthetics, Politics, and the Avant-Garde*. Stanford: Stanford University Press, 1993.

Higgins, Dick. *Pattern Poetry: Guide to an Unknown Tradition*. Albany: State University of New York Press, 1987.

Hillson, Jeff, ed. *The Reality Street Book of Sonnets*. London: Reality Street, 2008.

Hobson, E.W. *Squaring the Circle: A History of the Problem*. Cambridge: Cambridge University Press, 1913.

Hocquard, Emmanuel. *Un test de solitude*. Paris: POL, 1998.

Hoffmann, E.T.A. *Mademoiselle de Scudéri*. Translated by Andrew Brown. Richmond: Alma Books, 2020.

Houellebecq, Michel. *Rester vivant et autres textes*. Paris: Flammarion, 1997.

Hough, Graham. *An Essay on Criticism*. London: Duckworth, 1966.

Huizinga, Johan. *Homo Ludens: A Study of the Play-Element in Culture*. Boston: The Beacon Press, 1955.

Hunter, Richard. *Critical Moments in Classical Literature*. Cambridge: Cambridge University Press, 2009.

Husserl, Edmund. "Pure Phenomenology, Its Method and Its Field of Investigation." In *Husserl: Shorter Works*, edited by Peter McCormick and Frederick A. Elliston, translated by Robert Welsh Jordan, 10–17. Notre Dame, IN: University of Notre Dame Press, 1981.

Isou, Isidore. *Introduction à une nouvelle poésie et à une nouvelle musique*. Paris: Gallimard, 1947.

Jakobson, Roman. "Closing Statement: Linguistics and Poetics." In *Style in Language*, edited by Thomas A. Sebeok, 350–77. Cambridge, MA: Technology Press of Massachusetts Institute of Technology, 1960.

– "On Linguistic Aspects of Translation." In *The Translation Studies Reader*, 2nd edition, edited by Lawrence Venuti, 110–14. New York: Routledge, 2000.

– "Quest for the Essence of Language." In *Selected Writings*, vol. 2, *Word and Language*, 345–59. Berlin: De Gruyter Mouton, 1971.

Jakobson, Roman, and Linda Waugh. *The Sound Shape of Language*. Berlin: De Gruyter Mouton, 1987.

James, Alison. "Aleatory Poetics." In *The Princeton Encyclopedia of Poetry and Poetics*, edited by Stephen Cushman, Clare Cavanagh, Jahan Ramazani, and Paul Rouzer, 31–4. Princeton: Princeton University Press, 2012.

– *Constraining Chance: Georges Perec and the Oulipo*. Evanston, IL: Northwestern University Press, 2009.

- "Écritures en collaboration." In *Oulipo mode d'emploi*, edited by Christelle Reggiani and Alain Schaffner, 303–315. Paris, Honoré Champion, 2016.
- "Perec and the Politics of Constraint." In *The Afterlives of Georges Perec*, edited by Rowan Wilken and Justin Clemens, 157–70. Edinburgh: Edinburgh University Press, 2017.

James, Henry. *The Art of the Novel*. New York: Charles Scribner's Sons, 1934.

Jameson, Fredric. *Postmodernism, or, the Cultural Logic of Late Capitalism*. Durham, NC: Duke University Press, 1991.

Jeannelle, Jean-Louis. "Perec et le divers de l'histoire littéraire: Sur 'Le voyage d'hiver.'" In *Fictions d'histoire littéraire* (*La Licorne* 86), edited by Jean-Louis Jeannelle, 171–94. Rennes: Presses universitaires de Rennes, 2009.

Jenny, Laurent. *La parole singulière*. Paris: Belin, 1990.

Jetubhai, Khuman Bhagirath, and Madhumita Ghosal. "Ungendered Narrative: A New Genre in the Making." *Concentric: Literary and Cultural Studies* 44, no. 2 (2018): 272–93.

Jouet, Jacques. "De la lumière pour les navets." Interview by Xavier Person. *Le matricule des anges* 26 (1999): 44–5.
- "De la morale élémentaire." In *La morale élémentaire. Aventures d'une forme poétique, Queneau, Oulipo, etc.* (*La Licorne* 81), edited by Jacques Jouet, Pierre Martin, and Dominique Moncond'huy, 9–12. Rennes: Presses universitaires de Rennes, 2008.
- "Entretien de Jacques Jouet avec Camille Bloomfield." In *Jacques Jouet* (*La Licorne* 118), edited by Marc Lapprand and Dominique Moncond'huy, 293–313. Rennes: Presses universitaires de Rennes, 2015.
- *Fins*. Paris: POL, 1999.
- *Je me souvins*. La bibliothèque oulipienne no. 206. Paris: printed by the Oulipo, 2014.
- *Mountain R*. Translated by Brian Evenson. McLean, IL: Dalkey Archive, 2004.
- *Poèmes de métro*. Paris: POL, 2000.
- *Raymond Queneau*. Paris: La Manufacture, 1989.
- *Ruminations du potentiel*. Caen: Nous, 2016. [RP]
- "Subway Poems." Translated by Ian Monk. *Substance* 30, no. 3 (2001): 64–70.
- "With (and Without) Constraints." Translated by Roxanne Lapidus. *SubStance* 30, no. 3 (2001): 4–16.

Bibliography

Jonas, Hans. "The Nobility of Sight." *Philosophy and Phenomenological Research* 14, no. 4 (1954): 507–19.

Josipovici, Gabriel. "Georges Perec's Homage to Joyce (and Tradition)." *The Yearbook of English Studies* 15 (1985): 179–200.

Jules Romains et les écritures de la simultanéité. Edited by Dominique Viart. Lille: Presses universitaires du Septentrion, 1996.

Jullien, Dominique. "Zazie dans la brousse." *Romanic Review* 91, no. 3 (2000): 263–78.

Jurt, Joseph. "Les mécanismes de constitution de groupes littéraires: l'exemple du symbolisme." *Neophilologus* 70 (1986): 20–33.

Kafka, Franz. *The Trial*. Translated by Willa and Edwin Muir. Harmondsworth: Penguin, 1953.

Kant, Immanuel. *Critique of Judgment*. Translated by Werner S. Pluhar. Indianapolis: Hackett, 1987.

Kantor, Martin. *Understanding Paranoia*. Westport: Praeger, 2004.

Kaufmann, Vincent. *Poétique des groupes littéraire: Avant-gardes 1920–1970*. Paris: Presses Universitaires de France, 1997.

Kazanina, Nina, Jeffrey S. Bowers, and William Idsardi. "Phonemes: Lexical Access and Beyond." *Psychonomic Bulletin & Review* (2018) 25: 560–85.

Kim, Annabel. "Dans l'béton, dans la merde: Anne Garréta's Intractable Materiality." *Revue critique de fixxion française contemporaine* 21 (2020): 121-30.

– *Unbecoming Language: Anti-Identitarian French Feminist Fictions*. Columbus: Ohio State University Press, 2020.

Klütsch, Christoph. "Information Aesthetics and the Stuttgart School." In *Mainframe Experimentalism: Early Computing and the Digital Arts*, edited by Hannah B. Higgins and Douglas Kahn, 65–89. Berkeley: University of California Press, 2012.

Knuth, Donald. "Algorithmic Thinking and Mathematical Thinking." *The American Mathematical Monthly* 92, no. 3 (1985): 170–81.

Kohan, Martín. *Me acuerdo*. Buenos Aires: Godot, 2020.

Kojève, Alexandre. "Les romans de la sagesse." *Critique* 8, no.60 (1952): 387–97.

Kosofsky Sedgwick, Eve. "Paranoid Reading and Reparative Reading; or, You're So Paranoid, You Probably Think This Introduction Is about You." In *Novel Gazing: Queer Readings in Fiction*, edited by Eve Kosofsky Sedgwick, 1–37. Durham, NC: Duke University Press, 1997.

Koyré, Alexandre. *Études d'histoire de la pensée scientifique*. Paris: Gallimard, 1973.

Kroker, Arthur, and Marilouise Kroker. *Hacking the Future: Stories for the Flesh-Eating 90s*. New York: St Martin's Press, 1996.

Kronfeldner, Maria. "Explaining Creativity." In *Creativity and Philosophy*, edited by Berys Gaut and Matthew Kieran, 213–29. Milton Park: Routledge, 2018.

Krugman, Paul. "Competitiveness: A Dangerous Obsession." *Foreign Affairs* 73, no. 2 (1994): 28–44.

Ladha, Hassanaly. "From Bayt to Stanza: Arabic Khayāl and the Advent of Italian Vernacular Poetry," *Exemplaria* 32, no. 1 (2020): 1–31. http://doi.org/10.1080/10412573.2020.1743523.

Lamarque, Peter. "Poetry and Abstract Thought." *Midwest Studies in Philosophy* 33 (2009): 37–52.

Landy, Joshua. "In Praise of Depth: Or, How I Learned to Stop Worrying and Love the Hidden." *New Literary History* 51, no. 1 (2020): 145–76.

– *Philosophy as Fiction: Self, Deception, and Knowledge in Proust*. New York: Oxford University Press, 2014.

Lapprand, Marc. "Jacques Jouet: Un oulipien métrologue." *Magazine Littéraire* 398 (2001): 63–5.

– *L'œuvre ronde: Essai sur Jacques Jouet*. Limoges: Lambert-Lucas, 2007.

– *Poétique de l'Oulipo*. Amsterdam: Rodopi, 1998.

– *Pourquoi l'Oulipo?* Québec: Presses de l'Université Laval, 2020.

Lapprand, Marc, and Dominique Moncond'huy. "Avant-propos." In *Jacques Jouet (La Licorne 118)*, edited by Marc Lapprand and Dominique Moncond'huy, 7–10. Rennes: Presses universitaires de Rennes, 2015.

Laskowski-Caujolle, Elvira. *Die Macht der Vier*. Frankfurt: Peter Lang, 1999.

Lasky, Dorothea. *Poetry Is Not a Project*. Brooklyn, NY: Ugly Duckling Presse, 2010.

Lautréamont, Comte de (Isidore Ducasse). *Les Chants de Maldoror, Together with a Translation of Lautréamont's Poésies*. Translated by Guy Wernham. New York: New Directions, 1965.

– *Œuvres complètes*, edited by Marcel Jean and Arpad Mezei. Paris: Eric Losfeld, 1971.

Lécureur, Michel. *Raymond Queneau: Biographie*. Paris: Les Belles Lettres/Archimbaud, 2002.

Lederer, Jacques. "Préface." In *"Cher, très cher, admirable et charmant ami …" Correspondance Georges Perec et Jacques Lederer*, by Georges Perec and Jacques Lederer, 7–19. Paris: Flammarion, 1997.

Lefebvre, Henri. *Critique de la vie quotidienne I*. Paris: L'Arche 1977.

Bibliography

Leighton, Angela. *On Form: Poetry, Aestheticism, and the Legacy of a Word*. Oxford: Oxford University Press, 2008.

Lejeune, Philippe. *La mémoire et l'oblique*. Paris: POL, 1991.

Le Lionnais, François. *Les nombres remarquables*. Paris: Hermann, 1983.

– *La peinture à Dora*. Paris: L'Échoppe, 1999.

Leong, Michael. "Rats Build Their Labyrinth." *Hyperallergic*, 17 May 2015, https://hyperallergic.com/206802/rats-build-their-labyrinth-oulipo-in-the-21st-century.

Le Tellier, Hervé. *L'anomalie*. Paris: Gallimard, 2020.

– *Atlas inutilis*. Translated by Cole Swensen. New York: Black Square Editions, 2018.

– *Esthétique de l'Oulipo*. Bordeaux: Le Castor Astral, 2006.

– *Joconde jusqu'à cent.* Bordeaux: Le Castor Astral, 1998.

– *Joconde sur votre indulgence*. Bordeaux: Le Castor Astral, 2002.

– *The Sextine Chapel*. Translated by Ian Monk. McLean, IL: Dalkey Archive, 2011.

Levi, Primo. *If This Is a Man*. Translated by Stuart Woolf. London: Sphere, 1987.

Levin, David Michael. *The Philosopher's Gaze: Modernity in the Shadows of Enlightenment*. Berkeley: University of California Press, 1999.

Levin Becker, Daniel. "Introduction." In Anne F. Garréta, *Sphinx*, translated by Emma Ramadan, v–vii. Dallas: Deep Vellum, 2015.

– *Many Subtle Channels: In Praise of Potential Literature*. Cambridge, MA: Harvard University Press, 2012. [MSC]

Levine, Caroline. *Forms: Whole, Rhythm, Hierarchy, Network*. Princeton: Princeton University Press, 2015.

Lindfors, Bernth. "Amos Tutuola's Search for a Publisher." *Journal of Commonwealth Literature* 17 (1982): 90–106.

Lindon, Mathieu. *Je ne me souviens pas*. Paris: POL, 2016.

"Liquidation." *Littérature* 18 (1921): 1–7.

Longinus. "On the Sublime." In Aristotle, Horace, Longinus, *Classical Literary Criticism*, edited and translated by T.S. Dorsch, 97–158. Harmondsworth: Penguin, 1965.

Lucretius. *De Rerum Natura*. Edited and translated by W.H.D. Rouse. Cambridge, MA: Harvard University Press, 1975.

– *On the Nature of the Universe*. Translated by Ronald Latham. Harmondsworth: Penguin, 1951.

Lupton, Deborah. "The Embodied Computer/User." *Body and Society* 1, nos. 3–4 (1995): 97–112.

Lusson, Pierre, Georges Perec, and Jacques Roubaud, *A Short Treatise Inviting the Reader to Discover the Subtle Art of Go*. Translated by Peter Consenstein. Cambridge, MA: Wakefield Press, 2019.

Madden, Matt. *99 Ways to Tell a Story: Exercises in Style*. Chicago: Chamberlain Bros, 2005.

Madrid, Anthony. *I Am Your Slave, Now Do What I Say*. Ann Arbor: Canarium Books, 2012.

Magné, Bernard. "À propos de *W ou le souvenir d'enfance*: Cinq micro-lectures du manuscrit de Stockholm." *Formules* 6 (2002): 21–31.

– "Carrefour Mabillon 'ce qui passe, passe…'" In Georges Perec, *Poésie ininterrompue, inventaire*, edited by Bernard Magné, 55–67. Marseille: André Dimanche, 1997.

– "L'estampille ou comment Georges Perec a récrit certaines contraintes." *Forme et mesure: Mélanges pour Jacques Roubaud, Mezura* 49 (2001): 293–303.

– "La figure de l'orphelin dans l'oeuvre de Perec." In *Modernités 21, Deuil et littérature*, edited by Pierre Glaudes and Dominique Rabaté, 299–315. Bordeaux: Presses universitaires de Bordeaux, 2015.

– *Georges Perec*. Paris: Nathan, 1999.

– *Perecollages 1981–1988*. Toulouse: Presses universitaires du Mirail-Toulouse, 1989.

– Preface to *Le voyage d'hiver / Le voyage d'hier*, by Georges Perec and Jacques Roubaud, 9–13. Nantes: Le Passeur, 1997.

– "Quelques considérations sur les poèmes hétérogrammatiques de Georges Perec." In *Les poèmes hétérogrammatiques, Cahiers Georges Perec* 5, 27–85. Paris: Limon, 1992.

Maher, Thomas V. "Threat, Resistance, and Collective Action: The Cases of Sobibor, Treblinka, and Auschwitz." *American Sociological Review* 75, no. 2 (2010): 252–72.

Mallarmé, Stéphane. *Collected Poems*. Translated by Henry Weinfield. Berkeley: University of California Press, 1996.

– *Correspondance. Lettres sur la poésie*. Edited by Bertrand Marchal. Paris: Gallimard, 1995.

– "Crisis of Verse." In *Divagations*, translated by Barbara Johnson, 201–211. Cambridge, MA: Harvard University Press, 2007.

Manaster Ramer, Alexis. "Turkish Rhymes and Antirhymes in Phonological Theory." *Transactions of the Philological Society* 93, no. 2 (1995): 273–87.

Mancarella, Mariacarmela. "Harry Mathews traduttore: Il gioco e l'identità." PhD diss., Università degli Studi di Catania, 2011.

Bibliography

Manea, Raluca. "Michelle Grangaud's *Geste*: An Anti-Epic of Everyday Life." *French Forum* 40, nos. 2–3 (2015): 67–82.

Marías, Javier. "Guía para descartar lecturas." In *Harán de mi un criminal*, 303–5. Madrid: Alfaguara, 2003.

Marinetti, Filippo Tommaso. *Critical Writings*. Edited by Günther Berghaus. Translated by Doug Thompson. New York: Farrar, Straus and Giroux, 2006.

Marsal, Florence. *Jacques Roubaud: Prose de la mémoire et errance chevaleresque*. Rennes: Presses universitaires de Rennes, 2010. http://doi.org/10.4000/books.pur.39161.

Martial. *Epigrams Book II*. Edited and translated by Craig A. Williams. Oxford: Oxford University Press, 2004.

Marx, Karl. *Grundrisse*. Translated by Martin Nicolaus. London: Penguin Books, 1973.

Marx, William. *L'adieu à la littérature*. Paris: Minuit, 2005.

Mathews, Harry. *The Case of the Persevering Maltese*. Normal, IL: Dalkey Archive Press, 2003. [CPM]

– "An Interview with Harry Mathews." Interview by Lytle Shaw. *Chicago Review* 43, no. 2. (1997): 36–52.

– *Tlooth*. Normal, IL: Dalkey Archive Press, 1998. [T]

– *Le verger*. Paris: POL, 1986.

– *Les verts champs de moutarde de l'Afghanistan*. Translated by Georges Perec with the collaboration of the author. Paris: Denoël, 1975. [VCM]

Margolis, Joseph. "Genres, Laws, Canons, Principles." In *Rules and Conventions: Literature, Philosophy, Social Theory*, edited by Mette Hjort, 130–66. Baltimore: Johns Hopkins University Press, 1992.

Mark, Thomas Carson. "On Works of Virtuosity." *The Journal of Philosophy* 77, no. 1 (1980): 28–45.

Martín Sánchez, Pablo. "El arte de combinar fragmentos: Prácticas hipertextuales en la literatura oulipiana (Raymond Queneau, Georges Perec, Italo Calvino, Jacques Roubaud)." PhD diss., University of Granada, 2012.

– *Tuyo es el mañana*. Barcelona: Acantilado, 2016.

Mayer, Bernadette. *Sonnets*. New York: Tender Buttons Press, 1989.

McCleary, John. *Exercises in Mathematical Style*. Washington: Mathematical Association of America, 2017.

McHale, Brian. *Constructing Postmodernism*. London: Routledge, 1992.

McManus, I.C. "Symmetry and Asymmetry in Aesthetics and the Arts." *European Review* 13, supp. no. 2 (2005): 157–80.

Bibliography

Meizoz, Jérôme. "Ce que l'on fait dire au silence: Posture, ethos, image d'auteur." *Argumentation et analyse du discours* 3 (2009): 1–10. http://doi.org/10.4000/aad.667.

Mélois, Clémentine. *Dehors, la tempête.* Paris: Grasset, 2020.

Menger, Pierre-Michel. *The Economics of Creativity: Art and Achievement under Uncertainty.* Cambridge, MA: Harvard University Press, 2014.

Meschonnic, Henri. *Célébration de la poésie.* Paris: Verdier, 2001.

Métail, Michèle. "Femme, Oulipo, poésie sonore, musique: Entretien avec Michèle Métail." Interview by Camille Bloomfield. *Formes poétiques contemporaines* 8 (2011): 115–19.

– "Une petite musique chinoise." *Trames, Lectures de Raymond Queneau, no.1 Morale élémentaire* (1987): 69–83.

– "Poésie avec Michèle Métail." Interview by Laure Adler. L'heure bleue, France Inter, 24 October 2018, audio 53:00, https://www.franceinter.fr/emissions/l-heure-bleue/l-heure-bleue-23-octobre-2018.

– *Le vol des oies sauvages.* Saint-Benoît-du-Sault: Tarabuste, 2011. [VOS]

– *Wild Geese Returning.* Translated by Jody Gladding. Hong Kong: Chinese University Press, 2017. [WGR]

Métail, Michèle, and Louis Roquin. *L'un l'autre: L'esperluette.* Illiers-Combray: Marcel le Poney, 2008.

Millikan, Ruth Garrett. *Language: A Biological Model.* Oxford: Oxford University Press, 2005.

Monk, Ian. *Writings for the Oulipo.* Los Angeles: Make Now Books, 2005.

Montémont, Véronique. "JR007: La valeur communicationnelle du secret chez Jacques Roubaud." In *Le mystère dans les lettres*, edited by Christelle Reggiani and Bernard Magné, 177–86. Paris: Presses universitaires de Paris Sorbonne, 2007.

– "*Quelque chose noir*: Le point de fracture?" *Textuel* 55 (2008): 9–32.

Moret, Philippe. "Discontinuité du recueil et construction de l'œuvre." In *Poétiques de la discontinuité: De 1870 à nos jours*, edited by Isabelle Chol, 219–29. Clermont-Ferrand: Presses universitaires Blaise Pascal, 2004.

Motte, Warren F. "Clinamen Redux." *Comparative Literature Studies* 23, no. 4 (1986): 263–81.

– *Playtexts: Ludics in Contemporary Literature.* Lincoln, NE: University of Nebraska Press, 1995.

Mougin, Pascal. "Littérature conceptuelle: Réflexions sur une catégorie problématique." *Marges* 27 (2018): 82–95.

Możejko, Edward. "Constructivism." *Encyclopedia of Contemporary Literary Theory: Approaches, Scholars, Terms*, edited by Irena Makaryk, 18–20. Toronto: University of Toronto Press, 1973.

Bibliography

Mréjen, Valérie. *Ping-Pong*. Paris: Allia, 2008.

Mullen, Harryette. *Sleeping with the Dictionary*. Berkeley: University of California Press, 2002.

Müller, Herta. *The Hunger Angel*. Translated by Philip Boehm. London: Portobello, 2012.

Mumford, Stephen, and Rani Lill Anjum. "Powers and Potentiality." In *Handbook of Potentiality*, edited by Kristina Engelhard and Michael Quante, 261–78. Dordrecht: Springer Netherlands, 2018.

Murray, Penelope. Introduction to *Plato on Poetry*, edited by Penelope Murray, 1–35. Cambridge: Cambridge University Press, 1996.

Nadeau, Maurice. *The History of Surrealism*. Translated by Richard Howard. Harmondsworth: Penguin, 1973.

Nake, Frieder. "Information Aesthetics: An Heroic Experiment." In *Computers and Creativity*, edited by Jon McCormack and Mark d'Inverno, 61–95. Berlin, London: Springer, 2012.

Naukkarinen, Ossi, and Yuriko Saito. "Introduction." *Contemporary Aesthetics*, special volume 4 (2012), ARTIFICATION. https://digital commons.risd.edu/liberalarts_contempaesthetics/vol0/iss4/1.

Naville, Pierre. *Le temps du surréel*. Paris: Galilée, 1977.

Nehamas, Alexander. *On Friendship*. New York: Basic Books, 2016.

Nerval, Gérard de. *Poésies*. Paris: Gallimard, 1964.

Nguyen, C. Thi. "Games and the Art of Agency." *The Philosophical Review* 128, no. 4 (2019): 423–62.

Nicol, Bran. "Reading Paranoia: Paranoia, Epistemophilia, and the Postmodern Crisis of Interpretation." *Literature and Psychology* 45, nos. 1–2 (1999): 44–62.

Nietzsche, Friedrich. *Beyond Good and Evil*. Translated by Judith Norman. Cambridge: Cambridge University Press, 2002.

– *The Gay Science*. Translated by Thomas Common. Mineola, NY: Dover, 2006.

Noguez, Dominique. "Le grantécrivain: D'André Gide à Marguerite Duras." *Le Débat* 4, no. 86 (1995): 29–40.

– *La véritable origine des plus beaux aphorismes*. Paris: Payot, 2014.

North, Michael. *Novelty: The History of the New*. Chicago: University of Chicago Press, 2013.

Novitz, David. "Creativity and Constraint." *Australasian Journal of Philosophy* 77, no. 1 (1999): 67–82.

The noulipian Analects. Edited by Christine Wertheim and Mathias Viegener. Los Angeles: Les Figues Press, 2007. [NA]

Nufer, Doug. *Never Again*. New York: Black Square, 2004.

Nugent, Benjamin. *American Nerd: The Story of My People*. New York: Scribner, 2008.

O'Meara, Lucy. "Georges Perec and Anne Garréta: Oulipo, Constraint and Crime Fiction." *Nottingham French Studies* 53, no. 1 (2014): 35–48.

O'Neill, Ryan. *The Drover's Wives*. Sydney: Brio, 2018.

– *Their Brilliant Careers*. Melbourne: Black Inc., 2016.

Ording, Philip. *99 Variations on a Proof*. Princeton: Princeton University Press, 2019.

Oriol-Boyer, Claudette. "'Le voyage d'hiver': Lire / écrire avec Perec." *Cahiers Georges Perec I: Colloque de Cerisy, juillet 1984*, 146–70. Paris: POL, 1985.

Orsini, G.N.G. "Coleridge and Schlegel Reconsidered." *Comparative Literature* 16, no. 2 (1964): 97–118.

Orwell, George. *The Collected Essays, Journalism and Letters of George Orwell*, vol. 2. London: Secker and Warburg, 1968.

Oswald, Alice. *Memorial*. London: Faber and Faber, 2011.

Oulipo. *L'abécédaire provisoirement définitif*. Edited by Michèle Audin and Paul Fournel. Paris: Larousse, 2014.

– *All That Is Evident Is Suspect: Readings from the Oulipo 1963–2018*. Edited by Ian Monk and Daniel Levin Becker. San Francisco: McSweeney's, 2018. [AES]

– *Anthologie de l'Oulipo*. Edited by Marcel Bénabou and Paul Fournel. Paris: Gallimard, 2009. [AO]

– *Atlas de littérature potentielle*. Paris: Gallimard, 1981. [ALP]

– *La bibliothèque oulipienne*. Volume 1. Paris: Ramsay, 1987. [BO 1]

– *La bibliothèque oulipienne*. Volume 2. Paris: Ramsay, 1987. [BO 2]

– *La bibliothèque oulipienne*. Volume 4. Bordeaux: Le Castor Astral, 1997. [BO 4]

– *La bibliothèque oulipienne*. Volume 5. Bordeaux: Le Castor Astral, 2000. [BO 5]

– *La bibliothèque oulipienne*. Volume 6. Bordeaux: Le Castor Astral, 2003. [BO 6]

– *La bibliothèque oulipienne*. Volume 7. Bordeaux: Le Castor Astral, 2008. [BO 7]

– *Cher Père Noël*. Paris: Éditions j'ai lu, 2020.

– *Genèse de l'Oulipo 1960–1963*. Edited by Jacques Bens. Bordeaux: Le Castor Astral, 2005. [GO]

– *La littérature potentielle: Créations, récréations, recréations*. Paris: Gallimard, 1973. [LP]

– *Moments oulipiens*. Bordeaux: Le Castor Astral, 2004. [MO]

Bibliography

- *Oulipo*. Paris: Association pour la diffusion de la pensée française, 2005.
- *Oulipo: A Primer of Potential Literature*. Edited and translated by Warren F. Motte Jr. Lincoln, NE: University of Nebraska Press, 1986. [OPPL]
- *Oulipo Compendium*. Edited by Harry Mathews and Alastair Brotchie. 2nd ed. London: Atlas Press, 2005. [OC]
- *Oulipo Laboratory: Texts from the Bibliothèque Oulipienne*. Translated by Harry Mathews, Iain White, and Warren F. Motte Jr. London: Atlas Press, 1995. [OL]
- *Paris-Math*. Paris: Cassini, 2017. [PM]
- *Winter Journeys (Expanded Edition)*. Translated by Ian Monk, Harry Mathews, and John Sturrock. London: Atlas Press, 2013.

The Oulipo. Verbivoracious Festschrift Volume Six. Edited by G.N. Forester and M.J. Nichols. Singapore: Verbivoracious Press, 2017.

Owens, David. "Duress, Deception, and the Validity of a Promise." *Mind* 116, no. 462 (2007): 293–315.

Pagani, Francesca. "Potentielle et actuelle: La sextine au XXIe siècle." *Elephant & Castle* 14 (2016): 5–23.

Pages, Nicolas. *Les choses communes*. Paris: Fayard, 2001.

Park, Sowon. "Scriptworlds." In *The Cambridge Companion to World Literature*, edited by Ben Etherington and Jarad Zimbler, 100–15. Cambridge: Cambridge University Press, 2018.

Pascal, Blaise. *Pensées*. Paris: Seuil, 1962.
- *Pensées*. Translated by W.F. Trotter. Mineola, NY: Dover, 2003.

Paterson, Don. *The Poem: Lyric, Sign, Meter*. London: Faber and Faber, 2018.

Paz, Octavio. *The Collected Poems of Octavio Paz 1957–1987*. Translated by Eliot Weinberger. New York: New Directions, 1990.

Peirce, Charles Sanders. *Collected Papers of Charles Sanders Peirce*, vol. 2. Cambridge, MA: Harvard University Press, 1960.

Pellis, Sergio, and Vivien Pellis. *The Playful Brain: Venturing to the Limits of Neuroscience*. Oxford: Oneworld, 2009.

The Penguin Book of Oulipo. Edited by Philip Terry. London: Penguin, 2019. [PBO]

Perec, Georges. *56 lettres à un ami*. Paris: Le bleu du ciel, 2011.
- *An Attempt at Exhausting a Place in Paris*. Translated by Marc Lowenthal. Cambridge, MA: Wakefield Press, 2010.
- "Avez-vous lu Harry Mathews?" *Review of Contemporary Fiction* 7, no. 3 (1987): 82–3.
- *La boutique obscure*. Translated by Daniel Levin Becker. Brooklyn: Melville House, 2012. [BO]

Bibliography

- *Cahier des charges de* La vie mode d'emploi. Edited by Hans Hartje, Bernard Magné, and Jacques Neefs. Paris: Zulma/CNRS Éditions, 1993.
- *Dialogue avec Georges Perec.* Interview by Bernard Noël. Marseille: André Dimanche, 1997.
- *Entretiens, conférences, textes rares, inédits.* Edited by Mireille Ribière. Paris: Joseph K, 2019.
- *Entretiens et conférences.* Edited by Dominique Bertelli and Mireille Ribière. Paris: Joseph K, 2003. 2 vols. [EC I and EC II]
- *Espèces d'espaces.* Paris: Galilée, 1974.
- *I Remember.* Edited and translated by Philip Terry and David Bellos. Godine: Boston, 2014.
- *Je suis né.* Paris: Seuil, 1990. [JSN]
- "Lieux, un projet." Interview by Gérard Macé. In *Georges Perec* (boxed set of four compact discs). Marseille: André Dimanche/INA, 1997. Disc 3.
- *Life: A User's Manual.* Translated by David Bellos. London: Collins Harvill, 1988. [LUM]
- "The Machine." Translated by Ulrich Schönherr. *The Review of Contemporary Fiction* 24, no. 1 (2009): 33–93.
- *Die Maschine.* Translated by Eugen Helmlé. Stuttgart: Philippe Reclam, 1972.
- *Œuvres I* and *II.* Edited by Christelle Reggiani. Paris: Gallimard, 2017. [O I and O II]
- *Poésie ininterrompue, inventaire.* Edited by Bernard Magné. Marseille: André Dimanche, 1997.
- *Species of Spaces and Other Pieces.* Translated by John Sturrock. London: Penguin 1999. [SS]
- "Still Life / Style Leaf." Translated by Harry Mathews, *Yale French Studies* 61 (1981): 299–305.
- "Tentative de description de choses vues au carrefour Mabillon le 19 mai 1978." In *Georges Perec* (boxed set of four compact discs). Marseille: André Dimanche/INA, 1997. Discs 3 and 4.
- "Tentative de description d'un programme de travail pour les années à venir." *Cahiers Georges Perec 1: Colloque de Cerisy, juillet 1984,* 328–31. Paris: POL, 1985.
- *Things: A Story of the Sixties* and *A Man Asleep.* Translated by David Bellos and Andrew Leak. London: Vintage Books, 2011.
- *Three.* Translated by Ian Monk. London: Harvill, 1996. [TH]
- *W or the Memory of Childhood.* Translated by David Bellos. London: Harvill, 1989. [WMC]

Bibliography

Perec, Georges, Harry Mathews, Oskar Pastior, Brunella Eruli, and Guillermo López Gallego. *35 variations*. Paris: Le Castor Astral, 2000.

Perec, Georges, and Bernard Noël. *Dialogue*. Marseille: André Dimanche, 1997.

Perec, Georges/Oulipo. *Le voyage d'hiver et ses suites*. Paris: Seuil, 2013.

Perloff, Marjorie. *Unoriginal Genius: Poetry by Other Means in the New Century*. Chicago: University of Chicago Press, 2010.

Pettit, Philip, and Christian List. *Group Agency*. Oxford: Oxford University Press, 2011.

Phillips, Richard. "Georges Perec's Experimental Fieldwork; Perecquian Fieldwork." *Social & Cultural Geography* 19, no. 2 (2016): 171–91. http://doi.org/10.1080/14649365.2016.1266027.

Plato. *The Dialogues of Plato*, vol. 2. Translated by Benjamin Jowett. New York: Random House, 1937.

– *Phaedrus*. Translated by Robin Waterfield. Oxford: Oxford University Press, 2002.

– *The Republic*. Translated by H.D.P. Lee. Penguin: Harmondsworth, 1955.

Pliny the Elder. *Naturalis Historia (Natural History)*, vol. 3. Translated by H. Rackham. Cambridge, MA: Harvard University Press, 1940.

Plutarch. *The Parallel Lives*, vol. 3. Translated by Bernadotte Perrin. London: Loeb Classical Library, 1916.

Poe, Edgar Allan. "Von Kempelen and His Discovery." In *Collected Works: Stories and Poems*, 186–90. San Diego: Canterbury Classics, 2011.

Poiana, Peter. "The Hyperbolic Logic of Constraint in the Poetic Works of Jacques Jouet." *SubStance* 48, no. 2 (2019): 75–9.

Poier-Bernhard, Astrid. "Michelle Grangaud – Anagrammes, tercets et autres textes insolites." In *Oulipo poétiques*, edited by Peter Kuon, 119–40. Tübingen: Gunter Narr Verlag, 1990.

– *Texte nach Bauplan: Studien zur zeitgenössischen ludisch-methodischen Literatur in Frankreich und Italien*. Heidelberg: Universitätsverlag Winter, 2012.

Polizzotti, Mark. *Revolution of the Mind: The Life of André Breton*. New York: Farrar, Straus and Giroux, 1995.

Pollock, Sheldon. "Future Philology? The Fate of a Soft Science in a Hard World." *Critical Inquiry* 35 (2009): 931–64.

Ponge, Francis. *Entretiens de Francis Ponge avec Philippe Sollers*. Paris: Gallimard/Seuil, 1970.

– *Pour un Malherbe*. Paris: Gallimard, 1965.

Poucel, Jean-Jacques. "The Arc of Reading in Georges Perec's 'La clôture.'" *Yale French Studies* 105 (2004): 127–55.

Bibliography

- "Chiquenaude: Vie brève de la morale élémentaire." In *La Morale élémentaire. Aventures d'une forme poétique, Queneau, Oulipo, etc.* (*La Licorne* 81), edited by Jacques Jouet, Pierre Martin, and Dominique Moncond'huy, 15–54. Rennes: Presses universitaires de Rennes, 2007.
- "Family Vocation: Toward a Fictional Theory of Oulipian Influence." In *Formules 16: Oulipo @ 50 / L'Oulipo à 50 ans*, edited by Camille Bloomfield, Marc Lapprand, and Jean-Jacques Thomas (2012): 35–48.

Pound, Ezra. *The Cantos*. London: Faber and Faber, 1975.

"Portrait: A Life in the Bush of Ghosts." In *Critical Perspectives on Amos Tutuola*, edited by Bernth Lindfors, 26–7. London: Heinemann, 1980.

Prendergast, Christopher. *Mirages and Mad Beliefs: Proust the Skeptic*. Princeton: Princeton University Press, 2013.

Propp, Vladimir. *The Morphology of the Folktale*. Translated by Laurence Scott. Austin: University of Texas Press, 1968.

Proust, Marcel. *Against Sainte-Beuve*. Translated by John Sturrock. London: Penguin, 1994.
- *Du côté de chez Swann*. Paris: Gallimard, 1987.
- *Finding Time Again*. Translated by Ian Patterson. London: Penguin, 2003.
- *The Prisoner* and *The Fugitive*. Translated by Carol Clark and Peter Collier. London: Penguin, 2002.
- *La prisonnière*. Paris: Gallimard, 1989.
- *Swann's Way*. Translated by Lydia Davis. New York: Penguin, 2002.
- *Le temps retrouvé*. Paris: Gallimard, 1954.

Putnam, Hilary. "Literature, Science, and Reflection." *New Literary History* 7, no. 3 (1976): 483–91.

Quayson, Ato. *Strategic Transformations in Nigerian Writing*. Oxford: J. Currey, 1997.

Queneau, Anne-Isabelle, ed. *Album Queneau*. Paris: Gallimard, 2002.

Queneau, Raymond. "L'analyse matricielle de la phrase en français." In *Cahier de l'Herne: Queneau*, edited by Andrée Bergens, 55–60. Paris: L'Herne, 1975.
- *Aux confins des ténèbres: Les fous littéraires*. Edited by Madeleine Velguth. Paris: Gallimard, 2002.
- *Bords*. Paris: Hermann, 1963. [B]
- "Chansons d'écrivains." In Jacques Jouet, *Raymond Queneau*, 155–71. Paris: La Manufacture, 1989.
- *Elementary Morality*. Translated by Philip Terry. Manchester: Carcanet, 2007.
- *Entretiens avec Georges Charbonnier*. Paris: Gallimard, 1962. [EGC]

Bibliography

- "Erutarettil." *La nouvelle revue française*, 172 (1967): 605.
- *Exercises in Style*. Translated by Barbara Wright and Christopher Clarke. New York: New Directions, 2012. [ES]
- *Journaux 1914–1965*. Edited by Anne-Isabelle Queneau. Paris: Gallimard, 1996.
- *Letters, Numbers, Forms: Essays, 1928–1970*. Translated by Jordan Stump. Urbana, IL: University of Illinois Press, 2007. [LNF]
- "Meccano." In *Cahier de l'Herne: Queneau*, edited by Andrée Bergens, 61–66. Paris: L'Herne, 1975.
- *Odile*. Translated by Carol Sanders. Normal, IL: Dalkey Archive, 1988. [O]
- *Œuvres complètes I*. Edited by Claude Debon. Paris: Gallimard, 1989. [OC I]
- *Œuvres complètes II*. Edited by Henri Godard. Paris: Gallimard, 2002. [OC II]
- *Œuvres complètes III*. Edited by Henri Godard. Paris: Gallimard, 2006. [OC III]
- *Pounding the Pavements, Beating the Bushes, and Other Pataphysical Poems*. Translated by Teo Savory. Greensboro, NC: Unicorn Press, 1985.
- *Stories and Remarks*. Translated by Marc Lowenthal. Lincoln, NA: University of Nebraska Press, 2000.
- "Sur les suites s-additives." *The Journal of Combinatorial Theory* 12 (1972): 31–71.
- *Le voyage en Grèce*. Paris: Gallimard, 1973. [VG]
- *Witch Grass*. Translated by Barbara Wright. New York: New York Review Books, 2003. [WG]
- *Zazie in the Metro*. Translated by Barbara Wright. London: Penguin Books, 2000. [ZM]

Quillien, Christophe. *Je me souviens des années 70*. Paris: Hachette Littératures, 2006.

Quine, Willard Van Orman. "Methodological Reflections on Current Linguistic Theory." In *Semantics of Natural Language*, edited by Donald Davidson and Gilbert Harman, 442–54 Dordrecht: D. Reidel, 1972.

Raymond, Dominique. *Échafaudages, squelettes et patrons de couturière. Essai sur la littérature à contraintes au Québec*. Montreal: Les Presses de l'Université de Montréal, 2021.

Raz, Joseph. "Promises in Morality and Law." *Harvard Law Review* 95, no. 4 (1982): 916–38.

The Reality Street Book of Sonnets. Edited by Jeff Hilson. Hastings, UK: Reality Street, 2008.

Reggiani, Christelle. "Contrainte et littérarité." *Formules* 4 (2000): 10–19.

– "De la contrainte à la forme." *Sites* 25, no. 5 (2022): 539–47.

– *L'éternelle et l'éphémère: Temporalités dans l'œuvre de Georges Perec.* Amsterdam: Rodopi, 2010.

– "Être oulipienne: Contraintes de style, contraintes de genre?" *Études littéraires* 47, no. 2 (2016), 103–17. http://doi.org/10.7202/1045749ar.

– *Poétiques oulipiennes. La contrainte, le style, l'histoire.* Geneva: Droz, 2014.

Reig, Christophe. *Mimer, miner, rimer: Le cycle romanesque de Jacques Roubaud.* Amsterdam: Rodopi, 2006.

– "Nomen est (h)omen. Lettres et onomastique dans *Le voyage d'hiver* (Georges Perec) et ses oulipiennes séquelles." In *Le pied de la lettre: Créativité et littérature potentielle,* edited by Hermes Salceda and Jean-Jacques Thomas, 117–32. New Orleans: Presses universitaires du Nouveau Monde, 2010.

Reina, José Luis. "Entretien avec Jacques Roubaud, Paul Braffort, et Jacques Jouet, membres de l'Oulipo." *Lendemains* 52 (1989): 33–40.

Ribière, Mireille. "La poésie en question dans *La clôture et autres poèmes* de Georges Perec." *Le cabinet d'amateur: Revue d'études perecquiennes* (2015). http://associationgeorgesperec.fr/le-cabinet-d-amateur.

Rimbaud, Arthur. *Collected Poems.* Translated by Oliver Bernard. Harmondsworth: Penguin, 1986.

Riviere, Sam. "Sam Riviere on Christopher Reid's *Six Bad Poets*." *Poetry Review* 103, no. 4 (2013): 78–80.

Robbins, Michael. "Ripostes." *Poetry,* 1 July 2013, https://www.poetryfoundation.org/poetrymagazine/articles/70023/ripostes.

Rorty, Richard. "The Pragmatist's Progress." In *Interpretation and Overinterpretation,* edited by Stefan Collini, 89–108. Cambridge: Cambridge University Press, 1992.

Rowe, Mark W. "Poetry and Abstraction," *British Journal of Aesthetics* 36, no. 1 (1996): 1–15.

Roubaud, Jacques. $\in$. Paris: Gallimard, 1966.

– "L'auteur oulipien." In *L'auteur et le manuscrit,* edited by Michel Contat, 77–92. Paris: Presses universitaires de France, 1991.

– *La Bibliothèque de Warburg.* Paris: Seuil, 2002. [BW]

– *Ciel et terre et ciel et terre, et ciel.* Paris: Argol, 2009.

– "Compose, Condense, Constrain." Translated by Jean-Jacques Poucel. *Poetics Today* 30, no. 4 (2009): 635–52.

Bibliography

- *La dernière balle perdue*. Paris: Fayard, 1997. [DBP]
- *Description d'un projet*. Caen: Nous, 2014.
- *La dissolution*. Caen: Nous, 2008.
- *The Great Fire of London*. Translated by Dominic Di Bernardi. Elmwood Park, IL: Dalkey Archive, 1991. [GFL]
- *Hortense in Exile*. Translated by Dominic Di Bernardi. McLean, IL: Dalkey Archive, 2001.
- *Hortense is Abducted*. Translated by Dominic Di Bernardi. McLean, IL: Dalkey Archive, 2000.
- *Impératif catégorique*. Paris: Seuil, 2008. [IC]
- *The Loop*. Translated by Jeff Fort. Champaign, IL: Dalkey Archive Press, 2009. [L]
- *Mathematics*. Translated by Ian Monk. Champaign, IL: Dalkey Archive Press, 2012.
- "Le nombre d'Opalka." In Christine Savinel, Jacques Roubaud, and Bernard Noël, *Roman Opalka*, 27–46. Paris: Dis voir, 1996.
- *Our Beautiful Heroine*. Translated by David Kornacker. Woodstock, NY: Overlook, 1987.
- *Parc sauvage*. Paris: Seuil, 2008. [PS]
- "Perecquian Oulipo." Translated by Jean-Jacques Poucel, *Yale French Studies* 105 (2004): 99–109.
- *Peut-être ou la nuit de dimanche*. Paris: Seuil, 2018. [PE]
- *Poésie:*. Paris: Seuil, 2000. [P]
- *Poésie, etcetera: Ménage*. Paris: Stock, 1995. [PEM]
- *Poetry, etc: Cleaning House*. Translated by Guy Bennett. Los Angeles: Green Integer Press, 2006. [PECH]
- "Préparation d'une famille de contraintes." *Formules* 1 (1997–98): 204–8.
- *Quasi-cristaux*. Paris: Editions Martine Aboucaya et Yvon Lambert, 2013. Web edition by Valérie Beaudouin and Anne F. Garréta. https://blogs.oulipo.net/qc.
- *Quelque chose noir*. Paris: Gallimard, 1986.
- "Racontez-moi l'Oulipo." Interview by Camille Bloomfield. *Formes poétiques contemporaines*, 8 (2011): 195–210.
- *Some Thing Black*. Translated by Rosmarie Waldrop. Elmwood Park, IL: Dalkey Archive, 1990.

Rousseau, Jean-Jacques. *The Collected Writings of Rousseau*. Vol. 5. Edited by Christopher Kelly, Roger D. Masters, and Peter G. Stillman. Translated by Christopher Kelly. Hanover, NH: University Press of New England, 1995.

Bibliography

Roussel, Raymond. *How I Wrote Certain of My Books*. Translated by Trevor Winkfield. Cambridge, MA: Exact Change, 1995.

Rousset, David. *L'univers concentrationnaire*. Famot: Geneva, 1976.

– *A World Apart: Life in a Nazi Concentration Camp*. Translated by Yvonne Moyse and Roger Senhouse. London: Secker and Warburg, 1951.

Ruthven, K.K. *Critical Assumptions*. Cambridge: Cambridge University Press, 1979.

Saclolo, Michael P. "How a Medieval Troubadour Became a Mathematical Figure." *Notices of the American Mathematical Society* 58, no. 5 (2011): 682–7.

Salceda, Hermès. *Clés pour* La disparition. Leiden: Brill, 2019.

– "La réception de l'Oulipo en Catalogne et en Espagne." *Catalonia* 22 (2018): 3–31.

Salon, Olivier. *Le disparate, François Le Lionnais: Tentative de recollement d'un puzzle biographique*. Paris: Le nouvel Attila, 2016.

– "Traces et abandons oulipiens dans *Quelque chose noir*." *Textuel* 55 (2008): 169–80.

Samoyault, Tiphaine. *L'intertextualité. Mémoire de la littérature*. Paris: Armand Colin, 2010.

Sanders, Carol. *Raymond Queneau*. Amsterdam: Rodopi, 1994.

Sapir, E. "The Psychological Reality of Phonemes." In *Phonological Theory: Evolution and Current Practice*, edited by V.B. Makkai, 22–31. New York: Holt Rinehart and Winston, 1972.

Savinel, Christine. "Opalka ou l'éthique de l'assignation." In *Roman Opalka*, by Christine Savinel, Jacques Roubaud, and Bernard Noël, 5–26. Paris: Dis voir, 1996.

Schama, Simon. *Citizens: A Chronicle of the French Revolution*. London: Penguin, 1989.

Schimmel, Annemarie. *The Mystery of Numbers*. New York: Oxford University Press, 1993.

Schleiermacher, Friedrich. "On the Different Methods of Translating." In *The Translation Studies Reader*, 2nd ed., translated by Susan Bernofsky, edited by Lawrence Venuti, 43–63. New York: Routledge, 2000.

Seiffert, Colleen M., David E. Myer, Natalie Davidson, Andrea L. Patalano, and Ilan Yaniv. "Demystification of Cognitive Insight: Opportunistic Assimilation and Prepared-Mind Perspective." In *The Nature of Insight*, edited by Robert J. Sternberg and Janet E. Davidson, 65–124. Cambridge, MA: MIT Press, 1995.

Seneca, *Epistulae Morale*, vol. 2. Translated by Richard Gumere. Cambridge, MA: Harvard University Press, 1920.

Bibliography

Şentürk, Levent. *199+*. Eskişehir: Yortkitap, 2020.

Serres, Michel. *Hominescence*. Paris: Le Pommier, 2001.

Sheringham, Michael. *Devices and Desires: French Autobiography from Rousseau to Perec*. Oxford: Clarendon Press, 1993.

– "Raymond Queneau: The Lure of the Spiritual." In *Literature and Spirituality*, edited by David Bevan, 33–47. Amsterdam: Rodopi, 1992.

– "Les vies anglaises de Jacques Roubaud." In *Jacques Roubaud, compositeur de mathématique et de poésie*, edited by Agnès Disson and Véronique Montémont, 241–2. Nancy: Absalon, 2010.

Simonnet, Claude. *Queneau déchiffré*. Geneva: Slatkine, 1981.

Skrbina, David. *Panpsychism in the West*. Cambridge, MA: MIT Press, 2017.

Sperber, Dan, Fabrice Clément, Christophe Heintz, Olivier Mascaro, Hugo Mercier, Gloria Origgi, and Deirdre Wilson. "Epistemic Vigilance." *Mind and Language* 25, no. 4 (2010): 359–93.

Stallings, A.E. *Olives*. Evanston, IL: Triquarterly, 2012.

Stokes, Dustin. "Incubated Cognition and Creativity." *Journal of Consciousness Studies* 14 (2007): 83–100.

Stolnitz, Jerome. "On the Cognitive Triviality of Art." *British Journal of Aesthetics* 32 (1992): 191–200.

Strawson, Galen. *Selves: An Essay in Revisionary Metaphysics*. Oxford: Clarendon Press, 2009.

Stump, Jordan. *The Other Book*. Lincoln, NE: University of Nebraska Press, 2011.

Suits, Bernard. *The Grasshopper: Games, Life, and Utopia*. Peterborough, ON: Broadview Press, 2014.

Sutton-Smith, Brian. *The Ambiguity of Play*. Cambridge, MA: Harvard University Press, 1997.

Tableau complet de la valeur énergétique des aliments habituels. Paris: Éditions de la pensée moderne, 1957.

Tahar, Virginie. *La fabrique oulipienne du récit*. Paris: Classiques Garnier, 2019.

– "Les oulipiennes sont-elles des oulipiens comme les autres?" In *Femmes à l'œuvre dans la construction des savoirs: Paradoxes de la visibilité et de l'invisibilité*, edited by Caroline Trotot, Claire Delahaye, and Isabelle Mornat, 215–32. Champs sur Marne: LISAA éditeur, 2020.

Terry, Philip. *Oulipoems*. Tokyo: AhaDada Books, 2006.

– *Quennets*. Manchester: Carcanet, 2016.

Textos potentes. Edited by Pablo Martín Sánchez. Logroño: Pepitas de calabaza, 2019.

Thom, René. "Stop Chance! Silence Noise." Translated by Robert E. Chumbley, *SubStance* 40 (1983): 11–21.

Thomas, Dylan. "Blithe Spirits." In *Critical Perspectives on Amos Tutuola*, ed. Bernth Lindfors, 7–8. London: Heinemann, 1980.

Thomas, Jean-Jacques. *La langue, la poésie. Essais sur la poésie française contemporaine*. Lille: Presses universitaires de Lille, 1989.

– *Oulipo. Chronique des années héroïques (1978–2018)*. New Orleans: Presses universitaires du Nouveau Monde, 2019.

Tillion, Germaine. *Ravensbrück*. Translated by Gerald Satterwhite. Garden City, NY: Anchor Press, 1975.

Todorov, Tzvetan. *Genres in Discourse*. Translated by Catherine Porter. Cambridge: Cambridge University Press, 1991.

Tubbs, Robert. *Mathematics in Twentieth-Century Literature and Art*. Baltimore: Johns Hopkins University Press, 2014.

Turner, Simon. "Arranging Excursions to Disparate Worlds." In *Stress Fractures*, edited by Tom Chivers, 115–33. London: Penned in the Margins, 2010.

Tutuola, Amos. *L'ivrogne dans la brousse*. Translated by Raymond Queneau. Paris: Gallimard, 1953.

– "My Vernacular." *Transition* 120 (2016): 22–7.

– *The Palm-Wine Drinkard and his Dead Palm-Wine Tapster in the Deads' Town*. London: Faber and Faber, 1952.

Valéry, Paul. *Œuvres complètes I*. Edited by Jean Hytier. Paris: Gallimard, 1957.

Vanderschelden, Isabelle. "Perec traducteur." *Trans Littérature* 4 (1992): 13–19.

Viala, Alain. "L'éloquence galante: Une problématique de l'adhésion." In *Images de soi dans le discours. La construction de l'ethos*, edited by Ruth Amossy, 177–95. Paris: Delachaux & Niestlé, 1999.

Vidal-Naquet, Pierre. *L'affaire Audin*. Paris: Minuit, 1989.

Vrydaghs, David. "Le surréalisme fictif. Motifs critiques et réécritures historiographiques dans *Odile, Gilles* et *Aurélien*." In *Imaginaires de la vie littéraire: Fiction, figuration, configuration*, edited by B.O. Dozo, A. Glinoer, and M. Lacroix, 153–66. Rennes: Presses universitaires de Rennes, 2012.

Watkin, Christopher. *French Philosophy Today: New Figures of the Human in Badiou, Meillassoux, Malabou, Serres, and Latour*. Edinburgh: Edinburgh University Press, 2017.

Webber, Gale. "Constructivism and Soviet Literature." *Soviet Union* 3, no. 2 (1976): 294–310.

Bibliography

White, Gillian. *Lyric Shame*. Cambridge, MA: Harvard University Press, 2014.

White, J.J. "Goethe in the Machine." *Publications of the English Goethe Society* 41, no. 1 (1971): 123–4.

Wichner, Ernest. "Interview with Ernest Wichner." Interview by Valentina Glajar and Bettina Brandt. In *Herta Müller: Politics and Aesthetics*, edited by Bettina Brandt and Valentina Glajar, 36–53. Lincoln, NE: University of Nebraska Press, 2013.

Wierzbicka, Anna. "The Alphabet of Human Thoughts." In *Conceptualizations and Mental Processing in Language*, edited by Richard A. Geiger and Brygida Rudzka-Ostyn, 23–51. Berlin: Mouton de Gruyter, 1993.

– *Semantics: Primes and Universals*. Oxford: Oxford University Press, 1996.

Winnicott, D.W. "Communicating and Not Communicating Leading to a Study of Certain Opposites." In *The Maturational Processes and the Facilitating Environment: Studies in the Theory of Emotional Development*, 179–92. Madison, CT: International Universities, 1965.

– *Playing and Reality*. London: Routledge, 1991.

Wittgenstein, Ludwig. *Philosophical Investigations*. Translated by G.E.M. Anscombe. Oxford: Blackwell, 1958.

Wittig, Rob, for IN.S.OMNIA. *Invisible Rendezvous: Connection and Collaboration in the New Landscape of Electronic Writing*. Hanover, NH: Wesleyan University Press, 1994.

Women Writers of Traditional China. Edited by Kang-i Sun and Haun Saussy. Stanford: Stanford University Press, 1999.

Ziff, Paul. *Semantic Analysis*. Ithaca: Cornell University Press, 1960.

Zizek, Slavoj. *Everything You Always Wanted to Know about Lacan (But Were Afraid to Ask Alfred Hitchcock)*. London: Verso, 1992.

– "The Limits of the Semiotic Approach to Psychoanalysis." In *Psychoanalysis and ...*, edited by Richard Feldstein and Henry Sussman, 89–110. New York: Routledge, 1990.

Index

Literary works are listed under their authors. Figures and tables are indicated by page numbers in italics.

Abaclar, Camille: *Je suis le ténébreux* (anthology), 270
Abish, Walter, 269
acronym, 49
Actes sémiotiques (journal), 264
Adair, Gilbert, 269
Adler, Laure, 112, 120
æncrage, 134–5
Aeneid, 256
Agamben, Giorgio, 224
Aira, César, 21, 58, 73, 75, 112, 272–3
Aji, Hélène, 245
Alamo (Atelier de Littérature Assistée par la Mathématique et les Ordinateurs, Workshop for Literature Assisted by Mathematics and Computers), 76, 77
aleatory methods. *See* chance-governed methods
alexandrine, 40, 44, 274

Alféri, Pierre, 248–9, 254, 257
Algol poetry, 265–6
All that is Evident is Suspect (anthology), 5, 247, 257, 264
allusions, 118, 134–5. *See also* citations; intertextuality
ampersand, 122
anagram, 9, 49, 132–3, 272
anaphone, 259
anaphora, 132
Anjum, Rani Lill, 224
Anomalous (journal), 245
antecedents, literary, 94–6, 126, 226–8
Antelme, Robert, 206, 207; *The Human Species (L'espèce humaine)*, 119
An Anthology of Chance Operations ... (Young), 31
anticipatory plagiarisms, 49, 114, 217, 258, 268, 290n37
antirhyme, 257–8, 261
antonymic translation, 97, 217
Apollinaire, Guillaume: *Alcools*, 40; *Calligrammes*, 131
Aragon, Louis, 16, 22, 33; *Aurélien*, 16

Index

Archet, Anne, 272

Aristotle, 46, 223–4, 260

Arnaud, Noël: *Algol* (Algol poetry), 265–6; on fecundity and potentiality, 225; on Genette, 98, 99; on Oulipo's membership, 29; on political discussions within Oulipo, 22; in WWII Resistance, 24

Arnheim, Rudolf, 148

Artaud, Antonin, 22

Ashbery, John, 224, 269

asymmetries, 154–6, 295n60

Atlas de littérature potentielle (Atlas of potential literature), 15, 43

attention, 63–4, 93, 183–4, 187, 191

Attridge, Derek, 46–7

Auden, W.H., 195, 224; "Rimbaud," 51–2

Audiberti, Jacques, 24

audience and readers: constraints and, 60–1, 65; deep formalism and, 183–7, 191; hide-and-seek with, 175–7; paranoid interpretations by, 10–11, 179–83, 188–91

Audin, Michèle: collaboration with Monk, 274; Desarguesiennes constraint, 143–5, 144; justice for father's murder by French army, 23; marketing using Oulipo's brand, 16; mathematics and, 10, 29, 146; numerology and, 139

– *La formule de Stokes, roman* (Stokes's theorem, a novel), 146

– *One Hundred Twenty-One Days* (*Cent vingt et un jours*), 143, 194, 225

– "Rue Desargues," 144–6; *Winter Journeys* instalment, 231

Ausonius, 49

autobiography, 163–4. *See also* psychoanalytic autobiography; revelation and dissimulation

automatic writing, 32, 42, 79

automation: introduction, 8; Alamo workshop and, 76, 77; computer-assisted writing, 76–7, 289n11; machine as metaphor for literary inspiration, 85–6; *Die Maschine* (*The Machine,* Perec) and, 8, 82, 83–5; Oulipo's interests and, 73, 75–6, 77–8; PALF project (Perec and Bénebou) and, 8, 79–82, 85, 289n27; procedures and, 73; vs simulation, 8, 78, 85

avant-garde. *See* literary movements and schools

Avatars de Nerval (website), 270

Baetens, Jan, 245

Baldwin, Thomas, 219

Ball, Hugo, 19

Bamford, Alice, 243

baobab constraint, 54

Barthes, Roland, 39–40

Baskin, Jason, 191

Baudelaire, Charles, 41, 85, 214, 274

Beard, Richard, 269

Beardsley, Monroe, 67

Beaudouin, Valérie, 231, 274, 290n37

beautiful in-law (*beau présent*) constraint, 275–6

Becker, Daniel Levin. *See* Levin Becker, Daniel

Beckett, Samuel, 300n2

Index

349

Bedient, Calvin, 50, 99, 193

Bellos, David, 101–2, 106, 124, 176, 185, 231, 232

Bénabou, Marcel: on autobiography, 163–4; on constraints, 44, 64–5, 86, 90, 166; on inspiration, 90; on phoneme constraints, 258, 259; Roubaud and, 135; semantic constraints and, 266; writer's block and, 89
- "Entre Roussel et Rousseau, ou contrainte et confession" (Between Roussel and Rousseau, or constraint and confession), 163–4
- *Jacob, Menahem, and Mimoun: A Family Epic* (*Jacob, Ménahem et Mimoun, une épopée familiale*), 164
- PALF project (with Perec), 8, 79–82, 85, 289n27
- "Rule and Constraint," 44, 90, 258
- *Why I Have Not Written Any of My Books* (*Pourquoi je n'ai écrit aucun de mes livres*), 89, 164, 176

Bénichou, Paul, 192

Benjamin, Walter, 116–17

Benoist-Méchin, Jacques, 178

Bens, Jacques, 26, 30, 143, 231, 247

Bense, Max, 6–7, 14, 35, 36–7, 38, 283n86

Benveniste, Émile, 202

Berge, Claude, 22, 26, 29, 32, 274

Berkman, Natalie, 77–8, 264

Bernstein, Charles: *Shadowtime*, 272

Berrigan, Ted, 71

Bersani, Leo, 219

Bertelli, Dominique, 176

Berti, Eduardo: co-optation by Oulipo, 20, 247; *I Remember* (Perec) and, 231; marketing using Oulipo's brand, 16; N + die (S + dé) method and, 35
- *L'Ivresse sans fin des portes tournantes* (The endless drunkenness of revolving doors), 266–7
- "Mañana se anuncia mejor" (Better weather forecast for tomorrow), 225
- *Por*, 229
- *Winter Journeys* instalment, 231

Binet, Catherine, 175

biological metaphors, 225

Birkhoff, George D., 36

Bishop, Elizabeth, 224

Blanchette, Patricia, 244

Blanchot, Maurice, 300n2

Blavier, André, 20, 171

Bloom, Gary, 158

Bloom, Harold, 147

Bloomfield, Camille: interview with Jouet, 266; interview with Métail, 70; interview with Roubaud, 23, 77; on Jouet's productivity, 60; on minor crises within Oulipo, 19, 26; on the nature of Oulipo, 4, 100; on Oulipo vs avant-gardes, 19; on tabula rasa rhetoric among avant-gardes, 41–2; on translations by Oulipians, 99

Bohman-Kalaja, Kimberly, 203

Bök, Christian: on constraints, 276; disappointment with Oulipo, 127–8; *Eunoia*, 54, 245, 286n53;

Noulipo and, 269; on Oulipo's political reticence, 23–4, 25

Bongo, Pietro: *Numerorum mysteria*, 135

Bonnefoy, Yves, 266

Borel, Adrien, 24

Borges, Jorge Luis, 85, 116, 227; "Pierre Menard, Author of the Quijote," 187, 299n88; "Tlön, Uqbar, Orbis Tertius," 181

Bose, R.C., 274

Bot or Not (website), 76, 289n11

Bourbaki, 72, 87, 260

Bourdieu, Pierre, 18–19, 22

Bourguet, Dominique, 76

Bouveresse, Jacques, 37

Bracciolini, Poggio, 148

Braffort, Paul: Alamo workshop and, 76, 77; crisis of 1974 and, 26; departure from Oulipo, 19, 27, 282n56; elementary morality form and, 234; mathematics background, 29; "Prolégomènes à une occultation" (Prolegomena to an occultation), 263; on semantic constraints, 263

Brainard, Joe: *I Remember*, 226, 232

Breton, André: automatic writing and, 42, 79; chance-governed methods and, 32; *Exercises in Style* (Queneau) and, 33, 226; *La décomposition* (Garréta) and, 214; Queneau's homage to, 26, 41; surrealism and, 16–17, 19, 23, 28; Tzara's score for, 41

- *The Communicating Vessels* (*Les vases communicants*), 32
- "First Surrealist Manifesto," 42, 82
- "Liquidation" (with Tzara), 41

- *Mad Love* (*L'amour fou*), 32
- *The Magnetic Fields* (*Les champs magnétiques*; with Soupault), 19, 40
- *Nadja*, 32; "The New Spirit," 33, 226
- "Second Surrealist Manifesto," 214

Bridges, Robert, 49

Brivadois acrostic, 268

Brooke-Rose, Christine, 269

Brotchie, Alastair. See *Oulipo Compendium* (Mathews and Brotchie)

Brown, Lee Ann, 269

Browning, Robert, 47

Burgelin, Claude, 167, 173, 174–5, 179, 205–6, 208

Bürger, Peter, 22

Burt, Stephanie, 247

Butor, Michel, 119

Cadieu, Morgane: *Marcher au hasard* (Random walks), 148

Cage, John, 31

Caillois, Roger, 202, 209

Calame, Alain, 30, 72, 168, 171

California Institute of the Arts, 269–70

Călinescu, Matei, 191

Calle, Sophie, 60

Calvino, Italo: collaborative novel project and, 227; Genette on, 98; influence on Perec, 96; on literary machines of the future, 86; on semiotic squares, 264–5; translation by, 99; in WWII Resistance, 24

- *The Castle of Crossed Destinies*, 273

- "Cybernetics and Ghosts," 86
- "How I Wrote One of My Books," 264–5
- *If on a Winter's Night a Traveler* (*Se una notte d'inverno un viaggiatore*), 15, 227, 245, 264
- *The Path to the Nest of Spiders* (*Il sentiero dei nidi di ragno*), 24
Campion, Thomas, 49
Cantor, Georg, 141
Caradec, François, 30
Carelman, Jacques, 230
carmina figurata (pattern poems), 131
Carr, Brian, 179
Carrère, Emmanuel, 300n2
Cassam, Quassim, 78
Catton, Eleanor, 273
Cavalcanti, Guido, 95
Cave, Terence, 219
Cendrars, Blaise: "Prose du transsibérien et de la petite Jehanne de France" ("The Prose of the TransSiberian and of Little Jeanne of France"), 40
censorship, self-, 10, 65, 166
Cerquiglini, Bernard, 266
Chambers, Ross, 20
chance-governed (aleatory) methods, 31–6; Bense and, 6–7, 35; Breton and, 32, 33; *Exercises in Style* (Queneau) and, 32–4; vs forms, 35–6; history of, 31; Oulipo's relationship with, 6–7, 32, 34–5; Queneau on, 6, 14, 34, 38; surrealism and, 32
Change (collective), 22–3
Change (journal), 26
channelling, 95
Chapman, Stanley, 20, 247

Charbonnier, Georges, 3, 16, 34, 35, 140, 222, 226
cheating, 149, 201–2
Cheng, François: *L'écriture poétique chinoise* (*Chinese Poetic Writing*), 112, 113, 114–15
Chénier, André, 96
Chile, 203, 206
chimera, 215, 217
chimère (chimera) constraint, 302n53
Chomsky, Noam, 36, 260–1
Christensen, Inger, 269
chronogram, 49
chronopoems, 54
citations, 118, 214–15. *See also* allusions; intertextuality
Claburn, Thomas: *i feel better after i type to you*, 61
Clancier, Anne, 167, 168
Clark, Timothy, 88
clastic experimentalism, 7, 39–42, 43, 214
clinamen: introduction, 10, 147, 162; asymmetries and, 154–6, 295n60; eodermdrome and, 159–62; functions and effects as openings, 149–54; history and conceptual drift of, 147–8, 295n56; Oulipian adoption of, 148–9
Coetzee, J.M.: *Elizabeth Costello*, 117
cognition, incubated, 7, 64–5, 93
Coleman, Wanda, 71
Coleridge, Samuel Taylor: "Shakespeare's Judgment Equal to his Genius," 71
Colie, Rosalie, 47

352   Index

collaboration, 192, 227, 266–7, 273–5

competition, 200, 207, 208–9

complexity, 241

composition, literary: and antecedents, influences, and imitation, 94–6, 98, 126, 226–8; machine as metaphor for, 8, 85–6; originality and, 64, 124, 125–6, 241, 272; vs real-time description, 62–3; transformation and, 98; translation and, 124–5. *See also* clinamen; constraints; forms and formalism; translation

computers: computer-assisted writing, 76–8, 289n11; mathematics and, 78. *See also* automation

conceptual art, 8, 57–8, 73–5

Condorcet, Nicolas de: *Esquisse d'un tableau historique des progrès de l'esprit humain* (*Sketch for a Historical Picture of the Progress of the Human Mind*), 238–40

Consenstein, Peter, 251

Constitutions Unlimited (event), 276

constraints: introduction, 7, 43–4; artisanal approach to inventing, 267–8; attention and, 63–4, 93, 183–4, 187; attribution to individual creators, 46; biological metaphors for, 225; "cheating" when writing under, 149; choice within, 148; classification and types, 7, 50–6, 51; complexity and, 241; conventions and, 7, 44–50, 284n27; cross-media

collaboration and, 266–7; deep formalism, 183–7, 191; definition, 66; for eluding self-censorship, 10, 65, 166; evolution of, 55–6; forms and, 67–8, 71–2; hide-and-seek with readers, 175–7; historical precedents, 49–50; inspiration and, 86, 90, 93; Métail's critique of, 8, 70–1; naturalization of, 44, 45; non-member inventions, 268; originality and, 64; performance/publication constraints, 54–5, 56, 60–1, 65, 266; phonemes and sound, 257–62, 259; politics and, 275–6; potentiality and, 66, 225–6; power of, 70; product constraints, 7, 53–4, 55, 63–5; for prolonging interpretation, 178–9; proposed by Queneau, 140; proposed by Roubaud, 285n30; Queneleyev's Table, 53, 258, 261, 263–4; semantic constraints, 263–6; semiotic functions, 127; syllabic constraints, 263; writer's block and, 167. *See also* automation; clinamen; forms and formalism; mathematics; numerology; potentiality; process constraints

constraints, specific: acronym, 49; Algol poetry, 265–6; anagram, 9, 49, 132–3, 272; anaphone, 259; antirhyme, 257–8, 261; beautiful in-law (*beau présent*), 275–6; Brivadois acrostic, 268; *chimère* (chimera), 302n53; Delmas's method, 268; Desarguesiennes constraint, 143–5, 144; eodermdrome, 10, 156–62, 157,

194, 202; haikuized poems, 51–2; holorhyme, 98; homonyms, 81, 85, 238; homophones, 155, 164, 238; isograms, 57, 149, 153, 262; "kick-start" text ("texte à démarreur"), 132; landscape monostichs, 55, 132; lipogram, 47, 49, 50, 53, 63, 64, 67, 132, 238, 248, 259; lipophoneme, 258, 259; memory constraint, 162; monovocalic text, 43, 53–4, 132, 149, 245; N + 7 (S + 7) method, 34–5, 51, 76, 97–8, 214, 225, 226, 248, 271; N + die (S + dé) method, 35; nonina, 225, 274; palindrome, 49, 98, 157; phonetic palindrome, 258; prisoner's constraint, 108; quenina, 140, 143, 225; slenderizing, 269; "snowball" ("boule de neige"), 131; spiral permutation, 67, 68, 136, 143, 225–6, 274; *ulcérations* (threnodials), 42–3, 238; ventriloquist's constraint (Turkish verses), 258; *x* mistakes *y* for *z* constraint, 50, 140. *See also* poetic forms
constructive experimentalism, 4, 7, 42, 43, 65. *See also* constraints; forms and formalism
conventions, generic, 7, 44–50, 284n27. *See also* constraints
Corneille, Pierre, 274
Cortázar, Julio, 227
Costello, Elizabeth, 117
Cots Vicente, Montserrat, 213
craftsmanship, 8, 77, 78
Crawford, Lynn, 269

creativity, 7, 35, 124
cross-media collaboration, 266–7
Culler, Jonathan, 179–80, 181, 183
Curtis, Richard, 269

Da, Nan Z., 114–15
Dada, 17, 19, 31, 41, 43
Dangy-Scaillierez, Isabelle, 173, 189
Dante Alighieri, 91, 95, 135–6; *Divine Comedy*, 140–1, 297n16; *La vita nuova*, 135
Darrieussecq, Marie, 300n2
Daumal, René, 17, 91
Debon, Claude, 72, 171, 176, 233
Debord, Guy, 20, 202, 300n2
deception, 201–2
Decout, Maxime, 227
Dedekind, Richard, 141
deep formalism, 183–7, 191. *See also* constraints; forms and formalism
Deerhoof (band), 130, 267
De la Torre, Mónica, 272
Delay, Florence, 135
Delemazure, Raoul, 118
DeLillo, Don, 181
Delmas's method, 268
De Quincey, Thomas: "On the Knocking at the Gate in Macbeth," 213
Derain, André, 33, 41
Descartes, René, 142
Descombes, Vincent, 64, 219
Desnos, Robert, 17, 258
"Des Papous dans la tête" (radio program), 30
Despentes, Virginie, 300n2
destruction. *See* clastic experimentalism

diagram, 9, 132–3
Dickner, Nicolas, 272
Dionysius of Halicarnassus, 94–5
"the disparate," 26, 282n54
dissimulation. *See* revelation
and dissimulation
Döblin, Alfred, 254
Dos Passos, John, 254–5
Dourish, Paul, 93
Drayton, Dave, 275; *P(oe)Ms*, 275
Drexler, Jorge, 222–3
Drieu La Rochelle, Pierre, 24;
Gilles, 16
Drunken Boat (journal), 245, 258
Ducasse, Isidore (Comte de
Lautréamont), 41, 222, 228;
Poésies, 217, 218
Duchamp, Marcel, 27, 73
Duchateau, Jacques, 26
Duchêne, Ludmila: *Rationnel
mon Q* (Rational my ass / Q;
with Leblanc), 230
Duflo, Colas, 200, 202
Du Maurier, George: *Peter
Ibbetson*, 100
Duncan, Dennis, 90, 246–7
Durand, Pascal, 39
Duras, Marguerite, 192
Dussutour-Hammer, Michèle, 118
Dworkin, Craig, 75

Ecclesiastes, 125
Eco, Umberto, 10, 110, 124, 181–3
education, 30, 63–4
Egudu, Emmanuel, 117
Eleksographia (journal), 245
elementary morality (form),
232–41; introduction, 12;
adaptability and durability of,
240–1; first use in *Elementary*

Morality (Queneau), 232–3;
Les temps traversés (Grangaud)
and, 238–40; Oulipian responses
to, 238; Queneau's explanation
of, 233–5; "Roubaud's Principle"
(Perec) and, 236–8; Terry and,
240
Eliot, T.S., 214
Elkin, Lauren, 20; *The End of
Oulipo?* (with Esposito), 246
Éluard, Paul, 87; "Liberté"
("Freedom"), 24
emotive function, of language,
10, 163
empty structures, 222, 224
Encyclopédie de la Pléaide, 36
Engels, Friedrich: *The Communist
Manifesto* (with Marx), 82
Englert, Walter G., 295n56
eodermdrome, 10, 156–62, 157,
194, 202
Epicurus, 147, 295n56
equality, 133
Esposito, Veronica: *The End
of Oulipo?* (with Elkin), 246
Esposito-Farèse, Gilles, 270
Étienne, Luc, 258
Euripedes: *Medea*, 116
exercises, 5, 15–16, 30, 31, 99
experimentalism, literary: clastic
experimentalism, 7, 39–42,
43, 214; constructive
experimentalism, 4, 7, 42, 43, 65.
See also constraints; forms
and formalism

Fabb, Nigel, 46–7
Faerber, Johan, 300n2
fairy (folk) tales, 116–17, 198
family resemblance, 47–8

Faucheux, Pierre, 230
Faulkner, William: *Mosquitoes*, 93
Favard, Jean, 14
Faye, Jean-Pierre, 22
fecundity, 225–6. *See also* potentiality
Felski, Rita, 182
feminism. *See* gender
Ferguson, Deanna: "Cut Opinions," 289n11
Ficino, Marcilio, 87
first impressions, 127–8, 130
Flaubert, Gustave, 95–6
Flem, Lydia, 231
Fluxus, 31
folk (fairy) tales, 116–17, 198
Fontaine (journal), 24
forms and formalism: introduction, 7–8, 9–10; constraints and, 67–8, 71–2; deep formalism, 183–7, 191; definition, 66, 68; diagram and, 9, 132–3; disharmony with content, 139–40; hide-and-seek with readers, 175–7; icon and, 130–3; image and, 9, 131–2; index and, 9, 134–5; mathematics and, 143; Métail on, 8, 70–1, 120; Oulipo's ambition to invent a popular form, 70; paranoid interpretations and, 10–11, 179–83, 188–91; Peircian typology of signs and, 9–10, 130–6; posture and first impressions, 127–30, 130; potential fecundity of, 224, 225–6; power of, 70; for prolonging interpretation, 178–9; reuse vs uniqueness, 71; semiotic functions, 127; symbol and, 9–10, 135–6; value of,

35–6. *See also* clinamen; constraints; numerology; poetic forms; potentiality
Forte, Frédéric: collaboration with Deerhoof, 130, 267; on constraints, 66; elementary morality form and, 238, 241; jiǎnpǔ system, 262, 274; on Oulipo's potentiality, 275
– "99 notes préparatoires à ma vie avec Raymond Queneau" (99 preparatory notes to my life with Raymond Queneau), 59
– "99 Preparatory Notes to 99 Preparatory Notes," 58–9, 66
– *Dire ouf*, 129, 130
Fortier, Dominique, 272
Foucault, Michel, 171–2, 187
foulipo, 269, 270
found language, 75
Fournel, Paul: at California Institute of the Arts conference, 269; co-optation by Oulipo and, 27, 28; "Des Papous dans la tête" radio program and, 30; elementary morality form and, 238; on Oulipo's aim and purpose, 26, 86, 274; on Oulipo's future, 309n55
– *Chamboula*, 194
– *Dear Reader* (*La liseuse*), 225
Fowler, Alastair, 46, 47–8
Fowler, Don, 295n56
frames, 120
Frankfurter Werkstatt für potenzielle Literatur, 275, 310n83
free will, 147
Frege, Gottlob, 141, 214, 243–4
Freud, Sigmund, 79, 166, 168, 174, 179, 297n8

356   Index

friendship, 27–8
Front national (journal), 24
Front National (political party), 25
Frow, John, 47
Fulgentius, 49
furor poeticus, 86–7
Futurism, 17, 41, 43

Gadamer, Hans-Georg, 187, 191
Galileo, 142
Gallimard, Gaston, 24
games, 31. *See also* exercises; play
   and playfulness
gaps, between texts, 118–19, 173
García, María Dolores Vivero. *See*
   Vivero García, María Dolores
García Márquez, Gabriel: *One*
   Hundred Years of Solitude, 194
Garréta, Anne: departure from
   Oulipo, 20, 280n21; imitation
   by, 96; *I Remember* (Perec) and,
   231; Levin Becker on, 209;
   marketing using Oulipo's brand,
   16; on Oulipo's literary role,
   247; on paranoid interpretations,
   180; on playfulness, 11, 195;
   on Proust, 218–19
– *Ciels liquides* (Liquid skies), 209
– *La décomposition*
   (Decomposition), 209–20;
   introduction, 11, 209, 248; citations and intertextuality, 214–15;
   comparison to *Life: A User's*
   Manual (Perec), 302n51; desecration of and homage to Proust,
   96, 215, 216; dialogue with
   In Search of Lost Time (Proust),
   215, 217, 217–18; gamification,
   209–11, 213–14; Levin Becker
   on, 209, 219; Monsieur de

Cadillac's name, 212, 302n43;
   narrator in, 219–20; narrator's
   failure to follow constraints and
   reality breaking in, 211–13, 214
– *In Concrete* (*Dans l'béton*), 220
– *Pas un jour* (*Not One Day*),
   165–6, 176
– *Sphinx*, 5, 107, 194
Géhéniau, Florence, 187
gender: ambiguity in *Tlooth*
   (Mathews), 106–8; foulipo and,
   269, 270; neutralized in
   Elementary Morality (Queneau),
   141; Oulipo and gender diversity,
   20, 280n21; in *W or the Memory*
   of Childhood (Perec), 204, 205
generic conventions, 7, 44–50,
   284n27. *See also* constraints
Genette, Gérard, 47, 98–9, 193,
   215, 217, 288n7
geometry, 242–3. *See also*
   mathematics
Germany: "Deutschlandlied," 83–4;
   Nazi Germany and *W or the*
   Memory of Childhood (Perec),
   203, 205–6, 207, 301n39
Ghosal, Madhumita, 107
Gide, André, 192, 300n2
Gilbert-Lecomte, Roger, 17
Gladding, Jody, 113, 121
Goddard, Cliff, 265
Goethe, Johann Wolfgang von:
   "Wanderers Nachtlied II"
   ("Rambler's Lullaby II"), 83, 84
Goldie, Peter, 75
Goldsmith, Kenneth, 61, 75, 126,
   246; *Soliloquy*, 62
Gombrich, Ernst, 148
Goodwin, Ross, 76–7
Gowers, Timothy, 78

Index

grammatical translation, 97
Grand Jeu, Le (avant-garde group), 17
Grands Rhétoriqueurs, 49
Graner, Nicolas: Avatars de Nerval (website), 270
Grangaud, Michelle: anagram poems, 9, 132–3, 249; diagrammatic signification and, 132–3; elementary morality form and, 238, 241; equality and, 133; against Front National, 25; haikuized sonnets, 52
– *Geste* (Gesture), 248–57; Alféri on, 248–9, 254, 257; comparison to *Life: A User's Manual* (Perec), 254–5; connections and sequences within, 252–4; contents and characters, 250–1, 255–7; equality and, 133; form employed in, 249–50; influences on, 254, 255; language usage, 251–2; potentiality of, 257; reading experience of, 254
– *Memento-fragments*, 132
– "Poèmes fondus" (Melted poems), 52
– *Renaître*, 132
– *Souvenirs de ma vie collective* (Souvenirs of my collective life), 73–4
– *Stations*, 132
– *Les temps traversés* (Times traversed), 238–40
Grasset, Jean-Baptiste, 266
great writer (*grantécrivain*), 192, 300n2
Green, André, 201
Greenblatt, Stephen: *The Swerve*, 148

Greimas, Algirdas Julien, 264–5
Griffiths, Paul, 269
Grivel, Charles, 178
Guénon, René, 16
Guidoux, Valérie, 247

Hacking, Ian, 146
haikuized poems, 51–2
Halle, Morris, 260–1
Halliday, Michael, 40
Han Shan, 234
Han Yujoo, 246
Hardy, G.H., 143
Harig, Ludwig, 35
Hart, Kevin, 90
Hartje, Hans, 35
Hasan, Ruqaiya, 40
Hayes, Terrance, 71; "A Gram of &s," 272; *Hip Logic*, 272
Hazzard, Shirley, 218
Heaney, Seamus, 256
Heck, Maryline, 206
Hegel, G.W.F., 41
Heidegger, Martin, 196
Heine, Heinrich, 214; "Die Lorelei," 218
Hejinian, Lyn, 269
Helmlé, Eugen, 82, 84, 176, 301n39
Herbert, George: "Easter Wings," 131
hide-and-seek, with readers, 175–7
Higgins, Dick, 131
Hilbert, David, 87, 242, 243–4
Hinton, David, 115, 121–2
Hocquard, Emmanuel, 71, 255
Hoffman, E.T.A.: "Mademoiselle de Scudéri," 302n43
Hölderlin, Friedrich, 85
holorhyme, 98

358   Index

Hölty, Ludwig Christoph
    Heinrich, 83
Homer, 87, 91; *Iliad*, 269
homolexical translation, 97
homonyms, 81, 85, 238
homophones, 155, 164, 238
homophonic translation, 97
homosemantic translation, 97
homosyntaxism, 97
Hopkins, Gerard Manley, 70
Houellebecq, Michel, 268, 300n2
Hough, Graham, 47–8
Hugo, Victor, 192, 274
Huizinga, Johan, 200, 202
humour, 30, 193–4. *See also* play
    and playfulness
Hutchinson, Ishion, 194
hypertextuality, 99, 215

iambic pentameter, 46–7, 49, 64
I Ching (*The Book of Changes*),
    62, 114, 140–1, 176, 234
icon, 130–3
illumination, 92–3, 170, 172
image, 9, 131–2
imitation, 94–6, 98. *See also*
    influences, literary
incubated cognition, 7, 64–5, 93
incubation phase, 92–3
index, 9, 134–5
influences, literary, 94–6, 126,
    226–8
information theory, 36–7
infraordinary, 62
inspiration, 85–93; constraints
    and, 90, 93; critiques of, 8, 88–9;
    illumination and, 92–3; Le
    Lionnais on, 148; vs literary
    machines, 85–6; Plato and
    Socrates on, 86–7; Queneau

on and Oulipians' interpreta-
    tions, 89–93, 235; Roubaud's
    rejection of, 87–8; vs writer's
    block, 89
interjections, 163
internationale situationniste, L',
    (formerly L'internationale let-
    triste), 20
internet, 75, 180, 219–20
interpretation: deep formalism
    and, 183–7, 191; paranoid
    interpretations, 10–11, 179–83,
    188–91; prolonging using formal
    encoding, 178–9
intertextuality, 118–19, 125, 215,
    217, 227. *See also* allusions;
    citations
intralingual translation, 97, 98
Invisible Seattle (collective):
    Constitutions Unlimited event,
    276
"irrational sonnets," 143
isograms, 57, 149, 153, 262
Isou, Isidore, 20, 40–1

Jacques, Jacques, 96
Jakobson, Roman, 97, 98, 130–1,
    163, 262
James, Alison: on chance-governed
    methods, 31, 32, 34; on
    constraints and forms, 72;
    on Oulipo's nature, 274–5; on
    "The Winter Journey" (Perec),
    232, 304n32
James, Henry, 165
Jameson, Fredric, 175
Jarry, Alfred, 147
Jeannelle, Jean-Louis, 227
Jenks, Tom, 269
Jenny, Laurent, 193

Index

Je suis le ténébreux (anthology), 270

Jetubhai, Khuman Bhagirath, 107

jiǎnpǔ system, 262, 274

joking, pathological (Witzelsucht), 193

Josipovici, Gabriel, 175

Jouet, Jacques: chronopoems, 54; on clastic experimentation, 42; collaboration with Rosenstiehl, 274; on constraints, 46, 86, 93, 266, 285n33; "Des Papous dans la tête" radio program and, 30; elementary morality form and, 238, 241; on forms, 10, 71, 279n4; interview with Bloomfield, 266; *I Remember* (Perec) and, 231; landscape monostichs, 55, 132; Lécroart's portrait of, 132, *133*; non-Oulipian works, 5; on organizational tinkering, 7, 44, 67–8, 235, 284n20; performance/publication constraints and, 54–5, 56, 60–1; on potentiality, 225; productivity of, 60; projects and, 59, 60; on revealing compositional rules to readers, 177; on "Roubaud's Principle" (Perec), 237; on "The Winter Journey" (Perec) and *If on a Winter's Night a Traveler* (Calvino) titles, 227

– *Fins* (Endings), 67, *68*, 69, 132, 225, 287n91

– "Monostiques paysagers" (Landscape monostichs), 55, 132

– *Mountain R* (*La montagne R*), 194

– *Navet, linge, oeil de vieux* (Turnip, cloth, pocket grid), 132

– *Poèmes de métro* (Subway poems), 52, 59, 62

– "Poems of the Paris Metro," 274

– "projet poétique planétaire" (planetary poetic project), 55

– *La République roman* (The novel republic), 177

– *Ruminations du potentiel* (Ruminations on potential), 42

Joyce, James, 91–2, 95, 175; *Finnegans Wake*, 40, 125; *Ulysses*, 91, 178–9

Jullien, Dominique, 116

Jullien, François, 120

Kafka, Franz, 96, 227; *The Castle*, 205, 214; *The Trial*, 227

Kahn, Gustave, 40

Kamo no Chomei, 95

Kanganoulipo (writing collective), 246, 275

Kant, Immanuel, 148, 295n60; *Critique of Judgment*, 35

Keats, John, 46–7

Kennedy, John, 158

Kepler, Johannes, 142

"kick-start" text ("texte à démarreur"), 132

Kim, Annabel, 220

Klarsfeld, Serge: *Mémorial de la déportation*, 185

Klee, Paul, 84, 148

Knuth, Donald, 77

Koh, Julie, 246

Kohan, Martín: *Me acuerdo*, 231

Kojève, Alexandre, 30

Kosofsky Sedgwick, Eve, 182, 184

Kripke, Saul A., 214

360 Index

Kroker, Arthur and Marilouise, 220
Kronfeldner, Maria, 124, 272

Lacan, Jacques, 79
Ladha, Hassanaly, 68
La Farge, Tom, 123
Laforgue, Jules, 40
Laird, Benjamin: Bot or Not
 (website), 76, 289n11
Lamartine, Alphonse de, 214
landscape monostichs, 55, 132
Landy, Joshua, 191
language: conceptual art and, 75;
 vs constraints, 45–6; emotive
 function of, 10, 163; linguistic
 automatism, 79; poetic function
 of, 163; translation and, 101–2.
 See also phonemes and sounds;
 semantics
Lapidus, Roxanne, 284n20
Lapprand, Marc, 19, 232, 289n27,
 309n55
Laskowski-Caujolle, Elvira, 136
Lasky, Dorothea: *Poetry Is Not
 a Project*, 58
Latis, 284n27
Lautréamont, Comte de (Isidore
 Ducasse), 41, 222, 228; *Poésies*,
 217, 218
Lawson, Henry: "The Drover's
 Wife," 229
Lebdeğmez (un-touched lips), 258
Leblanc, Agnès: *Rationnel mon Q*
 (Rational my ass / Q; with
 Duchêne), 230
Lécroart, Étienne, 247, 266;
 "Portrait en creux (Jacques
 Jouet)," 132, *133*; "Portraits en
 creux" (intaglio portraits), 9, 132
Lederer, Jacques, 95

Lefebvre, Henri, 206
Leighton, Angela, 66
Leiris, Michel, 17, 65, 96, 172, 258
Lejeune, Philippe, 56, 57, 172
Le Lionnais, François: age when
 founding Oulipo, 19; on Algol
 poetry, 265–6; on "amalgam of
 mathematics and literature,"
 242; on antirhymes, 257, 261;
 on chance, 34; on composition
 and translation, 125; conceptual
 art and, 73; on constraints, 43–4,
 148; on creativity, 7, 35; the
 disparate and, 26, 282n54; on
 emotive function of language,
 163; on *Exercises in Style*
 (Queneau), 32; on forms, 28,
 35–6, 267–8; on future potential
 of Oulipo, 28–9, 31, 268; on
 interestingness of numbers, 142;
 on literary virtuosity, 219;
 manifestos, 28, 29, 35, 246;
 mathematics background, 29; on
 Oulipo's emergence, 15; Oulipo's
 establishment and, 3, 244;
 playfulness and, 162, 194–5;
 politics kept out of Oulipo, 22,
 25; on potentiality, 221; query
 to Oulipians on personal
 Oulipian projects, 235;
 questioning Oulipo's future, 247;
 recruitment procedures for
 Oulipo, 202; role in Oulipo, 4;
 on semantic constraints, 263,
 264, 266; on sonnets, 71; on
 structuralism, 265; in WWII
 Resistance, 24, 267
– "Idea Box," 222, 257, 264
– *Les nombres remarquables*
 (Remarkable numbers), 142

- *La peinture à Dora* (Painting at Dora), 24
- "Second Manifesto," 28–9, 36, 219, 263, 265

Leong, Michael, 272

Le Pen, Jean-Marie, 25

Leroux, Gaston: *The Mystery of the Yellow Room*, 82

Lescure, Jean: crisis of 1974 and, 26; on inspiration, 89–90; "Poèmes pour bègues" (Poems for stutterers), 258; political leanings, 22; on writer's role in N + 7 procedure, 98; WWII Resistance and, 24

Le Sidaner, Jean-Marie, 15, 153, 176

Le Tellier, Hervé: "Des Papous dans la tête" radio program and, 30; on inspiration, 89, 90; on literary machines, 86; mathematics background, 29; political leanings, 22, 25; Prix Goncourt won by, 245
- *L'anomalie* (The anomaly), 30, 100, 194, 245
- *Atlas inutilis*, 275
- *Joconde jusqu'à 100*, 229
- *Joconde sur votre indulgence*, 229
- *The Sextine Chapel*, 225

Lethem, Jonathan, 229

Levé, Édouard, 269

Levi, Primo, 207; *If This is a Man* (*Se questo è un uomo*), 24

Levin Becker, Daniel: co-optation by Oulipo, 28; on debate over revealing compositional rules, 177; on Garréta, 209, 219; *Many Subtle Channels*, 5, 20; on Oulipo, 20, 21; on *Tlooth* (Mathews), 107; translation of *Gestes* (Grangaud) by, 257

Levine, Caroline, 66, 68

Lévy-Leblond, Jean-Marc, 266, 267

liminal texts, 187, 231

Lin, Tan: *Ambient Fiction Reading System 01*, 61

Lindemann, Ferdinand von, 141

Lindon, Mathieu, 231

Li Po (Li Bai), 234

lipogram: classroom uses, 64; composition approaches, 63; vs conventions, 47; as diagram in *A Void* (Perec), 132; elementary morality form and, 238; as emblematic constraint, 248, 259; impacts on a text, 50, 67; as (product) constraint, 49, 53

lipophoneme, 258, 259

List, Christian, 22

Literary Center of the Constructivists, 43

literary composition. *See* composition, literary

literary experimentalism: clastic experimentalism, 7, 39–42, 43, 214; constructive experimentalism, 4, 7, 42, 43, 65. *See also* constraints; forms and formalism

literary movements and schools: Bourdieu on avant-garde group formation and dissolution, 18–19, 22; future orientation and, 28–9; Oulipo compared to and defined against, 14–16, 19–22, 25, 28–9; politics and, 22; Roubaud's caricature of, 17–18; surrealism as anti-model for Oulipo, 16–17, 22, 26; tabula rasa rhetoric, 41–2. *See also* Dada; Futurism; Le Grand Jeu; surrealism

literary prizes, 30. *See also* Prix Goncourt; Prix Médicis

Littérature (journal), 41

Longinus: *On the Sublime*, 95

Lucretius, 147

lushi (poetic form), 234

Lusson, Pierre: *A Short Treatise Inviting the Reader to Discover the Subtle Art of Go (Petit traité invitant à la découverte de l'art subtil du go;* with Perec and Roubaud), 161–2

Macé, Gérard, 57

Mac Low, Jackson, 269, 272

Macron, Emmanuel, 23

Madden, Matt: *99 Ways to Tell a Story*, 230

Madrid, Anthony, 277, 287n82

magical causation, 116–17, 124–5

Magné, Bernard: on "La clôture" (Perec), 151; on *Life: A User's Manual* (Perec), 118, 155, 174, 176; paranoid interpretations and, 179; on Perec's *æncrages*, 134–5; on Perec's numerology, 134, 184; on Perec's translation of *Tlooth* (Mathews), 109; on real-time description, 62; on "The Winter's Journey" (Perec), 227

main à plume, La (journal), 24

Maldiney, Henri, 279n4

Mallarmé, Stéphane, 39–40, 51, 95, 117, 214, 228, 274; *Un coup de dés (One Toss of the Dice),* 39–40

Mälzel, Johann Nepomuk, 78

Mancarella, Mariacarmela, 106

Manea, Raluca, 253

manipulation, 98. *See also* translation

Marías, Javier: "Guide to What Not to Read," 128

Marinetti, Filippo Tommaso: "Against Academic Teachers," 41; "The Foundation and Manifesto of Futurism," 41

Marker, Chris, 30

Marmande, Francis, 135

Marsal, Florence, 165

Mars-Jones, Adam, 214

Martial, 50, 286n46

Martin, C.B., 224

Martín Sánchez, Pablo, 16, 20, 99–100, 247, 288n8; *Tuyo es el mañana* (Tomorrow is yours), 225

Marx, Karl, 206; *The Communist Manifesto* (with Engels), 82

Massaro, Dominic W., 260

Massin, Robert, 230

mathematics: Audin and, 10, 29, 146; computers and, 78; Desarguesiennes constraint and, 143–5, *144*; *Exercises in Style* (Queneau) adaptations and, 230; geometry and literature, 242–3; inspiration and, 87–8; interestingness of numbers, 142–3; mathematical fiction as niche, 146; neo-Pythagoreanism, 137; numerology and, 142; Oulipians with backgrounds in, 29, 282n61; Queneau and, 37–8, 244, 282n61; Queneau numbers, 136, 137, 143; use by Oulipians,

4, 37–8, 77–8, 143.
See also numerology
Mathews, Harry: collaborative novel project, 227; at Constitutions Unlimited event, 276; on constraints, 65; on elementary morality form, 235; on eodermdrome, 156; haikuized version of "Rimbaud" (Auden), 51–2; on hide-and-seek with readers, 177; *I Remember* (Perec) and, 231; on Queneleyev's Table, 263; on slenderizing, 269; on translation, 97, 98; translation of *Elementary Morality* (Queneau), 233; *ulcérations* constraint, 43; on *A Void* (Perec), 21. See also *Oulipo Compendium* (Mathews and Brotchie)
– *Cigarettes*, 65
– "Fearful Symmetries," 110
– *The Sinking of the Odradek Stadium*, 15, 99
– *Tlooth*, translated by Perec, 105–12; introduction, 9; characters' names and gender ambiguity, 106–8, *107*; coded messages in, 108–9, *109*; compositional rules of, 106, 108, 112; influence on Perec's writings, 106, 125; *Life: A User's Manual* (Perec) and, 118, 125, 293n57; Perec's orientation towards the written word and, 105–6; title, 110–12; translation background and negotiations, 106, 110; transposition of phonemes, 109–10, *110*, *111*
– *Le Verger* (*The Orchard*), 106
Mayer, Bernadette, 71, 269

McCleary, John: *Exercises in (Mathematical) Style*, 230
McHale, Brian, 180, 181
McSweeney's (journal), 224
Mechanical Turk, 78
mechanisms. *See* automation
Mégret, Christian, 36
Mehlman, Jeffrey, 147
Meizoz, Jérôme, 127
Mélois, Clémentine, 30, 247, 266; *Dehors, la tempête* (Outside, the storm), 184
Melville, Herman: *Moby-Dick*, 214
memory-based imitation, 8, 94
memory constraint, 162
memory-image (*image-mémoire*), 165
Mendeleyev, Dmitri, 263
mental composition, 94
Meredith, George: *Modern Love*, 70
Merrill, Stuart, 85
Meschonnic, Henri, 193
Messages (journal), 24
Métail, Michèle: autobiographical anchoring in later work of, 122–3; on constraints and forms, 8, 70–1, 120; co-optation by Oulipo, 28; decision to learn Chinese, 112–13; departure from Oulipo, 19, 27, 120, 282n56; *Elementary Morality* (Queneau) and, 140, 176, 234; as first female Oulipo member, 20; gaps between texts and, 119; interview with Bloomfield, 70; translations by, 100; visits to China, 120
– "The Map of the Armillary Sphere" (Su) translation, 9, 113–15, *115*, 120–2, *122*, 125

- *Noun Complements* (*Compléments de noms*), 123
- *L'un l'autre: L'esperluette* (The one the other: The ampersand; with Roquin), 122–3
- *Wild Geese Returning* (*Le vol des oies sauvages*), 113, 114–15
metrical conventions, 40, 46–7, 49
métromètre tool, 274
Meyer-Bagoly, Suzanne, 140
Michelet, Jules, 238
Middleton, Christopher, 269
Millikan, Ruth Garrett, 49
modernism, 180–1
Mohammad, K. Silem, 272
Molière, 274
Monk, Ian: at California Institute of the Arts conference, 269; collaboration with Audin, 274; "Des Papous dans la tête" radio program and, 30; on freedom, 276–7; "Iris," 54; monovocalic texts by, 53; translation of Perec's monovocalic motto, 43; translation of *The Exeter Text* (*Les revenentes*; Perec), 54, 149; translations by, 99
monovocalic text, 43, 53–4, 132, 149, 245
Montaigne, Michel de, 27–8
Montrichard, Christian de, 231
Moréas, Jean, 40
Moret, Philippe, 233
Mortal Kombat (video game), 214
Motte, Warren, 147; *Oulipo*, 5
Mréjen, Valérie, 293n70; *Capri* (film), 125–6
Mullen, Harryette, 269, 271–2; *Sleeping with the Dictionary*, 271–2

Müller, Herta, 25; *The Hunger Angel* (*Atemschaukel*), 25
Mumford, Stephen, 224
Murray, Penelope, 87
Musca, Giosuè, 182
music: chance-governed methods and, 31; collaborations with musicians, 130, 229, 266; comparison to poetry, 94; *Elementary Morality* (Queneau) and, 67, 176, 234

N + 7 (S + 7) method: automation of, 76; chance and, 34–5; durability and productivity of, 225, 226; as emblematic constraint, 248; as playful decomposition, 214; as process constraint, 51; *Sleeping with the Dictionary* (Mullen) and, 271; translation and, 97–8
N + die (S + dé) method, 35
Nadeau, Maurice, 53, 56, 305n60
Nake, Frieder, 36
nationality, 20
National Writers' Committee (France), 24
"Natural Semantic Metalanguage" (NSM), 265, 266
Naukkarinen, Ossi, 61
Naville, Pierre, 17, 22
Nazi Germany, 203, 205–6, 207, 301n39
Nehamas, Alexander, 27–8
neo-French, 105
neo-Pythagoreanism, 137
nerds, 20–1
Neruda, Pablo, 85
Nerval, Gérard de: "Angélique," 227; "Artemis," 139; cited in *La*

décomposition (Garréta), 214; "El Desdichado," 270

Nguyen, C. Thi, 277

Nietzsche, Friedrich, 41, 202

Noguez, Dominique, 192, 300n2

nonina, 225, 274

non-text, 40

The n*oulipian Analects* (anthology), 270

Noulipo, 269–70

Nouvelle revue française (journal), 12, 24, 229, 234

Nufer, Doug: *Never Again*, 270–1

Nugent, Benjamin, 20

numerology: *Elementary Morality* (Queneau) and, 140–2; *The Last Days* (Queneau) and, 139–40; mathematics and, 142; *Odile* (Queneau) and, 140; Perec and, 134, 184–7; Queneau and, 137–42, 178; Roubaud and, 135–6, 136–7; *Some Thing Black* (Roubaud) and, 135–6; symbols and, 135; *Witch Grass* (Queneau) and, 138–9, 178. *See also* mathematics

Objectivism, 255

Olympic Games, 204, 207

O'Meara, Lucy, 219

O'Neill, Ryan: *The Drover's Wives*, 229, 275; Kanganoulipo and, 246; *Their Brilliant Careers*, 231–2

onomatopoeia, 261

Opalka, Roman, 60; OPALKA 1965/1–∞, 199

OpenAI, 76–7

Oplepo (Opificio di Letteratura Potenziale), 4, 275

opportunistic assimilation, 93

Optatianus Porfirius, 49

oral novel, 117

Ording, Philip: *99 Variations on a Proof*, 230

organizational tinkering, 7, 44, 67–8, 235, 284n20

originality, 64, 124, 125–6, 241, 272

Oriol-Boyer, Claudette, 231

Orwell, George, 25, 281n48

O'Sullivan, Maurice: *Twenty Years A-Growing*, 100

Oswald, Alice, 269; *Memorial*, 269

Otchakovsky-Laurens, Paul, 56

Ougrapo (Ouvroir de design graphique potentiel), 275

Oulipo: introduction, 4, 5–13, 276–7; age of founders, 19–20; aims of, 4, 267–8; appropriation by and influence on non-members, 268–73; automation and, 73, 75–6, 77–8; vs avant-gardes, 19–22; as brand, 16; chance-governed (aleatory) methods and, 6–7, 31–2, 34–5; channelling and imitation by, 94–6; characteristics of, 3–4, 38; collaboration and, 192, 227, 266–7, 273–5; comparison to surrealism, 6, 17–19, 22, 26, 28; conceptual art and, 73–5; constructive experimentation and, 4, 7, 42, 43, 65; craftsmanship and, 8, 77, 78; crisis of 1974, 26; critical assessments and literature on, 5, 245, 246–7; departures from, 19, 20, 27, 280n21, 282n56; differences within, 4–5; education and, 30;

establishment and ground rules, 3, 17, 244; exercises as public face of, 99; future hopes and potential, 28–9, 31, 247–8, 268, 309n55; gender diversity and, 20, 280n21; inspiration and, 85–6, 87–8, 89–93, 235; international importance and influence, 245–6; intertextuality and, 217; lack of a totalizing project, 26; mailing list, 270; mathematics and, 4, 37–8, 77–8, 143, 282n61; nationality and, 20; negative self-definition, 14; negative views of, 98–9, 127–8; nerds and, 20–1; as not a literary movement or school, 14–16; as not a scientific seminar, 29–31; originality and, 126; paranoid interpretations of works by members, 10–11, 179–83, 188–91; playfulness and, 192–5, 220; politics and, 22–3, 25–6, 276; Queneau's warning against taking too far, 244; radio and, 30; recruitment and inclusion mechanisms, 27–8, 202; related groups to, 275; serious and grave themes, 194; as social invention, 273; as underknown, 248; WWII Resistance and, 23–4. *See also* automation; constraints; forms and formalism; revelation and dissimulation; translation; *specific members*
- *L'abécédaire provisoirement définitif* (Provisionally definitive alphabet primer), 66, 192
- *All that is Evident is Suspect*, 5, 247, 257, 264

- *Atlas de littérature potentielle* (Atlas of potential literature), 15, 43
- *Cher Père Noël*, 229
- *Moments oulipiens*, 280n21
- *Oulipo Laboratory*, 264
- *Winter Journeys (Expanded Edition) (Le voyage d'hiver et ses suites)*, 231, 275

Oulipo Compendium (Mathews and Brotchie): introduction, 5; on *chimère* (chimera) constraint, 302n53; on elementary morality form, 235; on eodermdromes, 156; on *Exercises in Style* (Queneau), 32–3; inclusion of works by non-members, 268–9; lack of entry for potentiality, 66; playfulness in, 192; on slenderizing, 269; "snowball" ("boule de neige"), 131; on translation, 97

Oulipo Press, 246

Outranspo (Ouvroir de translation potencial), 269, 309n61

Over, Jeremy, 269

overinterpretation. *See* paranoid interpretations

Pages, Nicolas, 231

PALF project (Production automatique de littérature française [Automatic production of French literature], Perec and Bénabou), 8, 79–82, 85, 289n27

palindrome, 49, 98, 157

palindrome, phonetic, 258

paranoid interpretations, 10–11, 179–83, 188–91

paratexts, 176, 187, 231

Paris, Gabriel, 230
Parker, E.T., 274
participant tracking, 254
Pascal, Blaise, 235; *Pensées*, 217, 218
Pastior, Oskar, 25
Paterson, Don, 128, 153, 262
pathological joking (Witzelsucht), 193
pattern poems (*carmina figurata*), 131
Patterson, Ian, 302n60
Paulhan, Jean, 24, 99
Paz, Octavio: "Homage and Desecrations," 215
Peano, Giuseppe, 141
Péguy, Charles, 96
Peillet, Emmanuel. *See* Latis
Peirce, Charles S.: paranoid interpretations and, 182; typology of signs, 9, 130–6
Pellis, Sergio and Vivien, 201
The Penguin Book of Oulipo (anthology), 5, 247, 268, 269
Perec, Georges: *æncrage* and, 134–5; ambitions of, 172, 184; autobiographical writings, 57, 167, 172; beautiful in-law (*beau présent*) constraint, 275–6; channelling and imitation by, 95–6; on clinamens, 10, 148–9; collaborative novel project, 227; on constraints, 65, 93, 183; crisis of 1974 and, 26; deviations from constraints, 149–54; diagrams and, 132; elementary morality form and, 236–8; *Eunoia* (Bök) and, 54; on exercises, 15; gaps between texts and, 173; goal behind formal encoding, 178;

on hide-and-seek with readers, 176–7; on intertextuality, 118–19; lyric terror of, 152–3; monovocalic motto, 43; numerology and indices, 9, 134, 184–7; on overlap between poetry and Oulipism, 235–6; on paranoid interpretations, 11, 188–90; paratexts and hidden compositional rules, 176; Paris writings, 53, 57, 62, 120; on play, 195; potentiality in actuality and, 221; process constraints and, 55–7, 58; projects and, 56; psychoanalysis and, 10, 167–8, 172, 173–5; Queneau and, 96, 236–8, 305n60; surname, 173; translation by, 99; *ulcérations* constraint, 42–3; on violence, 206
– "35 variations sur un thème de Marcel Proust" (35 variations on a theme by Marcel Proust), 98
– *53 Days*, 11, 189–90
– *Alphabets*, 134, 149, 150
– *L'arbre* (The tree), 172
– "Attempt at an Inventory of the Liquid and Solid Foodstuffs Ingurgitated by Me in the Course of the Year Nineteen Hundred and Seventy-Four," 61–2
– *La boutique obscure*, 161
– "La clôture" (The enclosure), 149, 150–1, 183
– *La clôture et autres poèmes* (The enclosure and other poems), 10, 57, 150, 154, 184, 236, 248
– "L'éternité" (Eternity), 153, 235

368   Index

- *The Exeter Text* (*Les revenentes*), 54, 99, 149, 284n18
- *A Gallery Portrait* (*Un cabinet d'amateur*), 99
- "History of the Lipogram," 53
- *I Remember* (*Je me souviens*), 12, 226, 228–9, 230–1, 232, 233, 274
- *Konzertstück für Sprecher und Orchester* (Concertino for speaker and orchestra), 106
- *Lieux* (Places), 53, 56–7, 172
- *Lieux où j'ai dormi* (Places where I have slept), 230
- *Life: A User's Manual* (*La vie mode d'emploi*): asymmetries in, 154–6; Berge's assistance with, 274; borrowings from *Tlooth* (Mathews), 118, 125, 293n57; Anne Breidel's caloric intake, 185–6, *186*; comparison to *A Void* (Perec), 155–6; comparison to *Geste* (Grangaud), 254–5; comparison to *La décomposition* (Garréta), 302n51; comparison to *La dernière balle perdue* (Roubaud), 199; comparison to *Lieux* (Perec), 56; comparison to *Souvenirs de ma vie collective* (Grangaud), 74; comparison to "Un poème" (Perec), 152; comparison to *W or the Memory of Childhood* (Perec), 155–6, 175; composition of, 172; conceptual art and, 74–5; critical recognition and canonical status, 140, 245, 248; deep formalist approach to, 185–7; epigraph from *The Exeter Text* (Perec), 284n18;

hidden compositional rule, 176; Holy Grail legend and, 304n32; influences on, 9, 96, 106; inter-textuality and, 118; numerology and, 134; Oulipo's relevance and, 12, 247; on paranoid interpretations, 188–9; paratexts and, 175–6, 187; Prix Médicis won by, 15; product constraints and, 63; as psychoanalytic autobiography, 173–5; simultaneism and, 254–5; synopsis and structure, 154, 172–3
- *A Man Asleep*, 227
- *Die Maschine* (*The Machine*), 8, 82, 83–5
- *Notes de chevet* (Bedside notes), 230
- PALF project (with Bénabou), 8, 79–82, 85, 289n27
- "Un poème," 150, 151–2, 154, 235
- "Roubaud's Principle," 236–8, 244
- "The Scene of a Stratagem" ("Les lieux d'une ruse"), 167, 168, 172, 175
- *A Short Treatise Inviting the Reader to Discover the Subtle Art of Go* (*Petit traité invitant à la découverte de l'art subtil du go;* with Roubaud and Lusson), 161–2
- *The Sinking of the Odradek Stadium* (Mathews) translation, 15
- *Species of Spaces* (*Espèces d'espaces*), 56, 287n77
- "Still Life / Style Leaf," 152

- "Tentative de description d'un programme de travail pour les années à venir" (Attempt at a description of a work program for the years to come), 56
- *Things* (*Les choses*), 96, 119
- *Tlooth* (Mathews) translation. *See under* Mathews, Harry
- "Ulcérations" (Ulcerations), 149, 150, 244
- *A Void* (*La disparition*): diagrammatic signification in, 132; eluding self-censorship and, 65; as emblematic of Oulipo, 248; Genette on, 98, 288n7; *Life: A User's Manual* (Perec) and, 155–6; lipogrammatic constraint in, 47, 50, 67; Perec's preoccupation with the letter and, 106; reactions to, 21; translations of, 245–6
- *Which Moped with Chrome-Plated Handlebars at the Back of the Yard?* (*Quel petit vélo au guidon chromé au fond de la cour?*), 99
- "The Winter Journey" ("Le voyage d'hiver"), 12, 85, 226–9, 231–2, 233, 274, 304n32
- *W or the Memory of Childhood* (*W ou le souvenir d'enfance*): autobiographical elements, 57, 167; comparison to *Chêne et chien* (Queneau), 167; comparison to *La dernière balle perdue* (Roubaud), 207, 208; comparison to *Life: A User's Manual* (Perec), 155–6, 175; comparison to "Un poème" (Perec), 152; competition and

play, 11, 202–9; hide-and-seek with readers, 176–7; loss and mourning, 194; on mother and child, 296n72; Nazi Germany and, 203, 205–6, 207, 301n39; numerology in, 134; Perec's psychoanalysis and, 167–8, 173–4; Perec's surname and, 173; political critique in, 206–8; publication of, 56; W's society and class system, 203–5
performance/publication constraints, 54–5, 56, 60–1, 65, 266
periodic table, 263
Perloff, Marjorie, 272
Perrot, Michelle, 23
Pettit, Philip, 22
Phaneuf, Marc-Antoine K., 272
Philip, M. NourbeSe, 269, 272
philology, 115
phonemes and sounds, 257–62; antirhyme, 257–8, 261; avoidance of in constraints, 259–61; in Bénabou's classification of constraints, 258, 259; constraint possibilities, 261–2; lipophoneme, 258, 259; phonetic palindrome, 258; as subordinate to letters, 258–9; transposition of in *Tlooth* (Mathews), 109–10, 110, 111; ventriloquist's constraint (Turkish verses), 258
phonetic palindrome, 258
Pizarnik, Alejandra, 266
Plato, 86–7, 120, 260; *Ion*, 86; *Phaedo*, 120; *Phaedrus*, 86–7; *Republic*, 87
play and playfulness: introduction, 11; competition and *W or the*

Memory of Childhood (Perec), 202–9; deception and *La dernière balle perdue* (Roubaud), 195–202; gamification and *La décomposition* (Garréta), 209–20; vs great writers (*grant-écrivains*), 192; Oulipo critiqued for, 192–4; Oulipo's approach to, 192, 195, 220; Oulipo's defence of, 194–5; *Parc sauvage* (Roubaud) and, 161–2, 195, 196, 202; saving ourselves through, 161–2; Witzelsucht (pathological joking) and, 193

Poe, Edgar Allan, 78

poetic forms: alexandrine, 40, 44, 274; Algol poetry, 265–6; anagram poems, 9, 132–3, 249; chronopoems, 54; haikuized poems, 51–2; iambic pentameter, 46–7, 49, 64; *lushi*, 234; pattern poems (*carmina figurata*), 131; quenina, 140, 143, 225; rondeau, 44, 128; sestina, 67, 128, 136, 224, 225. *See also* elementary morality (form); sonnet

poetry: computer generated, 76–7; Oulipism and, 235–6; Plato and Socrates on, 86–7; posture in, 127; Roubaud's "playing" of, 94

Poiana, Peter, 59, 60

Poier-Bernhard, Astrid, 133, 241, 249, 254

politics, 22–3, 25–6, 275–6

Pollock, Sheldon, 115

Ponge, Francis, 10, 28, 279n4

Pontalis, Jean-Bertrand, 167, 172, 173–4

postmodernism, 180–1

posture, 127–30, *130*

potentiality: introduction, 11–12; antecedents and precursors, 226–8; elementary morality form and, 232–41; of empty structures, 222, 224; fecundity and, 225–6; invitations for others to build upon works, 228–32; lack of Oulipian theorization on, 66; of Oulipo, 274–5; potentiality in actuality, 12, 221, 222, 223, 224, 226, 241, 275; predisposed potentiality, 11–12, 221, 222, 224; Roubaud on, 66

Poucel, Jean-Jacques, 23, 25, 151, 183, 192, 237

Pound, Ezra, 39

precursors, literary, 94–6, 126, 226–8

Prendergast, Christopher, 209, 219

preparatory notes, 58–9

Prigogine, Ilya, 147

Pringle, Alan, 102–3, 104

prisoner's constraint, 108

Prix Goncourt, 30, 245

Prix Médicis, 15, 166

procedures, 73

process constraints: introduction, 7, 51, 51–3; development of by Perec, 55–6; exhaustibility of, 59; Jouet on, 266; literary composition and real-time description, 62–3; performative aspect, 60–1; productivity and, 59–60; product's value and, 57–8; projects and, 56–7; reader sympathy and, 60; reading experience and, 65; temperament and, 58–9; translation and, 97

Index 371

product constraints, 7, 53–4, 55, 63–5
productivity, 59–60, 86
projects, 56–8
Propp, Vladimir, 198
Proust, Marcel: "L'affaire Lemoine," 227; "Against Obscurity," 233; Bénabou and, 164; decomposition and recomposition of *In Search of Lost Time* in *La décomposition* (Garréta), 11, 96, 209–11, 214, 215–19, 216; destruction of *In Search of Lost Time* manuscripts, 176; *Finding Time Again*, 217, 218–19, 302n60; Garréta on, 218–19; PALF project and *In Search of Lost Time*, 82; Perec and, 172; Queneau and, 91
psychoanalytic autobiography: introduction, 10; "Le boulanger sans complexes" (Queneau) and, 169–70; *Chêne et chien* (Queneau) and, 167, 168–9, 170; *Life: A User's Manual* (Perec) and, 172–5; "Résipiscence" (Queneau) and, 170–2; *W or the Memory of Childhood* (Perec) and, 167–8
psychological automatism, 79
publication/performance constraints, 54–5, 56, 60–1, 65, 266
punctuation, 40
Putnam, Hilary, 261
Pynchon, Thomas, 181

qualia, 251
Quayson, Ato, 117
Queneau, Raymond: age when founding Oulipo, 19;

autobiographical writings, 167; on Breton, 26, 41; on chance, 6, 32–4; channelling and imitation by, 96; comparison to Bense, 35, 36–7; and constraints and conventions, 44, 50; on creativity, 6–7, 35; crisis of 1974 and, 26; elementary morality form and, 233–5, 238–41; on empty structures, 222; on forms, 35–6, 71–2; Genette on, 98; goal behind formal encoding, 178; hide-and-seek with readers, 176–7; hopes for Oulipo's future, 31; on inspiration, 8, 89–93, 234–5; on interestingness of numbers, 143; interviews with Charbonnier, 3, 16, 34, 35, 140, 222, 226; mathematics and, 4, 37–8, 137, 244, 282n61; misrepresentation as merely a comic writer, 30; on $N + 7$ method, 34; negative definition of Oulipo by, 14, 38; neo-French and, 105; numerology and, 137–42, 178; on oral novel, 117; on Oulipo as not a literary movement, 14–15, 16; on Oulipo as not a scientific seminar, 29, 30; Oulipo's establishment and, 3, 17, 244; on paranoid interpretations, 11, 183, 190–1; paratexts and, 176, 187; Perec and, 96, 236–8, 305n60; on playfulness, 31, 194; on poetry and Oulipism, 235; politics kept out of Oulipo, 22, 25; on potentiality, 221, 226; process constraint and, 51, 58; psychoanalysis and, 10, 168–70,

172; Queneau numbers, 136, 137, 143; Queneleyev's Table, 53, 258, 261, 263–4; recruitment procedures for Oulipo, 202; role in Oulipo, 4; Roubaud on, 77, 95; on sonnet, 240; surrealism and, 16–17; translations by, 100; Tutuola and, 118; on "Ulcérations" (Perec), 244; on unfinished works, 59; warnings against taking Oulipism too far, 244; on Witzelsucht (pathological joking), 193; writer's block and, 89; WWII Resistance and, 24

- *The Blue Flowers* (*Les fleurs bleues*), 99, 116
- "Bois flottés" (Driftwood), 297n18
- *Bords*, 37
- "Le boulanger sans complexes" (The baker without complexes), 169–70, 172, 175
- "The Café de la France," 170
- *Cent mille milliards de poèmes* (A hundred thousand billion poems): automation and, 75–6, 288n8; comparison to *Exercises in Style* (Queneau), 229; comparison to "the Map of the Armillary Sphere" (Su), 114; composition and structure, 3; as emblematic of Oulipo, 248; Le Lionnais on, 15, 221; potentiality of, 11–12, 221, 222–3
- *Chêne et chien* (Oak and dog), 167, 168–9, 170, 175
- *Children of Clay* (*Les enfants du limon*), 140, 183

- *Elementary Morality* (*Morale élémentaire*), 62, 140–2, 176, 226, 232–3, 241, 249
- *Exercises in Style* (*Exercices de style*): antecedents of, 226; chance and, 6, 32–4; comparison to *Cent mille milliards de poèmes* (Queneau), 229; comparison to *Elementary Morality* (Queneau), 233; inspiration for from music, 67, 226; invitation to other writers to build upon, 228–30, 232; Le Lionnais on, 15, 221; potentiality of, 12, 221, 226, 229; Queneau's fame and, 30
- *Fendre les flots* (Breaking the waves), 169, 170, 172, 175–6
- *The Flight of Icarus*, 26, 116, 117
- "The Foundations of Literature (after David Hilbert)," 12, 241–3, 244, 246
- *Hitting the Streets* (*Courir les rues*), 120
- "Humor and its Victims," 193
- "L'inspiration," 92
- *L'instant fatal*, 96
- *The Last Days* (*Les derniers jours*), 72, 139–40, 148
- "La mer des Sargasses" (Sargasso Sea), 297n18
- *Odile*, 16, 17, 89–91, 92, 139, 140, 244
- *The Palm-Wine Drinkard* (Tutuola) translation, 9, 100–5, 116–17, 124–5
- "Plus and Minus," 89, 91, 92
- "Pour un art poétique" (For a poetic art), 92

Index

- "Redundancy in Phane Armé" ("La redondance chez Phane Armé"), 51, 269
- "Résipiscence" (Resipiscence), 170–2
- "Strange Tastes," 178
- "Sur les suites s-additives," 282n61
- "A Tale for Your Shaping" ("Un conte à votre façon"), 75–6
- "Technique of the Novel," 14, 71–2, 137–8, 139, 162, 178, 250
- *Witch Grass* (*Le chiendent*), 5, 11, 14–15, 138–9, 178, 190–1, 299n93
- "The Writer and Language," 117
- *Zazie in the Metro* (*Zazie dans le métro*), 30, 89, 105, 115–17
Queneau numbers, 136, 137, 143
Queneleyev's Table ("Classification of the works of the Oulipo"), 53, 258, 261, 263–4
quenina, 140, 143, 225
Queval, Jean, 238
Quillien, Christophe, 231
Quine, W.V.O., 45, 214
Quintilian, 94
Quinzaine littéraire, La (journal), 26, 56

Rabelais, François, 96; *Gargantua*, 178
Racine, Jean, 274; *Phaedra*, 82
Radgett, Ron, 232
radio, 30
radio plays: *Die Maschine* (Perec), 8, 82, 83–5; *Konzertstück für Sprecher und Orchester* (Perec), 106
Raimbaut d'Orange, 95

Rakosi, Carl, 255
Ramanujan, Srinivasa, 143
Raymond, Dominique, 272
readers. *See* audience and readers
real-time description, 62–3
recitation, 94
recognition, critical, 248, 307n16
Reggiani, Christelle, 45, 67, 150, 153, 225, 230–1
Régnier, Henri de, 40
Reig, Christophe, 231, 232
Reina, José Luis, 136
Renéville, Rolland de, 17
Resistance (wwii), 23–4, 267
revelation and dissimulation: introduction, 10–11; autobiography and, 163–4; deep formalism and, 183–7, 191; *The Great Fire of London* (Roubaud) and, 164–5; hide-and-seek with readers, 175–7; paranoid interpretations and, 10–11, 179–83, 188–91; *Pas un jour* (Garréta) and, 165–6. *See also* psychoanalytic autobiography
Rhei, Sofía, 222
Rhodes, Dan, 269
rhyme, 261. *See also* antirhyme; holorhyme
Ribemont-Dessaignes, Georges, 17
Ribière, Mireille, 150, 206
Rimbaud, Arthur, 41, 214, 228
Riviere, Sam, 128
Robbins, Michael, 128, 287n82
Robert, Yves, 230
Robert-Foley, Lily, 269
Romains, Jules, 254
rondeau, 44, 128

374   Index

Roquin, Louis: *L'un l'autre:
L'esperluette* (The one the other:
The ampersand; with Métail),
122–3
Rorty, Richard, 179
Rosenstiehl, Pierre, 274
Rosenthal, Jean, 100
Roubaud, Alix Cléo, 135, 136
Roubaud, Jacques: Alamo
workshop and, 76, 77;
autobiographical writing and,
164–5; on automation, 77;
baobab constraint, 54; caricature
of literary movements, 17–18;
Change (collective) and, 22–3;
channelling and imitation by, 94,
95, 96; on clinamens, 149; on
complexity, 241; at Constitutions
Unlimited event, 276; on
constraints, 44, 45, 46, 66, 71,
259–60; constraints proposed by
removed from Oulipo website,
285n30; crisis of 1974 and, 26;
departure from Oulipo, 19, 27,
282n56; on eodermdrome, 156,
157; on exercises, 15–16; on
family resemblance, 47–8; on
forms, 72; Frankfurter Werkstatt
für potenzielle Literatur and,
275; against Front National, 25;
Garréta and, 165; goal behind
formal encoding, 178; on
inspiration, 87–8; interview with
Bloomfield, 23, 77; Le Lionnais
on, 266; mathematics
background, 29; memory
constraint, 162; metrical
conventions and, 49; numerology
and, 135, 136–7; on Oulipo's
ambition to invent a popular

form, 70; on Oulipo's nature, 8,
78, 274; on Oulipo's rules of
co-optation, 27; playfulness and,
11, 195; on "playing" poetry,
94; on politics kept out of
Oulipo, 22, 23; on potentiality,
11–12, 66, 221–2, 224; process
constraints and, 58; projects
and, 56, 60; sonnet and, 68,
71; on tabula rasa, 42;
translations by, 100;
typographical innovations by,
128; ventriloquist's constraint,
258; writer's block and, 89
– "L'auteur oulipien"
(The Oulipian author), 45
– *La Bibliothèque de Warburg*, 66
– *Ciel et terre et ciel et terre, et ciel*
(Sky and earth and sky and
earth, and sky), 196
– *La dernière balle perdue* (The
last lost ball), 11, 195–202,
207, 208
– *Description d'un projet*
(Description of a project), 56
– *La dissolution* (The dissolution),
66, 89
– *Dors* (Sleep), 136
– *The Great Fire of London* (*Le
grand incendie de Londres*), 56,
136, 137, 164–5, 176, 194, 248
– Hortense novels, 225
– *Impératif catégorique*
(Categorical imperative), 70
– "Le Pen est-il français?"
("Is Le Pen French?"), 25
– *The Loop* (*La boucle*), 95, 157
– *Mathematics*, 146
– "Mathematics in the Method
of Raymond Queneau," 77

- "Notes sur l'Oulipo et les formes poétiques" (Notes on the Oulipo and poetic forms), 44
- "The Oulipo and Combinatorial Art," 15–16, 17–18
- *Parc sauvage* (Wild grounds), 10, 136, 157–62, 194, 195–6, 202, 248
- *Peut-être ou la nuit de dimanche* (Perhaps or Sunday night), 19, 28, 247, 282n56
- *Poésie:* (Poetry:), 87–8, 94
- *Poetry, etcetera: Cleaning House*, 42
- "La Princesse Hoppy ou le conte du Labrador" ("Princess Hoppy or the Tale of Labrador"), 244
- *A Short Treatise Inviting the Reader to Discover the Subtle Art of Go* (*Petit traité invitant à la découverte de l'art subtil du go*; with Perec and Lusson), 161–2
- *Some Thing Black* (*Quelque chose noir*), 9–10, 135–6, 137
- "Tombeaux de Pétrarque" (Tombs of Petrarch), 136
- "Yesterday's Journey" ("Le voyage d'hier"), 231

Rousseau, Jean-Jacques: *Confessions*, 166

Roussel, Raymond: Aira on translating Roussel, 112; constraints and, 65; *How I Wrote Certain of My Books* (*Comment j'ai écrit certains de mes livres*), 106, 164, 172; *Not One Day* (Garréta) and, 166; "Parmi les noirs" ("Among the Blacks"), 81, 82; Perec influenced by, 96; revealing compositional rules and, 171–2

Rousset, David, 207; *L'Univers concentrationnaire* (*A World Apart: Life in a Nazi Concentration Camp*), 206

rules. *See* constraints

Russia. *See* USSR

Rutebeuf, 96

S + 7 method. *See* N + 7 method

S + dé (N + die) method, 35

Sade, Marquis de, 41

Saito, Yuriko, 61

Sala, Jerome, 269

Salceda, Hermes, 50, 99, 248

Salon, Olivier, 29, 136, 285n30; *Le disparate, François Le Lionnais*, 282n54

Samoyault, Tiphaine, 217

Sánchez, Pablo Martín. *See* Martín Sánchez, Pablo

Sanders, Carol, 140

Sapir, Edward, 261

Sartre, Jean-Paul, 300n2

Saunier, Greg, 267

Savage, Steve, 272

Schellekens, Elisabeth, 75

Schiller, Friedrich, 85

Schlegel, August Wilhelm, 71

Schleiermacher, Friedrich, 102, 187

Schönberg, Arnold, 262

Schönherr, Ulrich, 83

Schuldt, Herbert, 269

Schulz, Rémi, 184–5, 188

Schwartz, Laurent, 23

Schwartz, Oscar, 77; Bot or Not (website), 76, 289n11

science fiction, 8, 78, 85. *See also* automation

scientific seminar, Oulipo as not a, 29–31

scriptworlds, 120

Sedgwick, Eve Kosofsky. *See* Kosofsky Sedgwick, Eve

Seifert, Colleen, 93

Sei Shonagon, 230

self-censorship, 10, 65, 166

semantics: constraints using, 263–6; semantic representation, 75

semiotic squares, 264–5

semodefinitional literature, 97

Seneca, 94, 96

Şentürk, Levent, 246

Serreau, Geneviève, 110

Serres, Michel, 37, 147

sestina, 67, 128, 136, 224, 225

Séverin, Fernand, 85

Shakespeare, William: *Macbeth*, 213; sonnet 130, 271

Shannon, Claude, 35, 36

Shaw, Lytle, 177

Shelley, Percy Bysshe, 87

Shrikhande, S.S., 274

Sidney, Philip, 224

signs: diagram, 9, 132–3; icon, 130–3; image, 9, 131–2; index, 9, 134–5; Peircian typology of, 9, 130–6; symbol, 9–10, 135–6

Simias of Rhodes, 131

Simonnet, Claude, 72

simulation, 8, 78, 85

simultaneism, 254–5

slenderizing, 269

Slimani, Leila, 300n2

Slow movement, 78

"snowball" ("boule de neige"), 131

Socrates, 86–7

Sollers, Philippe, 22, 28

sonnet: in *Cent mille milliards de poèmes* (Queneau), 3, 76, 222,

223; and constraints vs conventions, 45, 47; development of, 68, 70; flexibility of, 71; haikuizing, 51–2; "irrational sonnets," 143; Queneau on, 240; by Rhei, 222

Sontag, Susan, 246

Sorrentino, Gilbert, 269

sounds. *See* phonemes and sounds

Soupault, Philippe, 41; *The Magnetic Fields* (*Les champs magnétiques*; with Breton), 19, 40

Spahr, Juliana, 269, 270

Spartacus, 208

Spenser, Edmund, 224

Spinetta, Luis Alberto: "Por" (song), 229

spiral permutation, 67, 68, 136, 143, 225–6, 274

Srinivasan, Amia, 202

Stallings, A.E.: "Fairy-Tale Logic," 198

Starynkevitch, Dimitri, 76

Stein, Gertrude, 95; "Red Faces," 289n11

Stendhal: *The Charterhouse of Parma*, 288n7

Stengers, Isabelle, 147

Sterne, Laurence, 96

Stolnitz, Jerome, 261

Stout, John, 249

Strawson, Galen, 62

structuralism, 265

Stump, Jordan, 138, 299n93

Stuttgart School, 14, 35, 37

Su Hui: "The Map of the Armillary Sphere," translated by Métail, 9, 113–15, *115*, 120–2, *122*, 125

Index

Suits, Bernard, 11, 200, 202, 208, 213
superstition, 139
surrealism: age of founders, 19; chance-governed methods and, 31, 32; comparison to Oulipo, 6, 17–19, 22, 26, 28; on inspiration, 87; lack of cohesion, 22, 28; psychological automatism and, 79; Queneau's experience with, 16–17; recovery of neglected works by, 41; as totalizing project, 26
Swinburne, Algernon Charles, 224
syllabic constraints, 263
symbol, 9–10, 135–6

tabula rasa, 41–2
Tahar, Virginie, 302n51
Tel Quel (journal), 22
temperament, 58–9
Terry, Philip: elementary morality form and, 240, 241; "Elementary, My Dear Watson," 240; *The Penguin Book of Oulipo* (anthology), 5, 247, 268, 269; *Quennets*, 240; translation of *Elementary Morality* (Queneau), 232–3; translation of *I Remember* (Perec), 231
Tesson, Sylvain, 300n2
Themerson, Stefan, 269
Thirion, André, 17
Thom, René, 148
Thomas, Dylan, 100–1, 105
Thomas, Jean-Jacques, 193, 263
threnodials (*ulcérations*) constraint, 42–3, 238
Tillion, Germaine, 207
Tillman, Lynne, 229

tinkering, organizational, 7, 44, 67–8, 235, 284n20
transformation, 98
translation: introduction, 8–9, 100; vs adaptation, 124; conventional translations by Oulipians, 99–100; and creativity and originality, 124; influence on the translator's original writings, 124–5; intralingual translation, 97, 98; linguistic normalization and, 101–2; as manipulation, 97–8; Métail's translation of "The Map of the Armillary Sphere" (Su), 9, 113–15, *115*, 120–2, *122*, 125; as negotiation, 110; Perec's translation of *Tlooth* (Mathews), 9, 99, 105–12, *107*, *109*, *110*, *111*, 118, 125, 293n57; Queneau's translation of *The Palm-Wine Drinkard* (Tutuola), 9, 100–5, 116–17, 124–5
translexical translation, 97
transplants, 97
Trollope, Anthony, 95
Troubadours, 49, 68, 234
Tubbs, Robert, 243
Turk, Mechanical, 78
Turkey, 258
Turkish verses (ventriloquist's constraint), 258
Turner, Simon, 247
Tutuola, Amos, 105, 118; *Feather Woman of the Jungle*, 118; *My Life in the Bush of Ghosts*, 118; "My Vernacular," 105; *The Palm-Wine Drinkard*, translated by Queneau, 9, 100–5, 116–17, 124–5; *Simbi and the Satyr of the Dark Jungle*, 118

Tye, Michael, 251
typography, 127, 128–30, *129*
Tzara, Tristan, 19, 41

ulcérations (threnodials) constraint,
    42–3, 238
Ultraism, 17
unpredictability, 7, 35. *See also*
    chance-governed methods
USSR, 208

Vaché, Jacques, 41
Vailland, Roger, 17
Valéry, Paul, 214, 290n47
Vanderschelden, Isabelle, 109
Van Valckenborch, René, 269
ventriloquist's constraint
    (Turkish verses), 258
Verdure, Jean, 22
Verlaine, Paul, 85
Verne, Jules, 96; *Michel Strogoff*,
    259
versification, 49
Viala, Alain, 26
Vialatte, Alexandre, 101
Vicente, Montserrat Cots. *See* Cots
    Vicente, Montserrat
Vidal-Naquet, Pierre, 23
Viegener, Mathias: *The* n*oulipian
    Analects* (anthology), 270
Viélé-Griffin, Francis, 40
Vila-Matas, Enrique, 229
Villani, Cédric, 23
Villon, François, 96
Vivero García, María Dolores, 213
Volontés (journal), 91, 139
Von Kempelen, Wolfgang, 78

Waldrop, Keith, 269

Wallas, Graham, 92–3
Walther, Elisabeth, 35
Watkin, Christopher, 36, 37
Waugh, Linda, 262
Weiner, Lawrence, 75
Wertheim, Christine: *The* n*oulipian
    Analects* (anthology), 270
Wexler, Peter, 158
White, Gillian, 153
White, J.J., 84
Wierzbicka, Anna, 265
Wiles, Andrew, 78
will, 147
Winnicott, Donald, 173–4, 177,
    201, 202
Wittgenstein, Ludwig, 48, 66, 70,
    214
Wittig, Monique, 107
Witzelsucht (pathological joking),
    193
women, in Oulipo, 20, 280n21.
    See also gender
Words without Borders (journal),
    245
Wordsworth, William, 214
World War II, Resistance, 23–4, 267
writers, great (*grantécrivain*), 192,
    300n2
writer's block, 89, 167

x mistakes y for z constraint,
    50, 140

Young, La Monte: *An Anthology
    of Chance Operations …*, 31
Young, Stephanie, 270

Ziff, Paul, 45
Zizek, Slavoj, 180–1